JIM GARRISON:

His Life and Times, The Early Years

by

JOAN MELLEN

JFK LANCER
PRODUCTIONS & PUBLICATIONS
SOUTHLAKE, TX

JFK Lancer Productions & Publications, Inc.
100 Stonewood Court
Southlake, TX 76092

JFK Lancer First Edition May 2008

The goal of JFK Lancer Productions & Publications, Inc. is to make research materials concerning President John F. Kennedy easily available to everyone. Our prime concern is the accuracy of history and the true story of the turbulent 1960s.

For additional copies of this publication, please contact:

Email: orders@jfklancer.com
Web: www.jfklancer.com

For information on other titles by Joan Mellen, see www.joanmellen.net

Printed in the United States
Cover design by Ken Jacobs
Book design by Debra Conway

ISBN Number 978-0-9774657-2-9

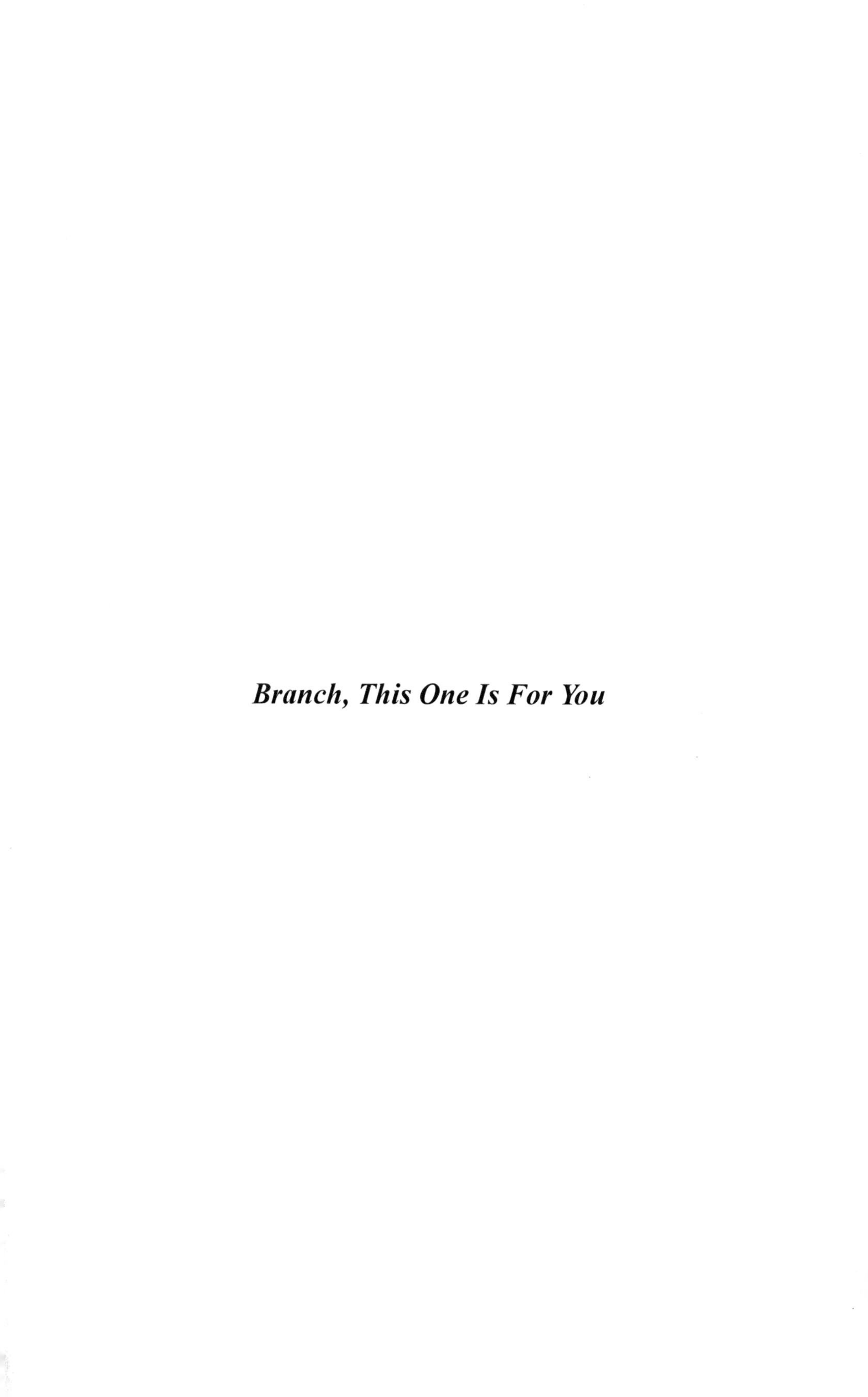

Branch, This One Is For You

Books by Joan Mellen

A Farewell to Justice: Jim Garrison, JFK's Assassination, and the Case That Should Have Changed History

A Film Guide to the Battle of Algiers

Big Bad Wolves: Masculinity in the American Film

Bob Knight: His Own Man

Hellman and Hammett

In The Realm Of The Senses

Kay Boyle: Author of Herself

Literary Masterpieces: One Hundred Years of Solitude

Literary Masters: Gabriel García Márquez

Literary Topics: Magic Realism

Marilyn Monroe

Natural Tendencies: A Novel

Privilege: The Enigma of Sasha Bruce

Seven Samurai

Voices From The Japanese Cinema

The Waves At Genji's Door: Japan Through Its Cinema

Women And Their Sexuality In The New Film

The World of Luis Buñuel: Essays In Criticism

Contents

Acknowledgements

This project is a consequence of the generosity and imagination of Debra Conway of JFK Lancer. I am deeply grateful to Debra for her recognition that knowing the story of Jim Garrison's life is crucial to any understanding of his investigation into the assassination of President Kennedy. It was my good fortune to discover in Debra Conway the most capable and talented of publishers.

I would like to thank as well the many people who so generously, and selflessly, contributed their time to helping me explore the New Orleans of Jim Garrison's time, and the details of Jim Garrison's life. For his extraordinary friendship, I would like to thank most Judge Louis P. Trent. Judge Trent, and his wife Lillian Cohen, provided a wealth of insight and information. Their kindness cannot be measured.

For their hospitality in both Louisiana and in Maine, I would like to thank Donald V. Organ, Jim Garrison's attorney on Garrison v. Louisiana, and his wife Joan Bovan. For life in the French Quarter of that era I would like to thank Robert Buras, whose integrity has been a beacon for me in my study of that bygone time. Louis Ivon and Dr. Frank Minyard were indispensable commentators for this story. John Volz spent many hours talking to me about the District Attorney's office. John Tarver taught me more than I could ever hope to know about the history and politics of the state of Louisiana. John R. Rarick was gracious, cordial and a constant support, and I am grateful to him and his late wife Marguerite for their hospitality, not least that trip over the Mississippi on a raft that made me feel as if I were reliving "Huckleberry Finn." I would also like to thank Jim Garrison's children, in particular Lyon Garrison, for the time they spent with me.

Many others helped. They include Dan Alcorn; Wilma Baker; Malcolm Blunt; William Alford; Peggie Baker; Judge Denis A. Barry II; Barbara Bennett; H. John Bremermann; Mickey Bremermann; Milton E. Brener; Loraine Chadwick; the late Lawrence Chehardy; John Clemmer; James A. Comiskey; Raymond Comstock; Louis Crovetto; L. J. Delsa; the late Jack Dempsey; Anne Dischler; John J. Dolan; Judge Adrian Duplantier; Clarence O. Dupuy; Judge Thomas A. Early; Lolis Elie; Phillip Foto; Warren Garfunkel; Liz Garrison; Max Gartemberg; the late Walter Gemeinhardt; Darrow Gervais; the late Vance Gilmer;

Alvin Gottschall; Fred Gore; C. Jackson Grayson, Jr.; Judge James J. Gulotta; Robert Haik; the late Walter Hammer; Sharon Herkes; the late Iris Kelso; the late Arthur Kinoy; the late Herman Kohlman; thr late Allen B. Koltun; the late Louise Korns; Phyllis Kritikos; Judge Rene Lehmann; Marcie Ann Little; William Livesay; Ray McGuire; James McPherson; the late Frank Meloche; Joseph A. Oster; Lester Otillio, Jr.; Rosemary Pillow; the late William Porteous III; Brucie Rafferty; Suzanne Robbins; Martha Ann Samuel; Ross Scaccia; Mike Seghers; G. Harrison Scott; Ralph Slovenko; Jay Teasdel; Wilmer Thomas; John Volz; Bruce Waltzer; Barbara Ward; Lenore Ward; Gus Weill; General Erbon Wise; and Joyce Wood.

I am grateful, as always, to Ralph Schoenman for his tireless devotion and support.

FOREWORD

In 1997, a decade ago, I began to write a biography of Jim Garrison. My goal was to tell the story of my subject, as the cliché has it, from cradle to grave. Garrison would be studied, like my earlier biographical subjects, Kay Boyle, Lillian Hellman, and Dashiell Hammett, for his strengths as for his weaknesses. I would be aided by the fact that, as I knew Boyle and Hellman, so I had been acquainted with Jim Garrison over a period of years, beginning in 1969.

I planned, of course, to devote a considerable portion of the book to Jim Garrison's investigation into the Kennedy assassination, and to why this man, alone among all public officials to this day, was able to bring before the bar of justice someone involved in the plot to assassinate President Kennedy. As I drove up and down the watery roads of Louisiana, I realized that I had to write as well about my own investigation and examine whether the multifarious documents released under the 1992 JFK Act confirmed Jim Garrison's findings, or rendered them irrelevant.

After seven years, a manuscript of 1500 or so pages emerged. The exigencies of twenty-first century publishing are grim, and Jim Garrison remained a figure attacked and discredited still, forty years after he began his investigation. Circumstances permitted only a book about Garrison's Kennedy work. That was "A Farewell To Justice" (2005), for which I utilized about a third of the research I had done.

Since the publication of "A Farewell To Justice," readers have inquired: What were Garrison's motives? What kind of man was he? In the elliptical style of that book, I could not convey the complexities of the man, or the contradictions in his character. Nor could I establish the extraordinary single-mindedness and purpose with which Jim Garrison approached his attempt to discover what had happened to the President whom he so much admired. I could not convey all Garrison lost, all he sacrificed in the process.

Had I been permitted to publish the long book required to explore Jim Garrison's life, I would have been able to consider whether the charges against him orchestrated by J. Edgar Hoover enjoyed any validity. Was Garrison, either as a district attorney or as a historian of the Kennedy murder, soft on the Mafia? Was he on the take?

Was he an egoist investigating the Kennedy assassination in pursuit of personal glory and fame? Was he careless and in violation of the law in his treatment of witnesses and suspects in the Kennedy case? Were suspects treated fairly and with equality by Garrison as District Attorney of Orleans Parish? Did he protect their rights? What were Jim Garrison's values and convictions, and in what ways, if he did, was he able to transcend his limitations?

It was the inspiration of my quixotic publisher Debra Conway that I return to where I began, to the story of Jim Garrison's life, and I am grateful to her for this act of imagination. When I re-read my original manuscript, I discovered that I had written as much a history of New Orleans in the 1960s as I had a biography of Jim Garrison. Inevitably, hence the subtitle "life and times," I had placed the man against the landscape of that steamy port of no return where immigrants from the mid-west, like Garrison's mother, reached the end of their search for sanctuary. Iowa-born Jim Garrison engaged with New Orleans, and with the state of Louisiana, recognizing that he had an advantage as an outsider. As Garrison himself pointed out, he owed no loyalty to the status quo.

As for the story of the Kennedy assassination itself, some have contended that had there been a conspiracy, within which Lee Harvey Owald was a mere "patsy," as Oswald claimed, and Jim Garrison believed, death-bed confessions would have made the work of historians far easier. If many people were involved in the planning and implementation of this event, why haven't they come forward?

The answer is that a number of people who had inside knowledge, contradicting the government's story, have brought information to the public. Each of these people, speaking from the vantage of his own personal involvement, has confirmed Jim Garrison's conviction that Lee Oswald was a low-level intelligence agent, part of a conspiracy, and set up to take the blame for the President's murder.

The government had been involved in this homicide, only then to perpetrate a cover-up of the events in both New Orleans and Dallas. The press, far from serving as the guardian of the public's right to know, assumed instead the role of gatekeeper, endorsing the disinformation that has flowed from government sources. Government and press alike have joined in a coordinated effort to ensure that the truth about the murder of President Kennedy will never emerge.

Yet clarifications of existing evidence, and further particulars, continue to surface.

On December 4, 2007, as I was preparing this book, with its focus on Jim Garrison's cleaning up of Bourbon Street, and attacks on B-drinking; his having been charged with "criminal defamation" by the judges of the Orleans Parish criminal court whose chicanery he exposed; and his role in the notorious Dombrowski case, I received a telephone call from one Donald Deneselya. I was not in search of information about the Kennedy assassination. Yet each fragment, each piece of the puzzle that accrues, comments simultaneously on the life of Jim Garrison and the choices that he made as a man and as a citizen.

Deneselya worked for the CIA in 1962 as a translator in the Soviet Branch of the Foreign Documents Division. In October 1961, at the age of twenty-one, he was recruited by the CIA out of the University of Pittsburgh. His father having been born in the Ukraine, Deneselya spoke perfect Russian, a highly valuable commodity during the "Cold War."

Among his tasks was to keep tabs on Russian industrial plants, for which he had assembled a collection of 5 x 8 cards. In this capacity, and in the normal course of his work, he reviewed a document, four to five pages long, that described a man who had defected to the Soviet Union. This man, a "re-defecting Marine," was returning to the United States, in the company of his family. The document outlines the man's detailed knowledge of the Minsk radio plant where he worked during his residence in the Soviet Union.

The Agency debriefed this man, whose name never appears on the document, in New York, in June 1962. The debriefer was a CIA employee named Andy Anderson, whose 00 designation marked him as an officer in the Domestic Contact Service of the Central Intelligence Agency. Anderson, far from working merely for Domestic Contact, was actually the New York representative of Robert T. Crowley, who headed up the CIA Contact Division, Support Branch, the primary function of which was Counter Intelligence. It was Crowley who was the first person handling the Robert Webster defection. It was Crowley of Counter Intelligence to whom Anderson reported in his debriefing of Lee Harvey Oswald, who, like Webster, and others, according to Deneselya, was part of a false defector program.

CIA has always and to this day denies that Oswald was debriefed upon his return from having "defected" to the Soviet Union. Just as CIA denied they even had an employee named "Andy Anderson."

Donald Deneselya's evidence makes clear that not only was Oswald debriefed by the CIA, but that he was debriefed in his capacity as a "false defector" and hence of interest to CIA Counter Intelligence. This debriefing establishes among other things, that Oswald was of continuing value to the CIA in 1962. The memo recording Oswald's debriefing would have been passed around to all the nine members of his section, Deneselya says. Some may be alive still.

Deneselya did not make a copy of the Oswald briefing report. There wasn't even a Xerox machine in his office. In 1962, the only copy machine they had was a Thermafax. Indeed, why would he bother to make such a copy, since this particular Marine, in 1962, was of no particular interest – unless you were in the loop and knew otherwise. Despite the several million documents now released to the National Archives, many from the CIA, the report has been suppressed and has never been allowed to surface.

Over the many years that have passed, Deneselya wondered: Why would a U.S. Marine have to re-defect from Moscow?

Deneselya today is certain of the basic truth that Jim Garrison also concluded: that Oswald was a CIA Counter Intelligence agent planted in the Soviet Union, exactly like Robert Webster, whom the CIA did admit to debriefing as a CIA asset; parallel to Oswald, Webster worked in a plant in Leningrad. The debriefing reports of these two agents differ only in that Webster's name is mentioned in his report, while Oswald's name is absent from his.

When Deneselya mentioned that he had discovered this debriefing document to a fellow CIA employee, someone in the Director of Central Intelligence's office, the man said the document referred to Robert Webster, not to Oswald. That the document had surfaced was treated as an unfortunate error to which some "spin," however improbable, had quickly to be attached. That Webster was not in Minsk but in Leningrad was an inconvenient reality best ignored. Around this time, Deneselya ran into James Angleton at the Army/Navy Club. He mentioned that he had seen the debriefing document of an American defector who had worked at a radio factory in Minsk.

"There is no way to find that document," Angleton said.

The nameless "re-defector" debriefed in New York in June 1962 upon his return to the United States satisfies the description of but one American "defector" who had been consigned to work at a radio factory in Minsk. He could only have been Lee Harvey Oswald. The debriefing produced other important information, including that Oswald's jobs entailed delivering U-2 material obtained at Atsugi air base in Japan to a dubious figure named Edwin Wilson. It is part of the historical record, of course, that Oswald was placed at Atsugi, situated in a position where he could learn about the U-2s resident there. In the report, Oswald provided the names of those he encountered to U.S. government agent Anderson, who debriefed him.

Donald Deneselya left the Agency in 1964. In 1978, learning that Senator Richard Schweiker was investigating the Kennedy assassination, Deneselya met with him twice. In 1978, Deneselya was also interviewed by the House Select Committee on Assassinations (HSCA) regarding his work with a KGB defector named Golitsin. He spoke as well of the Oswald debriefing report that he had witnessed, but his revelations were not included in the HSCA's final report.

In an HSCA "Outside Contact Report" dated September 26, 1978, and released under the JFK Act, Deneselya's information is examined primarily with respect to his work with Golitsin. Only secondarily is there a discussion of how Deneselya came to see the debriefing report. Deneselya recounts how his job was to maintain files on all of the technical and scientific industries in the Soviet Union and to translate from Russian to English. In that capacity, he was routed a contact form in July or August 1962 relating to a former Marine Corps corporal "redefecting to the U.S."

That report, which, of course, was in English, contained decisive information regarding the "size of the Minsk plant, the number of employees and the type of work," Deneselya recounts. Deneselya suggested that the HSCA contact the author of that memo and corroborate the existence of the report. Ken Klein, author of the HSCA report, did not reveal to Deneselya, although he does say so in his contact report, that they had already interviewed the man who wrote that memo, confirming, thereby, that it did exist.

The HSCA contact report deflects the reader's attention from the Oswald revelation by focusing on Soviet defector Golitsin's fantasies of a KGB plot to assassinate Richard Nixon, rather than on the more astonishing revelation that Oswald had been debriefed by the CIA upon his return from the Soviet Union. HSCA apparently never assimilated or chose not to register the importance of Deneselya's information about the report about a Minsk radio plant by American former Marine, whose name may have been suppressed on the debriefing report, but who could only have been Lee Harvey Oswald.

Klein's report of his interview with Deneselya was released by the CIA in the Record Series marked "Security Classified Files" – with 256 restrictions.

HSCA states that it plans to locate the Oswald debriefing memo through the Industrial Registry or the Foreign Documents Division. They consulted a CIA agent in the Soviet Realities section named Thomas Casasin, who had wished to debrief Oswald himself, and been put off by James Angleton, the Counter Intelligence Chief. Casasin had been astonished when he was told, falsely, that Oswald had not been debriefed by the Agency. He had assumed that had Oswald been debriefed, he would certainly have been informed. (See "A Farewell To Justice," pp. 176-177). In an attempt to be helpful, and anxious himself for the truth, Casasin suggested to the House Select Committee that the memo of Oswald's debriefing might be available in the Office of Research and Reports.

Of course the report of Oswald's debriefing was long gone. HSCA also asked Deneselya whether he knew a Talbot Bielefeldt, a friend of Ruth Paine, that "friend" of Lee and Marina Oswald, and of Ruth's mother-in-law, people with heavy CIA connections, although they did not explain why. Deneselya remarks that Bielefeldt was the head of the Soviet Branch of the Foreign Documents Division when he was there.

Deneselya's information, given that he himself was a CIA employee, alone should have rendered entirely specious, for the press as for the general public, the Warren Report's fictive conclusion that Lee Harvey Oswald was a mentally unstable "lone" assassin. Testimony that Oswald was debriefed by the government may be a very small fragment of the story. Yet isolated facts coalesce and dots connect.

To make his information known, in the early 1990s, Deneselya went on PBS's "Frontline" program about the life of Oswald. Before Donald Deneselya appears, Richard Helms comes on to deny that CIA ever debriefed Oswald upon his return from the Soviet Union. Deneselya describes the debriefing report on Oswald and notes that it was signed off on by a CIA officer by the name of Anderson. Helms returns to deny again that the CIA had any contact with Oswald when he returned to the United States.

On that "Frontline" broadcast, other witnesses chime in confirming the existence of 00 (Domestic Contacts) officer Anderson, which is but a fragment of the story, and the matter is dropped. Deneselya's astonishing information, that Oswald was a CIA spy, played no role in the program's conclusions; the implications of this revelation fade into oblivion. "Frontline's" narrator concludes: "In the end, there is only Oswald." Oswald alone, echos the narrator's ally, Oswald's own brother, Robert, who asserts, "To me, you can't reach but one conclusion," as he nails his brother as the murderer yet again.

"Frontline" signs off, impervious to the implications of the massive evidence describing what Jim Garrison figured out, that Oswald was never alone, while everyone seen with him was with the CIA. "Frontline" denies evidence it has itself just broadcast, in a schizophrenic effort to uphold the official story, even at the cost of its own credibility.

I made an appointment to see Donald Deneselya, to hear his evidence for myself. We met at a Holiday Inn on December 8, 2007, fifteen years after the death of Jim Garrison, who, alone among public officials, was persuaded that Lee Harvey Oswald was connected to the CIA. The biography of Jim Garrison turns implicitly to the many later corroborations of his evidence. New documents add weight to the inspired speculations for which Garrison was unable during his lifetime to provide documentation.

A few weeks later, Deneselya called me. He had read in "A Farewell To Justice" (p. 165) the discussion of Jack Edward Dunlap who had provided the Soviets with information about the U-2. Dunlap, I wrote, in keeping with the official record, had "committed suicide."

No, Deneselya says. Dunlap, who had been a courier for General Coverdale, moving between the NSA, the CIA and the White House, had, in fact, been murdered on the orders of William Harvey, CIA master of executive action capability. He had been found dead of carbon monoxide poisoning in his garage, Deneselya says, but it was not suicide: "Harvey took him out."

Harvey found using gas a convenient method in those days, Deneselya adds, particularly using cars. Another of Harvey's victims was one George Weiss, who had been involved in organizing security at the White House; he was an Agent high up in the CIA in Eastern Europe. Weiss too died of carbon monoxide poisoning in his garage, exactly in the manner that Dunlap died.

The name recalls the letter Garrison material witness Gordon Novel left in his apartment as he departed the Orleans Parish jurisdiction: It begins, "Dear Mr. Weiss." Novel's intention, was to make clear his own connections to the CIA, and the letter, found in his abandoned kitchen, seemed a fabrication motivated by Novel's wish to avoid Garrison's subpoenas. Yet there was, in fact, a Mr. Weiss in charge of White House security.

Willy nilly, survivors of this history have suddenly made their presence known. A New Orleans figure claiming to have taken part in the conspiracy came forward in August, and again in October 2007, writing without a return address to one of Jim Garrison's officers who had been involved in his Kennedy investigation.

"So you think that I am dead," he begins. "I am who they call the "2nd Oswald. I think that you know that I exist. Big Jim did." The question of why no one talked is answered in his first line: "The older I get, the more I feel the need to tell someone some facts about the whole Oswald, JFK, Garrison, Shaw, Russo fiasco."

This witness establishes his bonafides with some small details. With respect to that evening at David Ferrie's apartment, with Perry Russo, Clay Shaw and Ferrie in attendance, along with Oswald, he writes, "Shaw left his special pk. of cigarettes on a chair by the entrance."

The writer clearly knows far too much to be dismissed as a crack-pot. If nothing else, he suggests, he with his letters postmarked somewhere in Texas, that there may well remain people at large with some knowledge of the events of November 22nd, that some had been based in New Orleans, and that Jim Garrison was not unreasonable in devoting so much of his life to finding them.

Late 2007 seems a moment of emerging information. Since, paraphrasing the sublime novelist, Don DeLillo, in the story of the Kennedy assassination "everyone is connected," it should not be surprising that with both living in the state of Louisiana, the son of CIA field office second in command Hunter Leake should encounter Jim Garrison's law school classmate, John R. Rarick, who figures in the events of this book as well. At an annual Civil War event, "The Day The War Stopped," Judge Rarick had long played the role of a Confederate captain named W. W. Leake in a re-enactment of the burial of one Commander Hart. Rarick was replaced by Robert Leake, a great grandson of W. W. Leake.

At the 2007 event, Leake confided to Rarick of how many times his father had spoken to him about – Lee Harvey Oswald. Hunter Leake had, just before his death, talked of his knowledge of Oswald, and how after the assassination of President Kennedy he had destroyed some documents, and conveyed a good number of others to CIA headquarters. Here, however, was corroboration, not for publication, but in the course of everyday life where, again willy nilly, the truth forces its way to the surface.

Each fragment of information about the assassination of President Kennedy that emerges even at this late date, with the trail seemingly cold, returns us to the man who more than anyone else was determined to discover the truth. The story of Garrison's life, this prequel, illuminates simultaneously the character of the man and the nature of the cover-up of the facts concerning the Kennedy assassination.

This volume takes the reader not to the close of Jim Garrison's life, but to the moment when he declared that "nothing else matters" and devoted himself entirely to his Kennedy investigation. In the process, Garrison sacrificed, with no regrets, a promising political career. Like any conventional biography, my book opens on Garrison's family history and childhood and takes him through his formative years.

We observe him witnessing the atrocities of Dachau concentration camp at the end of World War Two. For Garrison, as he said often in later life, this was a moment of profound influence on his thinking. This volume closes on Garrison in the fullness of his prime.

My book is not hagiography, inventing the life of a saint. Jim Garrison remarked during his closing statement at the federal trial where he defended himself against the charge that he had taken bribes from pinball gambling interests that the last perfect person walked the earth two thousand years ago. I have chronicled the life of a person who was both a man of his time, a man of contradictions, and one who, despite persistent interference in his efforts from the highest authority, and its legion of collaborators, rose above the ordinary.

Jim Garrrison was a man who lived the history of his time. His unique passage is worthy of note.

Joan Mellen
Pennington, New Jersey
January 2008

"Speak of me as I am; nothing extenuate…."
William Shakespeare, "Othello."

JIM GARRISON:

HIS LIFE AND TIMES, THE EARLY YEARS

BY

JOAN MELLEN

CHAPTER 1:

Iowa to New Orleans

"It's just Mr. Jimmy."

"I thought I was living in the country I was born in," Jim Garrison liked to say when he was faced by media persistent in their refusal to tell the truth about the Kennedy assassination and demanding to know how he ever could have expected to bring anyone to justice for the murder of the President in a Louisiana state court. That country where a greater democracy seemed to thrive was pre-Depression America. He was born Earling Carothers Garrison on November 20, 1921 in a three-story, fifteen room Queen Anne-style mansion in Denison, Iowa. The house was built in 1881 at the height of his prosperity by Thomas Jefferson Garrison, Jim Garrison's grandfather. In this house, his father, Earling, and his mother, Jane Robinson Garrison, made their tentative home, and attempted to co-exist in harmony.

The Garrisons were Germans of "old Saxony stock," as one ancestor proudly recounts, who had settled in England. Arriving in North Carolina in 1644, they fought in the American Revolution. Freeborn Garrison, a minister, was said to be the first man in North Carolina to emancipate his slaves, and his descendant, Jim Garrison, making his life in Louisiana, despite the prevailing ethos, was no racist. Attempting to define for two Yankee visitors the "Sovereignty Commission," that temporary institution designed to thwart integration after Brown v. Board of Education, Garrison said, with his typical sardonic humor, it was about "keeping blacks from walking down white streets like Royal Street."

The first Garrison in the Garrison diaspora to enter the stage of history was the distinguished abolitionist, William Lloyd Garrison. Of this relation's extremist views, some Garrisons did not approve. So Judge Thomas Garrison Stansberry wrote: "I confess that I did not like very well to claim relationship with Lloyd Garrison of Massachusetts of Abolition renown...he was a talented man, but rather eccentric in his views with regard to the African race in America."

By 1764, some Garrisons had found their way to Patrick Henry County, Virginia, accounting for the given name of Jim Garrison's grandfather.

Thomas Jefferson Garrison was six foot six inches tall, the identical height of his grandson. A lawyer, known in town as T. J., he went to work each day dressed in a high hat and a Prince Albert coat, his flowing locks hanging out the back. He had come from poverty, dropping out of college almost as soon as he began, at age seventeen. T.J. went to work in a hardware and lumber business to save money for law school. He was twenty-seven by the time he graduated.

T.J. Garrison was a man of parts. Admitted to the bar in 1879, he went to work for the Chicago, Milwaukee & St. Paul Railway, and the Chicago and Northwestern Railway, becoming their General Counsel. On his staff was the young Clarence Darrow. When Darrow resigned to represent Eugene V. Debs, the great socialist leader of the railway workers, T. J. was relieved. He was a conciliatory man, a peacemaker, and he avoided litigation whenever he could.

Nor did T. J. Garrison "thirst for office." Preferring a quiet life, he married a Miss Emma Carothers, with whom he had four children. The youngest and the most spoiled, was Earling R., Jim Garrison's father, who managed to become a lawyer too.

T. J. built the palatial "Garrison House" in the part of Denison known as "Silk Stocking Row" because the rich people lived there. He owned a thousand acres of fertile Iowa farmland and was part owner of several private banks. When the Depression struck, T. J. lost everything, and the mansion had to be sold. "Why didn't we keep cash in a bank box, why didn't we keep a cash reserve?" T. J. lamented. In fact, he cared little for money and was no more cunning in its uses than his grandson Jim Garrison would be.

When Jim Garrison was born, an extended family was still resident in the mansion. Lillian, T. J.'s oldest child, lived at home as, in the parlance of that day, a spinster. She played the massive grand piano, a Weber with heavily carved legs, and wore dresses imported from Paris. Aunt Lillian's first love was music, and she was always among the first to appear at the local jewelry store when the new "red seal" records arrived from the Victor Company. There Lillian Garrison would sit, listening to the new records.

T. J.'s son Edgar became a judge for the Panama Canal Zone. Of this uncle, Jim Garrison would always be proud and among his possessions he kept photographs of Uncle Edgar in his white suit. Only T.J.'s youngest, Earling, born on June 2, 1898, and succumbing early to alcoholism, was a disappointment.

On January 22, 1921, Earling married Jane Anne Robinson and they settled in the Garrison mansion.

The Robinsons, no one more proudly than Jane, traced their ancestry to an Irish rebel named William McFarren, born in Ireland in 1722, and arriving in the Colonies in time to fight in the Revolution. The Robinsons were the tallest men in Marion County, Iowa. Jane's father, William Oliver Robinson, Jim Garrison's maternal grandfather, stood at seven feet three inches tall.

One day the circus came to Des Moines. The three Robinson boys, William Oliver and his two brothers, John S. Robinson and Charles M. Robinson, stood in the street with everyone else awaiting the parade. They did not suffer fools gladly. When tiresome people asked how the weather was up there, the Robinson boys would spit, and then say it was raining.

As the circus performers approached, people in the crowd urged the Robinson brothers to join the circus themselves. At once they stepped out into the street, marching three-abreast, just ahead of the circus performers, the tallest men in the world. It was said that they attracted as much attention as the elephants.

Later the circus manager outfitted them in high leather boots and stove-pipe hats, so that they seemed even taller. William Oliver liked to dress up as "Uncle Sam" as they traveled with the circus to Europe and as far away as Australia. In his later years, William Oliver continued to dress up on national holidays as Uncle Sam, decked out in a red, white and blue costume and huge stove-pipe hat. His eyes were fierce and he displayed a lavish handlebar mustache, the patriot of Knoxville, Iowa now. Among the dignitaries he greeted was President William Howard Taft. In his mundane life, William Oliver Robinson was a successful real estate and coal entrepreneur. Elegance marked him, as it would his grandson, and he had his suits tailor-made in New York City.

Jim Garrison thoroughly enjoyed his mother's stories about this grandfather, whom he never actually met. During the years of his investigation into the murder of President Kennedy, he liked to register at a hotel using the name W. O. Robinson. Names, nicknames, names self-selected, names discarded in favor of other names, would become his modus operandi, a source of amusement and an exercise of his copious imagination. He gave his youngest son, Eberhard, the middle name "Darrow," and another would be forever, "Snapper," because his wife Liz's pregnancy was difficult: Snapper would be like the jockey Snapper Garrison, quick to the finish, Garrison reassured Liz. Liz would not be Liz, but Edna, or Rochelda, because she abhorred roaches.

William Oliver married Dorcas Chapman. Their sixth child was Jane Anne Robinson, born October 1, 1899, and it is she who would become Jim Garrison's mother. Jane grew to six foot two, nearly six foot three inches tall. She was a strong-willed, intelligent woman. In the high school band she played the trombone, and she traveled with an independent band on Chautauqua circuits. Jane enrolled at Northwestern University, then dropped out. The year was 1919.

As the wife of Earling R. Garrison, Jane at once threw herself into community life. She joined "Entre Nous," an exclusive Denison social institution, and taught in the public school. Two years after the birth of Earling Carothers, she bore a second child, Judith Dorcas, born May 14, 1923.

Little Carothers, as he was called, to distinguish him from his father, was an active child, a child filled with curiosity and imagination. Mischief made life interesting. The telephone rang one day while Jane was giving him his bath. There was no little boy in the tub when she returned.

Jane raced out of the house and headed down Broadway in search of the missing toddler. She invaded store after store, only finally to discover Little Carothers at Cushman's. There he was strolling along, stark naked, but for the elaborate picture hat belonging to his mother that he had plucked from a hall chair on his way out the door. There was a world elsewhere.

Soon Carothers' disappearances became routine, then legendary. A baby-sitter turned around and he was gone. "He was right here, a minute ago," Mrs. Woolston pleaded. Later Carothers was found hiding in the oven. Another babysitter, named Mrs. Leo Gaughan, often called in "to sit with Carothers and Judy," found him equally obstreperous.

At the age of two, he was caught scribbling on someone's gravestone. At four, he could read, reading to be the passion of his adult life when a complete set of Shakespeare would ever occupy an honored place on his office desk.

In the autumn of 1926, Jim Garrison, not quite five years old, entered Kindergarten. At the end of the day, stern, square-jawed Jane Garrison arrived at the school to collect her precocious son. Carothers was nowhere to be found.

A fierce figure, holding herself to her full height, Mrs. Garrison demanded, "Where's my Earling?"

"There is no Earling in my class," the teacher said. Brushing past her, Jane Garrison strode into the room. At last she spied her son.

"Oh, you mean Jimmy!" the teacher said. Earling Carothers Garrison, aged four, had decided he did not like his name. Bypassing his difficult mother, he had kept secret his plan. He was changing his name. "Jimmy" was the name of the newspaper delivery boy. Little Carothers regarded Jimmy's shiny red bicycle with the appreciation it deserved. He decided to call himself "Jimmy." So he would be – "James Carothers Garrison" – until, entering politics, he made his new name legal as "Jim."

Inside the Garrison mansion, life had grown gloomy. Later Jim Garrison would remark that the atmosphere in his childhood home reminded him of "Arsenic and Old Lace." The men wore swallow-tail coats to dinner, the women long dresses. Before dinner, the men would shave for the second time that day. One night, before dinner, Jimmy ran upstairs and shaved off his eyebrows. Then he came down to the table.

Earling drank. Overshadowed by his brothers, he grew depressed. His wife had high standards and expected other people to live by them. One of Jane's favorite words was "glorious." Jane was a member of Daughters of the American Revolution and took that organization seriously.

When Jimmy was about six, Jane decided she could take no more. She would leave Earling, she would leave Iowa. Her brother, Ernest, lived in Chicago, and she headed there first, with her two children in tow. Earling found out and set off after her. He found his son and told him he was taking him out for ice cream, then carried him back to Denison, putting up at the Denison Hotel, father and son.

At once Jane hired a private investigator, who re-kidnapped Jimmy and returned him to his mother. Jim Garrison never would see his father again. In later years, if Jane Garrison deigned to mention her husband, it was always in disparaging tones. Jimmy never stopped yearning for his father, and he would become overly trusting of slightly older men, men who more often than not betrayed him. Over the course of his life, he would mention often how he missed not having had a father. Meanwhile, Jane Garrison became obsessed by this son who so came to resemble her that in later years her granddaughter Virginia would describe her as "Daddy in drag."

Back in Denison, alone and abandoned, Earling faltered. In May 1928 he was arrested in Des Moines for mail fraud; he had sent fountain pens to dead people C.O.D. with charges having been paid by the survivors. He used an alias, "Waldo Morrison," and served two years at the federal penitentiary at Fort Leavenworth, Kansas. In March of 1930, he was indicted again, this time for having stolen a cashier's check worth $1,196.40 from the home of a neighbor named Frank Woolston. Earling cashed it in a suburb of Des Moines, then bought a car, a typewriter and a suit. He became a vagabond and was identified from a photograph taken when he had been incarcerated at a military installation at Danville, Indiana.

Earling promised to lead a "reformed" life, even as he began his steeper five year sentence at the state penitentiary at Anamoon. By 1934, he was resident in Kansas. By 1940, he had moved to Arizona. He never attempted to make contact with his son.

As for Jane, she dropped off Jimmy and Judy with her brother Ernest, giving him three hundred dollars in cash for their expenses. Then she departed for Vincennes, Indiana, where she sold corsets door to door. By May of 1927, the year she was granted her divorce, she was selling real estate in Evansville, Indiana. She had by now collected her children, but they had nowhere to stay.

"We were stuck up in Evansville, Indiana, and the winters were mean cold," Jane would tell Jim Garrison later. "Then I had to face the Great Depression, raising you and your sister by myself. Your father had begun his world tour sampling the liquors of various countries, and when he found one with unusual alcoholic resources, he'd stay for a while." Nor would Jane ever forget the hardships she faced during the Depression. "You kids had so many holes in your shoes, I had to line them with cardboard. Do you remember that?" Jane said.

She sold insurance. Men failed, but not Jane. It was in Evansville that she had first looked into the oil business. Jane Garrison was among the earliest women to ply that trade, brokering oil leases as a middle-woman, taking her commission from the oil company, and eventually buying lease holds herself. Iron-willed, she took that trade to Louisiana, to the port city of New Orleans which was the end of the line for people running away from something. Jane arrived in New Orleans virtually penniless, without a place to stay or a regular job.

"No matter what it takes," she told Jimmy and Judy, "I'm going to get this family housed, clothed and fed. Some way, somehow, I'm going to get it done." And she did. Always Jane Robinson Garrison would remain proud of her ancestry, and when she died, her daughter Judith would receive a condolence card from the members of the Mississippi DAR. Jane had seen to it that Judith too became a member.

In later years, remembering his mother, Jim Garrison said that in the ring with her, "Mike Tyson wouldn't last a round." He drew his strength from her, his wife, Liz, would reflect. Oppressed by her domineering ways as he often was, he admired her grit, her determination, her sheer forcefulness.

In New Orleans, they moved from place to place. One walk-up was located on Walnut Street, near Audubon Park. The other children on the block knew Jimmy lived there, but they rarely spotted him, nor did they even know he had a sister. He lived like a hermit, reading, always reading. One of the boys, Bernie Jacobs, figured out that Jimmy didn't ride a bicycle like the other boys because he didn't have one. Jimmy did join the Boy Scouts, but was expelled for setting off a firecracker during a ceremonial meeting. Practical jokes leavened life, rendered his loneliness endurable. If he really got to know you, you could become the lifelong butt of his elaborate practical jokes.

He attended E. B. Krutschnitt elementary school. The teacher talked. Bored, Jimmy ignored her. He curled his hand around his pencil in a peculiar way so that the colored pencil rested between his middle and index fingers; the index finger curled around to meet his thumb. He was drawing pictures, caricatures, and portraits. He remained taller than the other children. One big foot stuck out in the aisle as he sat there doodling.

The G's sat together. Jimmy's seat partner was named Walter Gemeinhardt.

"You curleque your pen," Gemeinhardt said. He was as outgoing and chatty as a boy as he would be graciously effusive as a man and a New Orleans attorney. Jimmy remained silent.

"You're putting too much blue on the man," Gemeinhardt observed.

Jimmy "gave it a shrug." He didn't care what anyone thought. No one knew him well. After school, his giant of a mother, broad and heavy-hipped now, picked him up and took him the ten blocks back home. There were no social meetings with the other children. One day he disappeared. One of the children found out that his mother had taken him out of school and they had moved to Mississippi.

Jane found it impossible to maintain a home for herself and the children, whether in Louisiana or Mississippi. When they returned to New Orleans, the family moved into Fanny Campbell's boarding house at 3211 Prytania Street. Fanny's was a charming establishment, combining high respectability with bohemian largesse. Heavy Victorian furniture met sparkling conversation as the boarders shared dinner and gossip. From a socially prominent Creole family, Fanny dressed in a tailored jacket, a man's tie, long skirt and tennis shoes. Some thought you practically had to be in the social register to get into Fanny's, but it wasn't so.

Fanny liked interesting people, and delighted especially in helping those who had fallen on hard times. She opened her doors to anyone she liked. Commercial travelers, the elderly who had run out of options, divorced women whose social position was dubious – all could find a home at Fanny's. A Carnival queen told stories to the woman who wrote a society column or to the former Scripps-Howard retainer given to calling in false fire alarms. Paying the fine was small price to pay for the excitement. Jammering mynah birds added to the uproar. If you couldn't pay, Fanny would not withdraw her hospitality.

Best of all for Jane Garrison was that meals were served by black maids. You were expected to appear for dinner on time, and conversation ran high amid the red beans and rice and gumbo, not to mention the home-made cinnamon rolls, for which Fanny's was famous.

Men and women shared a bathroom, very outré for those times. An ice chest filled with beer was always available. Poking fun at the uptown world, Fanny rode on a banana wagon pulled by mules during one Mardi Gras, right behind the austere REX float. There Fannie sat, on a toilet bowl, dressed in feathers and bows, waving her scepter, which was a plunger.

In addition to Jane, there was another divorced woman living at Fanny's, a postal worker named Ruth Bayer Francis, later to become a Major in the Army during World War Two. In Jane Garrison, Ruth saw an intelligent, independent, determined woman. While Jane was out at night selling insurance, Ruth cared for Jimmy and Judith. Ruth didn't much enjoy the company of children, but Jimmy was such a sweet boy that she took to him at once.

Jane left Fanny's and they moved to the old Epley House, now cut up into apartments. They moved to the Quarter, to a house on Madison Street where their neighbor was Tennessee Williams. They moved down from Tujague's on Decatur Street.

Jimmy caught the St. Charles streetcar and traveled for an hour each way to attend the academically superior Alcee Fortier High School, class of 1939. He was a very tall gangling young fellow now, shy, unathletic and reclusive. He had retained his taste for the practical joke. Jimmy took big steps, but he didn't move very quickly. He had a lumbering walk.

Brilliant lawyers out of work during the Depression taught at Fortier, among them J. Skelly Wright, later to distinguish himself on the federal bench as Louisiana's advocate for desegregation. Among Jim Garrison's favorites was his English teacher, Miss O'Bier, who assigned her students to write the biography of one of their classmates. You picked the name of your subject from a hat. Students at Fortier went to school in suits, collar and tie. Jimmy was fastidious.

He joined the debating team where his dry wit and irony made the shy, reclusive Jimmy seem an entirely other person. His best friend, Alvin Gottschall, was surprised that Jimmy was so relaxed on stage when he was so shy otherwise. The Fortier debating team was to win the state championship in 1939. Gottschall was one of the few of Jimmy's friends who got to meet Jane Garrison. She talked in a mannish, forceful, even unpleasant way, he thought, and you couldn't change her mind about anything.

As for Gottschall, he would long remain a butt of Jim Garrison's practical jokes. Shortly after Jim Garrison took office as District Attorney, Gottschall received a telephone call from the police. He had twenty-one parking violations, he was told, and they were coming to pick him up. Indeed, Gottschall was escorted to what he would remember as the Jackson Street station. He had received a single ticket, Gottschall pleaded, in vain. Finally, they let him go, agreeing that there must be some mistake. The next day there was district attorney Jim Garrison on the telephone, laughing.

Claiming he had allergies, that his nose was clogged up much of the time, Jimmy played no sports. Often he was absent from school.

It wasn't that he was ill, his classmate Michael Bagot discovered, just that he didn't want to go to school. He was a loner.

One Saturday morning, Bagot and another boy found themselves in the neighborhood and rang the Garrison doorbell. Jimmy buzzed them in and they climbed to the third floor. It was the middle of the day. Jimmy was in his underclothes, lying on an unmade bed. He seemed surprised that they cared enough to visit. He seemed forlorn.

When he didn't feel like studying because he was bored, he didn't, and he didn't get particularly good grades. Jimmy daydreamed, staring out of the window, lost in space. In the cafeteria, he sat eating his lunch all by himself, day after day. Yet if you approached him, as future artist John Clemmer did, he was friendly and pleasant. He still liked to draw, and he would ask someone, "Do you have a pencil that I can borrow?" A boy named Herbert Barton sat in front of him, and Jimmy drew Barton's portrait. "How do you like this?" Jimmy asked, showing Barton the finished product. It was a well-constructed profile.

Jimmy decided to join Phi Lambda Epsilon fraternity which was considered important for social advancement. Its sponsor was Wilma Lilburn, the debating teacher, who chose the members of the debating team herself. "Take a slow, deep breath, and while looking over everyone from left to right, develop the feeling that you [are] the expert on your subject and you are going to enlighten those stupid fools in the audience," Miss Lilburn advised.

Initiation into Phi Lambda Epsilon was serious business. The officers dressed in robes and assembled in the "secret room" at the Roosevelt Hotel. About to be initiated, Jimmy began to giggle and then found he couldn't stop giggling. The President of Phi Lambda Epsilon threatened to kick Jimmy and Alvin Gottschall out before they even joined.

And then Jimmy was not quite so forlorn. He had attached himself to the parents of his friend Peggie Baker, an Uptown young lady. Peggie was a thirteenth generation descendant of John Alden and Priscilla Mullins. Peggie's great grandfather had graduated from Tulane, and her father was a pioneer anaesthesiologist – in New Orleans there were only two in that day – and he took to Jimmy at once. Peggie was warm, soft-spoken and elegant, with soft brown eyes.

After school, he went to the Bakers' Uptown mansion on State Street and did his homework, as if he lived there. To Peggie and her sister, Wilma, he talked about his family and it seemed to Wilma that he spoke of his absent father with disdain. The Bakers provided sanctuary for Jimmy from his over-solicitous mother, who seemed jealous of anyone with whom he spent time, who behaved as if she alone could fulfill his needs. Jimmy told Peggie and Wilma that his mother played chess with him.

On Saturday nights, the Bakers gave parties, a strategy by the parents to keep their attractive daughters safely at home. Somehow it came down to Peggie and Wilma and six or seven boys. Alvin, who had introduced Jimmy to the Bakers, believed they did this so they would have all the boys to themselves.

They danced. They listened to the radio. Jimmy lost himself in the music of the big bands, Glenn Miller's "One O'Clock Jump," Benny Goodman, Tommy Dorsey and others. Glenn Miller was their favorite. No one was more adept at identifying a big band from just a few seconds on the radio than Jimmy. As soon as the opening notes were played, you had to identify the orchestra, band leader and the song. Jimmy was always right. You could also call in to the station and request a record.

One night Jimmy picked up the phone and in a falsetto voice asked, "I want you to play 'Deutschland uber alles' in honor of Adolf Hitler."

The highlight of the evening came at eleven with the refreshments: ham, Swiss cheese, roast beef, bread and milk. Sometimes, it was just soda and cookies.

Swing music, the bands that came into their own at the turn of the 1940's, would remain important to Jim Garrison all his life. Decades later he was ordering tapes of Tommy Dorsey's "Sentimental" and "Tommy Dorsey's Dance Party," along with Gershwin, Glenn Miller, Benny Goodman, Harry James and Artie Shaw. In 1982, as a judge on the Louisiana Court of Appeal, Jim Garrison joined a group of local investors, including Willard E. Robertson, owner of the Volkswagen franchise, who planned to bring dance orchestras to a pavilion they wanted to establish at the 1984 World's Fair in New Orleans. It could, Judge Garrison thought, "be the beginning of the return on a sustained basis of the great 'swing' music which so many people still love."

"Mabel, who's downstairs?" Mrs. Baker would call down to her maid.

"It's just Mr. Jimmy," Mabel said. At the Bakers', Jimmy studied. He played the radio. He bought Peggie records when he had any money. He had discovered a family.

His sister Judith was not so fortunate. Judith walked around with a dreamy look and seemed always to want to be alone. Then she became despondent. Jimmy was obviously Mrs. Garrison's favorite; her daughter, people concluded, was someone she controlled, and, later, used. One day Judith ran away, and once more Jane Garrison had to hire a private investigator. When she returned, Jane put her in a hospital on the downtown side of Audubon Park, off St. Charles Avenue. Her spirit had been crushed, her will to live impaired.

Peggie Baker was Jim Garrison's first love. Their courtship was hampered, however, by his extreme poverty. If he took her to the movies, she had to pay her own way. With others, she could go to the Roosevelt Hotel where for a dollar you could dance to Latin American music and maybe enter the rumba contest and win a bottle of champagne. This was beyond Jimmy's means.

Yet Peggie brought him out. Shy as he was, when "Willie," as Jimmy dubbed Wilma, and Peggie spied a handsome young man who played in the Fortier band and asked whether Jimmy knew him, he lied and said he did. Then Jimmy invited Warren Malhiot to the Baker's "Dine and Dance." The next day, Mrs. Baker was on the telephone inquiring as to Warren's antecedents, as Uptown people did. Wilma and Warren were ultimately to marry. Mrs. Baker liked Jimmy, but she did not view him as an appropriate suitor for either of her daughters.

It wasn't only that he lacked family. Jimmy was different. He was, they all thought, "unpredictable." Pat Gore, a regular at the Bakers' parties, thought Jimmy used such big words that you almost thought he was cussing you out. Jimmy was unique among the young men in the Baker circle for his interest in ideas. He was already an intellectual.

"You know, everybody's a Unitarian," Jimmy said one night when religion was the subject.

"What do you mean? I'm a Presbyterian!" Willie demurred.

"Everyone interprets the Bible just the way they want to," Jimmy insisted. He alone read the newspapers and was interested in what was going on in the world. He talked about Louisiana politics as a joke. It was corrupt, too often with a showman at the helm. He was talking, of course, about Huey Long.

At midnight, Peggie's grandmother would clap her hands, signaling the end of the evening. One night, Jimmy just leaned back in his dining room chair, clapped his hands, and said, "what's that all about?" as if he didn't know.

"What a rude young man!" Peggie's grandmother said, but everyone knew Jimmy was teasing. His humor was not for everyone. Peggie was a picky eater and on one evening when she did not feel well, she spit her soup back into the bowl.

"Doesn't she have to eat it again?" Jimmy said.

Peggie was refined, the soup incident notwithstanding, beautiful and kind. She was musical, and elegant, a young woman of another era. She appreciated Jimmy and thought he was as warm, sweet and deep as anyone could be. For Peggie's high school graduation, since she planned to major in music and voice at college, Jimmy gave her an astonishing gift of two elaborate volumes of Beethoven Sonatas, a gift he could ill afford. When he went off to war and distinguished himself, he sent her one of his medals. Although her family was never to encourage this relationship, the loss of Peggie would be an immeasurable one for Jim Garrison.

Jimmy asked Pat Gore, one day. "Pat, why don't you come down to the Jackson Barracks on Sunday morning? You'll get some money and some exercise." In the spring of 1939, Jim Garrison was still a senior at Fortier, as he joined the Louisiana National Guard. Pat Gore didn't want to get up at five a.m. to take two streetcars, but he didn't need the money as much as Jimmy did.

James Carothers Garrison entered Tulane University, class of 1943. Ever mindful of his mother's precarious financial situation, he chose the School of Commerce and Business Administration. At once he joined the Forensic Council and Hullabaloo, and he was on the newspaper. When Russia invaded Finland, Jimmy led a movement for students to stop shaving until Russia ceased her aggression. He had become an activist.

By the end of the fall semester of 1940, having completed a year of college, Jimmy dropped out to enlist in the war that America had yet to enter. If his motive for joining the military so young was, in part, to escape from his possessive mother, that didn't work. When Jimmy was sent to Fort Sill, Oklahoma, Jane Garrison followed him.

CHAPTER 2:

Encountering Dachau

"What I saw there has haunted me ever since."
Jim Garrison

Jim Garrison loved serving in the military. His time in uniform, both during his training in America and in the European theater of war, was a cherished one. He had been politically sophisticated since high school, and the cause was just. He read the recruiting poster: "Serve with your neighbor and serve with an outfit that will serve New Orleans coffee." Jimmy needed no inducement. He joined the Washington Artillery nearly a year before Pearl Harbor. The cot on which he was to sleep was far too short – his feet hung over the bottom. He didn't mind.

His first sergeant was named Pershing Gervais. Street-wise, iconoclastic, and thoroughly amoral, Gervais was unlike anyone sheltered Jim Garrison had ever known. He was eight years older, his speech laced with obscenities, his bearing manly. Jim liked him. He sympathized too. Pershing had suffered adversity. He had grown up the son of deaf mutes, and had to bear the taunts of the other children. "That's the dummies' kid," they would say. Pershing had dropped out of school in the eighth grade – his quick intelligence was unmediated by formal education.

By the time he was twenty, Pershing Gervais had worked on the goon squad of a gubernatorial candidate, pouring little pint bottles of ink into ballot boxes. Caught, he denied everything. He celebrated his twenty-first year with an arrest: for carrying concealed weapons, a black jack and a pair of brass knuckles.

Jim Garrison enjoyed Pershing Gervais, and appreciated his manly influence. From the start, Pershing exerted, Garrison would come to acknowledge, with regret, a controlling influence on the younger man. Jim loved Pershing's stories, his bawdy, irreverent, cynical view of life. Pershing was "considerably more intelligent than most of the men around him," Jim Garrison told "Life" editor Richard N. Billings, as, years later, he attempted to explain the role of Pershing in his life after Pershing's manifold malfeasances had damaged the credibility of the Orleans Parish district attorney's office: Pershing "had a unique insight into human nature and a wayward sense of humor." Later still, Garrison would attribute his trusting Pershing Gervais to his obsession with not having had a father, a man who cared for him.

One night, recruit Jim Garrison was sleeping in what he called his "cold pyramidal tent." Pershing, the non-commissioned officer in charge of quarters, was making his rounds in the Battery area when he encountered a stray alley cat in search of food. "Never one to waste a golden opportunity," as Garrison later wrote of Gervais, Pershing brought the cat into Garrison's tent and tossed it up into the air. By the time the cat landed, "it had become transformed into a startling combination of wild cat and were-wolf." Jim wound up in hand-to-hand combat with the terrified cat, trying to pull the creature off him. Pershing had revealed himself: cruel, vicious and ever in pursuit of power over other men.

Yet they became friends, both becoming sergeants, both landing at Camp Shelby in Hattiesburg, Mississippi. The New Orleans newspapers heralded the departure of the fabled Washington Artillery, and granted it equal billing with the second inaugural of President Franklin Delano Roosevelt. Mornings in Mississippi the regimental song was played: It was "Dixie."

The urgent need for officers sent the first group from Camp Shelby to Officer Candidate School at Fort Sill, Oklahoma. It was now that Jane Garrison followed her son into his military service. If his motive had been to escape from her, it didn't work. His protests met with resistance. His friends were to perceive that Jane Garrison suffered nothing less than an erotic attachment to her son.

Jim Garrison trained first at the Field Artillery school, once the scene of United States Cavalry actions against the Comanche and Kiowa Indians. Geronimo, the Apache leader, had been imprisoned here. Sergeant Gervais, who claimed later to "love the army," but evinced no great ambition to serve on the field of battle, moved on to Camp Sutton in North Carolina.

From Camp Roberts in California, in the autumn of 1942, Lieutenant James C. Garrison wrote to still-Sergeant Gervais. He missed the Washington Artillery, Jim wrote. He was now "teaching materiel in an all-gun battery," with no "instruments or communications of any kind, nor any resemblance to a tactical outfit." Jim loved military language, and later it would become part of the parlance of the office of the District Attorney of Orleans Parish.

Still, he felt useless. Amid too many officers, he wasn't needed: "That makes you feel as desired and necessary as tent pegs in a honeymoon bed," he wrote to Gervais, already evincing his lifelong literary ambition. He had applied to be an aerial observer with the Field Artillery, but had been rejected for lack of flying experience. To this letter, Jim added a detail that he knew would appeal to Pershing. He thought he might spend his coming three day leave in Hollywood, "the town where Greer Garson and Theresa Wright live."

He remained an instructor, although he craved action on the field of battle. Instead, that November of 1942, in a "Special Training Battery," he taught reading, writing and arithmetic "(so help me) and care of personal equipment and foot drill" to "illiterates, mental neurotics, and [the] physically disabled." His pupils included "several dozen Cajuns who spoke only French and fifty Mexicans "who major only in Spanish." He tried to impress Gervais with his cleverness as he wrote about the "stolid Indian-speaking-only Indians padding around." This was not idealistic Jim Garrison's notion of serving in the military. "If this is the Artillery," he complained to Gervais, "my name is Shapiro." He signed this letter: "Shapiro."

Finally he was accepted into the Army Air Force Basic Flying School, and went off to train in Pecos, Texas. The town earned at the hands of urbane Jim Garrison the nickname, "Black Hole of Calcutta." He had been granted his wish to serve in the war.

Then he became uncertain. He said he told the Army that he "wasn't a damn bit interested in flying or the Air Corps" and applied for transfer back to the Artillery. "I merely sharpened my technique of cruising around upside-down, added a few complementary embellishments, and – Presto! Here I am!" he wrote Gervais, having failed to secure the transfer. But he continued to torture himself with having made the wrong decision. He longed now, he said, for the aiming circle, the firing tables. "I knew damn well that the day I began in the Air Corps, I would be missing the Field Artillery." When Gervais claimed to long for the Air Corps, Jim Garrison attempted to dissuade him:

> If you want a branch where the enlisted men rarely salute officers, and where a corporal's rating or higher means you don't have to wear stockings, can wear cowboy boots, can wear an officer's suit to work, or a dirty undershirt to Retreat. Where discipline is so low as to be all but absent, and where army customs and service habits that were law, with us, are consciously ignored. And where – this is the height: corporals can get K.P. and lieutenants C.Q! If that is what you want, in short, if you DON'T like the ARMY, then this is the branch for you, Gerv.

The field artillery was "the best [branch] in the service," Garrison insisted. Pershing should send him regimental insignia of the Artillery since he was collecting artillery crests. He liked the Artillery for its orderliness, for its discipline.

From Pittsburg, Kansas, he returned to Fort Sill. Jane Garrison now said she needed to be in Oklahoma pursuing her oil business. In 1943, with her son at last off to war, she moved to Laurel, Mississippi, purchasing oil and gas and mineral leases and working for the Lyon Oil Company. From her mineral interests alone, she derived a thousand dollars a year.

Meanwhile Jim Garrison had emerged a first lieutenant, trained to be a "liaison pilot" (Army Aviator). Before he could leave for Europe he had to lose thirty-five pounds. He did.

In France and Germany, from April 25, 1943 to March 28, 1945, Garrison flew a reconnaissance Piper Cub or "Grasshopper" over the front lines. An "L," standing for "Liaison," was painted on the wings of his plane. Behind Jim, sat an observer with a fifty pound radio; he was a spotter and his function was to communicate with the artillery battalions.

Garrison as pilot, his microphone before him, controlled the plane using the throttle at his left hand. His feet controlled the rudders. His right hand held a joy stick. He wore a left earphone, but kept the right above, up on his head, to hear the engine better. His plane carried no armor – which would have added weight. Garrison soon regained the thirty-five pounds he had lost, and had virtually to be squeezed into his olive green "Grasshopper." It didn't help when after his second mission the observer assigned to him weighed two hundred ten pounds himself.

You were fair game for anyone above or below you. When the "Grasshoppers" took off over the trees, people would put their hands over their eyes. Altitude was 1500 feet maximum, cruising speed 65 miles an hour. To be able to sight enemy artillery, you had to fly so low that you could be hit by someone on the ground with a rifle, and so slowly as to seem almost still. The "Grasshoppers" or L-4's, would fly for an hour over the front line before the next plane replaced them. The task was to locate the front line itself, so that you flew toward the enemy as far as you could until you encountered fire from a German Focke-Wulf, the new German jets which flew faster than the American planes, or the Messerschmidt fighters.

Garrison later explained that you could protect yourself only with "evasive maneuvers," diving, climbing, sudden banking off to the right or left, or going into a fake tailspin to create the impression that your plane had been hit and was out of control. Combat fatigue was inevitable, the stress constant. Casualties were as often psychological as physical. The survival rate for a reconnaissance pilot was sixteen weeks. Persistently they were ambushed by German fighter aircraft armed with machine gun wing cannon. By the close of every sixteen weeks, thirty liaison pilots had been killed.

Yet there was Jimmy, armed only with a .45 caliber pistol, piloting his "Grasshopper," which he had named "Roger The Dodger." Jimmy's childhood love of drawing had also been enlisted. He had painted the nose and engine cowling with a yellow, red and white copy of the Flying Tiger insignia, Roger's great white teeth gleaming. He said he liked to think of himself as one of Chennault's "Flying Tigers." On some days only the arrival of clouds saved his life.

In Germany, he joined the 7th Army before they crossed the Rhine. His closest call came during the siege of Nuremberg in April 1945. Near Firth, a German Focke-Wulf closed in on him. Machine gun cannon sprouted from its wings. Having been warned, the other Grasshoppers in the area had vanished. Jimmy had not received the message dispatched to warn him away too.

"Firtree, firtree. Splash!" came over the radio now. Jimmy banked sharply to the left, in time to see a shell exploding right in front of him. Then he heard a German fighter plane diving down upon him. He entered a spin downward and began to climb in the opposite direction. His observer warned him. He could feel the rush of the German plane passing.

He struck the nose of the Grasshopper in a vertical dive straight downward and headed for the ground so fast it seemed as if his wings would rip off. The windshield buckled. The dashboard was covered with dust. The German went hurtling by, missing him by inches. He attempted a vertical spin, pretending he had been hit. The Focke-Wulf zoomed pass again. Jimmy breathed a sigh of relief, only for the German plane to reappear right under him, machine guns blazing. "It sounded," he later recalled, "like popcorn popping." He was down to one thousand feet.

He climbed a little, then sent his plane into another nose dive, attempting to get below the tree line, dangerously close to the ground. He spotted a little hill and gunned "Roger the Dodger" low, its wheels finally spinning on the grass. Jim and his observer dove out the door. The German fighter plane flew by a thousand feet over their heads.

They were standing together smoking Camels when the ambulance pulled up. "We've come to pick up the bodies," the ambulance driver said. It was, Jim Garrison would remember, "the greatest adventure of my life." A few months later, the new group commander crashed "Roger the Dodger," falling to his death. Garrison received a brand new Grasshopper that he named "Roger the Dodger, II." In smaller letters, he painted "Lt. Jim Garrison."

Garrison flew thirty-five missions in France and Germany, receiving an Air Medal for meritorious achievement, an award of which he would be proud all his life. He had the medal matted and framed and it was so important to him that Jimmy Gulotta, the chief judge of the court where he served, and his good friend since law school, thought he might take Garrison down a peg, and threw the medal in its frame onto the floor. HE was the real war hero, Gulotta told him. HE had a silver star. Jim remained expressionless.

Lieutenant Jim Garrison arrived at the Dachau concentration camp on the morning after its liberation, April 30, 1945. Bulldozers were creating pyramids of the skeletal remains of its inhabitants. Jim walked among boxcars of naked bodies, people shipped from Buchenwald and left outside to die of starvation and exposure. "What I saw there has haunted me ever since," he said later.

With a small camera, he took photographs which he mounted in an album, and kept close to him for the rest of his life. He discovered that one of the victims he photographed had been "machine-gunned to death by the SS a few hours before the Allied troops arrived." He took a picture of a decapitated head. Years later, Jim Garrison would write about the experience and about lawyers "solemnly playing the game of justice while the bodies of the murdered innocent fell daily by the thousands on all sides of them, and judges nicely balanced discretion and the rights of men."

On February 6, 1945, in Laurel, Mississippi, Jane Garrison had married Lyon Gardiner, son of a rich man and scion of the family that had owned Gardiner's Island, off New York. They built a fine house paid for by his parents, and Jane at last had a home. Her second husband lacked a profession so that they existed on his capital and inheritance. Before long, Jane learned that her new husband was not only an alcoholic, but also a womanizer.

Jim Garrison decided to make the military his career. At war, he had experienced a sense of well being he had never before known. In 1946, he requested a recall to active duty. His request was declined "on the basis that his efficiency index was below 3.5." It was a time of military cut-backs, and there was pressure to demobilize. Only highly-connected people were permitted to re-enlist. Jim Garrison knew nobody who could help him.

He visited his mother at Laurel and met her new husband whom he liked so well that he would name his second son after him: "Lyon." He took a trip to Mexico where he caught amoebic dysentery, an ailment that would plague him for years to come. Then, qualifying with some credits he had received from Shrivenham University while he was in the army, on September 23, 1946 Jim Garrison entered the Tulane School of Law.

He took up residence at Fanny Campbell's boarding house. Fanny remembered him as a child, and she loved him now, this tall young man speaking in a stentorian voice. He remained a quiet, reclusive fellow to the party-loving younger set and spent his time in his small room by himself.

Jane came to visit and occupied a room next door to his. As long as she was there, he was silent, scarcely saying a word to anyone. Everyone could see, as his good friend Nigel Rafferty's girlfriend Brucie noted, Jane paid far too much attention to Jim. Mrs. Gardiner refused to dine at the table with everyone else, but demanded that she and her son sit at a little table for two. She was formidable, like a Valkyrie. These days Jim dressed in Brooks Brothers suits, paid for by his mother.

Once Jane was gone, he moved into an attic suite on the third floor of Fanny's Harmony Street annex that had once been a slave quarters. His roommates were Jack Grayson, who was from a distinguished Louisiana family from Fort Necessity and was now on the "States" newspaper; Nigel Rafferty; and the ladies' man of the group, Julius "Pooley" Alford. Nigel was short. People teased him and Jim with the 1939 World's Fair in mind. One was the obelisk, the other….

Dinner at Fanny's: Jim was by far the most learned of the young people at the table. Often he cited the classics. On some nights he was outgoing, on others he sat in silence. He could be the life of the party, one night strumming on a banjo at a local café, on others, he was glum, coming to the table, eating and then quickly departing. Fellow resident Mickey Parlour thought it was difficult to imagine Jim Garrison ever having been a teenager. He was quiet, and never pushed himself on other people. He was so shy and aloof that Jimmy Gulotta concluded that he was afraid of people. It was very difficult to get close to him.

Jim Garrison's appetite for practical jokes remained intact. He threw a snake (non-poisonous) into the tub while Jack was taking a bath: the idea was to see exactly how fast Jack could escape. Jack retaliated by surrounding Jim's bed with voodoo offerings; chicken bones; feathers, and dolls with pins stuck in their genitals.

"That's kind of silly, isn't it?" Jim said.

One night when Marcie Ann Little and Loraine Chadwick had a party in their suite and didn't invite Jim and his friends, Jim sprayed water from the garden hose into their room. No matter what the high jinks, Fanny didn't mind, not even when they eviscerated her trunk of Mardi Gras costumes and memorabilia. "It was my great happiness to see you all enjoying yourselves," Fanny said on that occasion.

The war was over, but Pooley dreaded being called up into the Reserves. Jim and Jack typed up orders for Pooley to report to the nearest Naval Reserve office. "Oh, my god, oh no!" Pooley groaned. The Navy greeted Pooley's written orders with disdain. "That's not our form!" they said.

Some of the pranks were less sophisticated: filling paper bags with water and dropping them on pompous passers-by from their attic window was one. Jim did not care what other people thought, but he was never cruel. Challenges of wit appealed to him most. The social graces were foreign to him. "That's Jim," people would say. He was singular, different.

Extended exercises of his imagination interested him. Jack taught at the Tulane School of Business Administration, and Jim helped him arrange a moot court experiment. A student wearing a red sweater entered a class in session, waved his paper and threatened his teacher, Grayson. "You son of a bitch, you gave me this 'F' and I'm going to get you!" the student threatened.

"I'll see you later. This is a class," Jack said, following the script.

"I'm going to see you now!" the student persisted. He left, changed his sweater to one of another color and barged into Jack's office where he threw the teacher to the floor, and simulated choking him to death. As Jack yelled for help, other professors, unaware of the ploy, rushed in to help.

At the moot court trial, the class was asked to describe the offending student, including the color of his sweater. This was the side of the law that Jim enjoyed, the battle of wits, the ambiguity and the drama. Years later, when he was practicing law, he would employ the same tactic in court, changing from an Atlanta Falcons tie, his morning costume, to a Saints' tie in the afternoon as a means of establishing for the jury the fallibility of an eye witness's testimony.

One night at Fanny's, Jim confessed that he wanted to go into politics. Marcie Ann and Loraine laughed at the idea that Jim Garrison, with his morose personality, so retiring, could ever succeed in politics. He was poor too, living on his veteran's benefits, out of which he paid sixty dollars a month to Fanny. When the women organized subscriptions to the symphony, Jim had to decline. He couldn't afford it.

Yet his ambition was real. On a weekend at Laurel, to which he dragged his old friend Alvin Gottschall, he talked about how he hoped to become a United States Senator. That night the daughter of Mrs. Gardiner's cook sang for the assembled guests. She was a skinny nineteen-year-old girl with an unforgettably powerful voice. Her name was Leontyne Price.

At the Tulane School of Law, Jim Garrison excelled, with a minimum of effort. Among his professors was the distinguished John Minor Wisdom, who taught Trusts and Estates. Another was Leon Hubert, whose class was in "Criminal Procedure," and who would later hire Jim Garrison as an assistant district attorney. Still later, Hubert's path would cross Jim Garrison's in another way: Hubert would serve as a lawyer on the Warren Commission, a body whose conclusions Jim Garrison, more than anyone else, would demonstrate were highly questionable.

C. J. Morrow, who taught "Torts," said that if Jim Garrison had worked, he would have been the best student he ever had. Yet Jim was lazy. He was lazy except when he was motivated, and then he was consumed. Garrison's grade point average at Tulane would be an undistinguished 79.16. His efforts on the Fortier debating team stood him in good stead and his moot court team won easily in 1947. The results were considered important enough to be printed in the afternoon newspaper, the "Times-Picayune."

Jim Garrison could be found sitting in the back of one or another classroom drawing caricatures of his professors, among them Mitchell Franklin, Eugene Neighbors and Ray Forrester. With only a few lines, he could produce a recognizable figure. His classmate Vance Gilmer thought he was so good that he could have had a successful career as a cartoonist.

The course was "Equity." The professor demanded a long outline with a history that bore no apparent application. When grades for the final exam were posted, Jim had received a point higher than his friend Warren Garfunkel. Garfunkel was perplexed.

"Let me ask you," Jim said. "Did you mention that outline he gave us?" Garfunkel had not – it had nothing to do with any of the questions on the exam.

"I threw it in," Jim admitted. "That's probably why I got the extra point." Garfunkel was surprised to see Jim Garrison, of all people, spooning out to these professors exactly what they wanted. A pragmatic thread was emerging in his character.

Jim Garrison made Law Review. Then, bored by the laborious writing demanded, he contributed no articles, and so was asked to leave. He won the American Jurisprudence Prize in Equity and the Ralph H. Schwartz Award in 1948 and 1949.

Politics filled the air. Most of the Tulane students were veterans. Jim Garrison was a patriot, and when the American Veterans Committee attempted to enlist the ex-GIs in a protest against President Truman's policy in Greece, Jim joined the opposition along with his classmate John R. Rarick. When they broke up the demonstration, according to

Rarick, they were called on the carpet by the Dean for violating the first amendment rights of the organizers.

He had been part of the liberation of the Dachau concentration camp, and numbered among his friends two Jewish classmates, Rene Lehmann and Garfunkel, yet he never mentioned to them that he had been at Dachau.

Often he felt ill and had to rest. To his friends, he seemed a hypochondriac even, carrying around a small pillow while complaining that his back bothered him. He slept a great deal, and explained to Jack Grayson that he had not been cured of his amoebic dysentery. He would go to bed in the afternoon to rest. Sometimes he couldn't sit up even to play cards. What he liked best was to read.

In his second year at Tulane he had been so overcome with exhaustion that he felt he could not continue. Was it a virus? Was it the aftermath of combat fatigue? He would go to class, then return to Fanny's to his bed where he could store up energy for the next day. The law school was being painted and he wondered whether he was allergic to the smell. Maybe he was allergic to wool, his own suits and the wool blankets, or to the lint. It seemed that in contact with wool, he suffered an asthmatic reaction and his air passages would close shut.

He withdrew from Tulane in June 1947, and transferred to the University of Virginia. In the spring of 1948, he returned to New Orleans. Now he had to sleep on a special iron cot with the mattress wrapped in cellophane so that the dust would not interfere with his breathing. There could be no wool blankets. His health would be fragile for the rest of his life.

As a law student, Jim continued to visit the Baker's. When she smelled pipe tobacco downstairs, Mrs. Baker would call out, "Mabel, who's downstairs?" although of course she knew. It was Jimmy wearing his uniform, of which he was very proud. Sometimes Peggie wasn't even there. Sometimes they talked. Mrs. Baker began to hope that he and Peggie would get together.

"If you feel someone is guilty, how can you defend them?" Peggie asked Jimmy one day.

"Someone has to defend everyone," Jimmy said. "Everyone has to have someone to take up for them."

Then he learned that Peggie was dating a naval officer. At once Jimmy stepped back. He refused to compete, as if he did not believe he had much to offer. Mrs. Baker was relieved that Peggie's new beau came from a distinguished family that had arrived in New Orleans in 1796.

Jimmy stopped visiting the Baker's now. He had taken it for granted that he and Peggie would be together but had never declared himself to her. He had assumed she knew he loved her, but just hadn't chosen to acknowledge it. He had never proposed marriage.

The blow was catastrophic. He was invited to Peggie's wedding in 1948, a very grand event at the Presbyterian Church on St. Charles Avenue. The groom had the bridal gown made so that it replicated the gown worn by Princess Carlotta in a photograph. Jim Garrison did not attend.

"Once you know love," Jimmy confided to Peggie's sister, Willie, "you can't be satisfied with anything else." He pretended, out of pride, to be referring to a girl named Ann Waguespack, but Willie knew. It was Peggie he was talking about.

Back at Fanny's, where everyone knew that he loved Peggie, Mickey Parlour couldn't resist a gibe.

"You lost your Peggie!" she said.

Jim Garrison would never forget Peggie Baker, the girl he had assumed he would marry, the love of his life. Twenty-five years later, celebrity Jim Garrison was on a Delta airlines flight bound for somewhere. The stewardess handed him a note. "I'm Peggie Baker's daughter, Mindy," it read. The district attorney who had investigated the Kennedy assassination, who had seen much sorrow and much of life by then, grabbed the startled air hostess and pulled her down onto his lap. Tears streamed down his cheeks.

Jim Garrison was to attend the funerals of both Peggie's mother and father. Nor were his feelings entirely unreciprocated. Fifty years later, Peggie née Baker says, "He is in my heart."

He turned to other women, although poverty continued to impede his social life, and his feelings remained distant. He and Jack Grayson were invited often to debutante parties, although Jim became notorious for not showing up. He became mildly interested in a fellow-boarder named Martha Ann Samuel. They went to Jackson Square to hear General de Gaulle speak. Jim wore his army uniform. He and de Gaulle were the tallest people in the crowd. One night he corrected Martha Ann's pronunciation.

"Martha Ann," he began, "You're an educated woman. The word is pronounced 'indefaTIGable.'"

Martha Ann held her ground. The room was polled. The consensus was that the pronunciation was "indeFATigable." Jim refused to change his mind.

Other infatuations followed. He spotted a tall, slim, angular young woman with dark hair who worked at the Engineering School, but couldn't figure out how to meet her. His friend Joe Allain pretended to represent a company sending gifts designed for brunettes to secretaries. Then Jim Garrison appeared. It did him no good.

Ill in the hospital, Joe had designs on his nurse, who had a twin sister. Jim discovered they were not identical after all. The sister was forty pounds heavier. After a drink, Jim came down with what he said was an attack of the fever he had contracted in Mexico and fled.

There was a girl named Jane Pitcher, a serious girl, a tall, willowy brunette, and he fantasized marrying her, but she didn't take to him. Jane went on to marry a man in the JUNIOR class, a low blow. Jim was devastated, but concealed his emotions. Women became what they looked like, as vacant as the model in the fluffy white jacket whom he escorted one New Year's Eve. He did not talk about Peggie as time passed, even as Jack Grayson could not remember his dating anyone. There was no one who could replace Peggie Baker.

James Carothers Garrison graduated from the Tulane School of Law on June 1, 1949. Rosemary Pillow was the only woman in the class and when her name was announced, all the men rose to their feet and applauded out of a genuine liberality of spirit. Rosemary brushed the tears from her eyes. Then she could not find a job in the law for years and had to work as a legal secretary. The war veterans in the class were accepted automatically to the bar, and didn't have to take a separate examination.

Jim decided he would become a Professor of Law and stayed on at Tulane for a Master's degree in civil law, with a specialization in gas and oil, an obvious Louisiana choice. One day, he stood in the midst of a group lamenting the sorry state of Louisiana politics and the immorality of those in high office. The issue of the class presidency arose. Being class president was an important office at Tulane.

"We ought to run someone against Floyd Lewis," Jim said. Lewis was an Uptown figure, a snob and close friend of Rufus Harris, whose father was president of Tulane. "Politics is something anyone can succeed at," Jim said. "I'll take the class renegade and I bet I can get him elected student body president.

"I'll bet you can't," Jim's friend Jack Bremermann said.

"I'm going to do it!" Jim said.

For his candidate, Jim chose Wilmer Thomas, an outsider from Mississippi, if from a highly distinguished family. His great grandfather had been in Congress. Wilmer had been dyslexic as a child, and his grandmother had cured him by paying him two dollars if he would read one of the books in his grandfather's library. It was a biography of Alexander The Great, and so began Wilmer Thomas's life-long fascination with history.

In a class of veterans, Wilmer had not seen combat. He seemed juvenile. He might pull your chair out from under you at Commons, the place where everyone met for coffee under a giant live oak tree. Brucie Rafferty would remember Wilmer throwing someone into the pool at the country club, and women knew to stay out of the reach of his wandering hands, because Wilmer would grab your rear end if you passed close enough to him. No one really took it amiss. It was "just Wilmer," very tall and blond and handsome and up to no good.

Like Jim, Wilmer was also an iconoclast, a rebel against authority. Wilmer considered himself a socialist. Wilmer Thomas, no relation, voted for socialist Norman Thomas in the presidential election of 1948.

With Jim Garrison, Wilmer also shared a love of mischief. He became notorious for stealing one book a day from the Tulane library so as, he claimed, to start his own collection; he figured that by the time he graduated, he would have his own library. At the same time, Wilmer greatly enjoyed his law studies, and Professor Ray Forester awarded him the unique privilege of requesting that Wilmer call him by his given name since the two met regularly for lunch.

Tulane lost nothing from Wilmer's library escapade. At the fiftieth reunion of his class, Wilmer was honored as the graduate who had made the most substantial financial contribution to the school: he had matched the total of all the other contributions. With an MBA from Harvard, he had gone on to become the most successful financially of his class; among his philanthropies was a sizable annual gift to the Metropolitan Opera in New York, on whose board he served.

Wilmer went along with Jim's scheme. Wilmer thought: the Dean controls everything at Tulane. The student government has no power at all. Why not make a mockery of the election for student body president! Wilmer believed that the two brightest people at Tulane were Jim Garrison and Edmund Reggie, an Earl Long supporter even then. Judge Reggie in later years would be brought up on charges of bank fraud. His daughter would go on to marry Edward M. Kennedy.

The convention in Louisiana politics at that time was that you had to run on a "ticket." Ever the provocateur, Jim, whose war record was known to everyone, who had come home from the war with a Nazi helmet in tow, decided to run Wilmer on the "Nazi ticket." The relief experienced by these veterans in the early post-war years is reflected in the zany slogan of Wilmer's campaign for student body president: "Hotsy, totsy, I'm a Nazi!"

Jim constructed a bulletin board, and dubbed it the "Wilmer board." Telegrams arrived mysteriously from Eleanor Roosevelt, Joe Stalin, J. Edgar Hoover, General Franco and Adolf Hitler himself. "I'm behind you, Wilmer," Stalin wrote. "I hope you'll be elected." John L. Lewis, head of the CIO, warned Wilmer, "Lay off my younger brother!" ostensibly the incumbent Floyd Lewis, no admirer of the militant labor leader. Jim sent some of the telegrams from the Communists to John Haygood, another candidate, because Jim knew he would be especially irritated. Jim also tacked up political caricatures he drew himself. His scheme was for a victorious Wilmer Thomas to don a suit of armor and ride down the steps of the law school on a white horse.

Dean Paul Brosnan summoned Jim Garrison and asked him to cease and desist. Then he called in Wilmer. Say you're getting rid of that bulletin board by order of the Dean, Brosnan suggested. Wilmer refused.

Scions of the Uptown elite, the "400" who had done so much to impede economic progress in Louisiana, who had resisted change for decades, were not amused, and they would oppose Jim Garrison for the rest of his life. It wasn't, Jimmy Gulotta would later reflect, that they approved of Clay Shaw, whom Garrison would charge with conspiracy in the murder of President Kennedy. Shaw was decidedly not of their class. Rather, they would dislike Garrison for his passionate desire to help the underdog. So outraged were they, foremost among them Walter Carroll, and Kennedy Gilly, one of Wilmer's campaign managers, that they didn't even want it to be known that they attended the same law school as Jim Garrison. So Wilmer himself speculated many years later.

Wilmer won the election. But Louisiana politics decreed that you had to win by a plurality, and so there had to be a run-off between the two candidates with the greatest number of votes. Wilmer was pitted against prim and proper John Haygood. Floyd Lewis, as a spoiler, threw his support to one of his own and Haygood won - but by just seven votes.

By June of 1950, Jim had completed all the requirements for his Master's degree but for his thesis, "The Louisiana Mineral Lease." He considered taking a job with an oil company.

"Jack, how do you like the FBI?" Jim asked Bremermann, who was now training to be an agent. Jim sent in an application for FBI training as a Special Agent. Then he took the summer off to try his hand at what he really wanted to do – which was to become a fiction writer. It would be his lifelong dream. If he could make a living as an author, Jim thought, he would give up the law.

Fanny had suffered a heart attack, and abruptly the boarding house was closed. Jim, Jay Teasdel, a friend whose father was president of Chevron Oil, Jack Grayson and Nigel Rafferty moved to the first floor of a house in the Garden district. Upstairs lived another World War Two veteran named Clay Shaw, who had connected with the International Trade Mart and was already interested in the restoration of French Quarter real estate. Jim and his friends knew Shaw only to say hello. He seemed effeminate, they speculated, these veterans of the tolerant bohemia presided over by Fanny Campbell. They gave Shaw no further thought.

Jim's elaborate schemes of mischief continued. At the stag dinner before Nigel Rafferty's wedding, Jim appeared with a heavy cannon ball. He clamped it onto Nigel's leg and pretended to swallow the key.

"I'll get it when I go to the bathroom tomorrow," Jim promised Rafferty. At three a.m. Nigel Rafferty went off to find someone to cut off the chain with a blowtorch.

One morning, as he was leaving for work, Jack Grayson spotted on the porch a telegram from his "States" editor. "Don't come to work this morning. You're fired!' it read. Remembering the Pooley incident, Jack went to work.

"We didn't send you any telegram," his editor said.

In a more elaborate prank, Jim pried a plank loose from the wall beside Jack's bed and inserted a carton of milk. The sour smell became so pronounced that Jack concluded there must be a dead rat behind the wall.

As a fledgling writer, Jim Garrison decided to focus on action and crime stories, often with a New Orleans background for color. Some of his stories were set during the war. At length he talked with Jay Teasdel about how to keep the action of a story moving. In one of Jim Garrison's early stories, "Footnote To Murder," the narrator turns out to be the killer. But the story falls flat because the reader is aware of his culpability from the start. Worse, his motive is explained didactically by the police, so that the reader is not granted the opportunity to enter the murderer's mind, enlisting his own psychological perspicacity.

"The Assassin," another Garrison effort, centered around a man he calls Gomez, who is attempting to uncover the killer of a politician named Prado. Prado was killed with a .38 caliber pistol, and Gomez suspects "the loyal bodyguards." The falsely accused assassin, Zapato, carries a .32. As Zapato dies, Gomez realizes that Zapato had very little to do with Prado's murder. Now he waits to discover which of the bodyguards will rise politically, following the strategy of "cui bono," who profits? It was a concept Jim Garrison would re-enlist years later in his investigation of the murder of John F. Kennedy.

With "The Assassin," it was as if Jim Garrison were imagining his own future. His Zapato would be Lee Harvey Oswald, another falsely accused "patsy," who would be murdered before the truth could emerge. Garrison himself would take the role of Gomez, and dedicate his life to uncovering the truth about a political assassination.

CHAPTER 3:

Police Characters

"Politics is something anyone can succeed at."
Jim Garrison

It was August 1950 and Jim Garrison now had no choice but to practice his profession and go to work for a law firm. He selected Deutsch, Kerrigan and Stiles, so highly social, so "uptown" an establishment that you practically had to be a member of the Boston Club to be hired there. The Boston Club, incorporated in 1842, was the oldest of the elite New Orleans clubs, formed by gentlemen devoted to a card game similar to bridge called the "game of Boston." Jefferson Davis was known to frequent the Boston Club when he visited New Orleans. By the late 1920's, you had to be nominated, then wait ten years before your name was submitted for election. At Mardi Gras, the King of Carnival, Rex, has been chosen exclusively from among members of the Boston Club.

With Jane's elaborate Revolutionary War antecedents, Jim Garrison qualified.

When Jim teased Jack Grayson now for being just a "lowly professor," who was "wasting his life," Jack retorted that lawyers were no better than leeches on society.

"That's exactly the way the Communists view the world!" Jim said.

At Deutsch, the senior partner, Eberhard Deutsch, became Jim Garrison's mentor. An intimate of Harry Truman's, with easy access to the White House, Deutsch was in a position to watch over the young lawyer's future.

Jim, Jack and Jay: the three friends moved to 722 St. Louis Street, a former slave quarters in the heart of the Quarter, where they had separate apartments. You entered through a courtyard, and a small room cost thirty-five dollars a month. Down the street was the Napoleon House, a bar that played classical music. One table had a chess board painted on it and chess tournaments were soon arranged. The prize was an old red wig – dubbed the "Herrick trophy" after another of their friends. Jim did not renew his acquaintance with Pershing Gervais.

The FBI continued to ponder the application of James Carothers Garrison. Jim had selected as references two of his law school professors. Others who wrote recommendations for him were Jack Bremermann, who was now serving with the Bureau, and Jack Grayson, who came from a family even more distinguished than Jim's, and would later become a leading education theorist. Another of Jim's references came from Peggie Baker's mother, Nellie May.

Jim told Mrs. Baker that he was worried about what the FBI would make of his sister being confined at the Mississippi State Mental Hospital for what was diagnosed, inappropriately, as "schizophrenia."

"I would consider it an immense favor if you didn't mention Judy," Jimmy told Mrs. Baker.

"Well, I won't," Nellie May Baker said. Mental illness was a stigma at the time, along with homosexuality. In New Orleans, homosexual acts were against the law and were called "crimes against nature."

Beside the FBI's question as to whether any family members had been confined in a mental institution, Jim wrote "no." He wrote "no" as well beside the question as to whether any members of his immediate family had been arrested for any offense other than a traffic violation. His goal in life, he wrote, was "Prosecution work as in D.A. office."

At Deutsch, Kerrigan and Stiles, Jim Garrison worked in the Admiralty Law section. He found he was becoming so exhausted that he had to take afternoons off to rest. He had relapses of the amoebic dysentery he had contracted in Mexico, a disease, if not properly treated, that led to fever and prostration. He saw a neuro-psychiatrist named Dr. Robert A. Matthews at Louisiana State University, who could find nothing seriously wrong, except that he was a garden-variety neurotic. Matthews told him that "his trouble was a deep-seated chronic, severe psychoneurosis."

When the FBI inquired about him at Deutsch, they were told that Jim Garrison was "one of the most promising young lawyers," and that he was "capable, poised and alert."

In January 1951, Jim Garrison was appointed Captain of the Artillery of the National Guard in the Army of the United States.

In February, the FBI accepted the application of twenty-nine year old Garrison, hired as a Special Agent at a salary of $5,000 a year. It stood him well that Jane Garrison Gardiner was head of the Civilian Defense Program at Laurel, Mississippi, and that he was a member of the 935th Field Artillery Battalion of the U.S. Army Reserves.

The FBI liked Jim Garrison. Reports during his training depicted him as "a pleasant, friendly personality…confident, forceful, and will undoubtedly inspire confidence in all persons whom he may contact." His intelligence was "above average." The FBI praised Garrison's "excellent attitude toward both his position as a Special Agent and toward the Bureau." The FBI also liked the way he looked. He dressed in a conservative manner, had "regular features" and was six foot six inches tall. "He gives the impression of being mature and intelligent," his supervisor wrote. "His conversation is direct and intelligent and he speaks in well-modulated tones."

While Jack Bremermann was posted to Boston, working on such exciting cases as the Brinks' robbery, Jim was posted to Seattle, where he was an investigator on the "applicant squad" working on humdrum background checks. A fellow agent later remembered him as "rather distracted and absent-minded." He spent much of his time "wool-gathering," his fellow agent thought.

Jim Garrison was, in fact, bored. Boredom would always be difficult for him to tolerate. Described years later as being a man "fond of Shakespeare and Greek drama," Garrison dissented. "Greek drama has always bored me," he said. Boredom was the kiss of death.

When the Korean War broke out, Garrison was given the choice of remaining with the Bureau or going to war. He had served in the FBI four months, from March to June, and it had been enough. "If I can ever – whatever the situation, place and time – be of any service to the FBI in the future, I shall certainly regard it as a privilege to render such service," Garrison wrote to J. Edgar Hoover, as he left the Bureau. On July 24th he reported to the field artillery at Fort Sill, Oklahoma.

Then, facing Army routine, on the first day, Garrison realized he "just couldn't make it." Memories of missions in his "Grasshopper" behind enemy lines, being pursued by superior German aircraft, flooded his consciousness. After the Civil War, they had called it "soldier's heart." After World War I, the term was "shell shock." For Garrison's generation, "post-traumatic stress syndrome" was termed "battle fatigue." In that Grasshopper, he had to fly suspended, like an observer in a World War I balloon, virtually motionless. It was those observers who had experienced the most stress, vulnerable as they had been to gunfire from below. Some had emerged from World War I virtually speechless.

Jim Garrison's memories included his flying toward the enemy as closely as possible until he was shot at. The stress of those close calls, flying an unarmed, flimsy airplane into German-held territory, the terror of being frightened all the time, reasserted itself. A return to combat suddenly seemed inconceivable.

On his first day at Fort Sill, he reported to sick call. Put on "quarters" for two weeks, he was hospitalized. On August 17th, he wrote to Hoover requesting that he be permitted to return to service with the FBI. "I find myself accomplishing little of value here," Garrison explained, "now that the Korean business seems to be gradually concluding." He would accept an assignment to any field office.

Hoover paused, and requested that Captain Garrison furnish for the Bureau "an honorable discharge or re-lease to inactive duty." Hoover took the "opportunity to wish you the best of luck during your period of military service."

On September 16th, an exhausted Jim Garrison was admitted to Brooke Army Hospital at Fort Sam Houston in Texas. "I know this sounds crazy," Garrison explained, "but this is how I feel." Chronic exhaustion had plagued him since his original discharge from the Army.

The doctors could find nothing wrong with him, either physically or mentally. They did note that his amoebic dysentery persisted. If Dr. Matthews had spoken of "severe psychoneurosis," the Army's Dr. Marshall L. Fowler found Garrison's troubles more commonplace. He was "well-oriented," Fowler noted, and described his own neurotic symptoms "openly and with insights." Neither doctor reported any "signs of pathologic personality." There were no delusions, no hallucinations, no disturbance of affect.

Jim Garrison was shy, the Army doctors concluded, and this would be true all his life. He was something of a hypochondriac, as all his friends knew. He was "introverted" and could be anti-social. His allergies were psychogenic in origin, like most allergies. The medical board at Fort Sam Houston concluded that James C. Garrison suffered from "either a neurasthenia, or a hypochondriasis," but either or both were "of a moderate degree."

The source of Jim Garrison's particular neurosis, Dr. Fowler determined, was his "over-solicitous" mother, who "made every effort to monopolize his affections." He suffered from a "marked mother dependency." It was already apparent that Jane Gardiner had cast a pall over his life, and he had grown to resent her for not having told him how to locate his father. As his fellow-residents at Fanny Campbell's had observed, Jane's very presence rendered him unhappy.

Nor did Jim's friends like her. Jane Gardiner had become known in New Orleans as being unscrupulous in her oil leasing deals. She rode around New Orleans in her husband's ancient Rolls Royce, her pride in her ancestry now inflated by her second husband's even grander lineage. Once Jim visited his friend Vance Gilmer at his law office. When Garrison was gone, one of the senior partners at Gilmer's firm asked him, "Do you know this young man's mother?" The implication was that it was not a good thing to have anything to do with Jane Gardiner.

While he was at Fort Sam Houston, Jane wrote him, but he did not reply to her letters.

Jim Garrison was relieved from active duty in the Army on October 31, 1951, "by reason of physical disability." He returned to New Orleans where he completed his Master's thesis, "The Louisiana Mineral Lease," the subject alone reflecting his symbiotic relationship with his mother. Written in a lucid style, unlike most academic writing, Garrison's Master's thesis predicts the writer he was to become. "The word 'lease' in Louisiana," Garrison writes, "was something of a legal homonym, meaning one thing in the Louisiana Civil Code and quite another in the oil industry." The oil and gas lease was "something new and distinct in itself – a development of the gasoline-engine era." He received the degree of Master of Civil Law on May 27, 1952.

Jane was sending him an allowance even now, and he borrowed money from Jay Teasdel. Jim wrote Jay a check for a million dollars in repayment, which Jay kept for the rest of his life as a souvenir.

Jim Garrison avoided a return to the practice of law for as long as he could. He was interested in the question of justice, Jay concluded, but didn't like the law itself. Garrison continued to pursue the possibility of becoming a full-time author, and now he sent a batch of short stories to A.L. Fierst, a New York literary agent.

If he had hoped to be told that he would be able to make a living as a writer, Garrison was disappointed. Fierst replied that his stories were "decidedly promising." Garrison "handle[d] language well" and had a "fresh imagination." Fierst was returning the stories, however, because Jim hadn't yet "made the most" of his talent and they required revision. You should "give your work your best efforts, please," Fierst said. Then he added a note of encouragement. "I don't mind telling you that I believe you will hit the mark in not too long a time," Fierst wrote. It would be eighteen years before Jim Garrison's first book, "A Heritage Of Stone," would be published.

Reading Fierst's letter, Jack Grayson couldn't resist a taunt. "It's all garbage," Jack bantered. "No respectable publisher will ever publish you!"

Jim, Jay and Jack now made a bet. Whoever first published a book or an article or story in a national magazine would buy the others dinner at Antoine's. Jack published an article in a business magazine, but that was ruled out as not counting. Nor did a Jack Grayson book published by Harvard University Press qualify. When Jack became chairman of the Price Commission under President Richard Nixon, Flora Lewis interviewed him for "The New York Times." Jim decided that didn't count either.

In 1970, G. P. Putnam's Sons, a major publisher indeed, brought out "A Heritage Of Stone." Garrison's literary agent, Max Gartenberg, brought the manuscript to an iconoclastic editor named Arthur Fields.

"I hate it but I'm going to publish it," Fields said. "I don't believe a word of it. Do you believe it?"

"Yes, I do," Gartenberg said, "I wouldn't send it out if I didn't believe it."

Garrison warned his editor that he would "read some very derogatory things about me in the national press...I hope you have a strong stomach."

"A Heritage of Stone" was a success, going into four printings.

Jay wrote novels, but they were not published by major trade publishers. Then, in 1976, Jim Garrison published a novel, "The Star-Spangled Contract," with McGraw-Hill, for which he received a $250,000 advance against royalties. "You're kidding!" Garrison told his friend Ralph Schoenman, who had sold the book for him as a personal favor and was reporting the size of the advance. Ralph told him that he didn't want any fee or commission. "Then I won't take the money," Garrison said. "It's not open for discussion."

"The Star-Spangled Contract" required some editing by story doctor and novelist Gordon Lish, but most of the writing was Garrison's. Nor was Garrison, predating short story master Raymond Carver, entirely pleased by Lish's changes. He found the edited version "lewd." Sex was one thing, Garrison remarked. Politics, history and the truth were another.

Ever sardonic, Jim inscribed a copy of "The Star Spangled Contract," "to my old friend Jay Teasdel, America's most distinguished unpublished author." All his life, he took a professional author's approach to writing. "Just do it. Don't talk about it," he advised his oldest son Jasper. Writers wrote; they didn't talk about writing.

A few years before Jim Garrison's death, he and Jack had dinner at Antoine's. Then they argued over who would pick up the check, still debating whose publishing career had been the more distinguished.

The shock of his losing Peggie receded, and Jim Garrison became something of a ladies' man. Dressed in a white jacket, flaunting a red tie, he cut a dashing figure bar-hoping in the Quarter. He became a regular at Pat O'Brien's, and at Lucky Pierre's. Often he came in alone. Since no woman could truly replace Peggie in his affections, he chose prostitutes, and once he told Jack, about to visit a particular establishment, to "use my name. Tell them Jim sent you." Peggie was a tall, stately, brunette, quietly intelligent, measured, and elegant. Jim, now and for the rest of his life, would cultivate a new "type," as he put it: his women would be petite, blonde, and far from his intellectual equal.

In many ways, his tastes were simple, with a hint of the juvenile, the predilections of the practical joker. He loved the movie "Harvey" where James Stewart played a rabbit. His vocabulary grew saltier, laced with irony. Still he cherished solitude, re-reading Dickens, fond of quoting the line, "it was the best of times, it was the worst of times." The sound of Glenn Miller's music brought tears to his eyes, summoning memories of Peggie.

When Jack got married, Jim didn't show up for the wedding.

"Where were you?" Jack demanded afterwards.

"I was reading a good book," Jim said. Marriage was no cause for celebration for Jim Garrison. Jack Grayson at once forgave him.

He returned to Deutsch, no happier than he had been earlier. "Be anything but a lawyer," he would tell Jasper years later. Colonel Deutsch advised him to try politics as an alternative and introduced him to the mayor of New Orleans, DeLesseps ("Chep") Morrison, who had breezed into office in 1946 under the banner of reform, of "good government."

Morrison had stood up to the "Old Regulars," who had controlled elections through highly disciplined ward leaders, and were synonymous with the politics of favor and influence symbolized by a truism supposedly uttered by Earl Long, brother of Huey. "Those who are with me in the first primary get the jobs," Uncle Earl said. "Those who are with me afterward get – good government." The double entendre escaped no one – "good government" was the slogan of the opposing group. Uncle Earl may have dressed in farm clothes purchased at a Supermarket, but he was no one's fool.

Morrison organized the Crescent City Democratic Association (CCDA), standing for "progress," and cultivating public opinion, which the Old Regulars had ignored. Morrison left unmolested the corrupt police department, appointing Provosty A. Dayries as Superintendent.

By 1951 in New Orleans there was a backlog of more than 200,000 unpaid traffic tickets. Chep Morrison appointed Jim Garrison to his first political job. It was May 1952 as Garrison became Deputy Safety Commissioner, at $485 a month. The appointment earned him an article in the "Times-Picayune" newspaper.

The Safety Commissioner was one Bernard J. McCloskey, a charter member of Morrison's CCDA. Jim Garrison at once asserted his independence. McCloskey was an Eisenhower supporter, and that Ike should gain a Democrat's vote was also news: "M'Closkey Says He's Backing Ike," the "Times-Picayune" announced. Jim Garrison now signed an advertisement; "We USED to like Ike...We're voting for ADLAI!" At the end of the year, Garrison was replaced and had to return to private practice.

When the Metropolitan New Orleans Safety Council decreed that the traffic court was still in shambles, on January 1, 1954, Chep Morrison appointed Jim Garrison as full-time traffic prosecutor. For the first time, the traffic violations bureau became "an arm of the law," and paying fines at police stations was no longer a possibility.

Garrison at once called a press conference - in the company of Municipal Court Judge Jewell A. Sperling - to present his preliminary report. He had new measures that he would be putting in place, the upstart deputy announced. Mandatory minimum fines for traffic violators who failed to appear in court for trial would be ten dollars for moving violations and five for parking. "Round the clock arrests" were instituted for those who ignored a summons. Jail sentences, and far stiffer fines, would follow "the last such warning." The power of the clerk, Louis A. Heyd, Sr., would be eviscerated – Heyd would no longer be able to choose when and if to reschedule cases when a violator failed to show up in court. Garrison called failure to appear in court "a flagrantly contemptuous action," and threatened that bond would be forfeited. He did offer a reprieve to those who came in voluntarily and paid their overdue fines.

A reporter asked whether the municipal court could handle the rush that might ensue.

"If the rush is so great that a staff problem is created," Garrison said, "it's the kind of problem which is welcome."

Garrison's press conference was the lead in the "Times-Picayune" for February 17, 1954.

Jim Garrison had become a tough-minded prosecutor. When the penalty for non-appearance on a traffic ticket was set, in fact, for $2.50, Garrison expressed his disdain. "A fine of $2.50 for thumbing one's nose at the court would have about the same effect as a slap on the wrist," he said. The laxity of New Orleans judges would plague him for years to come.

Jack Bremermann had married Mickey Parlour, whom Garrison knew from his days at Fanny's. Mickey received a traffic ticket for only pausing at a stop sign.

"Ask Jim, he'll fix it," Mickey told Jack. Dutifully, Jack telephoned his old friend. "Don't be surprised if you get a call from Mickey about a traffic ticket," Jack said.

"Yes, I'll help Mickey," Jim said. He paused. "I'll get her to the head of the line!"

He was honest and he was an idealist. Traffic fines went from $24,922 in a single year to $40,821. When he was passionate about a cause, no detail was too small, or insignificant, as would become apparent in his investigation of the murder of President John F. Kennedy. Jim even designed a special envelope to be included with parking tickets so that fines could be mailed prepaid. His term was renewed.

It was during his efforts for the traffic court that Jim Garrison established his life-long habit of enlisting the press in his causes. It was a way of circumventing New Orleans politics, a way of reaching the people directly. So the "lanky" young prosecutor confided that people hadn't been paying their traffic fines because "they really were not forced to do so."

Garrison had a formidable opponent, however, in traffic court Judge Sperling, who had no intention of allowing Jim Garrison to make a career at his expense – if he could help it. Garrison struck back, blaming the mess on "inertia on the part of the judge." It was "an absence of a will for change," Jim announced, declaring war on Sperling, who had spent his time thinking up "reasons why suggested changes would not work." Garrison went on the attack, accusing Sperling of "not regarding failure to appear for trial as a serious offense," one "more serious than most traffic violations themselves."

Garrison confided to the public that Sperling "seldom gave any fine at all for non-appearance in court," and had a "negative attitude" toward "any and all steps for improving the situation." Should the five and ten dollar mandatory fines not produce results, Garrison promised, "sharper teeth" would be added to the law. He would "work on their driver's licenses." He represented "the city," Garrison said, and "the city will win this fight."

The press devoured Garrison's passionate rhetoric, delighted with a politician who could turn a phrase. Jim Garrison's attack on Judge Sperling made the front pages. That the court clerk, not Sperling, actually processed traffic tickets, didn't matter. Judge Sperling objected to traffic violators being treated as criminals, which was not unreasonable. But Garrison was better copy. When Sperling accused his "young critic" of "looking for publicity to advance himself," the charge fell on deaf ears.

Nor was Judge Sperling Garrison's equal when it came to wit, metaphor, and colorful language. "Such responses," Garrison responded to Judge Sperling's rebuttal in a public statement, "have long been the price of exposing incompetence and misfeasance in public office." Enlisting Louisiana populism, Garrison declared, tendentiously, that "to be safe and secure from such attacks is much less important than to reveal the truth... for the truth is... always the property of the people and not of some politician whose sinecure might be jeopardized by it." Then he compared Sperling's "attempt to smear me" to "the defensive reaction employed by the giant squid which, when attacked, shoots a cloud of black substance into its attacker's eyes. Now, removing the squid-juice from our eyes...." he went on. In the years to come, this squid releasing black fluid into someone's eyes would become a regular participant in Jim Garrison's rhetoric.

Soon his attack on Judge Sperling became even more personal. Sperling spent "perhaps an hour in his office" each day, Garrison accused. He was also corrupt, exonerating those brought before him with whom he enjoyed "mutual friends." Judge Sperling had rejected Garrison's suggestions out of "his desire to preserve this pleasant status quo." The judge received $7500 of "taxpayers' money," Garrison said. He scoffed at Judge Sperling's lame response to Garrison's suggestion that the traffic court be open on Saturdays: "Saturday is a holiday all over the state of Louisiana."

It was all theatre, as Garrison dubbed himself "an ambitious young Cassius," and the judge's reply "a masterpiece of fiction." The traffic court had become the arena of a full-blown crusade, as Garrison reached ever deeper into his rhetorical grab bag. The Judge had forced an admission from him, Garrison said. "I intend to run for President of the United States, just as soon as I am old enough."

Garrison's friends concluded that he was really less interested in notoriety than in proving a point, and he wouldn't go out of his way to make you change your mind about him if you got it wrong. The Metropolitan New Safety Council praised Garrison for "an excellent job," and declared him the winner in his contest with Judge Sperling.

In the Louisiana way, before it was over Garrison and Judge Sperling had become collaborators. Jim sponsored a bill authorizing municipal traffic judges to suspend the licenses of habitual offenders and Sperling endorsed it. "This means that Judge Sperling will be able to get tough in cases where he feels the violator should have the book thrown at him," Garrison said, confirming that he did indeed have the heart of a prosecutor.

He praised the "untiring effort" of the police, a politically expedient thing to do. He recommended to the City Council that it be a misdemeanor to fix a traffic ticket. "Human nature being what it is,"

Garrison remarked, "I think we should assume that where fixing can occur, fixing will occur."

When on one day alone in June four hundred people had failed to answer their summons, Garrison recommended that the fine be raised to $30 on top of the traffic fine. Chep Morrison went before a city council committee and said Jim Garrison had pushed for "attachments" for persons who failed to appear in traffic court, "the biggest single reason why we are getting enforcement." Licenses would be surrendered in moving violations should the motorist not post bond. For the first time, proper records were kept.

Among Jim Garrison's accomplishments was the creation of a separate traffic court, to which a new judge would be appointed. Those in the running for this position included Garrison himself, and an assistant district attorney named Howard Taylor. Taylor's legal skills were rusty (he had been in Korea).

Chep Morrison wanted to give Garrison the job, and Taylor's best friend, a lawyer named Numa Bertel, who will reappear in this narrative, was worried. Bertel had intervened with Morrison to help Taylor, to no avail.

One day Bertel ran into Jim Garrison.

"I don't want to be a traffic court judge," Garrison confided.

"Can I tell the Mayor?" Bertel asked quickly.

"If you don't tell the Mayor, then I will," Garrison said.

Garrison had, in fact, just been appointed an assistant district attorney. "I want to be District Attorney one day," Garrison confided to Bertel. Behind the scenes, a different story circulated. Judge Adrian Duplantier insists that in a "parley" Leon Hubert, the District Attorney, was forced to take on Jim Garrison as an assistant in exchange for Morrison's appointing Howard Taylor to the traffic court. Yet Garrison had already been appointed by Severn T. Darden, before Leon Hubert took office, on May 3rd. Of course, Duplantier was Hubert's first assistant, and was in a position to know.

As an assistant district attorney, according to his fellow assistant Milton Brener, Garrison was more interested in ideas than anything else. In court, he was not a tough opponent. Yet his delivery to a jury was always excellent. If you give Jim time to sit back and think, "he is devastating," concluded attorney Donald V. Organ, who beat him in a burglary case.

He moved slowly and on some days it seemed as if he didn't care whether the sun came up or not. In the office, he was fond of writing satirical poems which he then circulated among his fellow assistants. He was already known to be compassionate and easy on plea bargains. Reporters like Herman Kohlman admired Garrison because he told them the truth. Kohlman was on the "Times-Picayune" police beat, and Garrison allowed him to view his files, something no other assistant would permit. "There, in my office," Jim directed Kohlman, leaving him alone with the files. "Close the door when you're finished."

Assigned to Section A, the court of William J. O'Hara, Jim Garrison prosecuted lottery operators; a man who obtained a room for purposes of prostitution; a nightclub owner who hired a fifteen year old stripper; and a doctor for using blue instead of black ink on a death certificate. The doctor was convicted and fined $400 (this conviction was reversed on appeal).

Garrison lost a case against two men charged with selling jewelry, without declaring whether it was gold or base metal. He lost a case where a bar owner was accused of gambling by paying off on a pinball machine. Together with Edward A. Haggerty, Jr., another assistant in Leon Hubert's office, and one day to preside over State of Louisiana v. Clay Shaw, Garrison prosecuted a nineteen year old black man named Thomas Goins for murder during a forty cent hold up; they got the death penalty on that one.

Let us leave Jim Garrison working as an assistant district attorney in Leon Hubert's office for a moment and pick up the story of his nemesis and former wartime acquaintance, Pershing Gervais.

Police scandals had filled the New Orleans news during the spring of 1953. "The cops own this town," reporter A. J. Liebling discovered, and it was so. No-doubt apocryphal but persistent New Orleans lore had it that Al Capone, forced to leave Chicago, decided to move to New Orleans. At the New Orleans train station, Capone was met by the Superintendent of Police. "Don't get off that train," he told Capone. "WE run this city." The police were doing quite well and had no particular desire to split the take from gambling and prostitution with the Mafia. It was an era when a police captain made more money than a bank president, and houses were robbed with police complicity, if not participation.

And at the heart of New Orleans police corruption stood Pershing Gervais. Pershing was a heavy set man now, with a bullet head, thin lips, a bulbous nose and broad shoulders, a man of prodigious physical strength. He was six feet tall and weighed two hundred and twenty solid pounds, a black-haired man whose ferocity of aspect was intimidating. New Orleans reporter Rosemary James would write, almost admiringly, that Pershing had "a gleam in his eyes that absolutely can be confused with the Devil's own."

On September 30, 1946, having neatly avoided any and all fields of combat, Pershing joined the New Orleans police department. He and his friend Joseph Giarrusso were assigned to motocycles, a hot and sweaty assignment and one not to Pershing's liking. Pershing had a solution. Pershing drove his bike to a bar at Broad and Jefferson Davis. After some time, he would emerge and stop a driver at random.

"What did I do, officer?" the perplexed driver might ask. Told he was speeding, he would pay. By the close of day, Pershing had written twenty tickets to Giarrusso's eight. Years later, Pershing remembered what he called his "little routine." He would tell a suspect that he "had absolutely no constitutional rights as far as I was concerned. I was a very illiterate man, and I was unaware of the Constitution. More than that, I didn't like the way [he] looked."

Pershing would tell a suspect he had "only two rights, the right to go to jail, and the right to get out of town." He reasoned that this tactic would eliminate the "floaters." Then he could concentrate on "your local bums. The ones who lived here." In 1950, he was one of three police officers charged with battery on a young motorist they caught driving under the influence. Pershing soon developed a racket of seizing narcotics from addicts and pushers alike, then turning them over to his own stable of pushers to sell for him. Pershing moved in with a prostitute.

Pershing's take-home pay was "a lousy $21 a week." Called to a store on a robbery, he would load up his car with groceries. His escapades grew more bold. One day he and fellow officer Sal Marchese burglarized a warehouse. They were speeding off with the stolen merchandise when they heard sirens.

"Jesus, Pershing, it's the cops!" Marchese said.

"Will you relax!" Pershing said. "We ARE the cops!"

Marchese was soon fired, but Pershing could not be linked to any of the robberies and drew only a suspension. Pershing remained close to Marchese, and in the years to come when he required an intermediary for joint enterprises with Mafia chieftain Carlos Marcello over at Churchill Farms in Jefferson Parish, Marchese complied. Driving a cab, Marchese also served as Pershing's bag man.

So institutionalized was police corruption in New Orleans that graft was distributed routinely by the captain in envelopes on Friday afternoons. One day the box of envelopes was missing. Pershing had taken them all and departed for New York with a lady of his choice. Then it did it a second time. "It wasn't illegal," Pershing reasoned. Pershing was censored, accused of "conduct unbecoming an officer" by associating with "police characters," and with a "woman dope fiend."

An epidemic of safecrackings descended on New Orleans. The victims were gamblers and other racketeers, who didn't report the thefts. Pershing was at the center of it, as a witness against him named Carl Tyson, a "police character" himself, testified. Pershing was in fact known as one of the best safe crackers in the city. Rumor had it that sheriff Johnny Grosch was so accurate in dredging safes from the canals and bayous because his informant was none other than officer Gervais himself. Grosch soon accumulated $150,000 in pay-offs.

Dressed in a white linen suit, Pershing frequented the whorehouse of Norma Wallace, sometimes as a customer, and sometimes, receiving customers. It was said that his highly endowed favors went to one "wealthy Uptown woman" for $1500.

Always Pershing knew how to protect himself, keeping dossiers on everyone he encountered. He rose in the ranks from sergeant to detective. Finally he was brought down. "Did you ever give money to former Sergeant Pershing Gervais in an envelope directly?" Sergeant Bray was asked when Pershing, to save himself, testified against his former police confreres. "Yes," Bray testified. "his name was on the envelope and I may have at occasional times given him his in his hand."

Pershing disarmed his detractors. "A man that don't take money can't be trusted," Pershing would say. He disarmed you too by telling the truth – or at least admitting that he was lying. "I told you I was lying but you didn't believe me," he might say. In a barber shop one day, listening to some chat, he turned to an old confederate. "Adolph, why must you lie? You and I helped carry the safe out!"

"I was corrupt in my early years with the police force," Pershing later explained, adding, "I was part of a totally corrupt police force." He denied that the Mafia had a stronghold in Orleans Parish and everyone believed him because if anyone knew, it would be Pershing. "Racketeers don't go anywhere without being invited," Pershing pointed out. "They cannot. It's impossible to set up organized crime, gambling and prostitution" without its being sanctioned by "the city officials, the city fathers…the politicians." Pershing himself saw no reason to share.

Yet had Pershing found anyone in Orleans Parish profiting from organized crime, he would himself have cut a deal with him. The Marcello organization operated out of Jefferson Parish, and would have had to deal with Pershing Gervais in or out of uniform if they hoped to make inroads in Orleans Parish. "You couldn't open a book [a gambling handbook], you couldn't open a lottery shop, you couldn't open a whorehouse, you couldn't even beg on Canal Street," Pershing later said, "unless the police said okay. That was crime that was organized!"

Whorehouse madam Norma Wallace confirmed that there was scant mob influence in Orleans Parish. "I had the nicest place in town," she was to say, "so why didn't they come to me? I asked everyone I know if they were ever propositioned [by the mob] or had ever been shook down. They all assured me, no." There were envelopes and payoffs, yes, but they all went to the police department. I would know, Norma added, one of my husbands even played golf with "The Little Man." This was Carlos Marcello, Mafia boss of Louisiana and Texas.

With his penchant for violence, Pershing was a man nasty when crossed. As the years passed, his long belly hung over his belt. A cigarette dangled from his lips as he sized you up. As Pershing put it, always he "played for results." He was street-wise and dangerous, the opposite of idealistic, intellectual Jim Garrison.

When the state police declared itself determined to move in and clean up New Orleans gambling and prostitution, Chep Morrison, his reputation as a reformist in jeopardy, brought to town one Aaron M. Kohn. Kohn had been an FBI Special Agent, if one without distinction; in 1932 Hoover refused to promote him. The FBI found Kohn "somewhat superior," "over–confident," and with a "know-it-all attitude." Kohn was "cocksure." Scandal followed in Kohn's wake and he ran over an eight year old black child who was badly injured, escaping without penalty. One of his FBI superiors thought Kohn would do better in an "eastern area," an apparent reflection of Bureau anti-semitism.

Worst of all was Kohn's sin of embarrassing the Bureau. One night in 1938 in West Virginia, Kohn insisted on going along on a police raid of a bordello. The next day the Wheeling "News Register" reported that "an FBI man had been found in the whorehouse at the time the police made the raid." Kohn's resignation from the FBI followed immediately.

Kohn alighted in Chicago where he became chief investigator of a city anti-crime committee. Annoyed by his blundering – he obviously had no police experience – the Chicago police, to get rid of him, inquired of the FBI whether Kohn had been guilty of affiliations with Communist Party front organizations. More scandal followed, including allegations that Kohn had offered bribes to Chicago police officers. Kohn pleaded he had been investigating "political murders." Within six months, Chicago had rid itself of Mr. Aaron M. Kohn.

New Orleans was Kohn's next stop, the end of the line for flotsam and jetsam from the Midwest. Kohn would be another one of those who had outstayed their welcome elsewhere and for whom the port of New Orleans was their final resting place. Appointed by Mayor Morrison to a "Special Citizens Investigating Committee," Kohn was soon heading a "Metropolitan Crime Commission." To gain credibility, he claimed to have been an administrative assistant to J. Edgar Hoover, and had helped to organize the FBI's "National Academy." In fact, Kohn had labored in the FBI fingerprint department.

"This is all poppycock!" Hoover said when he heard that Kohn had reinvented his FBI career. It was unusual for The Director to set the record straight on such matters, but this time he did. The FBI at once denied Kohn's request that he use its laboratory facilities.

Aaron Kohn was tall and thin, black-haired and bespectacled, his eyes under heavy lids, his appearance always dapper. Press conferences were his forte as he declared that the people of New Orleans were afraid "of their own city government." The story made page one. The press lapped up his stories as Kohn lied shamelessly, claiming he had worked on the Ma Barker and John Dillinger cases, although his only connection with the Dillinger case was that he had made an error and failed to send a fingerprint report to the St. Paul field office. The result was an FBI reprimand for "inexcusable carelessness."

Before long, Kohn turned the Metropolitan Crime Commission (MCC) into his version of a mini-FBI.

He solicited a stable of informants, and even made an appeal to the public that was published in the "Times Picayune." People should come to him with instances "in which a policeman had been prevented from enforcing the law," Kohn said. Among his most reliable informants would be – Pershing Gervais. Kohn's informants remained nameless and despite their accusations, they never had to testify under oath. "I always thought he was for sale," Jim Garrison's friend Vance Gilmer, who became an executive with Shell Oil, would say of Kohn.

All the while, Kohn's reports to his MCC file were laced with gossip and innuendo, short on facts, high on self-righteousness. He had no respect for anyone's civil rights and argued for a register of ex-convicts residing in New Orleans, which he planned to share with federal agencies. He wanted all teaching applicants fingerprinted and screened for prior criminal records, and offered policemen inducements to testify against their fellow officers. He even challenged whether bingo was legal.

The FBI took note of all this and warned its New Orleans field office: "Be most circumspect in any dealings with Kohn." When Kohn requested The Director's assistance, Hoover reminded his over-zealous former employee that the FBI did not inject itself in matters of state legislation.

Chep Morrison had imported a monster, and for decades Aaron Kohn would wreak havoc on the New Orleans justice system, pursuing his personal enemies with the help of those he should have been investigating. Morrison did attempt to minimize Kohn's power by bringing into the fold another former FBI agent, the person President Kennedy's accused assassin, Lee Harvey Oswald, would call "the Chief."

W. Guy Banister had been Special Agent in Charge of the Chicago field office, but he was born in Monroe, Louisiana, in, he claimed, "a log cabin." He began as a policeman, then rose to chief of detectives, gaining notoriety by winning a pistol-shooting contest.

Hoover noticed him, and he joined the "Division of Investigation" of the Department of Justice in 1934. During World War II, in Banister's best known black bag job, he stole the German code book from the German Embassy in Mexico City. Banister ended his career in Chicago with raids on the Puerto Rican Nationalist Party, whose militants had attempted to assassinate members of Congress.

In New Orleans, Banister was known as a hot-head and an anti-Communist zealot. Six feet tall, with iron grey hair, and a hatchet-handsome countenance, his blue eyes flashed with the intensity of the fanatic. Cutting a dashing figure, he wore a white shirt and a dark tie every day, his costume enlivened by a fresh rose or a carnation in his lapel. One of his secretaries, Mary Helen Brengel, remarked that he resembled the actor Charles Bickford. Jim Garrison dubbed him "Mr. Spic and Span." Banister was a deacon of the Baptist Church and had been a Sunday school teacher.

At once Banister and Kohn began to work together to investigate the police department. But by 1956, Morrison had ordered that Banister stop meeting with Kohn and sent him off to study Communist subversion in New Orleans for Mississippi Senator James Eastland's Internal Security Subcommittee. "New Orleans is a lot closer to Siberia than Chicago," Banister pointed out, clearly enjoying the assignment. "All they would have to do is drop an atom bomb in the river and you couldn't live in New Orleans for ten years."

A year later, at the Old Absinthe House, unduly provoked, Banister pulled a .357 Magnum revolver. "I've already killed two men and another wouldn't make any difference," he told the bartender. Morrison and Superintendent Dayries managed to finesse him out of the police department, but Guy Banister does not disappear from this story.

Pershing was given a sixty-day suspension for those two separate thefts of the police graft money. The charges were "unauthorized employment outside his police duties" and trips to New York with a woman who was a "known police character." A "police character" was someone who had been arrested more than once, was known to the police, and was affiliated with criminal circles.

As was his wont, Pershing denied what he could. He and the woman "never, absolutely never" had "immoral relations," Pershing testified. That "absolutely" was his trademark when he lied. She was "like a man to me," Pershing insisted; he had met her while he was on the narcotics squad and she was a drug addict.

Pershing liked to party, but he maintained his distance from the women who crossed his path. A woman "separates you from your money," Pershing said. His advice to his fellow police officers was: "Never take a Rolex. Cars, boats and clothes can be traced.

Steal money." His IQ was 143 and he found some way to remember everybody: names, faces, objects.

Pershing wanted to be reinstated in the New Orleans police department. But as of July 1953, Pershing was an ex-police officer. In 1954, he was operating a bar at 435 Esplanade called "The Bucket of Blood." Even judges feared him. Pershing double-crossed everyone, including Aaron Kohn, reporting to one Milton L. Durel, that Kohn was making accusations against him. Accused of being an informant, Pershing called it an "outrageous accusation." Yet Kohn continued under Pershing's spell and no one knew better than Pershing how to give Kohn what he wanted: all Pershing had to do was write a report peppered with names ending in a vowel.

As part of Morrison's police department probe, Aaron Kohn was called before the Orleans Parish grand jury. He withheld documents because they revealed the name of one or another of his confidential informants, Kohn said. Among his accusations was of an employee of a contractor who sat on the grand jury. This man frequented a whorehouse on St. Charles Avenue, Kohn insisted. Kohn knew because the man's truck was parked there frequently. It turned out that the man was on a painting job in the area. This was typical of Kohn's "information."

In the spring of 1955, Kohn earned a ten-day sentence in Parish Prison. From his cell, Kohn held a press conference, praising such police department notables as Guy Banister. Years later, furious at the young prosecutor who had sent him to jail, Kohn made a special trip to Washington, D.C. to testify at the confirmation hearing of that prosecutor, Adrian Duplantier, who had been appointed to a federal judgeship. Kohn didn't get far.

"Get out!" boomed Senator Russell Long as soon as he spotted the tall Kohn slinking into the room.

Kohn's first major scapegoat was Police Superintendent Joseph L. Scheuering, a martinet in jodhpurs and high boots, who carried a whip. Scheuering failed to weed out undesirables from the police force, Kohn complained. He couldn't control the relationships between police and "known police characters" and had associated with "individuals not consistent with law enforcement." Indicted for malfeasance, Scheuering was acquitted. The assistant district attorney in charge of the matter was Jim Garrison, whom Chep Morrison praised nonetheless for doing "a most effective job."

At the Bucket of Blood, Pershing was accused of permitting B-drinking, about which more later, and of employing as a bartender a convicted narcotics offender named Wilbert ("Blackie") Comeaux. The charges were "trumped up," Pershing argued.

Later, in another "Gervais," as lawyer William Alford would dub Pershing's scams, Pershing testified at the appeal hearing of a police captain named Eldred J. Paternostro, who was also seeking reinstatement to the police force. If once Pershing had fingered Paternostro as one of three "bag men" at the Third District police station, now Pershing took it all back.

"It was purely hearsay as regards Lt. Paternostro," Pershing said. "I did not consider this to be ultimately used as evidence." Had he ever received graft money or given any to Paternostro? Pershing was asked.

"Positively not," Pershing said. With Guy Banister's concurrence, however, Paternostro's dismissal was rendered permanent.

One day in February 1956, Aaron Kohn buttonholed Assistant District Attorney Jim Garrison in the corridor of the Criminal Courts building. Jim was prosecuting a former police desk sergeant named Gardin Lesovsky. He feared he might lose because one of his witnesses, a Captain Alfred Malone, had testified while under the influence. Jim's other witness, Captain Eugene Dakin, suddenly could not remember the answer to the most important question, although Jim had briefed him before the trial.

"Why don't you charge both Captain Malone and Captain Dakin with perjury?" Kohn suggested.

Garrison said that he couldn't make a clear-cut case against them. One did not accuse people of perjury lightly.

"It's not as important to convict these men of perjury as it is to make a record of the fact that they had committed perjury," Kohn said. The accusation might be as useful as a conviction. Kohn's relationship with Jim Garrison would be "as of oil to water" ever after.

During the summer of 1956, Jim spent a month in New York City at the "Practicing Law Institute." Diligently, he took notes on the nuances of jury selection: "Avoid theatrical people & artists (too tolerant). Women are good. If D is seller & addict, find out if some jurors think this is only social or medical problem." If the defendant is a young male, "then avoid 'Mother' types on jury…if defendant is woman, female jurors are good." Avoid accepting: "artists, psychologists, teachers, pregnant women, persons too anxious to serve, [and] deformed persons."

He was taught not to mention a confession in his opening statement if the confession had not yet been admitted into evidence, lest he leave open the possibility of a mistrial. You could show a witness anything, even an "old shoe," if it refreshes his memory. You could overcome the "sympathy factor" by making the jury conscious of its sense of duty. It might be wise to mention that a defendant is the father of ten children. Then, in your summation to the jury, you should "remind them of their promise to you. This makes them conscious of Moral Commitment." Colorful items of testimony should be quoted back to the jury later. Use the same language your judge uses.

Bored, Jim dreamed up story ideas. Inspired by a film he had just seen, "Three For Jamie Dawn," starring Laraine Day and Richard Carlson, he considered writing a story called "The Witness" or "The Juror." A good fictional strategy would be to focus on "one man's dramatic involvement in a situation."

He was nearly thirty-five years old now, and politics was taking precedence in his life over literature. Backed by Chep Morrison's CCDA, he ran unsuccessfully as a delegate to a state constitutional convention to re-write the Louisiana State Constitution, a convention that never took place. When the Morrison faction formed a new grouping, the Crescent Democratic Organization, Jim Garrison was a member of its executive committee.

CHAPTER 4:

Midnight Rider

"How do you know if you're in love?"
Jim Garrison

He was a good man swimming in a sea of thieves and scoundrels shielded by a corrupt police force that served and savored the politics of favor. From Napoleonic times in Louisiana, office was deemed a form of property from which the holder was expected to profit. "Maybe a man has to sell his soul to get the power to do good," Robert Penn Warren writes in "All The King's Men," his novel about Huey Long, with whose populist rhetoric Jim Garrison's was sometimes compared.

Assistant district attorney Jim Garrison in November 1956 prosecuted Peter Murtes, a state representative charged with public bribery. Murtes had arranged to accept automobiles from four used car dealers attempting to defeat a bill prohibiting used car dealers from also selling new cars. A dealer named Irving Rubin testified before the Orleans Parish grand jury, only to change his testimony at the trial.

Jim Garrison affected "surprise." Did he know the penalty for perjury? Garrison asked Rubin when he had him back on the stand. Rubin insisted the man he met had not been Murtes after all. The politician was acquitted.

Nowhere more than in the Orleans Parish courts was truth elusive. Investigating the charge that seven black teenagers arrested for killing a retired police sergeant had been beaten in prison, Garrison discovered that it was not so. His record of narcotics convictions was impressive. There was no ideological spin to his prosecutions, and he refused charges against a rookie police officer who had killed a burglary suspect on St. Charles Avenue.

In the summer of 1957, Aaron Kohn orchestrated corruption charges against both Chep Morrison and police superintendent Provosty A. Dayries. Kohn attempted to force District Attorney Leon Hubert to recuse himself and not serve as advisor to the grand jury since his grandmother and Dayries' father were half-sister and brother. They were "related by blood within the fourth degree," as only Napoleonic New Orleans could define it. A reporter, perplexed, asked Judge Frank T. Echezabal what this meant, what were the rules?

"I'm not running a law school!" Echezabal snapped. He ruled that Hubert could remain.

The charges against Morrison and Dayries were "malfeasance, misfeasance, and or non-feasance and maladministration." That Dayries had not been investigating lottery operations was among Kohn's charges. Dayries replied that if Kohn had information about violations, his responsibility was to inform the authorities. Kohn's tactics were "underhanded."

By 1957, Morrison's cloak as a reformist was threadbare. Now he struck back at Kohn, accusing him of attempting to foster his own political ambitions with these false charges. He challenged Kohn to let people know what he, Kohn, had ever done "to improve law enforcement in this city." But the Kohn juggernaut pressed on, and in July Hubert stepped aside.

Jim Garrison was appointed legal adviser to the grand jury to handle the Dayries matter. When grand jury foreman Marc Antony requested of Hubert that he assign someone to assist Kohn, and the Metropolitan Crime Commission in its efforts, Jim Garrison was chosen. He would work full-time on this matter alone. Were Dayries to be indicted, it was decided, the Attorney General of the state of Louisiana would prosecute.

Guy Banister was brought in as an unpaid investigator. Only a month earlier, Dayries had fired Banister from the police department over that incident when Banister drew his service revolver at the Old Absinthe House bar. Hardly an impartial participant, Banister had his defenders in New Orleans. Deceived by Banister's appearance of respectability and his history of law enforcement, civic organizations had demanded the resignation of Dayries for firing Banister.

Now Banister produced a twenty-three page memorandum for the Orleans Parish grand jury, which he immediately released to the press. It charged that Chep Morrison had ordered unjustly the dismissal of high-ranking police officers to end the investigation of police graft. Morrison himself, Banister claimed, had admitted in a telephone call that two or three "big ones" were to be "hooked" (dismissed), so that the probe might be brought to a conclusion.

On August 28th, Jim Garrison signed a grand jury document concluding that "no true bill" would be offered against Provosty A. Dayries for failure to enforce the law against public bribery within the New Orleans police department. Not a word was included about any malfeasance on Chep Morrison's part.

Grand Jury foreman Marc Antony now went public, insisting that the grand jury document signed by Garrison had been, in fact, only a letter attacking Guy Banister for releasing his memorandum to the press. Fierce Judge J. Bernard Cocke vowed that if Banister released any more statements to the press, he would convict him of contempt of the grand jury.

The matter was, in fact, far from resolved, and Antony requested that Chep Morrison appear before the panel.

Antony was, it turned out, one of Aaron Kohn's secret informants. Jim Garrison, Antony told Kohn, according to Kohn, had done a complete "about face." Garrison had told the grand jury he thought they had a good malfeasance case against Dayries, and perhaps also against the Mayor, for terminating the police graft probe. Then, on the morning of August 25th, Chep Morrison had visited Jim Garrison at his apartment at the Claiborne Towers. It was two days after that visit that Garrison had told the grand jury that the cases against Dayries and Morrison were too weak for prosecution.

Now Kohn had a juicy bone to gnaw. He insisted that Leon Hubert conduct a public hearing on the "alleged communication" (he could hardly name his source) between Garrison and Morrison on August 25th. Meanwhile Morrison denied that he had any personal contact with Garrison, except by telephone to inquire how to get hold of Mr. Antony in order to request permission to appear before the grand jury.

Chep Morrison had ensnared young Jim Garrison in a web of intrigue as he attempted to conceal his acquiescence in police corruption. Standing before the grand jury, Garrison admitted that Morrison had indeed visited him. He added that "nothing" had happened, that Morrison had not influenced him.

"There's nothing at all sinister in this matter," Garrison said. "The entire matter was presented by me to the grand jury and every juror knew about it."

Kohn offered a different version of events. He claimed that Jim Garrison had telephoned him to say he was drawing up indictments against Morrison and Dayries, only the next day for Garrison to admit that Morrison had met with him and pleaded to have the indictments dropped. Kohn accused Garrison of lying and saying he had not met with Morrison, which was not true. Kohn drew up thirty-five suggested questions to be asked of Jim Garrison.

Kohn charged that Garrison had been "playing the game" for Morrison and Hubert, but he was never to learn what actually happened. Indictments had indeed been typed up against Morrison and Dayries. They were to be handed down on a Monday. That weekend, Marc Antony had made one of his not-infrequent trips to New York. A married man with a family, he sought relief at gay parties and that weekend in New York he had been arrested. The news reached Chep Morrison, who asked Jim Garrison to fly to New York to obtain the police report on Marc Antony.

In the wee hours of Monday morning, Jim Garrison visited Marc Antony at his home and showed him the report. The Mayor did not wish to hurt him, Garrison said. They knew this could be embarrassing. Later that morning, Marc Antony told the grand jury he had thought it over. Morrison and Dayries hadn't done the right thing, but you had to look at the positives. Morrison had accomplished much good for the city, even if he did steal. The grand jury should "pre-demit," take no action at all.

Judge Cocke protested vehemently, denouncing the grand jurors, who, he charged, should be locked up instead of the crooks. He knew something was fishy, but he didn't know what.

Corruption splashed. So Jim Garrison completed his political apprenticeship under the dubious influence of Chep Morrison. Marc Antony lied to Kohn, insisting that Dayries had not been indicted because that would be unfair unless they also indicted Chep Morrison. Mayor, Superintendent of Police, Grand Jury foreman – worked in concert to circumvent the law.

Garrison returned to prosecuting more mundane cases. He convicted of negligent homicide the driver who caused the collision death of the daughter-in-law of Leander Perez, arch-segregationist czar of Plaquemines Parish, winning himself a powerful ally.

Ever anxious to make inroads into New Orleans politics, Governor Earl Long created two new sections in Criminal Court, "G" and "H." In an attempt to manipulate the District Attorney's office, and outfox Morrison, his major adversary, the man he dubbed "Dellasoups," Long offered "G" section to Leon Hubert. Abiding by Morrison's suggestion, Hubert declined. "There will be other judgeships," Morrison promised. "We'll back you." In the end, Hubert was on his own. He never became a judge.

Suspecting that he would soon be out of a job, in December 1957 Jim Garrison decided to run for the office of Assessor. Unfortunately, his opportunity came in a district where Chep Morrison had few friends. Garrison would be only a "sacrificial candidate," up against the pillar of the "Old Regulars," James E. Comiskey.

Garrison promised to serve "with complete impartiality and fairness." He urged voters to choose the entire Crescent City ticket "so that the remarkable progress of New Orleans in the last twelve years can be continued." He had cast his lot with Chep Morrison and there he remained.

On Election Day, Garrison and fellow assistant Milton Brener planned to post signs at polling places. Brener wanted to obey the rule: signs had to be in place before six a.m., when the polls opened. Garrison suggested they meet at 9:30, which was early for him.

They began cruising the district only at 10:30. The posters of Jim's opponent gleamed up at him. When he lost to Comiskey by 3 to 1 (the vote was 6885 to 1447), Garrison's reaction was sardonic. If I had only listened to your suggestion that I post additional signs, he told Brener, I would have won.

Garrison had lost, but he was on his way. As City Hall reporter James Gillis wrote, Comiskey's margin was "scarcely a glowing triumph."

In the race for district attorney, Malcolm O'Hara, who had been an assistant in Hubert's office, and the Morrison candidate, ran against a criminal defense lawyer named Richard Dowling. With Hubert on leave, O'Hara was the temporary district attorney. O'Hara already had a chequered past. He had been charged with malfeasance for unauthorized expenditure of city funds for extradition in a bail bond case. Qualifying as an expert on extradition, Jim Garrison had testified for him and O'Hara had been exonerated. Gratefully, he now named Garrison his First Assistant.

In the election, O'Hara won by thirteen votes in the first primary, and nine in the second. Dowling claimed fraud. Deeming it "impossible" that the vote be reversed, pronouncing the controversy "all over," Garrison made the mistake of not participating in O'Hara's defense from the start. Instead, he went out on the town, appearing at the Mardi Gras Lounge dressed in his Captain's National Guard uniform. There he met up with his old acquaintance Pershing Gervais. It was inevitable that they would encounter each other in that seething Casablanca on the Mississippi where everyone was connected.

It was one in the morning. Depressed, having had too much to drink, Garrison talked about how politics was based on lying and influence. Honesty and justice were irrelevant. He seemed disillusioned. Soon the conversation turned to sex. Jim confided that he fancied "a real pretty girl," who danced at the Conforto brothers' club, Chez Paree. Gervais, ever the pimp, offered to set Jim up with a very young girl, one "underage," and then film the festivities. "How about if she's only sixteen?" Gervais continued.

Unaware that he was being set up, trusting Gervais, as he trusted similarly devious older men, Garrison fell into the trap.

"Now, for Christ's sake, don't go up and tell all this to Kohn," Garrison said, well aware that Gervais was a Kohn snitch. Gervais did just that. Gervais immediately reported to Kohn that Garrison had handed him his business card with his telephone numbers, urging Gervais "to call him whenever he knows of a young girl." Gervais added that Jim Garrison had spoken of "play[ing] his cards right" and himself becoming District Attorney. He was the most convincing assistant in the office, Garrison supposedly had boasted, the one best able to "make the jury cry."

Gervais then introduced what would become his plum scam. "Suppose you could make $1,000," Pershing began. All Garrison had to do was "nolle prosse" ("nolle prosequi" or refuse charges), and then tell him about it.

"I wouldn't want any part of the $1,000. You can keep it," Garrison said, according to Gervais. One thing was certain. Money was of no interest to him, and never would be. He would not discourage Gervais in his exploits, no one could stop Pershing anyway. But he would not profit from them.

Gervais that night had another favor to request. He wanted a permit to carry a concealed weapon.

"You don't need a permit," Garrison said, according to Gervais. "Just go ahead and carry it."

"I'm not taking no chances," Gervais said. Garrison wrote down a "reminder."

It fell, finally, to Jim Garrison to handle the voting fraud charge in the district attorney race. Jim appointed Assistant Allen R. Fontenot and two investigators to work on a report to the grand jury. O'Hara, their colleague, had an advantage and Aaron Kohn at once seized on the issue. But Garrison promised not to leave "any stone unturned nor ignore any evidence developed by anyone." The "Times-Picayune" supported him: "The start Mr. Garrison has made indicates a purpose to make use of the facilities the law provides."

On March 21st, by a 4-2 vote, the State Supreme Court declared Richard Dowling the winner in the race for district attorney over Malcolm O'Hara by eight votes, and hence the Democratic nominee and certain victor. Seventeen fraudulent votes had been cast by election commissioners, wearing O'Hara badges. Seventeen more votes than names in the voting register had emerged from the machines. The commissioners were not charged. (Malcolm V. O'Hara would be elected as judge on the Orleans Parish criminal court in July 1962.)

In his final two cases in the Hubert office, Garrison distinguished himself. One involved a corporate raider named Sinclair Robinson. The charge was the theft of two million dollars worth of bonds stolen from a dredging firm named Williams-McWilliams and used to effect a takeover. Garrison also investigated a violation of office policy involving another assistant, Edward K. Pinner, who had brought proceedings against the sheriff, Louis A. Heyd, for failing to seize a $5000 bail bond forfeited in a narcotics case.

Out of work, Garrison was again rescued by Chep Morrison, who appointed him to a reactivated citizens' police advisory board, a "sounding board of public opinion on police matters." It was another Morrison fig leaf.

Nigel Rafferty, Jack Bremermann and Jack Grayson were all married now. Jim Garrison continued in his Storyville life. Intimacy was a danger, the suffocating intimacy imposed by his mother. He continued to frequent the Quarter. According to Kohn, he also attended "wild drinking parties given at the Quarter apartment of a rich Texan named Frank Carruth where there was a plentiful supply of naked women."

Jim Garrison was thirty-seven years old in 1958, and his mother was concerned about the effect his swinging life style would have on his future political career. At your age, you should be married, Jane said.

He had met in the elevator at Deutsch, Kerrigan, and Stiles a file clerk named Leah Ziegler. They went for a coke, as Liz Garrison would tell it. Harrison Scott remembers their meeting as a blind date.

Hating her name, she called herself "Liz." She was a spirited young girl, an extrovert at St. Mary's Dominican High School where the nuns threatened to cut off your hair if you bleached it. "I dare you!" Liz, always ready for fun, would call out to her friends. She was effervescent and warm, and everyone liked her. She was someone you just wanted to hug, lawyer Lillian Cohen would say.

One of her husband's friends later described her as a "Mississippi Magnolia," someone who thought in terms of the Orleans Club and the ante-bellum south, although she was not of "uptown" respectability but from Algiers. Jane Gardiner wanted her son to chose a wife from among the Uptown women who talked of bloodlines and whose daughters made their debuts. Jim didn't respect any of that, and had a lifelong aversion to snobbery and notions of exclusivity.

When she met Jim Garrison, Liz stayed off and on at Claiborne Avenue in a house that seemed a replica of Tara out of "Gone With The Wind." She never wanted to go home. Jim's friends never imagined that he would marry her. They watched him as he broke dates with her arbitrarily. They saw that he was inconsiderate.

"Aren't you supposed to pick up Liz?" Jack Grayson asked him one night.

"She'll understand," Jim said.

Jack decided that he thought of Liz as a plaything, and no more. She was like a little pixie, a little doll, and she seemed so much younger than he – it was fifteen years – that his friends joked about how he was robbing the cradle. She was young and innocent.

He complained about her refusal to have sex with him. Praising her legs, he consulted his friends on how to get her into bed. They in turn warned him that she was not his equal in intellect; it was a mismatch. Seeing that she resisted the discipline of her parents, they concluded that Jim was a father figure, but one who would let her do whatever she wanted to do.

Her friends warned her that he had a bad reputation, but Liz didn't listen. Numa Bertel remembers one evening where Jim held forth about politics seated in a high-backed chair, while Liz sat at his feet, like a little kitten at the foot of her master. She said little then, and seemed intimidated by him.

Jim was living at that legendary establishment of literary people, the Pontalba apartments on Jackson Square, home of the Baroness Pontalba, whose philosophy had been that you marry for power or for influence, but never for love. Love had long ago disappeared from Jim Garrison's agenda. Nor was marriage on his mind.

While he dated Liz, he continued with others, including the beautiful, blonde and very rich Evelyn Jahncke, of the cement company family, and in later years, when he was very poor, he would remember that lost opportunity. Jahncke did belong to the Uptown debutante world.

When Jane Gardiner met Liz, she complained that Liz was a high-school drop-out, a file clerk. Jim must marry better, a woman with money who could help him in his career. Leah Ziegler was not good enough for her son, and Jane was so outspoken on this subject that some of Jim's friends were horrified. "His mother ruined him," Bob Haik later concluded.

One day Jim ran into Peggie Baker. He was thinking of getting married, he said. "How do you know if you're in love?" Jim asked Peggie, wistfully. It was a decade since he had lost her, and he was a different man from the one who had assumed that he and Peggie would be together forever. Jim Garrison was now a man who had adopted the credo that sex had "nothing to do with morality."

When Liz told him that she was pregnant, he decided to go through with the marriage. So he later explained to his closest friends, Bob Haik and Denis Barry. Jane still did not approve, and so they eloped, winding up at Jane's house in Laurel, Mississippi where Liz announced that she had miscarried. She said it so matter-of-factly that both Jim and Jane Gardiner had to wonder.

Yet they seemed happy to those who knew them, partying at piano bars in the Quarter. Jim would sing, "You're the cream in my coffee," and Liz, who didn't have much of a voice, would talk the song through. They attended bar association conventions, Jim creating high jinks on the golf course, laying down on the green and turning his putter, as if he were playing, while his law partner, Denis Barry, signaled the next group to play through. Once Liz and Denis's wife Barbara arrived early and the men had just enough time to avoid being caught in a less-than-loyal moment. Liz was now pregnant with their first child.

On August 3, 1959, Jim Robinson Garrison, nicknamed "Jasper" forever after, made his appearance. They were to have five children, as if Liz matched his infidelities by having babies. It wasn't that she was opposed to birth control for religious purposes. She became pregnant out of choice. "I got another one!" she was to boast to her friend Lenore Ward. Lenore would laugh and say, "Me too!"

When Richard Dowling had taken office as District Attorney in 1958, he "threw out," as Milton Brener put it, all the Hubert assistants. Jim Garrison would once again have to practice law, although what he still desired most, as he told Bob Haik, was "to be a successful writer." With no alternative, he went out and canvassed for office space. One day at the National Bank of Commerce Building, the very building where Aaron Kohn had perched, Jim arrived to find Denis Barry chatting with the landlord.

"Why don't you two guys get together?" the landlord suggested. They would specialize in "personal injury and admiralty." Their office was tiny, no bigger than a bathroom. Jim would handle the criminal cases, Barry the civil. If there was anything Jim Garrison could not abide, it was appearing in civil court. He was reading Orwell's "1984," Koestler's "Darkness At Noon," and Shakespeare plays that dealt with the conflict between justice and the law: "The Merchant of Venice" and "Julius Caesar."

"How do you build a practice?" Jim asked Bob Haik one day, to Haik's astonishment. The lion's share of the work fell to Denis Barry, and he complained about it to a lawyer named Jordan Brown, who had an office across the hall. Jim had almost no money, and had to borrow from a finance company.

In court, he was often late. He would apologize to the judge, and invariably be forgiven. It went against his nature to hustle for cases, and, according to Christine Wiltz, writing about Norma Wallace, he even turned up at Conti Street to solicit business, handing the Madam his card.

"It's an advantage to know how to play both sides of the fence," Wiltz claims Garrison, the former prosecutor, had said. Wiltz reports that on the two cases Wallace sent him, Jim Garrison was negligent, although her book, "The Last Madam" (2000), offers no corroborative research or citations. After his investigation of the murder of President Kennedy, everything Jim Garrison said or did passed through a lens of subjectivity. No admirer of Jim Garrison, Barry says that he was "excellent as a trial lawyer."

Barry had never even heard the name "Pershing Gervais" until they took the case of a ten-year-old girl badly injured by chicken wire surrounding a flimsy Mardi Gras float.

With seven days remaining before the statute of limitations ran out, Barry asked columnist Howard Jacobs to run a story mentioning two lawyers who were looking for information. Suddenly, there was Pershing Gervais, offering them an 8mm film of the truck parade, sunlight sparkling, and the prohibited chicken wire clear and distinct.

Settlement talks began at once. "Let's go outside," Garrison, ever the chess player, told Barry. They killed ten minutes, then returned to accept $20,000. Garrison and Barry took no fee. They did have to pay off Pershing Gervais, who always "played for results," and never did anything for nothing.

Pershing was now in the bail bond business. When a client jumped a $10,000 bond, Pershing called policeman Patrick J. Horrigan, who was assigned to Richard Dowling's office. If the $10,000 were forfeited, Pershing pleaded, he'd be put out of business. Horrigan complied and Dowling didn't forfeit the bond.

Jim Garrison also represented the pilot and master of the tugboat "Claribel," which slammed into the twenty-four mile Lake Pontchartrain causeway. A Winn-Dixie trailer-truck was crossing at the moment of impact, and the driver, Bradford Coleman, gunned his engine and flew across the buckling sections of causeway, rising into the air over the water and landing safely on the other side.

"Good religion is the only thing that saved me," Coleman said. Jim turned the case over to Deutsch, Kerrigan and Stiles, and the federal courts.

What is notable is Jim Garrison's memorandum for the defendants, as he battles the motion for a change of venue from St. Tammany Parish. Six Parishes border Lake Pontchartrain, hence the absurdity of pinpointing a particular jurisdiction. Jim describes the Lake as "an irregular polygon of eccentric shape," expanding into a riff on exactly what constitutes a boundary. "Just where is the 'middle' of this huge lake with its sinuous, winding shoreline?" he asks. Even "how far is it across the Lake?" is an ambiguous question:

> If A has just sailed from Frenier, in St. John the Baptist Parish, to Green Point, near Mandeville, his answer will be "about 23 nautical miles." On the other hand, if B has just piloted a tug from West End Park, at the junction of Orleans and Jefferson Parishes, to Goose Point in St. Tammany, he will reply that it is "about 14 nautical miles." And both are in a sense correct....

In federal court, Judge John Minor Wisdom ruled against Garrison's clients, "putting [his] trust in the trial judge's compass." The case crawfished its way to the United States Supreme Court, where certiorari was denied.

During his years practicing law, Jim frequently represented the African American citizens of Orleans Parish. Three black youths were accused of murder; Jim's client was acquitted, as were the other two, represented by Sam (Monk) Zelden and Frank Shea, both of whom will return to this narrative.

Jim defended successfully a young man charged with robbing and beating a student near a Tulane University fraternity house. A young man named Bernard Jennings got into a fight when some sailors whistled at his girlfriend. Jim got him off. A Bourbon Street stripper named Christen Ramsey ("Panther Girl") was arrested on obscenity and weapons charges; Jim got her a suspended sentence and a $500 fine.

In another potential death penalty case, a sixteen-year-old named Lester Lee Hall, high on drugs, in the company of a fifteen-year-old girl called Constance, murdered a homosexual. It was just a robbery gone bad, Hall said. They were in the habit of "rolling" degenerates in the Quarter. Denis Barry believed that Constance, who was represented by mob lawyer G. Wray Gill, had fired the fatal shot. Owing to Garrison's elaborate closing statement, Hall escaped with a life sentence rather than the electric chair.

In the Fernando Rios case, in which a gay Mexican tourist guide was murdered by three Tulane students in the Quarter, Jim represented the Mexican government on behalf of the family, and served as a special prosecutor. Garrison and Barry filed a wrongful death suit in federal court in North Carolina on behalf of Rios' mother, only to miss the statute of limitations deadline. Their case was dismissed.

Favor was rewarded with favor. Chep Morrison was now running for Governor. Jim helped out when a newspaper quoted someone accusing Morrison of being "closely associated with Communists." After his defeat, Morrison asked that the libel charges be dropped. He appointed Jim Garrison an assistant city attorney, which would give him an easy $400 a month.

Soon the word was out. If Jim Garrison thought you were right, he would dismiss the case, whatever the law said. He was the man to see. He never accepted bribes. He did make himself adept at giving and receiving favors.

He carried with him everywhere a little black book. If you had done something to him that he didn't deem fair, your name would go into the book. Yet because he was a forgiving man, it was easy to get your name erased. He walked through the Quarter; he wrote a name into the book. Before long he would be seen engaging in friendly conversation with the individual whose name he had noted, and you knew, that person's name had been scratched out.

Denis Barry was discovering that Jim Garrison was never going to be a nine to five guy. He would drift into the office at 10:30, and set off to lunch by noon. He would drink martinis or old-fashioneds at Brennan's. Sometimes his lunch companion was Milton Brener, who would become a bitter enemy during Garrison's investigation of John F. Kennedy's death. After lunch, he would go home and take a nap.

In that Southern post-war world governed by the double standard, marriage did not cramp your style. Garrison and Barry, married men, lived as if they were swinging young bachelors. Tuesday afternoons at four was party time for a group that kept an apartment in an old slave quarters. Strippers would dance before ten or twelve men, including Jim and Denis. All manner of sexual activity followed, sharing women, three in a bed. Jim never did anything homosexual. Otherwise, anything went.

By 1960, Jim Garrison had found the practice of law worse than tedious. Having trouble meeting his share of the expenses of the office, he considered returning to work for Deutsch, Kerrigan and Stiles. Bob Haik loaned him some money.

Garrison thought now that he had paid enough dues, garnered enough allies, to run for a judgeship on the criminal court. Outrageous almost in a nihilistic way, even for New Orleans, he attempted the unthinkable: he would unseat a sitting judge.

Who could be easier to beat, Garrison thought, than Judge George A. Platt, twenty-four years on the bench, yet more often to be found at the racetrack when the horses in the first race set off than in court. Denis Barry termed the laconic Platt "senile." He looked like a walrus sitting in his chambers, considering cases from behind an antique roll-top desk, and never venturing into the courtroom if he could help it. It would be easy.

The Old Regulars, the Regular Democratic Organization (RDO), led by James E. Comiskey, and the Crescent City Democratic Association (CCDA) had an agreement that they both would endorse all incumbents. Defying tradition, this time the CCDA endorsed four challengers to sitting judges, Jim Garrison among them. Denis Barry remained dubious. "The rule is you never run against a sitting judge. He has political help, you don't. You're unknown," he told Jim. Jim didn't listen.

So he began, enlisting his wit and his considerable intellectual energy to overwhelm his lethargic opponent, Judge Platt. "You do not have a full- time judge," Jim declared. "He may be a sitting judge, but he is not sitting in the court room." Jim Garrison opposed the automatic re-election of sitting judges as a "dangerous and most undemocratic proposition."

He termed himself a fair-minded enemy of crime. "Mercy there must be," he said, "in temperate measure, for the first offender is frequently not beyond rescue as a potentially good citizen, but the indiscriminate benevolence with easy disregard of the nature of the crime, the character and record of the criminal, and the cost to the community, results in the complete undermining of every element of the law enforcement process." He sounded as if he were running not for a judgeship, but for the office of District Attorney. At one rally, he argued that "there is a constant cold war between professional criminals and the hard-working, law-abiding citizens of New Orleans" and that "the only way to deal with these hardened professional criminals is to handle their cases not only firmly but swiftly so that our lives and property will be protected."

Garrison dared to be contemptuous of his opponent. "He has practically never been reversed because he has practically never tried a case," Garrison intoned. "I'm not running against a sitting judge; I'm running against a reclining judge." Judge Platt had defended his record, citing four hundred cases he had disposed of in the past year.

"This figure," Garrison told a luncheon meeting of "Veterans For Garrison," "must include cases dismissed, charges reduced in narcotics and armed robbery cases, and various paroles granted." His sardonic wit often slid into sarcasm. "Conceivably it may include the number of flies swatted in that deserted area of Section B – the jury box." Then he zeroed in for the kill: "How many felony convictions have there been – if any – in the last year in Section B?"

He enlisted his law school classmate Warren Garfunkel, now a certified public accountant, to compile a list of the number of jury trials in Judge Platt's court in the past two years. Garfunkel learned that while other judges had tried as many as eighty-eight cases, Platt had tried only seven. Garfunkel was amazed when Platt declared, "I run on my record."

Armed with Garfunkel's statistics, Jim declared before the "Citizens Committee For Better Courts" that between June 1, 1958 and June 1, 1960, not a single jury trial had occurred in Judge Platt's court. "Section B is as silent and deserted as the North Pole," he said. Judge Platt was "a likeable man, a kind man," as indeed he was, but he was ready for retirement. Garrison promised to "get down to work." The "Times-Picayune" liked what the "young attorney" had to say and endorsed him.

It turned out that New Orleans was not ready to defy tradition. Jim Garrison lost, 27,141 to Judge Platt's 33,283. In thanking the voters, Garrison could only lament that fewer than half of the eligible voters "were interested enough to make their voices – and their votes – heard."

He continued as an assistant city attorney, strolling into the office after noon, and explaining in a line that may well be apocryphal, "I keep late hours." It was the kind of anecdote told about Jim Garrison after he began his investigation of the death of President Kennedy when people searched for, or invented, ways to discredit him, and conjured up scandal, or the hint of scandal.

He was a liberal, but he had to represent the city of New Orleans and charge three civil rights demonstrators with disturbing the peace and loitering. One defendant, Frank Arthur Nelson, was a Freedom Rider, his trip south designed to desegregate transportation lines.

Appalled by segregation, Garrison found a way out. He requested a dismissal of the Dutch defendant, Hugh Brant Corstius, "on the ground of freedom of the press." Garrison pointed to Corstius's press card from a Dutch newspaper.

District Attorney Richard Dowling stepped in and demanded that the case against the demonstrators be continued so that the police could prepare their case, and Garrison could do nothing about it. In court, Judge Andrew G. Bucaro found the two remaining defendants guilty of having attempted to plant seeds of chaos, turmoil and anarchy.

It was routine in Louisiana in the early sixties. Civil rights demonstrators, peaceful or not, were accused of "criminal anarchy." An assistant of now-mayor Victor Schiro testified that the picketing had caused an unpleasant commotion on the second floor of City Hall. The demonstrators were found guilty of disturbing the peace and given ninety-day jail sentences. It was one more example of the contradiction between the law and justice that Jim Garrison found so disturbing.

CHAPTER 5:

A Full-Time District Attorney

"If the people of New Orleans want a $17,500 per year man as their district attorney, I'm not their boy."

F. Irvin Dymond

Every Friday afternoon they met at Brennan's, five ambitious young lawyers, drinking twenty-five cent martinis and talking politics. They dubbed themselves the "Nothing Group" because they possessed neither money nor favor. Their names were Frank Klein, Frank Shea, D'Alton Williams, Denis Barry – and Jim Garrison.

In October 1961, Richard Dowling, poised to run for re-election, seemed vulnerable. As criminal court Judge Schulingkamp's clerk, Walter Hammer, put it, Dowling was an old man sitting in his office "with his ass closed." Corruption ran rampant. "They sold cases like crazy," observed Joyce Wood, typing Dowling's Bills of Information. "You could buy your way out of charges," future U.S. Attorney John Volz knew.

One of Dowling's assistants, Louis Lacour, the son-in-law of James E. Comiskey himself, leader of the Old Regulars, took five hundred dollars from a fired Eastern airlines pilot in trouble named David W. Ferrie. Ferrie had been charged with a "crime against nature," then attempting to intimidate his victim. The intermediary was a bail bondsman named Hardy Davis. The charge vanished. Ferrie was equally successful at bribing who needed to be bribed in Frank Langridge's Jefferson Parish District Attorney's office.

Dowling didn't care. He sat in his office, then went to dinner and then went home, in the New Orleans way. In the South particularly, liberals could be driven from office with fake McCarthyite charges. As Aaron Kohn had tried to explain to Jim Garrison, his insidious wheedling anathema to the idealistic young attorney, an accusation was as good as the reality. Out of the gumbo of innuendo emerged mention of three "citations" against Dowling made by the House Un-American Activities Committee (HUAC), organizations on the list of subversive Communist fronts to which he ostensibly made financial contributions.

In those Cold War times, Dowling deemed it expedient to explain: He had made a lot of money during the Depression and wrote checks to organizations about which he knew little.

The purveyor of these rumors was a local hanger-on of dubious integrity. His name was Jack Martin. Part-time Algiers journalist; part-time private investigator operating out of the office of disgraced police officer Guy Banister, now running a detective agency at the corner of Lafayette and Camp; oil painting artist; hustler for advertising; political operative; peddler of information with special access to police records; religious zealot; apparent drunkard – all of these described Jack Martin.

Some said his real name was Edward Stewart Suggs, although who knew if even that were true. Not his wife. His tie perpetually pulled down, Jack Martin was a small man, only about five foot nine, skinny, with weak blue eyes, thinning hair and the pallor of an alcoholic. He was a messy little guy, like a snake in the grass, Sharon Herkes, later to become Garrison's secretary, thought. A black pork pie completed Jack's costume: always a grey suit. He was an odd fellow who always knew more than he should have known. Reporter Herman Kohlman and Hoke May of the "State's Item" discovered that Martin's information was always worth checking out, and invariably correct.

What has become apparent is that Jack Martin's connections were high: in the police departments of several Parishes; in the Louisiana state government, and particularly with Attorney General Jack P. F. Gremillion, another figure shortly to come to the foreground; and in certain federal agencies, including the Federal Aviation Agency (FAA), with whose Richard E. Robey Jack corresponded, referring to Robey as "Dick." Jack was also on a first-name basis with Senator Russell Long. And when the Labor-Management Commission of Inquiry of the State of Louisiana needed help, they turned to "Mr. Jack Martin, a private investigator in New Orleans, Louisiana."

What Jim Garrison would never discover, not through all the years that he investigated the assassination of President Kennedy, was that Jack Martin worked for government intelligence.

It is difficult for outsiders to register how powerful the office of District Attorney was in New Orleans. In a vestige of the Napoleonic Code, on a mere Bill of Information dictated by the District Attorney, someone could be arrested and charged with a felony. No grand jury testimony was required. Moreover, were a grand jury to produce evidence, however credible that evidence, the District Attorney could on his own judgment refuse to prosecute (nolle prosequi). Only if a defendant insisted upon a trial to clear his name would they go to court. It was a check and balance against a corrupt police force from whom false charges and false testimony might be offered.

On one of those late Friday afternoon confabulations at Brennan's, Jim Garrison decided to run for district attorney. Frank Klein, who had just been elected president of the New Orleans Criminal Courts Bar Association, would also run. D'Alton Williams too would try his luck. Then, whoever came out ahead in the first primary would gain the backing of the other four.

It cost $250 to qualify to run. Jim had to borrow the money. He was now the father of two, Jasper, and Virginia, two months old, born August 21, 1961. Some of Jim's friends were dubious. A medical resident he befriended, Frank Minyard, thought Jim Garrison was "the last guy in the world who could get elected." Yes, Jim was scrupulously honest, but he didn't have the energy. What he liked best was to go home to bed with four or five books and remain there for the weekend.

On October 13th, Jim declared his candidacy. Richard Dowling had continued to practice civil law while in office. Jim vowed to restore "an aggressively competent, unquestionably honest, full-time district attorney's office." Among his affiliations, he listed the Society of Former Special Agents of the FBI, and the Sons of the American Revolution, which Jane had made certain that he joined. His campaign chest consisted of $5,000 borrowed from a bank by Denis Barry.

Garrison presented himself to voters as a reformer. He was "furious about how Dowling had allowed his office to be corrupted," he said.

He chose as his major campaign issue Dowling's failure to prosecute narcotics dealers, labeling the situation "unbelievable."

But no matter what he did, Jim Garrison's candidacy remained mired in the back pages of the newspapers. Frank Klein garnered the support of councilman Paul V. Burke, and the endorsement of the Conservative Political Association led by ex-police officer Hubert J. Badeaux. Jim was worried. "This guy might beat me," he thought. Denis feared that Jim might even run behind Earl J. Amedee, a Dowling assistant who, as an African American, stood no chance whatsoever in the New Orleans of that era. The strongest candidate in the field, however, was not a member of the "Nothing Group," but a highly successful criminal attorney named F. Irvin Dymond.

Desperate to gain an advantage, Jim decided to approach Mayor Victor Schiro, who himself was now running for re-election. Rain water dripping from the lapels of his coat, Jim turned up at Schiro campaign headquarters. He seemed an unlikely candidate, William Klein thought as, from behind a desk where he worked for Schiro, Klein watched Garrison enter, hat in hand. Then Jim asked his friend Bob Haik, who was close to Schiro and was running for the State Senate on the Schiro ticket, to request of Schiro that he add Jim to his ticket. Schiro refused.

"My ultimate goal is to become a judge," Garrison told Haik.

Garrison's defeat in the race for district attorney was a foregone conclusion. "You should be helpful to the congressman from the area," Haik advised. Only Jim's future was in question now.

"Are you still in the race?" Milton Brener asked Jim one day when they ran into each other in civil court.

"I've been finessed," Jim lamented. Schiro and Dowling had entered into a brokered agreement not to oppose each other, affording Dowling the endorsement of both political machines, the Old Regulars, allied with the Longs, and the Crescent City Democratic Organization. The situation seemed hopeless. Meanwhile the deadline for withdrawals and getting your money back had passed.

A public debate was scheduled. "I may as well stay in until the debate is over," Jim said. At a Young Men's Business Club of Greater New Orleans debate, he attacked Dowling's claim to have 225 narcotics convictions, "more than the whole state of Louisiana combined."

"That's just like saying a Plaquemines Parish fisherman catches more oysters than the whole state of Arizona," Jim countered, drawing on his quick wit. Dowling flushed red with anger. Jim resigned as an assistant city attorney shortly thereafter.

Inserting himself in the campaign was Aaron Kohn, who garnered headlines by beating his organized crime drum. Kohn called the "strip-clip joints" of the Quarter "an important element of the organized crime of this community," which they were not. In reply, Dowling attacked Kohn's "habit of misinformation." Dowling's reply, regarding the presence of the Mafia, "in Jefferson Parish maybe," did not seem forceful and the "Times-Picayune" sided with Kohn.

Kohn mailed all the candidates questionnaires. Would they serve full-time?

"Emphatically yes," Jim wrote. He declared himself "open to suggestions from the director of the Crime Commission" regarding his staff choices. Would he close the illegal strip-joints? He would.

"Was there organized or syndicated criminal activity in New Orleans?" Jim replied that such activity was "substantial, particularly with regard to hand-books" and to ownership of some Bourbon Street clubs. When Dowling denied he had ever received a questionnaire, Kohn produced a mail receipt.

A full debate of all the candidates took place on January 14th, 1962, and was covered by all four television stations. Six candidates sat, lined up in a row. An empty chair remained, reminding the audience that Richard Dowling had boycotted the event. Some thought the empty chair alone killed Dowling's chances. Jim sat up straight in his three-piece Brooks Brothers suit, a watch chain firmly in place. He sounded and looked like a district attorney.

Frank Klein had decided to yield his time to Jim, who suddenly appeared to have the better chance. When asked a question, Klein would say, "What do you think, Jim?" In modulated tones, Jim invoked the narcotics problem in Orleans Parish and the "incredible" failure of the incumbent. He called Dowling "the great Emancipator. He let everyone go free."

"If I'm not your cup of tea, vote for one of them," Jim concluded, naming others, particularly Klein. "But get a new district attorney."

A single question changed everything.

Each of the candidates was asked whether he would serve as a full-time district attorney. One by one, they promised piously to divest themselves of outside business. None had much to give up – except for one man, Irvin Dymond.

That evening, just before the debate, Dymond had attended a fund-raising party, where he consumed his share of martinis. Now, half-inebriated, slouching in his chair while puffing away on a cigarette, he thought to himself: it's customary for a district attorney to keep his civil practice. What's wrong with that?

"I make more than $17,500 a year and I intend to go on making more than $17,500," Dymond said. "If the people of New Orleans want a $17,500 per year man as their district attorney, I'm not their boy!"

Projecting sincerity, Jim Garrison at once declared that he would certainly serve full-time. He had never made $17,500 in a single year.

Back at the cocktail party, Dymond's supporters, glued to the television set, gasped. Seasoned politicians, they knew it was all over. The only remaining issue was whether Dymond should withdraw right away.

Jim Garrison now became the darling of the Uptown crowd, the 13th and 14th "Silk Stocking" wards. The segregationists in the 8th ward liked him too. Up to that moment, he had collected about a hundred dollars in contributions. Suddenly everything changed. Schiro's rebuff had forced him to run as an independent, which turned out to be an enormous advantage.

A week later, on January 22nd, Jim Garrison was endorsed by the "Times-Picayune," which regretted that in these days of "tickets," he "is not included on the ticket of any political faction." A vote for Garrison, however, was a "vote for law enforcement."

Reading the newspaper endorsement of Garrison, Dowling panicked, and went in search of some scandal in Jim Garrison's history. Dowling had his assistant, Burton G. Klein, write to J. Edgar Hoover by Special Delivery. "I would like to know if Mr. Garrison's separation from the Bureau was involuntary or voluntary and the reasons for such separation," Klein wrote. The Bureau replied that "Garrison's record was satisfactory."

No more than in the race for assessor that began his political career did Jim bother to put up posters. "Posters don't vote," he told Bob Haik. "Throw them away." Old-time political rallies bored him. He decided to wait until the waning days of the campaign, and then put all his money into television appearances. His model was the Kennedy/Nixon debates, Nixon, swarthy, sweating and nervous, Kennedy passionate, handsome, glowing, and assertive.

"If you raise one hundred dollars, spend $90 on television the day before the election," Garrison decided. "You reach the people directly and you bypass the machine." He was right, and one judge running for office reported attending three or four rallies at which there was always the same handful of people: "Everyone else was home watching Garrison."

On January 22nd, there was Jim Garrison on television, the set a courtroom. His topic was "your NEW District Attorney's Office." The show opened with a close-up of a hypodermic needle, a needle children had supposedly used to inject drugs. In fact, it was the type of needle used to inject horses. No matter, Jim stuck it into his arm.

Then he produced some powder. "This is what heroin looks like," he said of the granulated sugar he had brought along. Why hadn't Richard Dowling prosecuted more narcotics cases? Garrison then demanded. He named the dealers Dowling had not charged, names he had garnered from narcotics police who revealed to him the deals they had made with Dowling's office. Garrison promised that his office would never dismiss narcotics cases. All the pushers would go to the penitentiary.

One day candidate Garrison received a telephone call from a policeman attached to the vice squad. The man would not reveal his name, but he was Raymond Comstock, a tall, lean, hard-eyed officer with a strong sense of responsibility. He was honest, sardonic, and fair and he wasted no words. Comstock could grow livid over a news report. He was just what he said he was, fellow officer Robert Buras remembers, Comstock having once saved his life under fire, and you could never change him.

Comstock remembered Jim Garrison from one of his cases. In June of 1960, Comstock had arrested a female impersonator for possession of a marijuana cigarette. Garrison had defended the man and got him off, but Comstock was impressed.

Comstock had also arrested a woman named Frances Welch, who would go on to perform more than sixteen hundred abortions. The records were all there, Comstock said. Comstock told himself: If Dowling was re-elected, he would rather ride a horse in City Park than be a police officer.

He pondered what to do. Then he telephoned Jim Garrison.

On television, Jim excoriated Dowling for not prosecuting Welch. Then, driving the narcotics issue home, he accused Dowling of failing "to oppose organized crime." A January 26th "Times-Picayune" cartoon pictures Jim Garrison as comic strip detective Dick Tracy. "His bookmarks for a vital volume," the cartoon reads, citing Garrison's accomplishments. Garrison holds a poster reading "Law Enforcement for New Orleans."

With no political organization behind him, Jim watched the returns of this, the first primary, designed to narrow the field to two, at Councilman Burke's headquarters. Richard Dowling received 47,576 votes, Garrison, 45,719. "It's obvious the people of New Orleans have indicated they want a new district attorney," Garrison said, brashly. "When I am sworn in, I am going to give them just that."

The run-off would be on March 3rd, with the winner certain to be the new District Attorney in what was then a one-party state. No Republican, no political descendant of Abraham Lincoln, stood a chance.

Jim's campaign began with three people, himself, Denis Barry and a young woman, an unpaid volunteer, named Carol Boyd, who kept the schedule of "coffees" where the candidate would give a brief talk to a group of ladies and their friends. If he won, he told Carol, who was nineteen, she could have a job in the office. "You can type, right?" Jim asked. "Well, that's good," he added when he learned she could. He taught her to drink bull shots, vodka, with beef bouillon, celery and Tabasco. Jim would go down to WDSU-TV, do a commercial, and then go home. There was no staff.

Contributions came in from his old friends, Jay Teasdel and Vance Gilmer. There were also contributions from future enemies: Judge J. Bernard Cocke, Gerald Gallinghouse and Milton Brener. Since his friend Irvin Dymond had departed the field, Adrian Duplantier endorsed Jim Garrison, and helped Jim with the black vote - Duplantier was known for integrationist views. Garrison did not even have to endorse Duplantier's mayoralty bid in return. Instead, Garrison promised his office would be "free and independent of politics."

A citizens' group called upon candidate Garrison. "Mr. Garrison, may I ask what church you belong to?" a woman wanted to know.

"I'm a Unitarian," Garrison said. He attended the first Unitarian Church of which Reverend Albert D'Orlando was Minister. He didn't go into the fact that the Reverend had been accused of being a member of the Communist Party and there had been a split in the church. But a woman brought it up.

"Mr. Garrison, may I ask, when the First Unitarian Church split, did you go with the group that started a new church, or did you stay with Reverend D'Orlando?" Jim Garrison would not succumb to red-baiting.

"I saw no reason to change," he said.

Hardy Davis, who has already made an appearance in this story as the bail bondsman who bailed out David Ferrie, now re-enters the narrative. Operating in the shadows of Tulane and Broad, where the Criminal Court and District Attorney's office were then located, Davis had set bonds on such figures as Carlos Marcello and the neo-Nazi leader George Lincoln Rockwell, a cohort of Guy Banister. One afternoon late in 1961, Jack Martin, ubiquitous and miraculously prescient in divining when something was about to happen, had popped into Davis's office.

Martin was just in time to overhear a Dowling assistant, Walter E. Doane, attempt to shake down Hardy Davis for a campaign contribution. Should Davis not contribute to Dowling's re-election effort, he might find it tough going, Doane let him know. Davis promised to contribute, and not only contribute, but do it through Doane, so that Doane would get the credit.

Ever on the look-out for valuable information, Martin hovered just outside the door. As soon as Doane was gone, Martin slithered into Davis's office. "I know a shakedown when I hear one," Martin said. "That was a threat to hurt you in his section of court." Davis later confirmed the story in his memoir, "Aiming For The Jugular In New Orleans."

Jack Martin had no love for Jim Garrison, who had refused to accept a charge when Martin accused a man of giving him a bad check for his investigative services. Yet he gave Garrison a sworn statement about the Dowling office shakedown of Hardy Davis. Soon word leaked out that Garrison had Martin's statement. Dowling then summoned Hardy Davis and got him to write an affidavit stating that the information was false; Doane had not tried to extort money from him. There, for the moment, the matter rested.

On February 18th, Garrison and Dowling appeared together in a television debate. It was like Paul Newman running against Barry Fitzgerald, Bob Haik thought. No matter that he had been the victim of red-baiting, Dowling did his own baiting. He demanded to know whether Garrison had accepted money from segregationist Leander H. Perez, "the boss and czar of Plaquemines and St. Bernard Parishes." (Three months later, Perez would be excommunicated by the Catholic church for opposing the integration of the Catholic schools; unabashed he called for the protection of "children against the unmoral curse of forced racial integration").

A liberal, Garrison saw no reason not to accept the support of people whose views were not his own: businessman L. P. (Lou) Davis, who, at the suggestion of Guy Banister, would host at his home George Lincoln Rockwell when he visited New Orleans; Jack Rogers, counsel for the Louisiana Un-American Activities Committee; or his own classmate, Congressman John R. Rarick – with none did he share a world-view. Guilt by association was a notion entirely foreign to him.

Leander Perez's son supported Garrison out of gratitude for Garrison's having convicted the driver who killed Perez's wife. Even Adrian Duplantier, in later years no admirer of Jim Garrison, points out that the younger Perez was a respected lawyer; there was no reason not to accept a campaign contribution from him. To finance his campaign, Jim also borrowed money from his mother. He refused a contribution from sixteen pinball operators, a fact even Aaron Kohn had to note. Garrison's entire campaign would cost only $15,000.

Dowling made an issue of Jim's having changed his name from "James Carothers Garrison" to "Jim Garrison." He was unaware that Jim's real name was "Earling Carothers Garrison" and that he had become "James," "Jimmy," "Jim," when he was less than five years old, at his own initiative. Jim, who never saw the need to explain anything to anyone, did not enlighten Dowling now.

Dowling charged that Garrison had been involved in a conflict of interest in representing the mother of Fernando Rios in her wrongful death suit, while simultaneously representing the Mexican government. In fact, their interests were identical. The issue was bogus, lawyer Donald V. Organ thought.

Jim now produced Jack Martin's affidavit outlining how Walter Doane had attempted to shake down Hardy Davis. The document had Doane aggressively confronting Davis: "And you can't help us, after all we've done for you? We're going to be in office until May and I'll put you out of office by then!" All he was asking for, Doane adds, is "a lousy $1,000." Dowling produced Hardy Davis's denial, adding that Jack Martin had been "in and out of mental institutions," which was, in part, true. Then Dowling declared that as an assistant district attorney in a two year period, Garrison had tried only 13 jury cases, while dismissing 448. His successor had tried 46 cases, dismissing only 284.

Watching, concerned, Milton Brener thought that "Garrison looked as though he had hit by a wet mop."

And Dowling had yet another arrow to fling Jim Garrison's way. He challenged Garrison's statement that he hadn't returned to the FBI after his brief return to military service because he had been offered a better job with safety commissioner Bernard J. McCloskey. Dowling had done his homework as he revealed that Garrison had left military service in October 1951, while he went to work for McCloskey in May 1952. His final barb was that Garrison, unauthorized, had visited the foreman of a grand jury, Marc Antony, while Garrison was an assistant district attorney, which was true, the result of his midnight trip to New York.

Dowling then summed up: Garrison was "a hack."

As the campaign drew to a close, the attacks grew ever more vicious. Dowling ran an advertisement in the "Times-Picayune" on March 2nd entitled "Myth versus Facts: The Real Garrison Record." He challenged Garrison's "independence" on the ground that he accepted contributions from a racist, and attacked him as well for charging the wife of the publisher of the "Times-Picayune" with only resisting arrest. Drunk, she had hit someone with her car. Dowling then connected this to the conviction of the man who killed Perez's wife. Dowling added that Garrison had refused to accept charges when a "white woman" was raped in a French Quarter tavern.

Retaliating, Garrison played his stongest card. He produced a letter signed by Dowling thanking a strip-joint operator named Carlo Montalbano for his campaign contribution. Garrison suddenly had in his possession the canceled checks from other clubs, proving that Dowling had been shaking them down too. All this information came to Garrison courtesy of that Quarter habitué who knew all there was to know, Pershing Gervais.

Dowling was called before a grand jury. "Cash has no name," Dowling said in his defense. "I took checks to prove it was all above board, campaign contributions. I could have taken cash and no one would have known the difference!" Back at the office, furious, he admitted that he had been exposed. Joyce Wood, no fan of Dowling's, listened.

"Go get that investigator who took checks!" Dowling ordered. "He's fired!"

Finally, Jim attacked specious leaflets reading "Citizens for Duplantier and Dowling" that had to be counterfeit because Duplantier had, in fact, endorsed Jim Garrison. Among those listed as having paid for this particular piece of campaign literature were lawyers Benjamin E. Smith and Bruce C. Waltzer whose paths would soon cross Jim Garrison's in the Dombrowski case. Garrison suggested that some of the people in this "Attorneys for Dowling" advertisement had not granted permission that their names be used.

The day before the election, Jim Garrison went into civil district court and filed a $75,000 libel suit against Dowling. Dowling was livid, calling it "the oldest, cheapest and rankest political trick of a desperate candidate who is facing defeat." The suit had been filed too late in the afternoon for Dowling's answer to make the newspapers.

On the day of the election, an advertisement appeared in the "Times-Picayune." Headed "Attorneys for Garrison," and paid for by Denis Barry, it named Frank Shea and Frank Klein, D'Alton Williams, Milton Brener, Charles R. Ward, and Steven R. Plotkin. The final "Times-Picayune" campaign cartoon depicted an outsized, Rodin-inspired figure. The legend read: "This thinker thinks for himself." On a paper in his hand is written "Independent voters will be boss March 3rd."

On election day, Jim was heady with confidence. At the Roosevelt Hotel, he retired with his lady of the moment, a stewardess named Judy Chambers. Because she was present at breakfast, Bob Haik dubbed her "Scrambled Eggs." In the years to come, Jim Garrison would claim he had the license to do whatever he wanted since he had been trapped into his marriage.

"I'll see you at nine," Jim told his friends. "That's when I'll be ahead." He was replaying the scenario of John F. Kennedy, a man who in every respect he admired. On the day of Kennedy's inauguration, his biographer Richard Reeves would report, he had sexual relations with the actress Angie Dickinson. For these men of the World War Two era, a predatory attitude toward women was emblematic of your manhood.

The Garrison supporters gathered at the Royal Orleans Hotel where someone had rented a room. For a long time, the room remained empty.

Frank Shea ambled in. Frank Minyard and Shea sat with Jim and Liz and waited. As the returns began to come in, more people arrived.

When Jim at last made his way forward to deliver his victory speech, photographers asked Jim and Liz to walk together to the podium. Suddenly an arm shot out. Liz would have tumbled to the ground had someone not caught her.

"I belong there!" Jane Gardiner said. 'I'm responsible for him being here today. You've been only a hindrance," she accused Liz. "I should be up there with him." Someone heard Mrs. Gardiner tell Liz, roughly, "Get out of my way!" She was a dragon, "States-Item" columnist Iris Kelso concluded. To Vance Gilmer, she seemed like a promoter, and talked about her son as if he had been elected President of the United States.

Jim Garrison had received 78,851 votes to Dowling's 71,821. The whole town was astonished. Garrison had managed to undermine forever New Orleans' established political traditions. Back-room political organizations, the rigid compliance with "tickets," had been dealt a death blow.

Immediately Jim and Denis Barry contacted Aaron Kohn. On March 10th, Barry wrote to Kohn, promising to file charges against lottery owners, in keeping with Metropolitan Crime Commission recommendations. He requested Kohn's "thoughts and recommendations."

Ten days later, Jim submitted to Kohn a list of the attorneys he planned to appoint as his assistants. As he selected police officers to be attached to the district attorney's office, the name of a Kohn informant came up, police sergeant John Leavines, who had admitted to participating in police graft. On the advice of Frank Klein and Frank Shea both, Jim passed him over. Then Garrison told the press he had communicated with Kohn, hoping to neutralize his once and future adversary.

Garrison had still to wait for the official April election when he would face the perfunctory Republican candidate. With time on their hands, Jim and Denis Barry went on a whirlwind tour. No wives were invited, although an exquisite woman boarded the plane with Barry and Garrison. This was "Scrambled Eggs," herself, who turned out to be the daughter of a woman who ran a prostitution ring using college students.

Their first stop was Washington, D.C. where they would be house guests of Chep Morrison, who had been appointed Ambassador to the Organization of American States by John F. Kennedy. Morrison had been in touch with dictators, from Trujillo to Peron, but that hadn't disqualified him. Morrison had suggested to Kennedy that Garrison be considered as an alternate choice for appointment as United States Attorney. It was an empty gesture, perhaps, since Representative Hale Boggs controlled that particular piece of patronage.

The highlight of the trip to D.C. was to be a meeting with President John F. Kennedy himself.

A limousine met Garrison and Barry at the airport, flags of the American States flying. Then they were whisked off. "Scrambled Eggs" bunked elsewhere.

"Get up early. Bright and early," Morrison instructed Barry and Garrison. "We're having breakfast at the White House. We'll have grits! The President will be there!"

Garrison and Barry stayed out until four a.m., and overslept. Louisiana Senators Allen Ellender and Russell Long appeared for the breakfast with John F. Kennedy, as did Congressmen F. Edward Hebert and Hale Boggs. The two dashing lawyers from New Orleans never made it.

On Monday morning, they had an appointment with the Attorney General. Robert Kennedy kept them waiting in the anteroom for a full hour. Finally, they were ushered into his office. There Bobby sat with his feet up on his desk. His shirt was open, he sported no tie, and his sleeves were rolled up. His hair fell boyishly into his eyes. For a long time he remained silent.

"What can I do for you?" Bobby finally asked Garrison and Barry.

"I've just been elected District Attorney of Orleans Parish," Jim began. "As a former FBI agent, I want to work with the local FBI. I'm here to introduce myself...."

In a matter of moments, after a few remarks about organized crime, they were ushered out. It was clear that in Bobby's eyes, Garrison had committed the unthinkable, standing up his brother, the President of the United States.

Back in New Orleans, Jim Garrison told the press that he had "an enjoyable" meeting with Robert Kennedy, the opposite of the truth. They had an understanding "about releasing details of the conversation to the press," Garrison confided.

"How did it go?" Bob Haik asked Garrison.

"Well, I met Bobby," Jim said. Then he told Haik what had happened. Haik was astonished.

"Bob," Jim said, placing his hand on Haik's shoulder. "You can always meet a President. But you can't always get a piece of ass like that!"

In New York, Barry and Garrison visited the offices of both the New York and Kings (Brooklyn) County district attorneys. They studied the bonding procedures. Garrison was amazed to learn that legendary prosecutor Frank Hogan tried no cases himself while running an effective operation. He decided to model his own office after Hogan's. He looked at District Attorney Silva's desk. It had no stray papers on it.

"How do you keep your desk neat like that?" Jim asked.

"I'm an administrator," Silva replied. "I don't try lawsuits."

Ready to begin, Jim and Denis made a personal appearance before the board of directors of the Metropolitan Crime Commission. Fearing nothing, believing in the integrity of the operation he planned to run, Garrison all but gave away the farm. "Any DA's office which would consider the Crime Commission as an opponent in any way would have something basically wrong with it," Garrison said. Then he told Aaron Kohn that the files of the district attorney's office would always be open for his inspection, and he meant not just the closed files that were part of the public record, but open files as well. Knowing Aaron Kohn for what he was, Denis Barry was dismayed.

On May 4th, John F. Kennedy visited New Orleans to dedicate the Nashville wharf. His visit was sponsored by International House and the International Trade Mart. In advance of his visit, the Citizens' Council had attacked Kennedy for his "perpetual attack on the Southern way of life and his palpable sympathy for left-wing elements."

At a March rally to protest Msgr. Henry C. Bezou's announcement that he was desegregating the Catholic schools, candidate Jim Garrison had made an appearance. "Are you going to see John when he comes to New Orleans?" the crowd was asked.

"NO!" they screamed back.

On the day John F. Kennedy came to New Orleans, among those in the procession of fifteen cars was Clay Shaw, Managing Director of the International Trade Mart. Shaw had been invited by Congressman Hale Boggs. In his speech, Kennedy invoked the "strength of diversity," and praised New Orleans as "cosmopolitan in nature, tolerant in outlook, the product of many nations, many cultures, many races and creeds." Jim Garrison, the District Attorney-elect, was conspicuously not in attendance.

Three days later, on May 7th, 1962, Jim Garrison took his oath of office. Garrison "wears the badge of no local political party," said Eberhard Deutsch, introducing his protégé. "He need fear no repercussion for any of his actions."

Jim Garrison was an atheist.

"I'll never swear on a Bible," he told Denis Barry, and he did not.

"My office may not be a popular office in the next four years," Garrison promised. "But it will be honest and efficient. No favors will be granted. A little old lady with a problem will receive as much attention as the mayor of the city." It was a jibe at Victor Schiro, who had defeated Adrian Duplantier. His was a victory "for the people of New Orleans," Jim Garrison said, as he welcomed the demise of "the selection of officials in smoke-filled back rooms."

Chapter 6:

Taking Office

"I call this city a banana republic in the twilight zone."

Gordon Novel, New Orleans resident

He had taken office as District Attorney in that port of no return, a city with an atmosphere "like a smog," a place characterized by a deeply-seated "tolerance of the status quo." Had he been born in New Orleans, Jim Garrison reflected later, he could not have been an effective district attorney. Serving as a Garrison assistant, young Ralph Slovenko walked into court as a lawyer for the first time, and the judge opened his palm, literally. Slovenko thought New Orleans resembled the Dominican Republic much more than it did one of the United States of America.

Shortly after his victory, Jim had lunch at the Petroleum Club with his old friend Vance Gilmer. Lamenting the corruption endemic to the Orleans Parish district attorney's office, Garrison revealed that he had already been approached. He did not say by whom, but he was expected to run a compromised office.

Garrison promised Gilmer a morality the likes of which the office had not seen. His staff would be told: "We will do no favors." Richard Dowling had been driven around New Orleans in a Cadillac. Garrison's successor, Harry Connick, for a time would drive around in a Rolls Royce confiscated from a drug dealer. Jim Garrison rode in a Ford LTD with the seats moved back because he was so tall.

He designed a seal to be placed over his office door: "Causa Civium –Nullum Negotium Principium: "For the People – No Compromise." He had most of the law books removed from his office: "A good lawyer doesn't need law books," he said. He did retain a copy of "Criminal

Procedure." On his desk were thirteen antique volumes of the plays of William Shakespeare. On another desk in the room sat "An ABZ of Love."

He hired brilliant young assistants. Frank Klein would be First Assistant and Denis Barry a "Special Assistant." Milton Brener would head narcotics and go on to fulfill Garrison's campaign promises. The office was unrelenting on the issue of drugs, and no assistant could dismiss a narcotics case without first consulting Brener. Garrison considered hiring Harry Connick, but Connick did not make the final cut.

From his staff, Garrison expected dedication. You were to be on call twenty-four hours a day. You would not be paid for overtime either. "It was like paddling without a paddle," remembered Frank Meloche, who served the office as a police officer. A prosecutors' school would train new assistants. Later Garrison's assistants were required to take a course at Tulane University in "Law and Psychiatry."

They were bold and defiant. We can take on anybody, they believed. Nobody was above the law. Jim Garrison created one of the finest district attorney's offices in the country. John Volz later realized that an important reason why he was offered federal appointments, including that of United States Attorney, was that he was a product of the Orleans Parish prosecutor's office.

Garrison organized his office according to practices he had admired in the U.S. military. In the field artillery, he had noticed, "a consistent characteristic in the operation of the very best battalions" was that "the commanding officer had been a man who had delegated the details of running the organization to his 'executive officer.'" Garrison chose Frank Klein as his second in command because, he said, Klein "complemented me perfectly."

Arriving at Tulane and Broad, Klein at once hung a gruesome picture of the electric chair behind his desk. Families who came to plead for lesser sentences, or lesser charges, for their loved ones would have to sit facing that painting. On his desk, Klein placed a model of the guillotine. Klein believed in law and order: if you transgressed, you paid the penalty. With Frank Klein, tempering justice with mercy was not an everyday occurrence. He smoked four packs of cigarettes a day and was a stellar prosecutor.

Even as Garrison thought Klein complemented him, he could not resist ribbing his Teutonic assistant. In his study at home, Jim kept his wartime souvenir, that German soldier's helmet with holes marking the path of a bullet that entered in one side and exited out the other. One day at a meeting of his staff held at the house, Garrison said: "Frank, do you think it was one of your relatives who wore that helmet?" Former U.S. Marine Klein seethed. Only Klein and the chief investigator would report directly to Garrison, who didn't want people running into his office casually.

In contrast, Garrison became notorious for the mercy he afforded defendants and their families. He had a "heart of gold," his former assistant, William Alford says, and sympathized often to the extent of reducing charges should someone be lucky enough to gain his ear. He might not dismiss the case, but he would reduce the charges. "He's got such a nice Mama," Garrison might say of a defendant. "I don't want him to get the death penalty." Garrison was a prosecutor who opposed the death penalty and when a local university invited him to participate in a debate, he sent conservative John Volz with the instruction that, in violation of his own beliefs, Volz argue against capital punishment as a salutary exercise.

Lawyers knew: get an appointment with Jim Garrison and just stay put. The more time you spent with Jim, the better your chances were that the prosecution would recommend no jail time. A lawyer named Jim McPherson came in to argue that it wasn't necessary to prosecute a certain case. Jim listened. Then he put McPherson together with one of the assistants, and McPherson realized: Jim Garrison was no hard-nosed prosecutor who wanted to put everyone in jail.

Criminal defense attorney Ray McGuire arrived with a story. His client had driven the car in an armed robbery case. The client had already served the first of a nine-year sentence at Angola, the nickname for the Louisiana State Prison. Meanwhile, his cohorts, those who had actually committed the crime, had pled "not guilty" and received probation.

"It isn't fair," McGuire told Garrison. He wanted to file a motion for a new trial. Before their meeting was over, McGuire and Garrison had signed a joint motion, requesting that new trial. The case was dismissed. McGuire's client went on to become a Jefferson Parish deputy sheriff.

In another matter, McGuire approached Garrison on behalf of a man who had been arrested on Broad Street. His name, description and age matched closely that of a felon on the loose. The magistrate had set a very high bond.

"The police know it's the wrong man," McGuire told Garrison. "Only they have already sent in their report. Now they have no authority to release him." In an act unlike any Richard Dowling would have dared, Jim Garrison picked up the telephone and called the police officers who had made the arrest.

"Are you sure this is the man you wanted?" Garrison asked. When they admitted that he wasn't, Garrison requested the file and refused the charges. "I want this man out right away," Garrison said.

Jim Garrison made full use of the district attorney's extraordinary power to "nolle prosse" ("nolle prosequi") a case. He gave his assistants the freedom to re-examine cases no matter what the original office screener at the complaint desk had decided. They could reduce charges. They could dismiss a case. The police might have received incorrect information.

Jim Garrison was also an easy touch when it came to personal matters. An acquaintance named Earl Landry turned up and told Jim that his family was hungry. Jim at once co-signed a $1,000 note that he wound up paying himself when Landry stopped answering the bank's letters.

Jim requested of the deans of the Tulane, Loyola and Louisiana State University law schools to recommend their best graduates and the office took shape. Ray Forrester, now the Tulane Dean, recommended Michael Karmazin, a Duke All-American and former professional football player. All positions had by then been filled, but Garrison hired Karmazin anyway. He might not ever have seen the inside of a courtroom, but Karmazin was obviously a competitor, Garrison thought. It became a standard hiring question at Garrison's office: what sports did you play at school? Years later, when John Volz became Garrison's Executive Assistant, he asked that question of a brilliant young lawyer named Ralph Whalen. Whalen was astonished.

Volz explained. "We want people who know what it means to win and to lose."

Jim Garrison appointed the first woman assistant district attorney in New Orleans history, Louise Korns. Korns was first in her class at Tulane in 1954, although the prejudice endured that women were not tough enough to be prosecutors. Korns was her own woman in other ways. She drove a convertible, rarely wore stockings, this in formal New Orleans, and a dash of lipstick was her only make-up. Korns would remain with Garrison until the end. She was in charge of appeals, and did all the office's legal research.

When Korns returned to the office after having argued an appeal before either the Louisiana or the United States Supreme Court, Garrison would never ask her what had happened. Once he trusted you, he did not interfere. His judgment had been correct. Korns was tough and didn't become disconcerted under fire. One day, as she was addressing the Justices at the United States Supreme Court, William Douglas, bored, put his head down as if he were sleeping. Korns never lost her composure. If anything surprised Louise Korns, it was that Jim Garrison had no desire to present oral arguments himself, not even before the Justices of the United States Supreme Court where he could have cut a dashing figure and garnered press attention. Personal ambition, Korns observed, was alien to him.

In choosing assistants, Garrison also relied on his instincts. A letter arrived from a young lawyer named Ross Scaccia. "I like the way you won the election," Scaccia wrote. "You won it on merit alone. It's not often you see people rewarded for their abilities. I'm a struggling lawyer. I think I'm good, but I don't have any connections. I don't pressure for connections. I'm trying to succeed on merit."

"I like your letter," Jim Garrison wrote back to Scaccia. "You're hired!"

There would be full-time police investigators attached to the district attorney's office for the first time. (Dowling had used civilian investigators, some of whom had even worked for houses of prostitution). Among those chosen was Louis Ivon, who would be with Jim Garrison from the day he took office until the day he left. Ivon, affectionately, always called Garrison "Boss." Jim called Ivon - "Buck." Raymond Comstock was another officer who joined the Garrison staff. In character, Comstock never told Garrison that he had been the anonymous caller who had tipped him off about the Frances Welch abortion case.

By the time of his swearing in, Jim Garrison had not revealed whom he had chosen as his chief investigator.

"We still need a chief investigator," Barry pointed out.

"I'll take care of it," Garrison said.

The new staff adjourned to Brennan's for a celebratory lunch, Brennan's being the restaurant where it had all begun.

"Do you remember the guy who helped us out in the Mardi Gras case?" Garrison asked Barry.

Barry was dumbfounded. Pershing Gervais had been fired by the police department. His reputation was sullied beyond measure. He was also a civilian, and they had agreed that only police officers would serve as their investigators.

Pershing was a living embodiment of the view that you can't tell the police from the criminals. He was a criminal. Yet he had helped Jim get elected by providing the evidence that Dowling's people had been picking up bribery money from the Bourbon Street clubs.

Garrison made his case for Pershing Gervais: You had to know the streets to be able to catch criminals. Pershing knew everyone. And hadn't Pershing testified voluntarily in federal court about graft paid to the police? Hadn't Pershing been one of the few who came forward? Plus, Pershing had a first class mind. Others noted that Jim Garrison had a weakness for Damon Runyonesque characters, cynics keyed to the absurd. Garrison loved black humor and hated to be bored. No one was ever bored by Pershing Gervais.

Lou Ivon thought: it was just like Jim Garrison to give someone who needed a break a chance. Later, he and John Dolan would compare the hiring of Pershing Gervais to Jim Garrison's helping people in the office when their licenses to practice law had been suspended; Garrison paid them for months to do "research." If Garrison had to fire someone, he would find them a better job first. Garrison "helped Pershing become a person again," Ivon says. Still, those familiar with law enforcement believed that Raymond Comstock would have made a far better chief investigator.

Pershing did know the streets and was under no one's thumb, He was subject to no one's power. He knew where and when to spread money around. He was feared because, whatever he did, there seemed never to be any reprisals. Pershing also was acquainted with elements Jim Garrison could not possibly approach. In a den of thieves, Pershing was king. Through his fellow officer and friend Marion (Mike) Seghers, Pershing controlled the police vice squad. He would do the dirty work and take the heat. Everyone in the Quarter was terrified of him, not least physically.

Garrison's gambit of hiring Gervais would hinge on whether Pershing would be loyal to Jim Garrison, or whether he would consider only his own needs. Soon the answer became clear. A law unto himself,

Pershing would accept bribes, and then bust people, or not. It wasn't long before he was entirely out of control. Some close to Jim Garrison would conclude that without an examination of the relationship between Jim Garrison and Pershing Gervais, "you will end up with a distorted view of Jim."

When the "Times-Picayune" announced that Pershing Gervais had been hired by Jim Garrison and placed in charge of all investigations, that Pershing would help carry out "efficient law enforcement," an outcry went up.

"Why does everybody holler about my being chief investigator?" Pershing retorted. "If you want to catch a crook, what you do is, you get a better crook!"

Everyone knew that Garrison had made a mistake, that he had compromised the office. Some tried to intervene to get rid of Pershing, but Jim would not budge. He's very "naïve about people and often deceived by them," D'Alton Williams admitted to Aaron Kohn about his boss. It takes him "a long time to recognize the real character and purposes of people." This was never more true than in the misplaced faith Jim Garrison put in Pershing Gervais. Entering the office in 1963, John Volz dubbed Pershing "the Devil Incarnate."

It may also be that Jim Garrison was bedeviled by Pershing not because Garrison was so naïve, but because, a sophisticated man, his propensity was not to view people in absolutes, as all black or all white. In "The Star-Spangled Contract," Garrison has his villain, Quillier, speak to a "fundamental American flaw, a failure to entertain ironies, contradictions, complications."

"You want it all apple-pie easy – the good guys and the bad guys," Quillier says, speaking for the author. Jim Garrison was wise enough about human nature to know better. He was not so wise, however, in choosing to believe that he could keep an eye on Pershing Gervais.

For the three years that he served as chief investigator in the district attorney's office, Pershing Gervais continued to work as an informant for Aaron Kohn. If Denis Barry had been in the dark about Pershing's appointment until May, when Garrison was sworn in, Pershing knew as early as March that he had garnered that plum of a job. He informed Aaron Kohn. Kohn advised that Pershing would have to be careful about with whom he was seen. "Jim is a little naïve in certain areas," Gervais confided. Jim Garrison would not be a Johnny Grosch, Pershing predicted, in a reference to that sheriff famously on the take.

"Pinball, in my opinion," Gervais remarked to Kohn, in his smarmiest tones, "is number one. Number two, strip joints. While I'm against them, I just don't know how he's going to prosecute them." Kohn and Gervais conferred when WDSU television reported that Garrison had revealed that Kohn had cleared the appointment of Gervais. Kohn, liking the idea of his informant being at the heart of Jim Garrison's operation, stated that Gervais had been "co-operative and helpful" during Kohn's 1953 and 1954 investigations of the police department. He implied that their connection had ended then.

WDSU knew that Pershing had operated a whorehouse. They knew he had shaken down people. None of this was mentioned on the air. Meanwhile at the office, Gervais told Raymond Comstock: "We're going to do great things. Make a name for ourselves."

Comstock kept his own council, and only later expressed his displeasure. "That bastard would lie like a rug!" Comstock says about Gervais. Nor was Comstock pleased when Gervais told him, "I lead Garrison around by the nose. He doesn't know what he's doing."

Gervais is to Garrison, Comstock decided, as "Professor Moriarty is to Sherlock Holmes."

Pershing's power grew immense. A young law school graduate named Edward Sapir hoped to be hired as an assistant in the Orleans Parish district attorney's office. Sapir's friend, assistant Steve Plotkin, had to tell Sapir: "Pershing won't let you in, so Jim won't let you in."

Those who were sensible avoided Pershing. One night Pershing invited Ray McGuire to the fights.

"Not me, Pershing," McGuire said. "I don't take anything from you."

When you opened the door at Tulane and Broad, there was Pershing's office, just to the right. Not to be outdone by Frank Klein, whom Pershing hated, Pershing placed a copper object on his desk. It looked like a starfish.

"That's an electric chair skull cap," Pershing explained. "It was used to electrocute five men at Angola." One day the cap disappeared.

Pershing tried to investigate. "Why would anybody want something like that?" Pershing said. "He's gotta be a pervert!" Pershing arrived every day laden with gold jewelry, including a sparkling Rolex watch. His language was rich in expletives. Dr. Robert Heath of Tulane University had talked about experimenting with electrode implants to give people orgiastic pleasure. "I could get a girl from the French Quarter to do that without an implant," Pershing laughed.

Pershing taught a mynah bird to echo his obscenities and brought his pet to live at Tulane and Broad. It was black as a crow. Then Pershing hung a doll dressed like a nun in the cage. He taught his mynah bird to say, "Fuck you, sister!" The bird was called only "Mr. Bird," and when he flew into the front room where the switchboard operator sat, and repeated Pershing's obscenities, she would tell "Mr. Bird" sternly, "That's not nice!"

Mr. Bird could sing the "Star Spangled Banner," every word, sharp and clear. Sometimes he sang in Spanish. He sang "Sonny Boy" in the voice of Al Jolson. Another of his songs reflected the police environment:

The old red flannel drawers
That Maggie wore
She hung them on the line
And the sun refused to shine,
On those old red flannel drawers
That Maggie wore.

Having been left alone in the office all weekend, on Monday morning when everyone arrived Mr. Bird burst into a song that lasted all day long.

Lou Ivon enjoyed fine clothes. One day, conferring with Pershing, with whom he had to collaborate in the early days, Ivon hung his coat on a rack not far from Mr. Bird's cage. Mr. Bird promptly flew over and did his business on Louie's coat. Ivon was irate.

"Fuck you, Louie!" Mr. Bird shouted out.

Richard Dowling's staff had left the office in disarray. Open files were scattered everywhere. Pershing complained that it was a "filthy mess." Jim Garrison said that Dowling's "operation resembled a Chinese whorehouse in a hurricane." Garrison discovered that more than a hundred files were missing and hired people to sort it all out. By the end of May, his first month in office, he had moved against an abortionist, a thief and a heroin dealer. Brener nailed the drug dealer with a ten year sentence.

Jim Garrison had promised to reform the office, and he did. Bail bonding abuses would end, he declared. There would be no paying bondsmen their fee on the installment plan, encouraging a new set of crimes. This reform was enacted after they caught someone in an armed robbery only for the criminal to take a cab over to bondsman Nick Christiana's office to make his payment. Garrison charged Christiana with being a principal in the robbery.

Determined to enforce bond forfeitures, Garrison lobbied the legislature to reduce the amount of time in which bonding companies must produce defendants before bonds are forfeited, from sixty to fifteen days. Then he took the bond forfeiture money and renovated both his office and the offices of the judges of the criminal court. Certain that the judges would reimburse him, he took out a $45,000 bank loan for office improvements and built a private elevator, suitable for one person, that went from the street to his private bathroom. Garrison never requested that his budget be increased, however. "We don't need more money in the budget now," he said.

He placed a security guard at the now-single entrance to his office to control the comings and goings of shady characters who habitually loitered in the hallways of Tulane and Broad. "The DA's office used to look like an African bazaar with people milling in and out," he told the Young Men's Business Club, knowing how, with colorful language and startling metaphors, to reach the public. "Now we have a wooden rail, operated by an electric buzzer. This helps keep out the people who aren't supposed to be there." He wanted a time clock placed in the office. There was a staff meeting every Wednesday night.

On homicide cases, Garrison was particularly tough. Even if the outcome of a case were not certain, Garrison wanted to proceed. "Charge them anyway," he told assistant Philip Foto. Garrison wanted to make it a felony for anyone with a criminal record to carry a concealed weapon.

Yet he laughed at "crimes against nature," the term used for so-called "deviant" sexual behavior that Louisiana law thought it could control. "I'd have to put my whole staff on trial," Garrison laughed. If an act was between consenting adults," Garrison told William Alford, "it shouldn't be a crime." Then he broke into a chorus of one of his favorite tunes, "On The Road To Mandalay."

Garrison hated to prosecute anyone at all for a sex crime. When Ralph Slovenko left the office to practice criminal law, he accepted the case of a Tulane medical school professor set up by a cop for a homosexual act. The cop had wangled an invitation aboard the doctor's yacht on Lake Pontchartrain in what was obviously an entrapment.

Slovenko went to Jim Garrison, who agreed at once not to charge the doctor. For a year, Garrison had the office experiment with not charging anyone at all for a sex crime. You had to find another charge, or not. "The only crime against nature is a hurricane, a cyclone, or an earthquake," Garrison said.

With a liberal's affection for the first amendment, Garrison disdained obscenity charges in a community policed by self-styled moral zealots like former police officer Hubert Badeaux.

One day, the police arrested some actors for "public nudity" at "La Mise En Scène" theatre.

"We're not prosecuting them," Garrison said.

"You have to prosecute them," John Volz said. "They broke the law."

"Well, I don't believe in that law," Garrison said.

Volz was nervous. This definitely was not good politics.

"You're the District Attorney. You swore to uphold the law," Volz pleaded.

"I don't want them charged," Garrison said. And that was that.

To priests who were arrested for serious misconduct, whether with an adult or with a child, Garrison granted no favors, and the Catholic Church immediately became an enemy. Jim didn't care. William Alford prosecuted these priests, who had become accustomed, under earlier prosecutors, to secret meetings with judges Tom Brahney and Bernard Bagert. The priest would plead guilty and escape with a small fine and unsupervised probation while the Church swept the whole matter under the rug. Under Jim Garrison, these priests were prosecuted.

At a time and a place where liberal opposition to segregation was more than unpopular, Jim Garrison openly opposed segregation. He brought a fairness to the treatment of African Americans that led to many black families placing his photograph in their homes beside those of Dr. Martin Luther King, Jr. and John F. Kennedy. When Frank Minyard became Coroner of Orleans Parish, he observed many of these photographs, and grew to admire Jim Garrison all the more. Blacks were routinely beaten up by the police. "We won't tolerate this," Garrison said as soon as he took office.

Among Garrison's causes was also protection of the rights of any and all defendants. Already that May he opposed attempts to repeal a 1960 act granting indigent defenders the right to a transcript of their court cases. Such a denial, Garrison asserted, was "unconstitutional." It would make Louisiana "look bad nationally," he told the legislators.

Louisiana was "one of the few states which treats defendants with so little regard."

He called for an end to the practice of denying an appeal to anyone sentenced to six months or less in jail. He did not want constitutional rights arbitrarily placed in the hands of judges. It was the judges, he concluded, who were responsible for the foundering system of justice in New Orleans. Immediately he began to reduce the number of Parish Prison inmates awaiting trial.

By July of 1962, lottery operators were being charged. In the old days, they went to Parish Prison. On a newspaper clipping with the headline, "Charge 8 Here In Crackdown," Garrison scrawled, "this time it was the pen."

Under Louisiana law, the district attorney had parole power. Garrison refused to exercise it. He did not want the office "involved in political campaigns," he said. He did find it difficult to refrain from vanquishing old enemies with his verbal pyrotechnics. Victor Schiro was a favorite Garrison target. "Not since Hamlet tried to decide whether or not to stab the King of Denmark has there been so much agonizing over a political decision," Garrison said, referring to a Schiro default. If he could enlist Shakespeare, so much the better. Public officials, Garrison said, should serve the people "with absolute disregard of personal consequences." In that aspiration was contained the future story of his life.

A month after Garrison took office, he addressed the graduates of the New Orleans Police Academy. His theme was not law enforcement, but justice, which "must be brought into being by men like yourselves." On July 2nd, he wrote to Aaron Kohn, confirming that offer about which Denis Barry was so dubious. "Any file in this office is available for inspection by you," Garrison told Kohn. All Kohn had to do was contact Milton Brener or Denis Barry or himself. The Young Turks had nothing to hide. Two weeks later, Barry sent Kohn an inventory of all the vice and gambling cases that had remained on the docket when they took office.

Kohn at once took advantage of the offer. Only four days after Garrison took office, Kohn had requested that the office prosecute two former policemen, Donald Sauviac and Emile Nolan, for malfeasance or public bribery. It was a case that Dowling had abandoned. Kohn demanded that the grand jury at once examine why Dowling had had suddenly decided not to prosecute. A prosecution witness named Carl

Tew had refused to testify on grounds of self-incrimination. Kohn insisted Tew's testimony was not essential. To appease Kohn, Garrison assigned two assistants to the case.

Kohn now began to demand more files. He sent Barry a long memo with suggestions on pinball and gambling handbook prosecutions. He all but ordered Barry to arrest and prosecute lottery vendors. He told Barry that he must confer with Ed Roussel of the Internal Revenue Service Intelligence Division. Kohn even interfered in appointments, opposing Garrison's hiring of Dowling assistant Burton Klein because of Klein's partnership with Irvin Dymond. Klein had "divided loyalties," Kohn insisted. Attempting to run a rival district attorney's office out of the Metropolitan Crime Commission headquarters, Kohn kept up the pressure.

Conciliatory, Garrison promised to keep Klein on only until September. Jim Garrison, never one to hold grudges, liked Klein and when William Alford later considered charging him for writing bad checks, Jim felt sorry for Klein and refused to prosecute.

No one was more active against crime than Denis Barry who, scrutinizing the old cases left behind by Dowling, found ten charges pending against the "Vice Queen" of New Orleans, one Mickey Medina. When Medina jumped bond on a prostitution case, Barry's vice staff raided her residence. As she entered a taxi, flipping a marijuana cigarette into a storm drain, the crack team of Lou Ivon, George Eckert and Tom Duffy apprehended her.

Medina was set free and again failed to appear. When Garrison assistant, and now former "Times-Picayune" reporter, Herman Kohlman thought the bond should not yet be forfeited, Jim Garrison blew his top and threatened to fire Kohlman. All this was reported to Aaron Kohn by Pershing Gervais. Kohn demanded "forfeiture at once." Garrison had also to contend with the judges who considered that his crime fighting was overly zealous. When assistant John Shea told Judge Shirley G. Wimberly that Medina's bond was too low, Wimberly was indignant. "The Supreme Court would look with a jaundiced eye on a $25,000 bond for a misdemeanor," Judge Wimberly said.

In his final month in office, Richard Dowling had dismissed hundreds of cases. They ranged from narcotics possession to conspiracy to murder of a witness. Milton Brener began to prosecute narcotics cases still pending, and by the end of May had begun to win either guilty pleas or convictions.

Kohn then had an idea. "All of this builds up to a very strong case of at least malfeasance against Dowling and some of his assistants," Kohn decided. He passed his idea on to Pershing Gervais.

At Gervais's suggestion, Jim Garrison began to prosecute Dowling and his chief assistant, Abraham Kleinfeldt. Milton Brener opposed vigorously Garrison's using his time and energies in this way. Wouldn't it be enough if Garrison conducted his office in an exemplary fashion?

Anxious to appease Kohn, and manipulated by Gervais, who argued that you cut people off to reinforce your position, and make sure they won't be back to oppose you on another day, Garrison brought charges of malfeasance for dismissing valid cases against both Kleinfeldt and Dowling. Ambiguity colored the whole process since Dowling had reinstated two cases dismissed by Kleinfeldt.

Judge J. Bernard Cocke took a dim view of charges that seemed needlessly vindictive. He demanded that Frank Klein reveal whether he was attempting to force Kleinfeldt to implicate other people. On one occasion, Cocke rendered a "poking motion" to Klein's left shoulder. Klein insisted that the judge not "shove" him.

Furious, Cocke asked Kleinfeldt whether he wished to avail himself of his constitutional guarantees. Cocke dismissed one of the indictments on the spot.

Jim Garrison then demanded a re-hearing, appealed, and issued nine new charges against Kleinfeldt for "abusing the discretion granted him" and declining to prosecute criminals. Eight were lottery charges, small matters, and one involved a "handbook." Burton Klein now testified for Kleinfelt, charging Garrison's staff with violating the law governing the secrecy of grand jury proceedings. "My final comment is that Garrison not only is indiscreetly malicious, but is using this for his headline of the week," Dowling said.

Still it went on. When another of the indictments against Dowling was dismissed, Garrison again vowed to appeal. He put the cases in the hands of Frank Klein, Frank Shea, Louise Korns, Charles Ward and Alvin Oser. Only in 1971 was the last charge against Kleinfeldt erased – by the district attorney's office itself.

Over-zeal, a Gervais-style of vindictiveness, marred the first months of the new district attorney's office. The public, however, approved of the vigor of the prosecutions. On June 20th, before the Dowling-Kleinfeldt matter, a member of the Crime Commission, Pastor J. D. Grey of the First Baptist Church, wrote to Jim Garrison commending him "for the excellent manner in which you are conducting the affairs of the District Attorney's office."

In those early days, before Jim Garrison's investigation of the murder of President Kennedy, there was a carefree atmosphere. "Just another day at Tulane and Broad," Garrison said whenever something untoward occurred. "Thank you for coming in to work today, Numa," Garrison told Bertel on more than one occasion. Bertel was tickled each time he heard it.

"Well, Boss, if that means I don't have to come...," Bertel laughed. Bertel never wanted to be late because he didn't want to miss the fun.

Jim Garrison was no athlete, and he couldn't play on the office softball team, but he did arrive one day in a jersey, accompanied by a jazz band. He couldn't dance, but he did swing a hula hoop around his hips with some finesse. If things were too quiet, he decided it must be someone's birthday, and they would lock the doors and party. To those parties, you could not bring a date. You could not bring your wife. "The office that plays together stays together" was the motto. Local establishments sent over boiled crawfish and booze – free of charge.

Garrison made requests of his employees with irony. "If you can find one of my illustrious investigators, would you ask him to bring me a cup of coffee," Garrison asked Joyce Wood. Pointedly he made this request of a man, not of one of the women. Joyce got the coffee herself. Later Sharon Herkes would remark, "he'd die of thirst before he got his own coffee." Jim Garrison was, in this as in those other ways, a man of that World War Two generation of men expecting prerogatives owing to their gender.

Behind Garrison's back, they called him "Giant." He detested that, and hated even more the appellation, "Jolly Green Giant." One day someone put a poster of the Jolly Green Giant on Joyce Wood's door.

"Well, Joyce, I see you have my photograph on your door," Garrison said.

The office grew filthy, wastebaskets not emptied, cigarette butts everywhere. D'Alton Williams was the office administrator, but he wasn't doing a very good job. One night, very late, Jim Garrison emptied all the overflowing trash cans into Williams's office. He added a note: "I really appreciate your keeping the office so neat. Thank you, Jim."

"I think the Giant's trying to tell me something," Williams said the next morning when he discovered the mess. Garrison was subtle and sensitive and he did not like to embarrass you if he could help it. Sometimes, however, he lost touch with what was going on. Joyce Wood remarked one day that others had received raises, but she hadn't.

"Oh, Joyce, why didn't you come to me?" Garrison said. He gave her a hundred dollar a month raise on the spot. In later years, Sharon Herkes made the mistake of asking Garrison's chief assistant, John Volz, for a raise. "There isn't enough money," Volz said. When Herkes recounted the conversation to Jim Garrison, he told Volz, "Take it from Moo's (Andrew J. Sciambra) salary. He hasn't been productive lately." Sharon got her raise.

He never carried money, and tossed his National Guard checks into his desk drawer where they languished, uncashed, for months.

When everyone got to know him, they learned to shield him from the incursions of his mother, Jane Gardiner, not least when he had made a lunch date with her, and then had failed to appear.

"He was supposed to meet me for lunch," Jane complained one day to Garrison's secretary. "I've been waiting an hour." He was out of town, but he had never bothered to cancel. It seemed then to those in the office that he feared his mother.

Meanwhile Jane cultivated his staff, complimenting Sharon on her blonde hair, and telling her she had a "lion's face." (When Herkes related the incident, Garrison the caricaturist sat down and drew for Herkes a picture of a lion). Jane invited Sharon to visit her at the Ochsner Clinic where she was undergoing a test, and in the middle of telling Sharon stories, commanded her daughter Judith, "I have to be changed." Judith Garrison rushed forward with a fresh sanitary pad, knelt down, reached under her mother's skirt and affixed the new pad. How odd to do this in front of a stranger! Sharon thought, but Jane kept talking as if nothing unusual was happening.

In those carefree years before his Kennedy investigation, Garrison favored lunches at the Vieux Carre or at Jimmy Moran's La Louisiane. At a big table for ten, Garrison gathered the people he liked best: D'Alton Williams, Billy Glennon, future judges Lou Trent and Frank Shea, oil man Joe Rault and Frank Klein. Garrison enjoyed playing practical jokes on members of the group, including arranging that a dump truck pour oyster shells on someone's lawn.

Pershing Gervais was not invited to these lunches.

As people came and went, Jim Garrison sat at the big table in the middle of the room at Moran La Louisiane, under the crystal chandelier. The regal center of attention in that ornately decorated room with its deep rose brocade wall coverings, he seemed, then, entirely happy with his lot in life.

CHAPTER 7:
An Upstart D.A.

"I never think of consequences."
Jim Garrison

Jim Garrison began his reform of bail bond abuses with a sting. He sent Max Gonzales, a friend from his Army days, into Parish Prison undercover with the alias "Joseph Max Lopez." Lopez had supposedly been imprisoned for possession of a stolen car. It was illegal for bail bondsmen to solicit bonds in prison. Gonzales didn't have long to wait before he was approached.

Soon he had flushed out Peter Hand, a former state legislator and convicted gambler. Hand not only was soliciting in prison, but was operating as a bondsman without a license. To save himself, Hand then implicated bail bondsman Hardy Davis, the very Hardy Davis whom Jack Martin had discovered was being shaken down by one of Richard Dowling's assistants. Caught with the money, Davis pleaded that he had given Hand no commission; he had kept the full $75 for himself.

At the center of the bail bond frauds was Pershing Gervais. Patrick Horrigan, the former Dowling investigator who had done Pershing that favor by not forfeiting a $10,000 bond, wanted to set up in the bail bond business himself. Pershing let him know. Pershing would have to be "kept informed" of everything or Horrigan would not operate for long.

When Peter Hand was arrested, Pershing told him, "Didn't I tell you I was lying to you? You just didn't believe me!" It was that typical Pershing response. Meanwhile Denis Barry, in the company of two investigators, arrested Hardy Davis. "This is merely the start against illegal bonding activities," Frank Shea said, speaking for the Garrison office.

For Jim Garrison, bail bonds abuses would be a major issue, and he went to war with the state legislature over it. When a bill supported by the lobbying bail bondsmen sailed through the legislature with only one dissenting vote in the Senate, Garrison was indignant. The bondsmen gained the right to have six months to produce a defendant, rather than eight weeks. Garrison called this new law "incredible."

Garrison proposed an ingenious law against loan sharks, making it a crime to lend money above a given rate. Up to a certain percentage, a loan made at an illegal rate did not have to be repaid. At a certain point, a jail sentence would be imposed on the lender. That the powerful loan companies were certain to finance his opponent when he ran for re-election did not trouble Jim Garrison. This bill languished in committee. The legislature eventually met in executive session – to figure out whether they should try to remove Jim Garrison from office.

Garrison enlisted his wit and sardonic humor. "When I was elected," he told a young "States-Item" reporter named David Chandler, "I fell down the rabbit hole and landed smack in the middle of Wonderland. Nothing I've seen since has surprised me."

"Alice In Wonderland" was one of his favorite books, and he would turn to it again as a source for metaphors of the absurd when he faced the quixotic task of investigating the murder of President Kennedy. Garrison said that he liked that he had "no obligations" to any politicians. As "the first person in history to be elected city-wide without any organized support," no one could expect favors from him.

Day or night, you were likely to run into Pershing in the Quarter, as if he were a man perpetually leaning against a lamppost. His long belly hanging over his tight pants, Pershing Gervais stood at the center of a circle of informants, thieves and low-lifes, Quarter scam-artists who spent their time in foul play. Fleecing tourists was the least of their transgressions. Among them was David Aycock, known as "Butch." Butch lived with a tall, skinny red-headed drag queen named "Tempest." Tempest's real name was Darryl Gibson.

Another of Pershing's entourage was an ex-Marine, a tough, hot-tempered waiter at the Court of the Two Sisters restaurant named William Livesay. Livesay's forearms bulged, like Popeye's, six inches of muscle. His hands were huge and beefy, his eyes blue and shrewd. Livesay and Pershing shared the same lover. Livesay's official girlfriend, a stripper at the Circus Club on Bourbon Street, was pregnant.

The night manager at the Court of the Two Sisters was Eugene C. Davis. Nicknamed "Mother," Davis walked around, an officious busybody, rattling the keys in his pocket. It was his pleasure to dispense favors, like a minor Mafia don. Whenever a "queen" was busted, Davis was the man to see. In 1958, Davis himself had been arrested for a "crime against nature."

One night in May 1961, Livesay got into a fight at a bar with a man named James Smith. Smith had dared to tell Livesay, "You're sitting in my seat!" Before it was over, Smith had been slashed across the face with his own knife. Livesay was now charged with attempted murder. Desperate, in search of a lawyer, Livesay consulted Eugene Davis. Davis had already allowed Livesay to use his upstairs room for sundry purposes. Livesay was sure Davis would help him.

Indeed, Davis had a suggestion. Livesay should consult a lawyer named Dean Andrews, a fat, round-faced, jive-talking Cajun operating out of neighboring Jefferson Parish. Andrews was known to handle sex offenses as well as take cases like this.

Dean Andrews used profanity at every third or fourth word, but in such a way that you weren't sure that he was cursing. In law school, if he gave the wrong answer in class, he would hit his desk, and yell "TILT" to the sound of a pinball machine. In court, if a judge asked him what his objection was, Andrews might reply, "You're the judge. You ought to know!" After his graduation from Tulane, Andrews had opened a stand on the waterfront bearing the sign, "Psychiatrist is in." Dean Andrews was an ambulance chaser in search of longshoremen who had been injured, and a small-time mob lawyer when he could get the work.

"Can I use your name?" Livesay asked Davis.

"Just tell him 'Mr. Bertrand' sent you," Davis replied. A quick study, Livesay at once understood. It was code. Davis himself wasn't "Bertrand." Rather, "Bertrand" was the name you used if you were a young male in trouble in the Quarter.

It turned out not to be necessary for William Livesay to visit Dean Andrews. Hardy Davis did Livesay a favor. The knifing victim, Smith, was on his way to Angola on a robbery charge anyway. Smith preferred not to encounter new enemies at the state prison and signed an affidavit stating that in the fight with Livesay he himself had been the aggressor. The charge against Livesay was dropped.

Free to continue to prey upon tourists looking for excitement in the Quarter, Livesay soon discovered a married woman from Kentucky. He took her to a motel, drugged her with chloral hydrate and slipped the diamond rings from her fingers. It was just another night on Bourbon Street. Discretion wasn't Livesay's strong suit. He bragged about the incident to a police character named Harold Sandoz, another of Pershing's many informants.

Pershing despised Hardy Davis. His animosity dated long before Jim Garrison became district attorney. Gervais was deeply sensitive about his son, who had been arrested on a narcotics violation. Pershing discovered that Hardy Davis had been gossiping about his son.

"I'll beat the shit out of you!" Gervais threatened Hardy Davis one day in the street.

By now, Livesay had also become one of Pershing's informants. It was Pershing who had been the mastermind of a robbery of a Royal Street residence carried out by Butch Aycock and Livesay, who had then asked Eugene Davis to fence a Hi-Fi and television set. Why would Hardy Davis go to so much trouble to get those attempted murder charges against you dropped? Pershing asked Livesay. All the while, Pershing was scheming to draw Hardy Davis into his net.

Gervais came up with a plan. Livesay would telephone Hardy Davis and say he wanted to talk about stolen property found in his possession. Could they meet on Saturday morning at the Gaslight Lounge? This was an establishment partly owned by Pershing, although the name on the deed was "Lester Otillio," a police officer attached to the district attorney's office. Otillio had a side job: he was a hairdresser, arranging the hair of the dead at several funeral parlors.

When Hardy Davis arrived at the Gaslight, Livesay proposed that for a quiet conversation it would be better that they talk at an apartment on Dauphine Street that belonged to the Gaslight bartender, William Rarick.

It was now June of 1962. In only two years the Gaslight would become notorious. After the death of President Kennedy, Dean Andrews, our roly-poly fast-talking Cajun lawyer, would tell the Secret Service that the men who accompanied Lee Harvey Oswald to his office "possibly frequent the Gaslight Bar [sic] in the French Quarter." Hardy Davis would suggest that Oswald was a member of a "homosexual clique," but would say no more. That Hardy Davis was homosexual himself, although married and in the closet, of the "Rock Hudson" type, Livesay says, adds credence to Davis's statement.

William Rarick had a typical New Orleans shotgun apartment: a combination bedroom and living room, kitchen and bathroom. Under Pershing's direction, the police drilled peepholes in the bathroom door, and set up their movie camera. A tape recorder was situated under the bed.

Livesay was attractive. Hardy Davis took the bait. Then, just as Livesay had his penis in Davis's mouth, with the movie camera grinding away, the police converged on the two.

"There were about nine inches of my dick (give or take a couple of inches) swabbing his tonsils," Livesay says.

"You guys busted in too quick!" Livesay told the police. "You might have waited a few minutes. What was the hurry?" Livesay was wild and free. There were no limits and life was savored for the moment, with no regrets forthcoming.

Davis was driven to the First District station, where he was booked on a "crime against nature" charge. Livesay was taken to Tulane and Broad. The police sat him in a little room, adjacent to Jim Garrison's office. Livesay typed out his own statement, using two fingers. It said that Hardy Davis had solicited Livesay for sexual purposes.

Suddenly Livesay heard someone shout, "Quick! Hide him! The Boss is here. Don't let him see him!" Jim Garrison had known nothing of this set-up; it had been "a Gervais operation," Lou Ivon says. Lester Otillio, who was close to the action, confirms Ivon's statement: Jim Garrison had no idea about Pershing's plan to entrap Hardy Davis.

Livesay peeked through a crack in the wall, and there was Jim Garrison himself. So he didn't know about this, Livesay thought. Soon Livesay was hustled out the door and returned to Rarick's apartment.

"What are you going to do with the film?" Livesay asked Gervais some time later.

"Oh, he'll pay, he'll pay," Gervais said, referring to Davis, and Livesay wondered whether Pershing meant revenge or money or both.

Now Pershing turned on Livesay. He called Livesay "a professional homosexual or involved with them, is in constant trouble and unreliable fundamentally." Compromised by Gervais, Jim Garrison was now compelled to uphold his chief investigator in his vendetta against Hardy Davis. An office document reads that Davis had been accidentally caught by the police "committing an indecent act with another man."

It was Livesay who would pay. His friends now shunned him. That you don't bust a bail bondsman (whom anyone might need at a given moment) was the rule of the street. Violence now erupted from within Pershing's group. Believing that Butch Aycock had informed to Gervais on a burglary of $10,000 worth of American Express money orders he committed with a group of others, Harold Sandoz beat up Aycock with a blackjack. Aycock was scheduled to be a state witness against him; Sandoz was determined that this not happen. Furious, Pershing then beat up Sandoz. "The hoods probably thought this boy was some sort of stool pigeon," Pershing told the press, referring to Aycock.

Livesay visited Butch Aycock at the hospital. His face was a mess of raw meat and bruises. "They'll get you too," Butch whispered to Livesay.

On a Friday morning in August 1962, at 9:30 a.m., having gotten off work at the Court of the Two Sisters, and after making the rounds, as was his habit, Livesay sat at the Gaslight Lounge enjoying a drink. A man walked in. Livesay looked up and recognized Perry Tettenburn, a friend of Eugene Davis's who lived with a blond drag queen named "Pepper." In the swamp of Quarter gossip, Livesay had heard that Perry Tettenburn had been trying to get his address. Now Livesay assumed that Tettenburn had been enlisted to punish him for his role in the entrapment of Hardy Davis.

Having fought as a heavyweight, Livesay knocked Tettenburn out with no trouble. Then Livesay went over to the bar, took a few swigs of his drink, and grabbed one of the wrought-iron bar stools. One of the legs was missing its protective pad. As Tettenburn lay unconscious, Livesay lifted the bar stool, and slammed it into his head. The exposed bar stool leg, a lethal weapon now, penetrated six inches into Tettenburn's skull. Passing through three lobes of his brain, it killed Tettenburn instantly.

It was a measure of Pershing's then influence in Jim Garrison's office that the state charged William Livesay not with manslaughter, but with murder. Livesay's lawyer was Richard Dowling, who seemed, Livesay thought, more interested in attacking Gervais, and through him, Jim Garrison, than in defending him. Hubert Badeaux, that do-gooder and moralist, involved himself in the case to help chief of police Joseph Giarrusso compile a dossier on Pershing. Badeaux gave Livesay a lie detector test, and, without Livesay's knowledge, made tapes that later would be played for the Orleans Parish grand jury. Claiming to be helping Livesay, Badeaux in fact offered him no assistance whatsoever.

At the trial, taking the stand, Hardy Davis said little. He admitted that he was currently charged with a "crime against nature," but did not outline the entrapment scene, which would have helped document Livesay's claim that he had acted in self-defense against Tettenburn.

Taking the stand as well, Eugene Davis took the fifth amendment. The prosecution claimed that the film of Livesay and Hardy Davis had been over-exposed and was not available as evidence, although later the police watched it at a stag party. Dowling and his co-counsel, Peter Compagno, decided that it would be better if Livesay did not testify on his own behalf.

Found guilty of murder, twenty-three year old William Livesay was given a life sentence at Angola. Later, Judge Haggerty and Louisiana Attorney General, Jack P. F. Gremillion, supported Livesay in his appeal of this harsh sentence. Jim Garrison, feeling compelled to abide by his strongly stated opposition to capital crimes, had been dealt a check mate by Pershing Gervais. "No one should, simply because he gave information to this office on a few isolated occasions, be given the license to take a human life with a resultant punishment of only a few months in prison," Garrison said. He opposed any mitigation of Livesay's sentence.

Garrison knew he was wrong, and his later actions reveal that he was not too proud to admit it. Self-defense, properly established, would have resulted in only a manslaughter charge for Livesay. Jim Garrison referred to the incident three years later, in 1965, when he was running for re-election. He admitted publicly his abhorrence of what had been done to Hardy Davis, and, in fact, had seen to it that Davis was never prosecuted on the "crime against nature" charge.

"Our own investigators arrested Davis," Garrison said, taking responsibility for an arrest he never would have encouraged. "It was my conclusion that in so doing they had clearly violated the defendant's constitutional rights." Governor John J. McKeithen, who had been elected largely on the strength of Jim Garrison's support, pardoned Livesay after he had served six years.

Efforts to "clean up" the French Quarter had begun in the 1920s. The enforcement of prohibition, which resulted in the closing of the houses of prostitution of Storyville, the cabarets and bars, hurt New Orleans and the Quarter more than Jim Garrison's effort ever would. Garrison had promised to zero in on "clip-joints." Free of the "clutch of professional politicians" who stood in the way of justice, as he saw it, he was fearless. "I never think of consequences," he would say later. The lethargy of the community continued to appall him. "If you want to get a mule's attention," Garrison said, "hit him with a piece of stove wood."

When Garrison took office in May 1962, Bourbon Street was back to B-drinking, open prostitution, drunk-rolling, and other forms of separating a tourist or a visiting sailor from his money. "B-drinking" meant drinking for the bar because for every drink a tourist bought, the girl got her cut, usually one-third for each drink, with two-thirds going to the establishment.

The Quarter prided itself on its own particular vernacular: Taxi drivers were "Vidalia hustlers"; a "Vidalia," the sweet onion, was an out-of-towner who was an obvious easy mark. The police might be called in to "cool the beef." A stripper named "Dixie Dawn" (Theresa Selensky Doe) later would testify for the district attorney's office and explain. A "mingled club" meant that strippers mixed with customers. A "score" referred to the commissions for "B-drinks." A "mark" was a well-dressed male customer who spent money freely. When a stripper took one glove off, that meant, "it's a strip." More than one glove, that was something else. You got fifty cents for one drink, a dollar for a double, five dollars for a small bottle of champagne, and between ten and thirty dollars for a large bottle.

A stripper or bar girl would ask you to buy her a drink. Whatever the John ordered, the girl would choose a champagne cocktail, which was actually ginger ale with lemon. It might cost as much as five dollars. If she ordered a mixed drink, it would be a coke with a little whiskey poured over the top so that it smelled strong. If she believed that the customer carried a sizable bankroll, she would suggest that they order a bottle of champagne. This was where the big money was.

As they ordered, the girl would promise that they would meet out front after she was off work. For now, they drank the champagne. She would request a glass of ice water, which was served in a plastic, red-frosted glass, half-filled with ice, but containing no liquid. When she took a sip of champagne, she would spit it into the red-frosted glass, so as not to become drunk. When the "water" glass was full, discreetly, the waiter would replace it with a fresh red glass.

When the John became drunk, they no longer bothered with real champagne. The bartender would fill an empty bottle with a cheap sauterne and club soda, stick a cork in and shake it up. Voila! Champagne! Pretending to be drunk herself, the girl would cuddle up to her customer, all tender and loving.

If they were ensconced in one of the booths in the back, "bust-out booths," the girl might rub a man's legs, administer oral sex, or just a hand job. Or, as she disrobed, he might touch or kiss her breasts. These were called "bust-out booths" because if someone walked in who looked like he might be with the vice squad, the bartender would hit a buzzer, and the girl would "bust out" of the booth and make her get-away.

Occasionally she might pour a knock-out drop into a man's drink, and he couldn't complain to the police because the police, or most of them, covered for the clubs.

The bartender would place a special swizzle stick with a particular mark on it into the stripper's drink. That swizzle stick was her receipt, and she would take her swizzle sticks to the bartender at the end of the evening. On a good night, a girl might have collected as many as forty swizzle sticks. If a girl placed a swizzle stick across the top of her drink, it meant she was waiting for someone, or was just not interested. The customer could refuse to buy her a drink if he didn't fancy her. The Flamingo also had a code of its own: "no smoking while stripping."

The women were paid in cash. That was necessary because you didn't trust the bartender.

At the end of the evening, the girl would tell the man that it was almost time for her to get off work. At four a.m., the bartender turned out the lights. The John had to leave. Having cashed in her swizzle sticks, the girl ran out the back door. After a while, the impatient John waiting for her outside might begin to yell, or bang furiously on the front door. If he returned the next night, angry, she might say, "I was looking for you" or make a more elaborate excuse about her mother having been in a car wreck or that her father had suffered a heart attack.

Only in the most disreputable places would the John be given a "Mickey" if he didn't pass out quickly enough. Then he was rolled and dumped in the back alley. At a reputable club, a John who had passed out would be thrust into a cab and the driver paid five dollars to transport him to the nearest hotel.

If the John, left to wait out front alone, created too great a disturbance, the police would threaten him with jail, or cart him off. The ethos of the Quarter in the days before Jim Garrison's office conducted its raids was that you knew what you were getting. The police too knew the drill, knew that the barker outside soliciting customers, "we've got the hottest girls in town and they take it all off," was simultaneously signaling those inside of the exact positions of the police at any given moment. When the police approached a club, the doorman would throw a switch that sounded an alarm or flashed a red light inside. In the Monkey Bar, the eyes of a fake monkey inside lit up in warning when the police drew near. The girls would get up from the bar or the bust-out booths and vanish.

As long as they didn't actually see the girls running, or observe the signal, the police did not intervene. The regular New Orleans police on the Bourbon Street beat, anxious to attack actual crime, honest officers like young Robert Buras and his partner, Norman "Big Red" Knaps, sympathized with the clubs. Working within a landscape of iniquity, they developed their own code: they would not tolerate crime - if they noticed it.

Less scrupulous police officers were on the take. "You don't want your wife to find out about this," an officer might say softly to an angry John. Then the bar would hand the cop half the disputed amount of money as his commission. Girls paid off the police on occasion. One was "Hot Water Sue," famous for giving blow jobs with hot water in her mouth.

After Garrison began, the barker outside a club would invariably attempt to engage the police in conversation to give the girls time, but also to show respect for the police. This was the dance. The police, in return for the favor, knew that if a policeman was alone and got into a fight, the doorman and the club owner would come to his aid. There were no radios then. What everyone wanted was to make it through the night with as little trouble as possible.

The night supervisor of police, Joseph (Big Mo) Guillot, had sent in the "four horsemen," four honest policemen, to police the Quarter. They were young and were told to stay clean and enforce the law; their loyalty was not to the district attorney but to the police department. One night Buras and Knaps found a dentist from Baton Rouge in a booth at the back of one of the bars with not one, but two girls. He laughed when the officers questioned him. No, they had not solicited him for drinks. "My daddy didn't raise no queers," he said.

Jim Garrison declared his war on vice in New Orleans on May 29th, 1962, only weeks after he took office. When Garrison went to Washington, D.C. on July 9th to fulfill his National Guard obligation at a defense strategy seminar at the National War College, Denis Barry took over the operation. Barry and Michael Karmazin went to the Circus Club where they were promptly solicited for B-drinks. The manager and two women, "Candy" Laine and Diane Sully, were arrested. The girls were brought "downtown" and then released. His effort to clean up the Quarter, Garrison would say, was not about small fry.

So it began. At first, Garrison's staff met in a courtroom, distributed cash, marked the bills and went themselves to the clubs. At the Texas Lounge on Canal Street, Denis Barry and George Eckert appeared. A bar girl named Mary Vann invited Eckert to the "bust-out" booth where she unzipped his trousers, exposed her breasts and began ordering drinks. Soon she had ordered one of the thirty dollar bottles of champagne. She removed Eckert's penis from his pants and was rewarded – with marked money.

Soon Garrison's staff was criticized for behaving as if they were a "second constabulary." And before long, they were easily recognized, so that undercover agents had to be found. For help, the office enlisted Aubrey Young, a bartender for the Marcello organization, who was later to work for John McKeithen when he became governor of Louisiana.

Pershing asked lawyer Don Organ to pose as a tourist. Organ declined. A private investigator with fewer scruples named Warren Moity, who had testified for the Kefauver crime committee, agreed. Jim Garrison had represented Moity in a libel suit against the district attorney, sheriff and deputy sheriffs of Iberia Parish. Moity and his partner, Malcolm Dodge, working for expenses only, as a favor, and affecting heavy Cajun accents, posed as rice farmers. Carrying marked money, with tiny radio units strapped to their bodies, they allowed themselves to be lured into "sex tents" or "sex booths" at the back of a bar. As part of another sting, Garrison's secretary, Lucy Sobecki, posed as a Madam, attempting to uncover prostitution by soliciting girls to work for her.

"We had to invent brand new methods that had never been used before," Garrison explained later. Ancient ordinances, like those requiring ample lighting at the clubs, were dusted off. If he could define a house of prostitution as one of "assignation," Garrison discovered, "B-drinking" became a crime. The ages of the clientele being served drinks were duly noted. A "no mingle" law was passed, and the police were required to ask a customer with a girl if she had asked him to buy her a drink. The police had to request the customer's identification and write it down in a notebook. The ablest people in Garrison's office prosecuted these cases: Denis Barry, Milton Brener, and Frank Klein. Barry spent nine straight days in court on padlock cases and was victorious in every one of them.

Later Pershing exempted clubs paying him off from being padlocked. But over at least one eight month period the places chosen to be padlocked were not selected by Gervais, although he was present with Raymond Ruiz, acting as Pershing's liaison with the police. Joe Oster and Harry Roberts, of a group called Southern Research, worked undercover with Jim Garrison's upright assistant James Alcock, who would later prosecute the conspiracy case against Clay Shaw. "There was no hanky panky," Oster says.

Nor, if there seemed to be an arbitrary quality to the padlocking, was it because Jim Garrison and his office exempted clubs with mob ownership. The 500 Club, the Old French Opera House, and the Third Sister Hideaway, all clubs in which Marcello-connected mobster Frank Caracci had an interest, were hit. The operator of the Flamingo, Frank Sinopoli, had borrrowed the money to buy his place from Carlos Marcello's brother, Peter. Denis Barry argued in court that Sinopoli was only a front for Marcello.

"If I have to explain that I'm not connected with racketeers," Garrison would say later, "it's very much like making General Grant explain that he's not in secret sympathy with the Confederates." If Carlo Montalbano's club was exempted, it was because he had been instrumental in helping Jim Garrison get elected. When during his investigation of the murder of President Kennedy, and later, Garrison would be accused of softness toward Carlos Marcello, even by some seemingly dubious of the conclusions of the Warren Commission, that would be a slander easily disproved by anyone in possession of the facts.

It is also true that before long Pershing saw to it that some of the clubs giving him payoffs escaped censure entirely. Pershing was now collecting from card games at the Gaslight Lounge, at the Cove and at the Spot. He also extorted money from the Music Box, and other establishments, those payoffs not part of recorded history.

Garrison chose to go into civil court against the clubs rather than into criminal court where the clubs would receive slaps on the wrist, and maybe a five hundred dollar fine. Instead, many clubs were shut down for a year. Garrison's office won every case. Seven clubs would be shut down permanently.

Jim Garrison was certainly bad for business, and as Pat O'Brien's chanteuse Barbara Bennett would remark years later, Quarter people would not help Jim Garrison identify Clay Shaw as the "Clay Bertrand" who had telephoned Dean Andrews and asked him to represent Lee Harvey Oswald in Dallas because they remained angry over the Bourbon Street raids. Bennett and many others could have testified with no ambiguity that Shaw was Bertrand. Among these potential witnesses was also a dress shop owner named Rickey Planche, who bought a house Clay Shaw had owned previously; Planche too knew Shaw as "Clay Bertrand." That Shaw used the alias "Bertrand" was universally known in the Quarter. But believing that Jim Garrison had destroyed the culture of the French Quarter, these witnesses did not come forward during his investigation.

Those who blamed Jim Garrison most were Quarter prostitutes and "exotic dancers" ruined by the padlocking, along with the club owners. Garrison was a hypocrite they began to say, as if his having enjoyed Quarter life himself meant that even as district attorney he should nonetheless turn a blind eye to corruption and crime. Even fabled whorehouse madam Norma Wallace, once lawyer Jim Garrison's client, was arrested. Wallace pled guilty on July 2nd.

Some hated Jim Garrison for not being corrupt, and slandered him. A dancer at the Poodles Patio, Suzanne Robbins, charged that she was arrested because she had rejected Jim Garrison's sexual advances. She did "interpretive dancing," Robbins claimed. All she did was remove her cape! Arrested twice, Robbins never danced again. When she went to court in her white gloves, the charges against her were dismissed. Later Robbins would spread rumors that Garrison picked up drag queens.

Jim Garrison was dismantling an entire culture, and an era of Quarter life came to a close. Much of value, from music to exotic dancing, vanished. The sleaze of street prostitution, the vulgarity of manufactured gaiety, replaced the old Bourbon Street. Local residents abandoned the Quarter and moved elsewhere. At fault, perhaps, was not so much Jim Garrison's crack-down of crime, as the Quarter's not having had the foresight to police itself.

One night Buras and Knaps were instructed to arrest an exotic dancer named "Linda Brigette" - if she included the round red velvet couch scene in which she touched herself, simulating orgasm, that was everyone's favorite part of her act. Brigette was, Buras thought, "the prettiest, sexiest, finest girl on the street." Brigette danced at the 500 Club run by Frank Caracci.

Caracci was a pudgy, soft-looking man, five foot six or seven, with a receding hairline and a small mustache; he resembled the Mafia operative that he was. Yet he was a reasonable man, and not unkind. Frank Caracci did not permit men to be rolled at his club, and was always fair to Linda Brigette. Linda also danced at her husband Larry Lamarca's club, the Gunga Den.

Brigette was a tiny Cajun woman, with blue eyes and black hair, only four feet ten inches tall. That she looked like a little girl added to her charm. Linda never totally stripped, she was not even raunchy. A mother of two, she took her name from the actress Brigette Bardot (her real name was Georgia Lambert) and liked to read comic books. Linda's large breasts had been augmented at the Hotel Dieu hospital under the supervision and care of nuns. This was, after all, New Orleans. Linda's posterior also had been improved.

One night she came on stage and did her dance with her newly implanted breasts red and sore, the surgical line still showing, and people thought how hard Larry Lamarca, her husband, worked her so that she had to dance at the Gunga Den even right after surgery. Nor was Linda Brigette much of a dancer. She had enrolled at Joan Bovan's dancing school only for them both to realize: Linda had two left feet. Joan taught her to make it seem as if she could dance.

Larry Lamarca was so jealous that he waited for Linda outside the door when she went to the toilet. It did him no good. Linda took lovers.

Linda Brigette's act was called "Dance Of A Lover's Dream," and it made her the toast of the town. She did part of the act on a swing. In another segment, she simulated being in a glass of champagne, as if she were floating in bubbles. By the end of the act, she was lying on the red velvet couch. To the beat of a sexy song, Linda simulated orgasm - that brought the house down every night. Bright lights came on and when the music stopped, Linda screamed, a shrill, act-stopping, ear-piercing scream. Then she rose from the red velvet couch and paraded around in her negligee.

Among those who enjoyed Linda Brigette's act were French Quarter regulars, Jim Garrison and Denis Barry. Sometimes they were accompanied by Garrison's assistant Frank Shea and Donald V. Organ, who would marry Linda's dancing teacher, Joan Bovan.

Buras and Knaps were ordered to keep an eye on Brigette. Most nights they concluded that, red velvet couch or not, she had not shown or put her hand into any part of her vagina. Deciding that her act was not obscene, they refused to arrest her. Their superiors keep up the pressure. One night, during the Garrison raids, under greater pressure, as Buras and Knaps watched, Linda did touch herself, and they arrested her for lewd dancing.

Much would be written about Frank Caracci, for whom Linda danced, and about what Aaron Kohn would call the "Karno-Caracci syndicate." The police found Caracci fair, his business clean. "Things are really different out here now," Caracci told a well-dressed man outside the 500 Club one night during the Garrison raids. Caracci was sitting on a stool, acting as his own doorman. Robert Buras came by. "What would you do if I tried to give you a ten dollar bill, right now or later?" Caracci said.

"I would arrest you," Buras said. Buras added that he never saw anything around Caracci's club that he needed any help on. Caracci laughed.

"That's not what the old timers would have said," Caracci remarked. Buras shrugged and walked on. He had to worry not only about drunks and criminals, but also about Kohn's Crime Commisson and the DA's people, who could hurt you if you messed up. Most of the time now Garrison's men did not make the Quarter arrests – the police did. The police were, as Buras says, in today's parlance, "where the rubber meets the road."

Buras remembers Pershing Gervais as a man of dishonor who could never be trusted. Sometimes Pershing would take money and still bust people. The padlocking was not even-handed, and the Spinato brothers, Buras believes, were nailed only because they did not give Pershing enough money. "Why would a good man like Jim Garrison want a man of dishonor close to him, except to provide cover?" Buras wondered. In Pershing, Garrison had a man who didn't have to worry about his reputation because he had none.

Jim Garrison suffered the presence of Pershing Gervais without profit. No one in Louisiana would have believed that Jim was not profiting personally – unless you knew Jim Garrison. Leading an organization of bar operators, Hubert Badeaux insisted that Jim Garrison had to be concealing some agenda with all these attacks on the clubs. "What stumps us is his motive," Badeaux said. "What's he want? We've already ruled out a shakedown. He's not interested in money."

Garrison couldn't resist a reply. "I've got the simplest motive in the world – I just want to run the best DA's office New Orleans ever had." He made himself plain and the press printed what he said. "I didn't make the laws against B-drinking, prostitution, gambling and drunk-rolling," Garrison said. He was going to "end the rackets here, and the only way anyone can stop me is to kill me." If "judges, police and miscellaneous officials" attacked him, yelling "what's the matter with Garrison?" so much the worse for them.

Carol Boyd, who now worked for the office, and who sometimes went with Lou Ivon and fellow officer Fred Williams to the clubs as an observer, noticed that Jim Garrison did not care who ridiculed him or laughed at him. If he believed in something, he followed through, like a pit bull. He never worried about what people thought. So he would be during his investigation of the assassination of President Kennedy. No amount of press abuse would stop him.

"The police here are like an army that had a mission to capture an enemy hill," Garrison said, developing one of his elaborate conceits. "Years ago they went out, surrounded it, and then dug in. They've been dug in for so long that they've forgotten what they're supposed to do. They've made friends with the enemy, and even exchange birthday and Christmas gifts. So why capture the hill and end all the fun?"

The Livesay murder case was enlisted as part of Garrison's rationale for his determined effort to clean up Bourbon Street. On August 6th, Garrison mentioned Sandoz's pulverizing of David ("Butch") Aycock in his call for a new "state of emergency" in the Quarter. Frank Klein announced that it would be a "four year campaign…to make the French Quarter safe for people who live there and visit there." On August 8th, members of the District Attorney's office invaded six Bourbon Street clubs: the French Casino; the Old French Opera House; Larry Lamarca's Gunga Den; Guys and Dolls; Frieda's Parisiennes. "In two and a half hours our man spent $2000 and he was trying to conserve his money," Garrison told the press.

Jim Garrison vowed the raids would continue. The next day raids were made on: Guys and Dolls; Blue Angel; Chez Paree; Gunga Den; and the Poodle Patio. Jim Garrison appeared in fatigues, pulling up onto the sidewalk in his maroon Oldsmobile convertible. After a series of fender benders, he would cease to drive at all, and either be driven by officer Steve Bordelon, or take United cabs.

One night Buras and Knaps arrested a girl, the bartender and the manager of the Gunga Den. They had arrived in uniform, and the girl and the bartender defied them. The B-drinking went on, as if the place was protected. That was showing the police disrespect, Buras thought. They made the arrests only for Larry Lamarca to arrive in the company of Frank Klein himself. Klein asked the police to give the Gunga Den people a pass. It doesn't matter, he then added drunkenly. He would "take care of it at the office." The charge simply wouldn't be accepted.

"Don't worry yourself," Buras said angrily. "Because this is going to municipal court and you won't see the case." As they waited for the paddy wagon, the manager said that the bartender was applying for American citizenship the next day. An arrest would ruin his chances. Could they substitute someone else? Buras and Knaps swore the bartender to secrecy and did just that. The case never came to court.

City officials had no alternative but to jump onto Jim Garrison's bandwagon. Mayor Schiro called for a review of liquor licenses of the bars on Canal Street. The President of the City Council announced he would introduce an ordinance requiring fingerprinting of all employees in places with "live entertainment." In September, councilman James E. Fitzmorris introduced an ordinance outlawing the use of sidewalk barkers in front of the clubs. Business on Bourbon Street fell by ninety per cent. Yet, if conventions were now ignoring New Orleans, and taking their business elsewhere, that had less to do with Jim Garrison's campaign against French Quarter vice, and more with hotels refusing still to accept "colored" guests.

Cleaning up Bourbon Street gave Jim Garrison an enormous amount of publicity. Throughout August, the "Times-Picayune" and the "States-Item" newspapers ran front page stories as Garrison rattled home his point: "The economics of Bourbon Street" depended on crime, forcing the "peeleries [to] operate on the fringes of the law."

National publicity followed. An article appeared in the "Saturday Evening Post" called "The Vice Man Cometh." It ran under the by-line of a second rate reporter named James Phelan. In fact, the article, all but five hundred words, was written not by Phelan, but by Garrison friend David Chandler. Garrison had been best man at his wedding.

Chandler's article was titled "Garrison: Demagogue Or Crusader?" and it called Jim Garrison's "the best DA's office New Orleans ever had." With the hindsight of history, Garrison would have done well to cast a cold eye on James Phelan if only, then, for his willingness to publish someone else's words under his name. Phelan, reporting to the FBI, would be among those enlisted to use any means necessary, including sophistry, lies, bribery and blackmail, in the effort to destroy Jim Garrison's investigation into the death of President Kennedy.

Jim Garrison's favorite novel was Ayn Rand's right-wing paean to individualism, "The Fountainhead." "Only the individual can do anything," he insisted. He viewed "the political establishment" as society's great danger, terming it "a Goliath that has 1,000 legs, [and] weighs 800 tons." He promised that he would not "be pushed around by all the power in the state."

Jim and Liz lost their third child, a boy, who had been named "John Lyon," after Garrison's stepfather, Lyon Gardiner. They had dinner with the Chandlers and Patricia Chandler thought Garrison was the "great man" in his marriage, which was, of course, the standard of the time. Jim and Liz argued, and Patricia's sympathy was entirely with Liz, who was "funny and friendly."

Domestic life had not claimed him. He still liked to eat at Moran La Louisiane, considered the best restaurant in New Orleans for those in the know. If "Diamond Jim" Moran had been a bodyguard of Huey Long's and was close to the Corolla organization, no one cared. Jimmy Moran never sent the district attorney a bill once he realized that his bills would only be ignored. If he went to the District Attorney with a bill, everyone would think that Jimmy Moran had lost his mind.

When Jim Garrison went up to Baton Rouge to lobby for bail bond reform, he seized the opportunity for an assignation with a nineteen-year-old stenographer. It took place at the Capitol House Hotel, and was an event Aaron Kohn noted in his special Garrison dossier. Garrison saw no need to be particularly discreet. He "shot at" every woman he met, Walter Hammer thought.

Garrison was among the first to receive a key to the new Playboy Club on Iberville Street. Then he irritated Denis Barry because too often he had to borrow money from Barry to pay the check, loans never to be repaid.

Jim had a couch in his private office, and one day Charlie Ward walked in on him having sexual intercourse with his secretary. Garrison raised his head.

"And what can I do for you today, Charlie?" Garrison said.

Never shy, Aaron Kohn confronted him directly. His personal behavior would destroy public confidence in his anti-vice campaign, Kohn said. Garrison replied that it was nobody's business but his own. Once he told Kohn that he had "reformed." Garrison often repeated his credo that sex had nothing to do with morality.

By August, Aaron Kohn was praising Jim Garrison's efforts on several fronts: bail bonding, lottery violations, parole abuses, and the clip-joint operators. "It has been refreshing and reassuring to observe the powers of the district attorney being applied vigorously against criminal elements which in the past have been permitted to acquire pseudo-respectability, and a false immunity from the law," Kohn, Garrison's future blood enemy, told the press.

In a personal letter to Garrison, Kohn repeated his praise. He noted Garrison's "considerable progress…within a relatively short period of time." By the close of 1962, Kohn was applauding Jim Garrison for initiating "a period of unprecedented use of the DA's powers to break up traditional crime situations in the community."

Chapter 8:

Sacred Cows Garrison v. Louisiana

"A thief, a grafter and a ruffian."

Judge J. Bernard Cocke

The Bourbon Street crackdown was financed from its inception by the "fines and forfeitures" fund, a pot consisting of bail bonds forfeitures and fines paid by petty criminals. This money resided under the control of the judges of the Criminal Court. When Jim Garrison took office in May 1962, there was a scant $1200 in the kitty. By August, there was $40,000 available for routing crime in the Quarter. Opposing Garrison from the start, the eight judges decided unanimously that it was the police, not the district attorney, who were authorized to investigate crime. No district attorney before Jim Garrison had done so.

Garrison sent the judges a list of his expenses: hotels, automobiles, trips from out of town for his undercover people. He had tossed out Richard Dowling's vintage World War II steel desk, and purchased a walnut desk for $602, but this was at his own expense. He did expect that the cost of the new carpets and draperies to replace Dowling's pink and green monstrosities would be covered.

"Do you think you could buy me a parenthetic microscope? I've never had one and I can't get one," Orleans Parish Coroner Nicholas Chetta asked Jim Garrison. The cost was seven hundred dollars.

"You'll have one tomorrow," Garrison said, never imagining that he would face opposition from the judges. He bought also: an air conditioner for the smoke-filled steamy investigators' office. He bought four two-door Chevrolets, stick shift models, without radios because these were cheaper. The whole town now watched the developing conflict between Garrison and the judges. When a new floor was laid in the DA's outer waiting room, the event made the "States-Item" "Police Beat" column.

Jim Garrison was not an efficient, or even an "able administrator." He knew this, and when he couldn't account for five thousand dollars worth of charges, he placed D'Alton Williams in charge of accounting. Williams was unable to locate bids on the four Chevrolets. Pershing paid off informants without securing receipts or creating vouchers, and that created a problem.

Jim Garrison will have to "walk a narrow line for the next four years," Iris Kelso predicted. Kelso attributed the hostility of the judges to Garrison's having attacked the owners of the lottery companies rather than the small fry, the vendors selling on the streets.

Garrison forwarded a bill to Judge William O'Hara, and when O'Hara went off on vacation, Garrison told Judge Shirley G. Wimberly that O'Hara had promised to endorse the purchase, a partial truth. This was all the pretext the judges required. In August, they froze the fines and forfeitures fund, refusing to release any more money to the district attorney's office.

The brightest and most influential of the judges was J. Bernard Cocke. A short, fat man, only about five foot four inches tall, with a bulbous nose and a red face, Judge Cocke sat on the bench with a fifth of Scotch in his pocket. He was known for his foul mouth and ran his courtroom as a reign of terror. If you weren't punctual, you might wind up in jail. If a jury came back with a verdict not to his liking, he cursed them out. Judge Cocke was a virtual Huey Long reincarnated, a man who would throw a steak on the floor if it didn't meet with his approval. In the sultry New Orleans heat, he came into court naked under his robes.

Yet J. Bernard Cocke was an honest man. No one had the nerve to offer him so much as five dollars. An able jurist, and humane, in 1954 he had spoken out vehemently before the state legislature against harsh mandatory sentences for first-time drug offenders. New Orleans police narcotics agents were planting drugs on suspects, Judge Cocke charged.

Having virtually run the Dowling office, Judge Cocke detested Jim Garrison for his independence. He despised Pershing Gervais even more. "Go get your degenerate boss and tell him I want to see him," Judge Cocke told officer Frank Meloche one day, referring to Gervais.

Like any successful bully, J. Bernard Cocke more often than not seized the offensive. Frank Shea, the assistant assigned to his court, was fifteen minutes late one day. "The district attorney's office is too busy chasing around Bourbon Street to have an assistant present," Judge Cocke sputtered from the bench. He threatened to send the sheriff to pick up Shea. On September 10th, Shea was replaced by Steven R. Plotkin, twenty-six years old. It was an unlucky assignment for Plotkin.

Among Judge Cocke's grievances against Jim Garrison was that he had not been consulted when Max Gonzales was sent into Parish Prison in the Peter Hand-Hardy Davis arrests. "He slipped that man into Parish Prison without even telling me what he was doing!" Cocke protested, outraged. "There I was, signing the necessary papers without knowing what was going on!" The Dowling days were over.

Among the other antagonists in Jim Garrison's burgeoning warfare with the judges was Edward A. Haggerty, Jr., an alcoholic and a roustabout. Steeped in the politics of favor, Haggerty sat surrounded by his father, who was clerk of the court, and his brother, Dan, the deputy clerk. Dan was a master at palming the ball so that if he wanted a certain case assigned to his brother, it was as good as done. The balls were marked "A," "B," "C," "D," or "E," etc. and the decision as to which judge a case was assigned was easily subverted. Judge Haggerty behaved so capriciously that he would sometimes grab a file out of the hand of the assistant district attorney assigned to his section, then tell the defense, "Don't plead. They don't have shit on you!"

If Edward Haggerty feared anyone, it was not Jim Garrison, but two very tough cops, Edward O'Donnell and Raymond Comstock, who has already entered this narrative. They could arrest a judge out on the town for being drunk and disorderly – or they could toss him into the back seat of the police car and drive him home. The police still ran New Orleans, and their power over him made Haggerty hate them. In court, he couldn't resist interrupting a policeman testifying, saying, "That's enough!" If the officer kept on talking, Haggerty would shout, "I said to SHUT UP!"

Bernard Bagert and Thomas Brahney were the Catholic judges who let offending priests escape with something less than a reprimand. Judge Platt was more often than not at the racetrack. Judge Schulingkamp was a virulent racist. One day he astonished listeners with his response to a question regarding why, their having committed the same crime under virtually identical circumstances, he gave a black man a one year sentence and a white man three years.

"The white man should have known better," Judge Schulingkamp explained. Compared to Judge Schulingkamp, his clerk Walter Hammer said, years later, "Ronald Reagan was a leftist."

The judges now retaliated against Jim Garrison. On October 11th, Judge Wimberly dismissed a case against three Bourbon Street night clubs charged with inadequate lighting. The law was unconstitutional, Judge Wimberly ruled.

"There is a conspiracy among the judges to wreck my administration," Garrison told his staff.

Jim Garrison declared war on the judges. As his venue, he chose a luncheon at Kolb's restaurant sponsored by the Temple Sinai Brotherhood. There, on October 30th, 1962, he launched into a full scale attack on the judges of the Criminal Court for laziness, and for taking so many holidays that Parish Prison was bursting at the seams. In a prison with a capacity to hold 523 people, 758 languished. Soon Garrison was dusting off the charges he has levied against his earlier judicial adversaries, Judge Sperling and Judge Platt.

The judges are behaving as if they're "the sacred cows of India," Garrison charged. "'Who does he think he is?' they will ask," he added. "Well, I am a district attorney who wants to clear his dockets." He counted up 206 holidays a year enjoyed by the judges, "not counting the legal holidays like All Saint's Day, [Huey] Long's birthday, and St. Winterbottoms' Day." The crowd roared with appreciative laughter. The worst was J. Bernard Cocke, Garrison said. "Cocke will not allow a case on Fridays." For Judge Cocke, Friday was a holiday.

Cocke retaliated. "Garrison is persona non grata as far as I'm concerned," Judge Cocke said. He pronounced himself "disenchanted" with the new district attorney.

The judges announced that they would be meeting "en banc," in a united front. "To my knowledge it will be the first time all of the judges worked on Friday," Garrison retorted. He went on television to appeal to his popular constituency. This was a considered tactic. "The only way to get these sacred cows back to work is by public reaction," he said. Then he took out a personal loan of $5,000 so that he could continue to finance his crackdown on French Quarter vice.

On Wednesday, November 7th, a peace conference was held between Jim Garrison and the judges. Judge Cocke did not bother to attend. Asked afterwards if he had apologized, Garrison replied, "No comment." Then he poured fuel on the raging fire. "The message is clear," Garrison said. "'Don't rock the boat, son. You are not supposed to investigate anything.' This raises interesting questions about the racketeer influences on our eight vacation-minded judges." He cited an example: he had observed Judge Schulingkamp having lunch with a Mafia personality.

Pershing Gervais, who kept those dossiers on people, and knew what there was to know, had an idea. Pershing suggested that Aaron Kohn testify before the Orleans Parish grand jury about the racketeering connections of the judges. Then, during the afternoon, the judges would be subpoenaed to appear.

Kohn refused. He did share what he knew about the judges with Pershing. Judge Schulingkamp had repeatedly paroled lottery vendors. Judge Haggerty and "Big Mike" Callia had attended a party where the women were naked. Judge Shirley G. Wimberly was the father-in-law of A. J. "Kay" Occhipinti, who had ties to Carlos Marcello. Judge Platt's mother had owned one of the lottery companies.The only judges on whom Kohn had nothing were Tom Brahney and Judge Cocke.

Now Denis Barry and D'Alton Williams obtained the addresses of the lottery company owners for use in subpoenas to the grand jury. They would be questioned about financial contributions made by the judges. Ed Roussel, chief of the Intelligence Division of the IRS, helped.

Invited by newly elected Judge Malcolm O'Hara, the son of Judge William O'Hara, to Lois's Crescent Lounge, Frank Shea and Barry, on a mission, had drinks with Judges Haggerty and Bernard Bagert. There they encountered Frank Caracci counting the coins from the juke box and pinball machines.

Judge Haggerty introduced Shea, Barry and D'Alton Williams to Francis Giordano, an ex-con and Marcello associate who had been to prison for narcotics and safe burglary. Giordano actually complained to Barry that when the pinball machines were seized by the Dowling office (pinball gambling was illegal in New Orleans at the time) they were returned. Jim Garrison, defying custom, was not releasing the machines. It seemed inconceivable that Jim Garrison was not as corrupt as the district attorneys who preceded him.

Unable to resist being the center of attention, Aaron Kohn testified before the Orleans Parish grand jury on November 8, 1962. He described how Malcolm O'Hara's brother was tied to the Mills-Litolff gambling dynasty through marriage. O'Hara was an officer of the Modern Finance Company, which used Mills' gambling money. Kohn outlined three generations of Mills' involvement in lottery, handbooks, gambling casinos, and football pools, along with payoffs of graft to bag men for public officials.

On that same morning of November 8, Jim Garrison was charged formally by the eight judges with criminal defamation. Asked if he would dismiss the charge, Garrison said, "that's ridiculous." Ten minutes later, Frank Klein attempted to do just that. "I don't think this is a good case," he said. "I don't think the allegation is true and the case is unsubstantiated."

Judge Cocke immediately instructed Judge Haggerty's father, the clerk of the court, to continue processing the charge. On Saturday, as if nothing had happened, Garrison outlined his ten point "crash" program to solve the problem of overcrowding in Parish Prison. The "Times-Picayune" praised his effort. Public opinion was also on Jim Garrison's side. A "Jefferson Resident" wrote to the "States-Item" that Garrison should "be given a gold medal." He wondered why "every politician in the Crescent City is out to stop him."

The judges now developed a strategy. They decided that if before it took only one judge to approve an expenditure by the district attorney's office, now it would take five out of eight to sign off on every dollar sent to Jim Garrison. The judges met in Baton Rouge with Louisiana Attorney General Jack P. F. Gremillion to reinstate the charges that had been dismissed by Frank Klein and to ensure that Garrison would be prosecuted.

An Earl Long protégé, Gremillion was not the brightest of men. "If you want to hide anything from my attorney general," Long said, famously, "Just put it in a law book." The "P. F." stood for Paul Faustin, but people called him "Jacques Pierre Francois" because he traded on his French ancestry. Gremillion signed letters to close friends: "JPFG," his trademark.

The judges demanded that Jim Garrison not only apologize, but publicly recant his allegation about their involvement in racketeering. "Apologize for what?" Garrison demanded. "I've been the one who has been aggrieved." At a church meeting, Garrison invoked the case of John Peter Zenger, the 18th century editor and publisher accused of "seditious libels" of a public official, and whom a jury had acquitted.

"It's amazing how swiftly the courts can move down here under certain circumstances," Jim Garrison remarked.

Gremillion charged him with criminal defamation, and Judge William H. Ponder was chosen to hear the case. Garrison let it be known that Judge Cocke had a photograph of Ponder at a fishing camp in his office. When Gremillion pronounced the situation "grave," Garrison ridiculed him. "If this was Hungary, Russia or someplace, it would be grave," he said. "But this is America. Have they forgotten the First Amendment?" Then he added, "People say worse things about President Kennedy every day."

Garrison's defense would rest on the First Amendment. On WWL-TV on November 23d, he addressed the citizens of Orleans Parish. "If you criticize me, you won't be charged with defamation, and if any public official does charge you for criticism, I will dismiss the case." It was, for Garrison, about justice, free speech, and the rights of the individual.

Jim Garrison had the great good fortune of having his friend Donald V. Organ sign on to represent him. "I had a great lawyer," Garrison later told Richard N. Billings. Organ at once challenged the appointment of William Ponder. "The entire judiciary of the State of Louisiana is an interested party in this case," he said.

The Bourbon Street raids continued. On December 1st, five clubs were padlocked. The judges then attacked Garrison's undercover man, Warren Moity, having discovered that Moity had once submitted an application to join the Louisiana bar that contained false information. Moity himself was under indictment for defamation. He had also once been accused of impersonating an FBI agent, and of extorting $500 from a nightclub operator. At first they thought they had Moity on an accusation of his having stolen a mink coat, only for it to emerge that the coat had been signed over to Moity as guarantee for a $1500 fee he was owed for work done.

Richard Dowling's law partner, Peter Compagno, entered the fray, accusing Moity of being "loud, boisterous and rough with women" at a "sex party," and for threatening a prostitute that he would "stomp her guts out!" A prostitute named Dolores Kennedy accused Moity of hitting her, and Garrison dropped the prostitution charge against her. This was in line with Garrison's general instruction that the object of the operation was to close offending establishments, not to charge small-time bartenders, barkers and prostitutes.

Owing to the able work of Milton Brener, through December of 1962 the district attorney's office chalked up fifty-one narcotics convictions. Only two defendants were acquitted.

Bernard Cocke returned from another month-long vacation to accuse poor Steven Plotkin of allowing the statute of limitations to run out on a battery charge in a case that had begun under the Dowling administration. "Your office is too busy blaming the vacation-minded judges!" Cocke blasted Plotkin. Plotkin better not bring any vice cases in his court.

Garrison tried to soothe Plotkin. Just put your finger under your chin and flip your goatee at Cocke, Garrison advised. A week after stripper "Dixie Dawn" testified for Jim Garrison, her husband was beaten up. Pershing, who excelled at law enforcement when he wanted to, caught the assailant easily. Yet when the case ended up in Judge Cocke's court, with Plotkin prosecuting, the charges were reduced to "simple kidnapping."

Jim Garrison kept up his war against Judge Cocke, and Cocke continued to reply in kind. Sentencing three lottery vendors, Judge Cocke wondered aloud why the district attorney didn't prosecute the operators, but instead continued their cases. Garrison replied in the press: "Inasmuch as this is the same J. Bernard Cocke, who, as district attorney [an office Cocke had once held], was publicly criticized for failing to bring to trial more than one hundred and thirty grand jury indictments, I am complimented by the higher standard which he applies to my office with regard to a few months' delay in trying three misdemeanors."

Two days later, in a direct attack on Judge Cocke, the Orleans Parish grand jury requested that Judge Cocke "be ordered to show why he was not in contempt." The charge was that Judge Cocke had violated the secrecy of the grand jury in the case of Dixie Dawn's husband. In open court, Judge Cocke had asked questions he could only have framed from the secret proceedings of the grand jury.

For Jim Garrison's defense, Don Organ was well aware from the start that he would not be paid. He agreed to represent Jim because he knew that the case was headed for the United States Supreme Court. As for the issue of the fines and fees, it was an open secret that the reason the judges wouldn't release the money for Garrison's investigations was that they simply wanted to keep it for themselves.

Garrison remained unperturbed. "My conscience is as clear as that of a new-born babe," he said. His entire staff stood behind him. "I may not last as the DA very long," he told Aaron Kohn, "and if I go out, my assistants will probably be booted out too, but at least we'll scratch their eyes going down." Then he enlisted his sense of humor. "I don't mind going to prison, except that those damn beds are too short for me," Garrison said. He planned to continue as district attorney from prison. "I may not be as available as I'd like to be," he said, "but I could still scribble notes and slip them through the bars to Frank Klein."

From seven p. m. to one in the morning on January 9, 1963, Pershing and Aaron Kohn reviewed Crime Commission files in search of further unseemly connections enjoyed by the judges. One of Pershing's informants told him that the other players in Judge Brahney's heavy-stakes card games were Alex Berger of Canal Loan – and the ubiquitous Frank Caracci.

The legalities were as ambiguous as they always were in New Orleans. When Don Organ insisted that a case involving the right of freedom of speech had to be tried by a jury, his motion was denied. Judge Ponder would speak throughout the trial as if the outcome of the case were a foregone conclusion.

On the facts, the judges had a weak case. What did "subject to racketeer influence" mean? The term "sacred cows" was clearly an opinion. The judges' declaring Garrison's vice investigation unconstitutional was itself unlawful.

In court, Jim Garrison sat in his chair pointedly ignoring the proceedings. Instead of focusing on the case, he donned his hat as an author and penned a three thousand word satirical parody of Shakespeare's "Richard The Third." He titled it "King James The First." If he ever expressed emotion openly, something he did rarely, Lou Ivon remembers, it was about his writing, what he loved best.

In a forest, Lord Bernard (J. Bernard Cocke) and seven dukes meet to denounce James, who "plots against us all." These nobles fear "our lives, families, holidays are in jeopardy and may not last the year," the juxtaposition of unlike elements, "families" and "holidays" revealing that Garrison borrowed his technique from the best of the 18th century satiric poets. One of the nobles disagrees with Lord Bernardo: "So long as this new king does not seek to take from us our lawful claim to lay witness to the daily double, then what concern have we with how this new prince amuses himself?" The joke, at Judge Platt's expense, would have escaped no one.

Lord Bernardo has other complaints against this "upstart king." He has surrounded himself with desks and chairs of "rare woods" and with "silken drapes and chartreuse rugs." Indeed the color of Jim Garrison's new carpet was chartreuse. George (Platt) demurs: "So long as the steeds are permitted to run their traditional course…." But when the new king "seeks to bar our honored sport of witnessing the steeds," one of the new "rules of the Court of St. James," the new king loses his sole supporter.

"What of our Fridays?" Sir Oliver (Schulingkamp) pipes up.

Jim Garrison does not exempt himself from the fun in this hilarious satire. He terms himself a "long-legged jack-a-napes, this raggedy-ass James." He acknowledges the accusation that he loved power, that he would be "saint" as well as "king."

At the end, Bernardo, the ringleader, rallies his forces against the "newly crowned king" who seeks to "rob us of our baronial powers, our reputations and our hours for reflection."

"Enough! Enough!" the dukes cry out in unison as they repair to their "en banc discourse."

"Woe upon him whose tragic fate is sealed by our vote of five out of eight," Lord Bernardo threatens, a joke on the new law regarding fines and fees expenditures.

During the trial, each of the judges took the stand. Don Organ knew that the judges were not racketeers, and that, although it was foolish for judges to consort with shady bail bondsmen and lottery operators, it was not criminal for them to have done so. Testifying, the judges managed nonetheless to make themselves seem petty and self-serving. William O'Hara insisted that the whole dispute was about his refusal to approve the $985 bill for a carpet and drapes for Jim Garrison's office without "competitive bids." Organ pointed out that Richard Dowling had never been refused expenditures from the fines and fees fund, yet had purchased a $6,000 Cadillac without producing competitive bids.

"Do you think a Cadillac is a more extravagant purchase than $985 for rugs and drapes?" Organ demanded. The audience burst into laugher.

Organ went on. "Didn't you tell Denis Barry, 'I stopped Grosch [the sheriff] and I'll stop Garrison'"?

"I told Barry no such thing," William O'Hara lied.

Judge Platt dragged into court a plaque awarded to him by the Louisiana Bar Association for thirty-five years of "distinguished and loyal service" on the bench. He lied about his mother's owning a lottery business, until Organ produced the bill of sale. Judge Schulingkamp, Organ demonstrated, had paroled people for Frank Costello, who brought big-time gambling to New Orleans, and for Mike Callia, a gambler, whom Schulingkamp then lied about knowing. Schulingkamp had also paroled Peter Hand.

"There's nothing wrong with paroles," Schulingkamp said dryly. "It relieves the crowded situation that Mr. Garrison talks about in the Parish Prison."

On the stand, Judge Haggerty complained that people hollered "moo" after him, a consequence of the "sacred cows" remark. Haggerty admitted that he attended a Callia-organized victory party for Judge Schulingkamp, and that he knew a rash of dubious figures: Andrew Monte, Jerome Conforto, and Mike Roach.

"Good morning, your honor," Don Organ told Judge Cocke on the second day of his cross-examination. Aware of how deeply Judge Cocke hated Pershing, Organ baited him deliberately. Judge Cocke fell for it, admitting that it was Jim Garrison's alliance with Pershing Gervais that led to his alienation from Garrison.

"Has Pershing ever been convicted of a crime?" Organ asked, disingenuously.

"Pershing Gervais is a liar, a grafter and a ruffian!" Judge Cocke burst out. "Any man who confesses under oath that while he was a sergeant on the police force he took $10 and $15 a week in little brown envelopes is a thief and a grafter, whether he has been convicted or not!"

Organ drew on other weapons to discredit Judge Cocke. Frank Klein had discovered that in Cocke's 1942 campaign for district attorney, his opponent had accused him of being associated with "gangsters and criminals," his entire record "one of favoritism and intimidation." So Judge Cocke and Don Organ faced off. As Judge Cocke had pointed his finger at Organ, now Organ pointed back. Had he filed any charges against Cicero Sessions? Organ wanted to know, referring to an old case.

Afterwards, Jim Garrison, Don Organ, Iris Kelso and Pershing walked down the courthouse steps together. "I'm no ruffian!" Pershing protested in mock outrage. That he was a thief and a grafter he did not deny.

Organ announced that he had subpoenaed twenty-three witnesses for the defense. He would also put Jim Garrison on the stand. Then he did not call a single witness. The state has not proved the elements of Jim Garrison's crime, Organ said. He didn't require witnesses because his case had been made by the eight judges themselves.

If Jim Garrison were "found guilty...then freedom of speech is walking a dangerous and narrow path," Organ argued. He produced seventeen points of law, the instructions a judge might have given to the jury, had there been one present. It was Organ's way of asking the judge to so charge himself. He was suggesting to Judge Ponder what law he should apply in assessing the facts before him.

As they awaited the verdict, Judge Ponder sent out a message. If Jim Garrison would recant on the racketeering comment, the judges would agree to drop the case. "Not a chance," Jim Garrison said. It would have amounted to political suicide.

Judge Ponder ruled that he had found "malice" in Jim Garrison's statements, and that Garrison did not "have any reasonable belief as to the truthfulness of his statement" about the judges' racketeering. Free speech did not mean Garrison could "cry fire in a crowded theater," that boiler plate exception to the absoluteness of the first amendment.

On February 6th, Jim Garrison was found guilty of criminal defamation and sentenced to a thousand dollar fine. He could have received a year in jail, but there had been, Judge Ponder granted, "some provocation." Pershing thought that Jim should take the thousand dollars and use it to commission a very garish painting of J. Bernard Cocke. Garrison was tempted, but Frank Klein talked him out of it.

Following his conviction, Garrison issued a statement. "I believe that the right of an American to speak freely was violated in this case," he said, taking the high road. "I intend to continue to exercise my right to criticize any public official who attempts to interfere with or limit the operation of my office." He would, of course, appeal. Then he went out and gave many speeches about the history of freedom of speech from Athens and the Magna Carta to the present, revealing how well he would have done as a professor of law.

National publicity flowed Jim Garrison's way as the "Washington Post" ran a series of articles both on his vice investigation and on Garrison v. Louisiana. Garrison was "a virtual Perry Mason," James E. Clayton wrote. Garrison was "sincere," Clayton thought. In New Orleans, Garrison was supported by both liberals and conservatives. L.P. (Lou) Davis, on behalf of the Conservative Committee for Constitutional Government, praised Jim Garrison for "his valiant fight to rid the city of crime." Charles Rivet, Secretary of the New Orleans Bar Association, told Aaron Kohn that he "personally approved of the recent pressures that District Attorney Garrison had been bringing on the courts." Judge Cocke had told Rivet that he would throw anybody in jail who pried into his records.

New Orleans politics proceeded as usual. Mayor Schiro told Clarence Chink Henry, President of Negro local 1419 of the International Longshoremen's Association, that unless his local supported Schiro's candidate for Orleans Parish Civil District Court in the second primary, members of the local might find themselves arrested for loitering while they awaited job assignments; the local's new building on South Claiborne might be subject to an increase in its taxes.

On June 5th, the Louisiana Supreme Court affirmed Jim Garrison's conviction. "For some time my attorneys have been working on my appeal to the United States Supreme Court," Jim said airily. Three days later, he appeared at Don Organ's office, as if the Supreme Court's granting certiorari was a given.

"I got a call from Deutsch," Garrison began. "He wants to put the facilities of his office on the research. He'll refund $5,000 of the expenses." Organ listened. There had, of course, been no payment for expenses, nothing to refund. Other than a practical joke of a check for $175,000, Garrison had not paid Organ a cent. And no further research was required. Organ had already constructed the entire case, aided only by fellow lawyer, Louis P. Trent, so that Deutsch had virtually nothing to do.

Garrison came to the point. In exchange for this $5,000, Eberhard Deutsch, the Colonel himself, who called presidents by their first names, and knew the Chief Justice personally, would argue the case before the United States Supreme Court as lead counsel. It was unfair and outrageous, because Organ had done all the work. During all the time they were preparing for trial, no word had come from Deutsch, Kerrigan and Stiles offering office help with the research on the constitutional issues. Deutsch was already famous for raiding other lawyers' clients. He had made his name in a grandstanding ambulance chase when a munitions ship exploded in Galveston harbor and he had cleverly filed a class action suit.

"Your name will appear on the case," Garrison added. Deutsch was willing to pay all future expenses, including the trip to Washington. It was clear to Organ that much more than five thousand dollars was involved.

"Don, you know my situation," Jim added. Organ did know. Jim lived from hand to mouth. Organ sympathized with Garrison in his plight. Deutsch had been his mentor and now he could not refuse this unjust demand.

"Jim, go ahead," Organ said. "But I won't be on a case with Eberhard Deutsch." Garrison was clearly relieved.

"Well, Don, I'll always appreciate what you did for me. I'll be your friend forever," Garrison said.

Organ vowed that he would never do anything for Jim Garrison again. Then he put the matter behind him. A few years later, David Chandler, now a bitter Garrison enemy, his loyalties elsewhere, would write that Don Organ called up Clay Shaw the day he was arrested and offered to represent him without charge. Organ says that Chandler was lying, that he did no such thing. Organ had never spoken to Clay Shaw.

Certiorari was, indeed, granted.

Short and dumpy, Jack P. F. Gremillion arrived at the United States Supreme Court with the legs of his trousers barely hitting his ankles. He was a country bumpkin, out of his depth. In contrast, Eberhard Deutsch was dressed in pin stripes, complete with waistcoat. He greeted the Justices as if they were old friends.

During argument, Gremillion was an embarrassing figure. "Mr. Garrison even predicted what the decision of this court would be," Gremillion confided. "He said he expected to lose this case in the state courts and to bring it to this Supreme Court, which would reverse the decision."

"Did he say it would be a unanimous decision?" Justice Harlan inquired. Subdued laughter wafted through the courtroom. Unwisely, Gremillion reminded the Court that it had been "criticized vociferously in my state." The states' rights card would not, however, play here.

"Have there been any other charges against people in New Orleans for talking about judges, either state or federal?" Justice Black asked Gremillion. The reference was to distinguished Judge J. Skelly Wright, who had been abused roundly in Louisiana for having the temerity to order the desegregation of the New Orleans schools.

When Gremillion dragged out a homespun story of a schoolboy who told a judge's son that his Daddy was a crook," Justice Potter Stewart asked, "Did you prosecute him for defamation?"

All Eberhard Deutsch had to do was invoke New York Times v. Sullivan, that decision reinforcing freedom of speech, and handed down on March 9, 1964, only a month before the Supreme Court agreed to hear the Garrison case.

Jim Garrison had planted himself in the middle of the room, and when his friend Bob Haik came to sit down next to him, he waived Haik away. His arms stretched akimbo, he preferred to sit alone, a figure likely to attract the attention of the judges. In the taxi on the way to Deutsch's suite at the Mayflower Hotel, Garrison explained why he didn't want his friend to sit next to him in the courtroom.

"I wanted them to concentrate on me," Jim said, according to Haik.

"You lost!" Haik predicted.

"How many former district attorneys were up there?" Jim said. "Three! I had three going in. I wanted to draw the attention of the three ex-DA's." Among them were Justice Black and Justice Douglas.

At the hotel, there was a knock on the door. Then Pershing Gervais walked in. His collar was open. He wore no necktie, and, as always, his belly hung over his belt. Unlike Haik, Pershing had no doubt about the outcome of Garrison v. Louisiana.

"Isn't this a wonderful day to fuck a little boy in the ass!" Pershing said.

Justice Brennan's opinion for the majority invoked "the great principles of the Constitution." He argued for freedom of speech, "even where the utterance is false," and declared that "speech concerning public affairs is more than self-expression; it is the essence of self-government." Boldly, Justice Brennan emphasized, in those days when the United States was closer to a political democracy, that Jim Garrison did not have to be correct: "Erroneous statement is inevitable in free debate. It must be protected if the freedoms of expression are to have the 'breathing space' that they 'need to survive.'"

Justice William Douglas added, elegantly: "It is a commonplace of life that heat and passion subtly turn to malice in actual fact." Garrison's utterances did not meet the new rigorous standard of malicious intent. Louisiana's defamation statute, the Court noted, dated back to the times of duels over one's honor, to retrograde Napoleonism. These anachronisms wilted in the light of the Warren Court.

Jim Garrison had the good grace to thank Don Organ first, and then Louis Trent, who had assisted him. Only then did he praise Eberhard Deutsch "who argued my case so magnificently before the United States Supreme Court."

In the autumn of 1964, Jim Garrison addressed the student body at the Tulane School of Law. His subject was "The Lawyer and the Bill of Rights." Justice, Garrison said, "must be brought into being by men like yourselves." Amid his customary references to Hamlet, the Magna Carta and the imprisonment of John Peter Zenger, he urged the future lawyers to place themselves in the "mainstream," yet also to remain in the path between the world of "should be" and the world of "is." They must not be like Hamlet, bemoaning their fate. The government would apply counter pressures to anyone daring to make real the ideal of "should be," he warned. It was as if he were predicting what would happen to him when he investigated the assassination of President Kennedy.

Garrison differentiated himself from those prosecutors who lamented that defendants have "too many rights." Rights must be "fought for and re-asserted time and time again," he said. Keeping at bay his customary sardonic humor, he said: "There is nothing quite so dangerous to the cause of freedom as virtuous men who are not particularly interested in the Bill of Rights."

Nor was this idle talk. Garrison had already put his confidence in the first amendment into practice. Racist Citizens' Council-supported school board candidates demanded action by the district attorney's office, charging that Max Lerner's "America As A Civilization," assigned by a junior high school civics teacher, "contains Communist philosophy."

Frank Klein refused their request to censor Lerner's book. "There is no element of this controversy which justifies action by this office," Klein declared. He referred to a Louisiana Supreme Court decision of 1958 entrusting the "entire field of subversive activities" to federal legislation. The state had "no power to prosecute Communist activities."

In June 1963, police officers walked into the Doubleday Book Store on the six hundred block of Canal Street and seized "Another Country," a novel by James Baldwin, declaring it "obscene." That the bookstore was a gay hang-out no doubt played a role in this singling out of a novel by distinguished African American writer Baldwin, who happened to be homosexual. The bookstore manager, Frank Rossetter, and a seventeen year old clerk, were arrested and charged with disseminating indecent literature. Frederick A. Soulé, head of the vice squad, argued that assistant city attorney Edward Pinner had termed Baldwin's book "the most filthy and pornographic book I have ever read." That was enough for him.

When he learned of these arrests, Jim Garrison was livid. "The idea of a police officer walking into a legitimate bookstore, removing a book from the shelf that is written by a respectable author and has been critically acclaimed, and then arresting the store manager is outrageous," he said. "All that is needed now is to have a ceremony in which the books are burned." Garrison refused the charges.

Mayor Schiro, describing Baldwin's novel as "indecent," then ordered the City Attorney to pursue action in Municipal Court, out of Garrison's jurisdiction.

Speaking at the Carrollton Avenue Presbyterian Church, Garrison termed Schiro's action "un-American, unconstitutional, and obviously a totalitarian police-state move." The police action had been a "cheap political expedient." The Citizens Council now attacked Garrison, arguing that "obscene books are just as damaging to public morals as obscene floor shows." At this ignorance, Garrison was incredulous.

Garrison defended the first amendment as energetically as he could, and as often. In the Baldwin case, there was no clear-cut victory. Doubleday's lawyers promised that the bookstore would not re-order "Another Country." For two years, distributors would withhold it.

Jim Garrison addressed the issue again at Tulane a month after the case against the Doubleday bookstore and James Baldwin's novel had finally been dismissed. "The Bill of Rights," Garrison said, in one of his most apt conceits, "lives in a kind of oxygen tent. And a 24-hour watch is needed because someone is always turning off the oxygen – always in the interest of justice, of course." He condemned the silence of the courts, of the members of the Bar, and of the newspapers when James Baldwin's book was first confiscated.

In other speeches, he returned to Garrison v. Louisiana. Garrison told the United Press International Newspaper Association of Louisiana that "all criminal defamation statutes [should be] ruled unconstitutional." They were obsolete laws enlisted "by the authorities as a form of reprisal against those who criticize those in public office."

In the years to come, Jim Garrison attempted to mend his fences with at least some of the judges. "Dear Ben," Jim Garrison wrote to Judge Bagert in 1966, "I am always interested in any complaints about possible shortcomings of our office because it gives me a chance to make improvements."

At the time the judges remained unregenerate, and police superintendent Joseph Giarrusso had to issue a message to all branches of his department noting that the judges of the Criminal Court "have been issuing orders to police officers contrary to established public procedure." While extending "every courtesy that is due a member of the judiciary," they were "politely to refuse to disobey police regulations."

Judge Haggerty nurtured his hatred of Jim Garrison for years. Garrison assigned a tall, broad-shouldered feisty assistant originally from Alabama named William Alford to Haggerty's section. Haggerty pursued his usual practice of grabbing a file out of the hand of the assistant district attorney and addressing the defense on what the state had against his client. One day Alford jerked his file back out of Haggerty's reach.

"You're not going to see my files anymore, Judge," Alford said.

"I'm calling Charlie Ward!" Haggerty threatened. By now, Ward was Garrison's First Assistant, and Alford's immediate superior. When Alford returned to the office, Ward patted him on the back and laughed. Alford now began to mark in the docket book what time Judge Haggerty arrived and what time he departed. It was 1966, two years after the "sacred cows" decision. Yet most of the judges remained "vacation-minded," and were invariably gone by noon.

The day after Edward A. Haggerty succeeded in his maneuver to have State of Louisiana v. Clay Shaw assigned to his court, William Alford was assigned to another judge's section.

Chapter 9:

Chess

"Truth is stranger than fiction."
Jim Garrison

That contempt citation against Judge Cocke for violating the secrecy of the grand jury in the beating of "Dixie Dawn's" husband, "Gerald Doe," kept the pot boiling. Then, on February 13th, 1963 only a week after Jim Garrison's defamation trial ended, the Orleans Parish grand jury added another charge, indicting Judge Cocke for malfeasance. This time he was accused of refusing to approve $2,416.60 worth of hotels, meals, drinks and travel incurred by Warren Moity and Malcolm Dodge in their undercover work. Irony mounted upon irony: only that week Moity had been convicted of defaming the Iberia Parish district attorney.

"Why indict just one judge?" WWL-TV asked.

"If you resist the iron fist," Jim Garrison replied, having been given equal time, "you are causing turmoil. If you protest, you are a publicity seeker."

In this elaborate chess game, chess being a lifelong Garrison preoccupation, he wrote to Jack P. F. Gremillion. "Respectfully," he requested that Gremillion "personally prosecute" the case against Judge Cocke. It was only appropriate since "the integrity of the judiciary may be involved." When Gremillion declined, Garrison responded: It was "one thing when the judges ask [Gremillion] to prosecute the DA, but quite another when the DA asks him to prosecute a judge." With his customary irony, Garrison pleaded that he had wanted only "to obtain for Judge Cocke a disinterested prosecutor."

Before a parent-teacher association meeting, Garrison pointed out that Judge J. Bernard Cocke "has always controlled the DA's office." When he was elected, Garrison said, his "choices were to accept the situation in peace, or to fight."

Frank Klein prosecuted the case against Judge Cocke for violating the secrecy of grand jury proceedings. Robert Ziblich defended Judge Cocke, searching for precedents where the "veil of secrecy" of the grand jury might be penetrated legitimately. Ziblich's co-counsel, George Gulotta, attacked Jim Garrison – for not being in the courtroom.

"Objection!" Frank Klein called out.

On February 20th, Judge Cocke was acquitted on the contempt charge. In the malfeasance case, Garrison himself appeared in court to cross-examine his adversary. It was the first case he would be prosecuting since taking office.

What do you think of the Bourbon Street night clubs and the padlocking actions taken against some of them? Garrison asked. If his purpose had been to provoke his adversary, he succeeded.

"You can burn Bourbon Street down for all I care," Judge Cocke burst out. "I don't associate with homosexuals or go to the homes of stripteasers. I don't care if you padlock or don't padlock!" He had refused to approve Moity's expenses because he knew him "to be the thief and crook that he is."

The law, Garrison countered, reads that "a judge" shall approve expenditures, not, as Judge Cocke and his colleagues devised at their en banc rendezvous in Baton Rouge, that five of the eight judges sign off on every request from the District Attorney's office.

"A judge doesn't mean 'one judge,'" Judge Cocke said, revealing how long familiar he had been with making the rules as he went along. He was found not guilty on all charges. Judge Wimberly then accused Jim Garrison of "public fakery." The judge has every right to criticize me, Garrison replied, and "need not fear being charged by me with defamation." By March 1963, the fines and forfeitures account stood at a plump $60,000.

Knowing that Denis Barry had opposed his appointment to the district attorney's office, Pershing kept a dossier on Barry, reporting all the while to Aaron Kohn. He learned that Barry had purchased a new Rambler and a Lincoln Continental for his wife. He had joined an expensive country club.

It had taken a year, but at last Denis Barry could produce irrefutable evidence of Pershing's corruption. Barry caught Pershing taking a $2500 bribe from the Old Absinthe House, and this time the recipient was willing to testify.

"If you don't do something, I'm going to the Crime Commission," Barry told Jim Garrison. Yet Garrison still did not fire Pershing Gervais. In February 1963, Barry resigned from the district attorney's office. He had meant to stay only for one year anyway, he said. Denis Barry and Jim Garrison would not speak to each other for several years. A week after his resignation from the district attorney's office, Denis Barry told Aaron Kohn that Pershing had made a deal with Charles Quartararo and Frank Caracci in which Gervais would protect one of the clubs in return for a secret share of the business. Years earlier, Jim Garrison had represented Quartararo and Gervais in a matter regarding the Gaslight Lounge, in which Gervais had a concealed part-ownership, with Quartararo among those fronting for him. Barry had long suspected that Gervais had been accepting graft since he had been in the district attorney's office. He had hoped to expose Gervais in a way that would not injure Jim Garrison.

Jim Garrison had replaced Steven Plotkin in Judge Cocke's section with William A. Porteous III. If only for the sake of Porteous' illustrious father, an "Old Regular" like himself, Cocke would surely contain his anger against this particular Garrison assistant. Porteous was a Princeton graduate who went on to be first in his class at Tulane. He made law review and was invited to clerk for Judge John Minor Wisdom, only to be called away for military service.

"If you just stick to doing your duty as an assistant district attorney and stay out of my fights with your boss," Cocke told Porteous, "you and I will get along perfectly well." Not that there weren't lapses. "You tell your boss not to bring all this trash around here," Cocke told Porteous one day.

When the judges wanted Porteous to testify to the exemplary record of Judge Cocke's court, Jim Garrison did not object to his doing so. It was then that Porteous realized: Jim Garrison's public rhetoric notwithstanding, he knew Judge Cocke was highly capable, if cantankerous, and respected him.

Porteous hadn't been in the district attorney's office more than four days when Pershing wanted to know if Porteous wished him to provide him with women. Despite his light tone, Porteous realized that Gervais was someone who could get you in trouble, someone in whose debt you did not want to fall. Porteous declined Pershing's offer.

Jim Garrison turned his attention to police superintendent Joseph Giarrusso, who had accused his office of hurting the tourist industry, and of not making use of the evidence Giarrusso's own office had collected. Giarrusso's reports, Garrison said, were "the purest garbage" and "would not provide a solid basis for padlocking a bird cage." Garrison waxed poetic: "The supposition is that there are certain permanent realities, the sky, the river, lottery, handbooks, B-drinking and other eternal absolutes."

When Giarrusso produced statistics demonstrating the competency of the police, Garrison replied that "he leans upon his statistics as a drunk leans upon a lamppost – more for support than for illumination." Criticized for not proceeding against Norma Wallace after a Giarrusso raid, Garrison explained that he padlocked only businesses which attempted to continue. Then he launched into one of his habitual military conceits, the story of an army that has an enemy hill surrounded:

> With the passage of time the condition of a stalemate has produced in this army traditions and comforts which are not lightly to be thrown aside. Every Christmas the army and the enemy exchange messages of good will and flagons of rum. The army, having been there for years, strongly defends the position at the foot of the hill against all critics. Its leaders point out that the critics do not understand all of the problems and that no one else is doing a great deal more. They cite statistics showing the periodic captures made of the men on the hill by their scouting patrols, their undercover agents and their tactical squads. But the hill remains occupied and everyone on both sides is quite contented because it has always been this way. Of course, if the army ever captured the hill the secret sweets and comforts of a friendly enemy would be gone, and the statistics would end.

It might have been a parable written by Franz Kafka.

In the spring of 1963, Garrison raised the issue of "systematic [police] brutality." He called it "an old New Orleans custom," and indicted nine police officers. Giarrusso retaliated by pointing out that Garrison previously had refused to accept charges against four of these officers, to which Garrison replied that the original evidence had been "doctored" and "fully orchestrated." Now Giarrusso threatened to investigate Garrison's own men. The charges against the officers were dropped. Kohn suggested that a "Mayor's Special Committee" be appointed to resolve their differences, while Garrison wanted the mayor alone to be involved since Giarrusso was "only an underling."

Garrison stepped up his rhetoric. Terming Giarrusso as intransigent as "the Rock of Gibraltar," he accused the police chief of being interested only in "preserving the status quo of the rackets," and not "acting effectively against organized crime." One night his investigators had heard a police major named Adolph Mayerhafer warn some women that the DA's investigators were in the area. "They obstruct our efforts with a great big, invisible, solid brick wall," Garrison charged. Meanwhile the Mayor was "like somebody from the United Nations. He thinks everything is wonderful."

Behind the scenes, local politicians waged war against Jim Garrison for his efforts against crime in the French Quarter. Ever ubiquitous, Hubert Badeaux colluded with the police in demanding injunctions against the arrests of the women at the clubs. Mayor Victor Schiro refused to replace one of Garrison's police investigators who had retired.

In a meeting designed to coordinate police efforts with those of the district attorney's office, attended by Garrison, Mayor Schiro and Police Superintendent Joseph Giarrusso, tempers flared. Garrison walked out after half an hour. The meeting had been "very unsatisfactory," Garrison told the press. "Nothing but words."

The next day, Giarrusso offered yet another challenge. "If Mr. Garrison has any knowledge of any officers being derelict in their duties, he has the power to charge them accordingly," Giarrusso said. Garrison said he did not wish to single out individual police officers. The problem was higher up, "at the very top of the police force."

Now Pershing arranged a secret meeting between Jim Garrison and Mayor Schiro at the New Orleans airport. For an hour and a half, Garrison complained about obstruction of his efforts by the police department. Later Schiro publicized a private letter from Garrison requesting that the police of the First District renounce their "monumental disinterest" in B-drinking. He was directing Giarrusso to cooperate with Jim Garrison, Schiro said.

The courts were mostly on Garrison's side. When thirteen club owners went into civil court and requested an injunction to stop the district attorney's raids, the request was denied.

Unable to attack Jim Garrison directly, Giarrusso focused on his Achilles heel, Pershing Gervais. Giarrusso volunteered to make public his own income tax returns. "But I'll bet the Chief Investigator of the District Attorney's office isn't willing to do the same thing," Giarrusso added. In yet another truce Garrison and Giarrusso agreed that "traditional police attitudes have been conditioned to tolerance of organized crime," and let it go at that.

Pershing was cleared by the Orleans Parish grand jury of the beating of Harold Sandoz, and of a man named Daniel Polka, an incident witnessed by no fewer than six police officers. Repeatedly, Garrison found himself in the position of having to defend Gervais. On April 15, he wrote a six-page letter to Mayor Schiro complaining about the "continued 'investigation' of a member of my staff – my Chief Investigator, to be specific." Garrison had discovered that Giarrusso had enlisted members of Alcohol Beverage Control; FBI agents; Hubert Badeaux – and others in an effort to stop Gervais.

All Garrison could argue was that the whole upper structure of the police department had been corrupt, and that Gervais had belonged to a tainted operation. At one point, Pershing agreed to take a polygraph if Giarrusso and his aide, Major Presley J. Trosclair, Commander of Police Intelligence, would also take one. It is Trosclair to whom Jack Martin would repair after Guy Banister pistol-whipped him on the day of the assassination of President Kennedy.

"Joseph Giarrusso is a perjurer and a liar and Trosclair is a perjurer and a liar, so how can I go down and cooperate with those bums?" Pershing told Kohn. He blamed Hubert Badeaux for his troubles. He also blamed Jack Martin, whom Kohn called a "pseudo-detective." Kohn had concluded that lawyer John E. Lanne, Hubert Badeaux, Guy Banister and Jack Martin formed a "lunatic-fringe" in the community. Gervais accused Giarrusso of tipping off Frank Caracci just before the undercover agents went into the Old French Opera House, although later he ordered that Caracci not be charged because he was a valuable informant. Indeed, Caracci was paying Gervais for protection of his operations.

No one could tell Jim Garrison anything now that Denis Barry was gone. Frank Klein was exasperated enough with the Gervais situation to confide in Aaron Kohn. "Gervais's opinions supersede those of anyone else in the office," he complained.

Now both Giarrusso and Jim Garrison were zeroing in on Mafia-owned clubs. Giarrusso personally led raids in an "Operation B-Drink" on a Marcello redoubt, Caracci's Old French Opera House. Garrison moved on the Old Southport, a casino with a chequered provenance – it was owned jointly by Carlos and Anthony Marcello. Garrison proceeded, although the casino was just over the Jefferson Parish line. The focus on the Old Southport was one more example of Garrison giving the Mafia no quarter.

Garrison enjoyed this foray into Jefferson Parish. It would make Jefferson district attorney Frank Langridge look silly, Garrison thought. "It will look like a situation in which a grown man has been tugging and tugging in an effort to lift a weight off the floor. He says that it is impossible and gives up. Then a little kid comes along and easily picks it up with one hand."

Informing to Regis Kennedy of the FBI field office, Kohn revealed everything he learned about the Orleans Parish district attorney's office. Then Kohn sent a personal contribution of forty-one dollars to Jim Garrison's voluntary fund for investigative expenses of the district attorney's office, a fund needed given the judges' appropriation of the fines and forfeitures account.

That spring of 1963, Jack Martin filed a suit against Jim Garrison and Pershing Gervais in Civil District Court for threatening him with arrest, demanding damages of $50,000. He requested that Jack P. F. Gremillion investigate both Garrison and Gervais; the court papers do not reveal for what. Martin's charge was "a conspiracy to harass, molest, intimidate and persecute your petitioner." Jim Garrison and Pershing Gervais had revealed confidential information obtained by Martin "in connection with a formerly private investigation." For corroboration, Martin names Major Presley J. Trosclair of police intelligence. The check Martin used to cover the costs of his suit was signed by Guy Banister.

Three days later, Jack Martin withdrew his suit, pleading that he was suffering "severe nervous strain and breakdown." Jim Garrison remained perplexed by the episode. "Truth is stranger than fiction," he said.

Garrison would always relish the chess game of politics. In April of 1963, Frank Klein, again serving as Jim Garrison's stalking horse, suggested at a meeting of Young Democrats of Louisiana that there was a "distinct possibility" that Jim Garrison might run against

Jack P. F. Gremillion for Attorney General of Louisiana. Could an Attorney General supersede a District Attorney who had "refused, failed, or neglected to perform his duties?" The issues were arcane and concerned that raid into Jefferson Parish, although they bear as well upon Gremillion's role in Garrison v. Louisiana.

Louise Korns drafted a statement for Jim Garrison entitled "Powers and Duties of the Attorney General."

"It appears that the Attorney General not only has the power but the duty to take action when the law enforcement machinery has broken down as it has in Jefferson," she wrote. Assuming he had Kohn's support, Garrison wrote that "the Attorney General has been playing the old shell game. He has said that he is ready to act if the courts order him to do so, knowing, it would appear, that there is no matter before the courts which would cause them to order him to do anything."

Garrison seized the offensive, attacking Gremillion for not moving against organized crime "in a number of Louisiana Parishes…he cannot look into the flourishing rackets of Jefferson," Garrison said sarcastically, because "it would not be proper."

In May, Jim told a group called "Students For Better Government" that he planned to run in the December 1963 primary for Attorney General. John McKeithen, the gubernatorial candidate, running against Chep Morrison, among others, made a public announcement that he was thinking of adding Jim Garrison to his ticket. On June 3rd, Garrison formally announced: "Louisiana…having had something of a vacancy in the post…needs an attorney general. I am applying for the job."

Jim Garrison had made his share of political enemies. Adrian Duplantier, now a powerful State Senator, beckoned McKeithen one day in the corridor of the Montelone Hotel on Royal Street. McKeithen, who was from the north of the state, and in search of New Orleans support, told Duplantier that he was considering putting Jim Garrison on his ticket.

"There's one problem in supporting Jim Garrison," Duplantier told McKeithen. "He might win." When McKeithen demanded an explanation, Duplantier told him that Jim Garrison was a loose cannon whose grandstanding was alarming. You never knew what he would do next.

"I understand," John McKeithen said.

Garrison was well aware that the newspapers would not support his candidacy unless he had a better relationship with the police. His quarrels with Schiro and Giarrusso were far from over, and everyone knew it. On June 6th, Jim Garrison announced that he might enter the race for attorney general – as an independent.

It would not be easy. Gremillion was corrupt – he would ultimately go to prison for lying to a grand jury. He was ignorant, prompting McKeithen to joke that he didn't know "of anything else to do but shoot him." At this, Gremillion offered to meet him on the steps of the Capitol at high noon! But Gremillion was entrenched in the mire of Louisiana politics, and would not be easy to dislodge. He had been in office since Earl Long's 1955 campaign. That year he was voted by his fellow attorneys general as "the nation's most outstanding attorney general."

Apparently Jim Garrison had no desire to be Louisiana's attorney general, or he thought he might lose. On August 12th, he withdrew from the race. "I do not consider the incumbent competent," he said, "and I hope someone runs and beats him." He preferred to remain in the district attorney's office "after the progress we have made." He knew perfectly well, as did everyone else, that district attorney of Orleans Parish was a far more powerful position than attorney general of the state of Louisiana, strange as that may seem.

"I dislike politics – especially old time machine politics," Garrison added. This was true, and always would be.

Garrison now threw his considerable influence behind John McKeithen. McKeithen was director of the Third Public Service Commission District. He was a nobody, sixth in a field of nine candidates. Among them was a local yokel named the Reverend Clyde Johnson, running as an independent. In that incestuous cauldron of Louisiana politics, Johnson would become a major witness as Jim Garrison prepared his case against Clay Shaw.

John McKeithen was a tall, lanky, rigid-looking, hatchet-faced Protestant with big wood-chopper hands. He affected the role of the ignorant country boy, having been born in the hamlet of Grayson. McKeithen cultivated the persona of a man of the people, champion of the poor. Dressed to the nines in a two-thousand dollar suit, he would ask potential supporters, "Won't you he'p me?"

J. Marshall Brown, a New Orleans insurance man who dabbled in politics and served on the State Board of Education, was McKeithen's actual first recruit. Brown then talked to Jim Garrison, and the two agreed that Chep Morrison could not win. Yet McKeithen was given little chance. His only asset was that he was a protégé of Earl Long.

At once, McKeithen dissociated himself from the "tyranny" of Washington, an appropriate move in a place where states' rights was the political norm. "I say throw off the yoke and tell Washington that you, too, stand for Louisiana and against dictatorship in America," McKeithen challenged his opponents.

McKeithen stood firm against civil rights legislation and despised John F. Kennedy. This gained him the support of Guy Banister, who took out a full-page ad to denounce Chep Morrison as an "integrationist." McKeithen ran out of money and so took a campaign contribution of $5,000 from Louisiana reserves colonel Erbon Wise. In exchange, if McKeithen were elected, Wise would become head of the Louisiana National Guard with the rank of Adjutant General. Years later, Governor Edwin Edwards would sell the same post for $25,000.

Garrison joined the fray with energy and enthusiasm in what seems like a replay of his campaign to make Wilmer Thomas president of the Tulane law school student body. Chep Morrison, the front runner, had been his mentor, but Garrison learned of a deal Morrison had forged with Richard Dowling. Running for a judgeship in 1960, Dowling had dropped out of the run-off in exchange for a pledge of support for his re-election from Morrison. Morrison apparently had not been loyal to Jim Garrison. Jim had attended a November 1962 Morrison cocktail party marking the beginning of Morrison's entry into the 1964 gubernatorial race, but this bespoke no commitment.

The received wisdom remained that no one from Catholic New Orleans could gain enough state-wide support to be elected governor of Louisiana. Morrison could not win, and Garrison was more than ready to move on.

"Come to Antoine's and meet the next governor of Louisiana!" Jim told Bob Haik, as he invited him to lunch.

"Who is he?" Haik asked. When he heard the unfamiliar name, Haik was incredulous.

"Are you crazy?" Haik told Jim Garrison. Only twelve people showed up for that lunch. A woman judge named Anna Levy gave a party for "the next governor, John McKeithen," and the Morrison people were astonished. Only five people turned up at that party, among them Jim Garrison, lawyer Clarence Dupuy and Marshall Brown. Jim Garrison was so active for John McKeithen that some wondered whether they had entered into a secret agreement that should U. S. Senator Allen Ellender not serve out his term, Jim Garrison would be appointed as his replacement. McKeithen's New Orleans campaign manager was Garrison friend Willard E. Robertson.

On November 15th, Jim Garrison took out a full-page advertisement in the "Times-Picayune." It was titled: "Why I believe John McKeithen Is The Man For Governor – Jim Garrison." Garrison names McKeithen's opponents only as "X" and "Y" (who has run for governor twice, and was obviously Morrison), and whom Garrison pauses to attack personally: "This man wears blinders so that he doesn't have to look at Washington." "Z" was a Long relative named Gillis Long.

McKeithen aide Gus Weill had to admire Garrison then: should Chep Morrison have been elected governor, Weill thought, he would have gone after Jim Garrison with an ax.

For his victory, John McKeithen awarded full credit to Jim Garrison. "More than anybody else, Jim was my only ally in the primary," he said. "He got me into the run-off." But McKeithen's coat tails were weak, and Jim Garrison was to treat him with irony in the coming years. One day Garrison told the office switchboard operator that he wasn't taking any calls, "not even if it's Jesus Christ." An hour later, McKeithen called.

"Governor McKeithen," the operator said, "If he's not going to take a call from Jesus Christ, I know he's not going to take a call from you."

The attacks on Pershing Gervais did not abate. On May 10th, Jim had told a student group that Gervais had, after all, been recommended for the job by the Metropolitan Crime Commission. Kohn at once denied it, and pressed for public clarification. "That's the first ultimatum I've had in some time," Garrison said haughtily. But in a press release of June 25th, Garrison had to admit the truth: "The Crime Commission neither cleared nor made recommendations for appointments to this office." Gervais was not mentioned by name.

Pershing Gervais flew to California on a bribe-tainted extradition. That particularly virulent abortionist Frances Welch had murdered a twenty-four-year-old woman, then had headed west. Welch had been arrested in Richard Dowling's time, only for Dowling to sit on the case. This same Frances Welch was the reason Raymond Comstock had helped Jim Garrison in his campaign.

Comstock prided himself on his rectitude. Observing how corrupt bail bondsman Nick Christiana had, in the early days, become a habitué of Jim Garrison's office, Comstock had warned Pershing: "You're surrounding yourself with assholes." "I wouldn't imagine even Carlos [Marcello] associating with a man of his caliber," Comstock said, referring to Christiana.

Now Comstock watched what was going on in the office. He concluded that too often Jim Garrison took Pershing's advice over that of Frank Klein. Without Pershing, Comstock thought, Jim Garrison would have made a great district attorney: "He had those stinking judges on the run." Comstock knew: Judge Platt continued to make deals with defendants and lawyers in his chambers. You could buy an allotment to Section B by paying the Deputy Clerk. In Section E, Judge Cocke was acquitting 98 per cent of misdemeanor cases without a jury trial.

To summarize: Comstock had first arrested Frances Welch in 1958 when he seized her note book listing 1,530 abortion payments between April of 1957 and October of 1958 alone. After one month in Garrison's office, he had arrested a man named Frank Dane, who was helping Welch evade charges. "Let's try the Welch case," Comstock had urged. Nothing was done. In March of 1964, only when a woman died, was Welch charged with manslaughter and seven counts of abortion.

Comstock was furious, and consumed with guilt. "I busted that nigger wench," he said later. In 1964, two years after Comstock first arrested her, Welch had finally killed one of the women on whom she performed her abortions. Had Dowling prosecuted Welch, and had Garrison, her twenty-four-year-old victim would have lived.

Garrison assistant Herman Kohlman pleaded, unconvincingly, Comstock thought, that the Welch case files were missing and witnesses were refusing to cooperate. Comstock seethed. Then Pershing brought Welch back and split the reward money given to him by the bail bondsman, Chris Baum, with the police officers involved. Comstock took his $150, went home and ate his supper. Then he got into his car, drove to Pershing's house, and handed him back the money.

"You deserve it," Pershing said.

"I hate everything Chris Baum stands for," Comstock said. "I can't take his money."

I'm also taking $150, Pershing volunteered. Comstock did not believe him. No one would believe that Pershing would take so little.

Later Jim Garrison told Richard Billings: "we put every one of the abortionists in the penitentiary." Over the years of his first term as district attorney, he did convict Juliette Pailet and Mrs. Ann Corinne Sharp, who killed a woman in a botched abortion the month Garrison entered office. Sharp had evaded the law for years as every one of her sentences was commuted by Governor Earl Long. Jim Garrison had to request help from Aaron Kohn. "Judging from her past method of operation," Garrison wrote Kohn, "It is safe to presume that she has not gone into total retirement." In the Sharp case, nearly nineteen months elapsed between one judgment imposing sentence - for Sharp's killing a nineteen year old girl, on November 12, 1963 - and any action being taken.

Arrested for "criminal abortion" in October 1962, Juliette Pailet had referred to herself as a "midwife." Lawyer John E. Lanne was accused of making an extortion payment to a woman on whom Mrs. Pailet had performed an abortion, and of not reporting a crime, the abortion, of which he had knowledge. One day Pailet arrived in court bearing a doctor's note stating that she was in an "acute psychotic phase." Her lawyer was F. Irvin Dymond.

Jim Garrison demanded that Judge Schulingkamp recuse himself, while Dymond also asked Schulingkamp to recuse himself because he was "catering" to Jim Garrison. He "feels that the good will of the district attorney is essential to his political career," Dymond said. Everyone knew Judge Schulingkamp despised Garrison, but rhetoric prevailed. A Kohn spy found that Pailet, far from being too ill to stand trial, was ensconced at Touro Infirmary where she spent long hours on the telephone.

It was not easy to convict Juliette Pailet, even with Milton Brener as prosecutor. The trial began on September 26, 1963. Pailet rolled into court in a wheelchair. She administered only pain pills, Dymond insisted. Milton Brener termed Pailet the operator of a lucrative racket "dealing in misery." He put Raymond Comstock on the stand. And even as she was on trial, Pailet continued to perform abortions.

When Garrison's office indicted Lanne, Judge Brahney dismissed the indictment. Lanne was under "no legal duty" to arrest and charge Pailet, he ruled, even as Lanne knew of her illegal activities. Undaunted, accompanied by Guy Banister, Lanne showed up at the FBI field office to complain about a wire tap put on Pailet's telephone by the New Orleans police department.

Eventually, Pailet was sentenced by Judge Schulingkamp to seven years at hard labor at the Louisiana State Penitentiary at Angola. When Governor Jimmie H. Davis, John McKeithen's predecessor, gave her a ninety day reprieve, Jim Garrison threw up his hands. "Governor Davis may call it an act of 'human kindness' if he wishes, but it looks like an old-fashioned fix," Garrison said. Pailet would serve less than two years.

In his ten point program suggesting new legislation, Jim Garrison had proposed changing the law so that people killing women in abortions could be charged with murder instead of manslaughter. Because the current law required that the person testifying be an actual victim, and to have been pregnant, Garrison proposed removing the word "pregnant" from the statute to permit the use of undercover policewomen. This bill passed.

Two years after he joined the district attorney's office, Raymond Comstock resigned. He was skeptical even about allowing Bourbon Street clubs to change their operations and re-open, as Jim Garrison was permitting them to do. "We had them on the run and we were winning. There wasn't any use in stopping," Comstock told Kohn later. After the padlocking of "Guys & Dolls" in March 1964, the Bourbon Street campaign ended.

"I understand you're leaving. You're welcome back any time," Garrison told Comstock.

"Thanks," Comstock said, expressionless and nothing if not taciturn. Jim Garrison did not ask Comstock why he was leaving. Comstock offered no explanation.

Despite the presence of Pershing Gervais, the accomplishments of Jim Garrison's office were considerable. Assistant district attorneys now had to work full-time; none could remain in private practice as of September 1, 1963, and Milton Brener left. The courts began to do business on Fridays. The number of inmates awaiting trial in Parish Prison was reduced. There was stricter foreclosure on bail bonds. Jim Garrison even called for raising the salaries of the judges on the Criminal Court of Orleans Parish to the level of other judges in the Parish. He wanted more money for the "under-staffed Legal Aid Bureau."

Accepting a Kohn suggestion, Garrison instituted a policy where he had to be notified any time an assistant or investigator was contacted by anyone other than the attorney of record regarding a case. He issued a press release: in contrast to the final year of the Dowling administration, which tried 70 cases and lost 42, Garrison's office had tried 101 cases and won 86.

Yet Jim Garrison remained frustrated by New Orleans politics. In a 1964 speech before a District Attorneys' conference on "Reform Versus Inertia," Garrison said that the major obstacle to law enforcement was not criminals as much as it was "good people, who, not being accustomed to change, have difficulty recognizing progress when it finally appears."

CHAPTER 10:

From Dombrowski To Dealey Plaza

"There are no meetings for him to go to because if he is a Communist, he's the only one in the city!"
Jim Garrison

New Orleans had been the largest city in the Confederacy. In 1963, nine years after the Brown v. Board of Education decision mandating integration of the public schools, Plessy v. Ferguson, the 1896 Louisiana case accepting the standard that school facilities be "separate but equal," was alive and well. If the ante-bellum way of life was to fade in Louisiana, it would not come without a bitter struggle.

Jack Rogers, counsel to the Louisiana Un-American Activities Committee, together with a state representative up for re-election named James Pfister, came up with a strategy to postpone the inevitable. If efforts for integration could be exposed as riddled with Communism and with Communist agendas, integration would be dealt, if not a death's blow, then, at the least, a crippling setback.

Behind this effort was Senator James Eastland of neighboring Mississippi, who chaired the U. S. Senate Internal Security Subcommittee. At the behest of Chep Morrison, Guy Banister had testified before the Louisiana Un-American Activities committee in the hope of being hired by Eastland. "The Negro race is not capable of the leadership or organizations for sit-ins," Banister had declared in 1960, shortly before the election of John F. Kennedy. Communists were surely at the head of the civil rights movement.

As he called for an exposure of "subversive influence in the state," Banister helped to lay the groundwork for what would become the

"Dombrowski case." The immediate task was to demonstrate that those financing civil rights activity in Louisiana were in fact Communists, people taking their orders from the Kremlin. Jack Rogers, James Pfister and Senator Eastland were encouraged in their efforts by FBI director J. Edgar Hoover himself.

The Southern Conference Educational Fund, operating out of New Orleans, and led by a man named James Dombrowski, was indeed helping to finance the work of Dr. Martin Luther King, Jr. If he wasn't a member of the Communist Party, it must also be said, Dombrowski was a sympathizer. Under the U.S. Constitution, this was not a crime. Yet James Dombrowski would be arrested, along with two lawyers, Benjamin E. Smith and Bruce Waltzer, under a newly enacted Louisiana law against subversion called the "Subversive Activities and Communist Control Law."

It was not a law evenly applied. No one in Louisiana suggested that a young man named Lee Harvey Oswald, distributing Communist, pro-Castro leaflets asking for "Fair Play For Cuba" on the streets of New Orleans during the summer of 1963, be charged with subversive activities. Nor was it that the Joint Committee On Un-American Activities of the Louisiana legislature could claim that they did not know about Oswald and his leafleting.

They heard testimony about Oswald from a former Naval Intelligence officer named Robert Morris, who stated that the "Fair Play For Cuba Committee" was "Communist-financed, Castro-financed [it wasn't]...Communist-controlled and Communist-directed." It was aimed, Morris elaborated, on getting the United States to "do nothing about Castro," even as he would soon be a "direct military threat." Of course, "Fair Play" had nothing to do with the unholy mixing of the races. Communism was not really the fear – it was that the very idea of white and black people living and working side by side confounded many in Louisiana.

It should also be said that tarring the civil rights movement with Communist influence and control was not unique to Louisiana. The FBI pressed President Kennedy to separate Martin Luther King, Jr. from two of his most valuable associates, men with Communist Party affiliations, Stanley Levison and Hunter Pitts ("Jack") O'Dell. Kennedy demanded that King break relations with these advisors. In an infamous walk with Dr. King in the White House Rose Garden, Kennedy whispered, "They're Communists. You've got to get rid of them." No foreigner to red-baiting, Kennedy said at one point, "King is so hot these days it's like Marx coming to the White House." A Cold War liberal, he didn't like it.

Jim Garrison, whose profound belief in the first amendment made the Subversive and Communist Control Law anathema, was duty-bound to enforce it. He had only just refused to charge the Doubleday bookstore for violating obscenity laws by selling "Another Country." Now he was faced with arresting the Dombrowski defendants, who were residents of Orleans Parish.

On October 4th, 1963, Jack P. F. Gremillion set the Dombrowski case in motion. Armed with warrants signed by Judge Thomas M. Brahney, and charging "criminal conspiracy," the Louisiana State Police raided the Southern Conference Educational Fund headquarters on Perdido Street in New Orleans. Assisting were Major Russell Willie, director of the State Police Bureau of Identification and Investigation, and Major Presley J. Trosclair, chief of the Intelligence Division of the New Orleans Police.

The Congress of Racial Equality (CORE) had worked hard in Louisiana during the summer of 1963 to mount a significant voter registration drive. In August, Willie had used electric "cattle prodders" on CORE demonstrators to make them stop singing "We Shall Overcome."

James Dombrowski was arrested at gun point, in the process the police pulling apart his aluminum crutches. The homes of Dombrowski and lawyers Benjamin Smith and Bruce Waltzer were raided. Included among the bounty yielded by these raids: a letter to President Kennedy requesting that he appoint an African-American to the United States Supreme Court (Kennedy's one appointee would be a conservative Republican, Byron "Whizzer" White; the first African American on the Court would be Thurgood Marshall, appointed by Lyndon Johnson); a photograph of Dr. Martin Luther King, Jr. in the company of James Dombrowski; a cancelled check for $167.74 made out to King for New York expenses; evidence that Mrs. Edith Stern, who owned WDSU television, a highly respectable figure and hardly a Communist or Communist-sympathizer – she would go on to become one of Clay Shaw's most enthusiastic advocates – had contributed $5,000 to the SCEF; and a letter to James Dombrowski from one of his supporters, Carl Braden, who suggests that the pressure put on King by President

Kennedy to rid himself of known Communists in his movement, people like Jack O'Dell, "helps to explain why he [King] has been ducking us."

Dombrowski, Smith and Waltzer were charged with three offenses. One was "participation in the management of a subversive organization." This was an absurdity since the SCEF was not on the Attorney General's list of Communist front organizations. The second was "being a member of a Communist front organization." Third was "remaining in Louisiana for five consecutive days without registering with the Department of Public Safety. It was all bogus; Dombrowski, Smith and Waltzer had done nothing illegal. The new Louisiana law was obviously unconstitutional. And yet, the case proceeded.

Speaking at a meeting of lawyers discussing how to help civil rights workers who had convened in New Orleans the very weekend of the arrests, Benjamin Smith was indignant. They were being called "Communists" because they were for "the moral right of Negroes to be free," Smith said. "If you want to call me a name, call me an integrationist!"

For his defense, Dombrowski hired Milton Brener, now in private practice. Brener argued before Judge Cocke that the seized materials demonstrated no illegal activity, and that the entire raid was illegal. Brener pointed out that the items seized were not even the same materials spelled out in the search warrants. He cross-examined Jack Rogers, who was testifying as an expert witness for the prosecution.

Brener inquired whether Dombrowski had advocated the violent overthrow of the government, as the Smith Act specified you had to do to be declared "subversive." Dombrowski supported "identified Communists," Rogers replied, ignoring the question. An honest answer would have put an end to the entire charade. Throughout, the Kennedys remained silent, although they could have challenged the entire Dombrowski prosecution under the 1957 Civil Rights Act.

Judge Cocke ordered Dombrowski, Smith and Waltzer released on the ground of insufficient evidence. His quarrels with Jim Garrison notwithstanding, Judge J. Bernard Cocke was an able and fair jurist.

Jim Garrison had not been informed in advance of the raids. Nor was he even aware of what the Un-American Activities Committee was up to, although he was well acquainted with Jack Rogers. (Mayor

Schiro and Governor Jimmie H. Davis had been informed). The New Orleans FBI field office was not notified of the raids either. It wasn't that the Committee did not have confidence in Mr. Hoover, Rogers later explained. It was because "we have no confidence whatsoever" in Hoover's boss, Attorney General Robert F. Kennedy. Jim Garrison read about the Dombrowski raids in the newspapers.

On a historic WDSU radio symposium held on October 31, 1963, "Conversation Carte Blanche," Jim Garrison appeared, along with James Pfister, Jack Rogers and the three Dombrowski defendants. Garrison speaks only at the conclusion of the broadcast, praising Judge Cocke's dismissal of the charges. This was "correct," Garrison said. His own role, by law, was to "represent the State's interest." Since he had no evidence against the defendants, Garrison made clear, he had merely gone "through the formality of a hearing where there was no evidence to present." Nor did he expect that evidence against the Dombrowski defendants was likely to emerge. Garrison adds that he is "satisfied with the procedure as far as the legality of the seizing of the documents" is concerned.

This bold move by the Louisiana Un-American Activities Committee struck fear into the hearts of all public officials, Jim Garrison not excluded. He had been blindsided, and at first he was cautious. "Speaking as an individual," Garrison said, he could not "feel completely happy about the arrest of the lawyers in the circumstance, or even the other person" [Dombrowski]. "I am very much concerned about the rights of the individual," Garrison added. Under the circumstances, at this historical moment, it was a courageous defense of Dombrowski, Smith and Waltzer.

Later, when he was investigating the murder of President Kennedy, Garrison would call James Dombrowski "the last living genuine liberal in New Orleans." "I don't think he's a Communist," Garrison said, "but he was [for] his time liberal enough…so whenever he gets sick, the FBI sends a doctor over to his house."

Elaborating on the riff, Garrison added, "There are no meetings for him to go to because if he is a Communist, he's the only one in the city." The year was 1968. For sixties Louisiana, this was strong language. "There is always a danger," Garrison said, "particularly in fighting Communism, that we may end up imitating Communism."

Garrison added that he believed that "the Committee overstepped its bounds ordering the arrests." There was no danger that the attorneys "were about to leave town," nor was the information acquired "so new as to require an immediate physical arrest." He repeated what he had said on the radio, that he had not "seen any evidence," once more implying that there was none to see. "This is just my thought as an individual," he felt compelled to add.

As the Dombrowski case made its way through the courts, according to William A. Porteous, representing the district attorney's office, Jim Garrison's strategy was to evade, circumvent and contribute as little as possible to this prosecution as he could. Dombrowski's lawyer, Milton Brener, concurs. The Louisiana State Police had placed the SCEF documents they had seized in their raids into a moving van. Then, in the dead of night, under the command of State Police Colonel Thomas Burbank, the van had been driven over the Louisiana state line to Woodville, Mississippi there to be retrieved by Senator Eastland. Now these materials were in the legal custody of the U.S. Congress.

Garrison filed a motion for a subpoena of the records. He could not proceed, he said, without full possession of the "facts." Examining the search warrants used to invade the homes of the three defendants, Garrison concluded that they were legally defective. "This is a mess," he told Porteous. "How could they have screwed up these search warrants so terribly?" Even the addresses of the defendants were incorrect. It was against the law not to describe exactly what materials were being sought and the state had not done that. Porteous and Garrison both concluded that the warrants must have been written not by a lawyer, but by a clerk for the Joint Legislative Committee.

In a perfunctory attempt to comply with Garrison's subpoena for these records, the state police dumped a bunch of documents at Tulane and Broad. "We're taking this material on advisement," Frank Klein said. Garrison's office was neither accepting nor rejecting the charges against Dombrowski, Smith and Waltzer. The evidence would have to go before the Orleans Parish grand jury.

Klein complained that they had been offered only a small portion of the documents, personal records and papers that had been confiscated. Until all the evidence was turned over by the police, Klein said, no action could be taken. By now he knew full well that the evidence had long departed the state of Louisiana.

Not to be thwarted by the Orleans Parish District Attorney, on November 14th Gremillion convened his own grand jury. Jim Garrison was expected to prosecute Dombrowski, Smith and Waltzer for "violations of the State Communist Control Law." Frank Klein wrote a letter requesting photographs of the documents, only for James Pfister to insist that he had turned everything over, which was false. Judge Malcolm O'Hara now ordered Pfister to turn over copies of the records, demanding, at the same time, that Klein accept them.

As Jim Garrison stalled, the Dombrowski defendants seized the offensive and took their case into federal court. The Louisiana Subversive Activities and Communist Control Law was obviously unconstitutional and they would prove it. At once they gained a temporary injunction from Judge John Minor Wisdom, restraining all state officials, including Jim Garrison, to his relief, from prosecuting Dombrowski, Smith and Waltzer. The Joint Legislative Committee replied that SCEF was a "Communist front and a subversive organization" and demanded that the matter be pursued by the District Attorney of Orleans Parish. "The prosecution is properly in his hands," they declared.

When Judge Wisdom's injunction was dissolved on January 10th, Jim Garrison had no alternative but to have Dombrowski, Smith indicted by the Orleans Parish grand jury. This was done on January 29, 1964. William Porteous thought that Waltzer did not hold it against Jim Garrison's office, and Waltzer in later years agreed that it was "all Gremillion's show."

Porteous emerged with the Pyrhhic victory of enabling the state prosecution of Dombrowski, Smith and Waltzer. In June, Judge Platt ruled that the arrest warrant and the search warrant were illegal, with all the seized material now inadmissible as evidence. More, the DA's office had failed to prove that Dombrowski was a supporter of "identified Communists." Platt ruled that the state had exceeded its authority. Quietly Jim Garrison joined a stipulation with Milton Brener for the return of the documents held by the district attorney's office to James Dombrowski.

In federal court, Judge Ellis wrote for the majority, reinstating the case against the Dombrowski defendants, and citing, among others, Thomas Jefferson. John Minor Wisdom wrote valiantly in dissent:

> "States' rights" are mystical, emotion-laden words. For me, as for most Southerners, the words evoke visions of the hearth and defense of the homeland and carry the sound of bugles and the beat of drums. But the crowning glory of American federalism is not

> "States' Rights." It is the protection the United States Constitution gives to the private citizen against all wrongful governmental invasion of fundamental rights and freedoms.

Judge Wisdom declared forthrightly that Louisiana was abusing the law by "punishing the plaintiffs for their advocacy of civil rights of Negroes." He noted that Communism had nothing to do with it.

Jim Dombrowski's chief counsel in federal court, legendary civil rights lawyer, Arthur Kinoy, argued that the Louisiana statutes violated the first, fourth, eighth and fourteen amendments, and the fundamental guarantees of free speech, press, assembly and the right to petition the government for a redress of grievances. He named Jim Garrison as a defendant, individually and as district attorney, for violation of the defendants' rights.

The United States Supreme Court granted certiorari and Porteous had to argue for "the appellee Garrison and his responsibility for the indictments." In his defense of Jim Garrison, Porteous had to defend the doctrine of states' rights: "Can we deny the State the basic right of self-preservation?"

Louise Korns authored an apologetic brief "pro se" on behalf of Garrison. No charges against Dombrowski, Smith and Waltzer had been accepted from the police, no affidavits sworn out in the Clerk's office, and "in a spirit of comity and through agreement between the district attorney and the three defendants, all state court proceedings had been held in abeyance since June 15, 1964." She requests that the U.S. Supreme Court pass on the constitutionality of the Louisiana statute.

When the Dombrowski case went before the U.S. Supreme Court, during argument, Chief Justice Earl Warren had a question: "How many Communists would you have to find to make it [SCEF] Communist-infiltrated?"

As he had Garrison v. Louisiana, so now Justice William Brennan authored the Dombrowski opinion, one in favor of the defendants. Louisiana's subversive law was so "sweeping," Justice Brennan says, "as to impair the constitutional right to free expression." Worse, the law had been applied in "bad faith," and "entirely for the motive of deferring the appellants' civil rights efforts." The Dombrowski prosecutions had "a chilling effect upon First Amendment rights." Freedom of expression, Justice Brennan argued, had a "transcendent value to all society, beyond even to those exercising their rights; the very society would be the loser." One case Justice Brennan cited was Garrison v. Louisiana, Jim Garrison's defense of his right to criticize the Criminal Court judges.

Two weeks later, thumbing their noses at what Louisiana citizens call the "fed," the Louisiana State Senate, an "entirely corrupt body" according to Governor McKeithen's former aide, John Tarver, voted to retain the Joint Legislative Committee on Un-American Activities by a vote of 37 to 2. That the Dombrowski prosecutions had been in conscious and knowing bad faith is demonstrated in a letter from Senator Eastland to the Director of the Mississippi State Sovereignty Commission, a body devoted to thwarting efforts at integration and African American voting rights. "The staff advises me that they have nothing on these people," Eastland writes, referring to Dombrowski, Smith and Waltzer. The entire Dombrowski case had been a cynical fishing expedition.

As for Jim Garrison, Milton Brener reiterates that Garrison did the "absolute minimum." Brener does not fault the district attorney's office for its role in the Dombrowski case. William Porteous agrees: Jim Garrison's duty under the law was to defend the constitutionality of the state statute, which amounted to his proceeding with the indictments.

Arthur Kinoy dissents. In an interview with the author shortly before his death, Kinoy maintained that Jim Garrison could have done much less; he could have challenged the newly minted Communist subversive laws or simply not charged Dombrowski, Smith and Waltzer, compelling Gremillion to reinstate the charges. For veteran civil rights lawyer Kinoy, Jim Garrison was just another district attorney in the deep South. Given the fire emanating from Baton Rouge, it seems clear that only the United States Supreme Court, and the liberal Warren Court at that, could have prevailed.

A little more than a month after the arrests of Dombrowski, Smith and Waltzer, President John F. Kennedy was shot in Dallas. After interviewing Lee Harvey Oswald's New Orleans mentor, David Ferrie, Garrison turned the investigation of the President's death over to the FBI, and the Secret Service.

By 1964, the crime rate in New Orleans had risen at a rate triple the national average. Murders had increased by 34%. Jim Garrison began a war on two fronts: against crime and against the entrenched New Orleans political establishment, which profited from crime too profoundly not to resist change. "People worry about the crime 'syndicate,'" Garrison said, "but the real danger is the political establishment, power massing against the individual."

Garrison began by accusing the state of operating a "supermarket of paroles." Beginning in the spring of 1963 through 1964, he pursued the issue of "quickie paroles," an arena for bribery and graft. Convicted felons were purchasing paroles even before they had begun to serve their sentences. Garrison's test case involved three drug dealers named James Martin, Sidney Hebert and John J. Scardino, who had kidnapped and beat up an undercover narcotics squad officer. Martin and Hebert paid a bribe of $3,500, served twenty-eight days, and were soon trolling the Quarter, courtesy of a parole dispensed by Governor Jimmie Davis. Left behind in Angola to serve a prior conviction, Scardino spilled the beans.

Knowing he could expect no relief from corrupt politicians, Garrison again appealed to public opinion in the Louisiana tradition of Huey and Earl Long. No one notices you unless you do things that excite the public, Garrison remarked to assistant John Volz. It was a blood and guts school of politics, epitomized by Opelousas-born Jim Bowie, who fought a duel out on a sand bar in the middle of the Mississippi River before he moved to Texas and covered himself in glory at the Alamo.

Even when you gained a conviction, Garrison discovered, there was no guarantee of how much of the sentence would be served. "The use – and users – of political paroles," he complained, "present a tremendous enforcement problem." Scardino's testimony against his confederates warranted a press conference.

The parole board, Garrison accused, had turned "loose upon the city of New Orleans hardened criminals convicted of every conceivable offense – including possession of a sub-machine gun, white slavery, selling narcotics and cutting off a man's head!" He refused to attend a state parole board hearing, calling it "a wily, serpentine evasion of action," and termed the crime of Martin and Hebert "an assassination plot" against the policeman they had kidnapped and assaulted. He accused the Louisiana Pardon Board of "unleashing…a small army of convicted career criminals onto the community."

Garrison applied for an open hearing so that the public might hear his allegations of malfeasance, public bribery and "corrupt influencing" along with "conspiracy to commit such offenses on the part of the state parole board."

Such public hearings were rare, and Garrison's request landed on the desk of Judge Edward A. Haggerty. Garrison stepped up his pressure. He might, he threatened, mischievously, "even request help from the Attorney General (if you will excuse the expression)." When it came to Jack P. F. Gremillion, Jim Garrison could not resist irony.

Haggerty agreed, and Garrison immediately subpoenaed Governor Jimmie Davis, who evaded service by having his cook, Magnolia, accept the summons. All five members of the parole board were subpoenaed. They begged the Louisiana Supreme Court to stop the hearing, to no avail. Among their many motions was one to remove the press and the public from attending the hearing.

"Democracies in general prefer open proceedings and are suspicious of a closed one," Garrison said dryly.

At the hearing, Jim Garrison himself conducted the questioning of the parole board members. "When did you start taking bribes?" he demanded of Warren C. Holden, chairman of the board. It was a Louisiana hayride. At one point, Garrison accused lawyer Monk Zelden of signaling to a witness. Garrison suggested that Zelden not be permitted to sit in the defense counsel's chair, and Haggerty agreed. Ignoring Zelden's protests, Garrison counted off the names of all the repeat offenders who had been paroled.

Testifying on April 3rd, John J. Scardino revealed the scale for the purchase of paroles; it ranged from $500 to $1,500.

Three times in three days, the hearing was recessed to await a Supreme Court decision on a defense motion. Why didn't the parole board simply correct "the miscarriage of justice which they brought about by their indefensible release of Martin and Hebert?" Garrison demanded.

Garrison asked Judge Haggerty to call the next witness. "This witness may be waiting in the hall to testify, your honor," Garrison said, tongue in cheek. "I suggest that he be called." For dramatic effect, Garrison then busied himself searching through a sheaf of his papers. Then he came up with the name.

"His name is Davis – Jimmie H. Davis," Garrison reported.

The Governor was, of course, not in the building.

On the stand, Martin admitted that he had been told the day after he was sentenced that he could buy a quickie parole. Had he applied for this parole even before he was sentenced? Garrison asked. Martin then requested the privilege of the fifth amendment.

"Perhaps 'paroles' is not exactly the word," Garrison told the press. "This is more like a legalized jail-break." Garrison's critics now included Harry Connick, first assistant to the U.S. Attorney, Louis Lacour. If Garrison had anything, he should have put the parole board on trial, Connick, and other of Garrison's detractors, insisted. He knew he couldn't convict anybody. The entire hearing amounted to "an attempt to gain publicity."

Garrison remained impervious. He knew the paroles of Martin and Hebert were the result of a "fix," and laughed at the objection of the parole board that he had attacked the reputations of "respectable citizens and witnesses" without granting them the right to defend themselves.

"The octopus," Garrison said, weaving a variation on his squid metaphor, "when on the defensive ejects a stream of black, inky fluid which obscures and confuses the observer. The parole board has used the same technique." Martin and Hebert had meanwhile continued "in the flamboyant enjoyment of their freedom." Nor did it bother Garrison when he was attacked by John Fournet, the Chief Justice of the Louisiana Supreme Court.

"If bringing out the truth about this Board's disservice is harassment," he replied, "then perhaps we have." To the charge that the parole board hearing had been a fishing expedition," he replied, "the thrashing and turbulence indicates that we have caught hold of a very large fish."

Garrison's support came from the public. The Retail Merchants Bureau praised his office for enforcing the "bad check" laws. The "States-Item" approved of his effort to get rid of the quickie paroles in an editorial entitled "The 'Railroaded' Paroles." When the Supreme Court sent down guidelines ("a fantastic new galaxy of ground rules"), Garrison lamented that "this is probably the last open hearing that will ever be attempted in Louisiana."

Garrison's attack on the structure of corruption in Louisiana was as much literary as political. Replying to criticism from the Criminal Courts Bar Association, he invaded the animal kingdom to develop one of his most felicitous conceits:

> Their righteous concern now about the open hearing on quick pardons is that of foxes who are denouncing a proposed investigation into the disappearance of chickens from the hen-house. Naturally, the objection of the foxes to such an investigation is based – in their public statements – on the loftiest of reasons: The inquiry may be bad for the health of the chickens, it may unnecessarily disturb the other animals on the farm and it is an outrageous violation of barnyard etiquette.
> But behind the state's reasons for the foxes' objections to the henhouse of investigation is the simple fact that foxes like the taste of chicken.
> If it were not for the foxes, there would be no missing chickens.

Thirteen lawyers resigned from the Criminal Courts Bar Association over this issue. Iris Kelso wrote in the "States-Item" that Garrrison had "focused the public's and the legislature's attention on law enforcement legislation as a means of combating crime." Herman Deutsch, brother of Garrison's mentor Eberhard Deutsch, wrote that Jim Garrison was not only certain of re-election, but was in a position for "escalating what has begun as an exceptionally promising career."

John McKeithen was inaugurated on May 12, 1964, replacing Jimmie Davis. He declared he was "anxious to get District Attorney Garrison's suggestions and recommendations on revision of the state's parole and pardon system." Jim Garrison had done more than anyone to put him in office, a fact of which McKeithen was, more often than not, mindful.

McKeithen offered Jim Garrison a bank charter, which would have made him a rich man. Garrison instructed Louise Korns to research a memo, "Obtaining A Charter For A State Bank." Korns produced a document that outlines how to apply to the banking commissioner for a certificate of authority to open a new bank. The application had to include setting out the qualifications and standing of the persons organizing the bank, the economic need of the area for a new bank, and the availability of federal deposit insurance. It all seemed too complex, too time-consuming – and boring. Money was of no interest to Jim Garrison anyway. He turned down the extraordinary opportunity.

Incredulous, John McKeithen tried to persuade him to accept the offer. "We'll do it together," he promised.

"I don't have time," Garrison said. Marshall Brown happily accepted the charter and later sold it for $750,000.

One day when Garrison was visiting McKeithen, a call came in from the Attorney General of Arkansas to discuss the formation of a loan company, to be called the Louisiana Loan and Thrift.

"How'd you like to represent a new business?" McKeithen said, anxious to help Garrison in any way. Garrison had to explain that he had made a campaign promise not to maintain a private law practice. Garrison recommended Representative Salvador Anzelmo in his place. Ultimately the Louisiana Loan and Thrift Company would be indicted for selling bond investment certificates without registering them with the SEC, and for corruption and various other species of fraud and the misappropriation of funds.

McKeithen thought of yet another way to reward Jim Garrison. McKeithen suggested that Garrison open a law office and staff it with bright young people. Business would flow from the governor's office and from the state. When Garrison left office himself, he would have a prosperous law firm ready and waiting for him. Garrison rejected this idea as well. If money meant nothing to him, the law bored him.

In the summer of 1964, Jim Garrison was named an "At-Large" delegate to the Democratic National Convention in Atlantic City. It was the convention where civil rights leaders, the incomparable Bob Moses and Fannie Lou Hamer, challenged the seating of the official Mississippi delegation. Garrison was suffering from a flu he caught during the annual convention of district attorneys in New York. There was another reason that he remained in Louisiana: The week before the convention, Liz gave birth to their fourth child, Elizabeth.

By October 1964, Garrison boasted of having sixty-seven more convictions than Richard Dowling for a similar period. Garrison enlisted his old law school classmate Warren Garfunkel to compile a statistical chart comparing his regime for its two year period with Dowling's. He had 189 guilty verdicts at trial to Dowling's 122. Cases tried were 244 for Garrison against 195 for Dowling.

Legislation calling for a professionally trained parole board and preventing parole until an inmate served at least a third of his term was proposed by Garrison's adversary Adrian G. Duplantier, and Salvatore J. Anzelmo. Up to that point, the Angola warden had been releasing prisoners who had served only half their sentences. It was commendable of Representative Anzelmo to help "slow down the stampede of ex-cons into New Orleans," Garrison said tartly. Anzelmo would have had a better chance, however, "if he'd filed a bill to send a rocket to the moon loaded with pralines or to make all bail bondsmen honorary colonels."

Garrison was far from pleased by the legislature's response to his efforts against crime. Favors and back-room deals remained a matter of course. The Louisiana legislature now voted down all of Garrison's prison reform bills. "The only way to explain it is wholesale bribery," Garrison charged. The legislature's response was to censure him 39-0 in the Senate and 99-0 in the House. "I am greatly honored," Garrison retorted. "I got even more votes than the bail bondsman bill." Then he added, "The guilty fleeth where no man pursueth."

Back in Orleans Parish, he got two bondsmen to sign affidavits swearing they had been offered $1,000 to assist in the passage of the new bail bond bill – that allowed six months instead of sixty days before a bond was forfeited. This legislature deserves the title "bail-bonding legislature," Garrison taunted his enemies in Baton Rouge. Then he charged bail bondsman Nick Christiana with contempt of the grand jury. That Christiana was known to be close to Carlos Marcello mattered not at all.

From Fort Polk, where he was serving his National Guard duty, Garrison attempted to get the paroles of Martin and Hebert revoked, even enlisting Aaron Kohn, who had approved publicly of Garrison's "muckraking of the Parole Board." Always, Garrison insisted that "structure changes" were required in the parole and pardon system, "a complete reconstruction" of Louisiana's approach to parole and probation. The board was now being run "for the benefit of those with money or influence."

Among his requests of the legislature was that "crimes against nature" be prosecuted, if they were prosecuted at all, without consideration of the background or the position in life of the defendant, by whom he meant those priests who had been escaping with a reprimand. He was a populist in his approach, and did not waver in his support for the underdog. There was talk of his running in 1966 for the U.S. Senate seat held by Allen J. Ellender.

"New Orleans is occupied territory today," Garrison said at the close of 1964, "occupied by an army of ex-cons, armed with everything from

Top: Jim Garrison as District Attorney of Orleans Parish

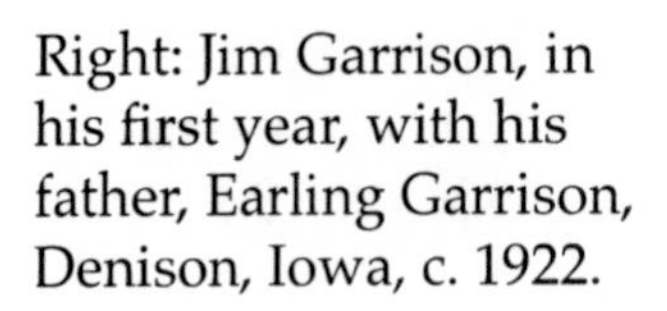

Right: Jim Garrison, in his first year, with his father, Earling Garrison, Denison, Iowa, c. 1922.

Top: Jim Garrison's uncle Edgar Garrison, a judge in the Panama Canal Zone.
Bottom: Garrison in the Army, Garrison is seated at the right of the first row.

Top: Garrison in the Army, standing at left.
Bottom left: Jane Garrison Gardiner in 1962, the year of her son's election as District Attorney of Orleans Parish.
Bottom right: Detail of Garrison at the Tulane School of Law.

Photographs taken by Jim Garrison at Dachau Concentration Camp, the day after Liberation.

Top: Painting of Peggie Baker: “Once you know love, you can’t be satisfied with anything else.”

Bottom: Revels at Fanny’s

Top: James Dombrowski under arrest. Left to right, Carl J. Braden, Lt. Paul Dyer; Detective R. Frey, and Dombroski.

Bottom: Jim Garrison with Governor John J. McKeithen (seated): "Governor McKeithen, if he's not going to take a call from Jesus Christ, I know he's not going to take a call from you…."

Top: Charlie Ward and Pershing Gervais at Tulane and Broad, 1965 c. Times-Picayune.

Bottom: The capture of Leonard Caesar.

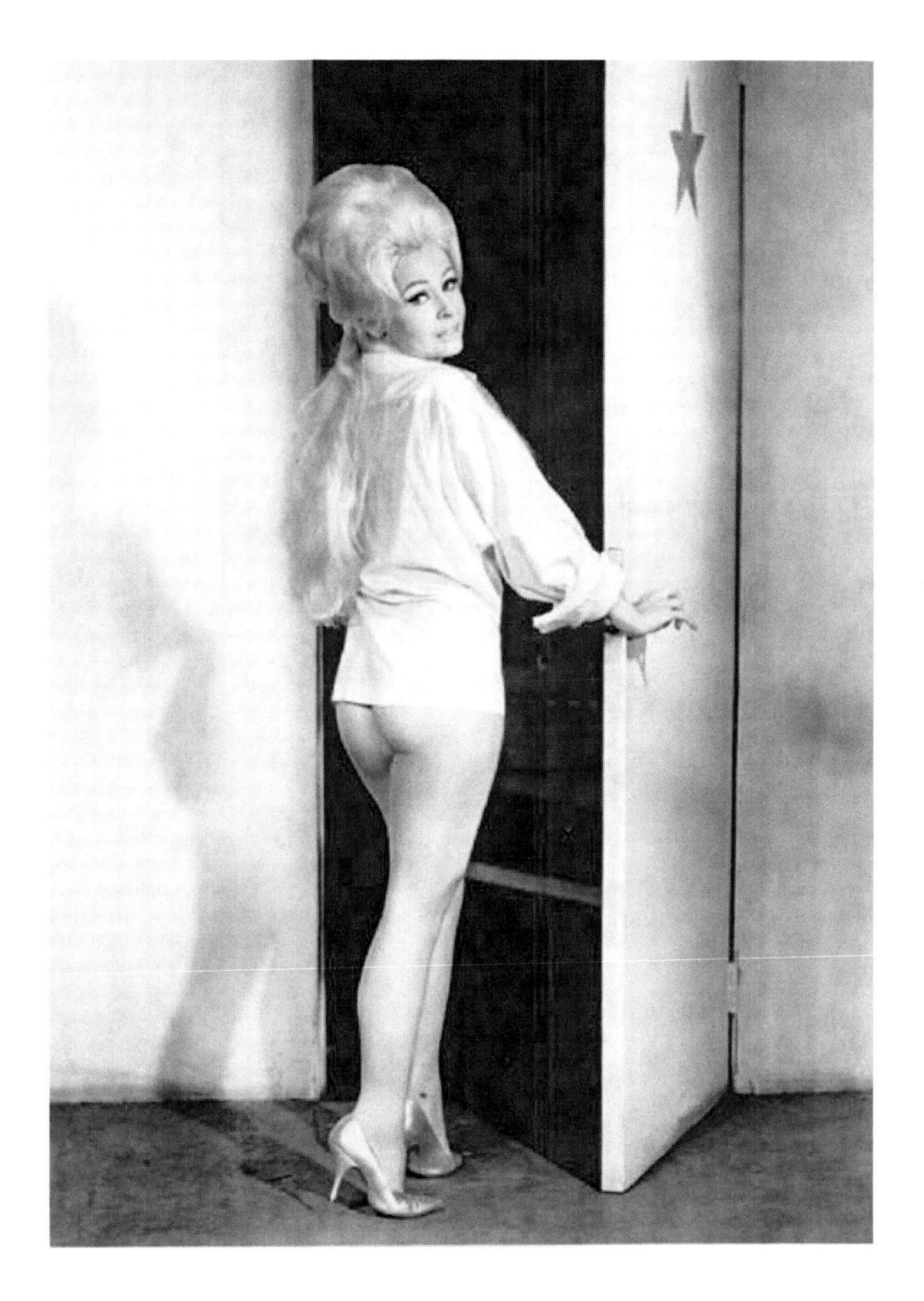

Top: Linda Brigette: "Oh, pardon me!"

Next page, top: Linda Brigette: Counterclockwise: Larry Lamarca, Linda, singer Frankie Laine, Judge Louis P. Trent, Lillian Cohen.

Bottom: Jim Garrison with his lawyer, Donald V. Organ (Garrison v. Louisiana)

Top: Jim Garrison with Jesse Core, c. 1965. Core is at the right.

Right: John R. Rarick; "I have a Constitution to follow."

Top left: Garrison, Liz and baby Eberhard: Photograph by Lynn Pelham. Courtesy of Lynn Pelham and Mrs. Pelham.

Top right: Jim Garrison with his children, Jasper, Virginia, and, foreground, Snapper.

Bottom: Jim Garrison and Phyllis Weinert on their honeymoon, Puerto Rico, 1976

Campaign advertisement, Garrison's 1965 re-election campaign.

switch blade knives to stolen guns." He hammered away at how those appointed to the parole board "are as qualified for that responsibility as apes are to fly jet airliners." This was the high price "of electing ignorant men to high office in Louisiana." John McKeithen appointed a new parole board.

Garrison opened yet another front. He became engaged in a systematic effort to replace the judges of the Orleans Parish Criminal Court, the "sacred cows" who had been his nemeses. Practically, he hoped to break the blockade against expenditures from the fines and forfeitures fund. Personally, he enjoyed the pleasures of king-making. It was the campaign for Wilmer Thomas yet again, writ large.

The common practice was that when there was a vacancy, the new judge would be nominated by the governor. This was a favor Jim Garrison did exact from John McKeithen.

"Who do you want?" McKeithen would call and ask Garrison whenever there was a vacancy. When Shirley G. Wimberly died, Garrison decided to elevate assistant Frank Shea. It seemed a good idea. Shea was an erratic and irascible person who had been so difficult to work with that Garrison had removed him from the fray and made him first, grand jury adviser, and then a special prosecutor. Shea had tried few cases, having been fired by Richard Dowling as soon as Dowling took office.

When Garrison hired him, Shea was virtually starving, living with his family in a prefabricated house in a subdivision off the Chef Menteur Highway. Among his many shortcomings, Shea was an anti-Semite. "You're not going to be happily married to a Jew," Shea told Lou Trent when he was about to tie the knot with lawyer Lillian Cohen.

In keeping with Jim Garrison's practice of never firing an employee if he could help it, and always, instead, finding the untenable employee a better job elsewhere, Jim Garrison severed Frank Shea from his office by making him a judge. It wasn't all that easy. Shea had to run in a field of nine; his chief opponent was Naval Intelligence officer and lawyer, Guy Johnson.

Jim Garrison wrote the advertisement, predicting that Frank Shea would be a "truly independent judge," free "of organizations and assessors." "Independent" voters should choose him. Shea, Garrison wrote in yet another jibe at the sacred cows, favored "recognition of the right of any American citizen to criticize public officials, including judges."

In the run-off, the seven defeated candidates all threw their support to Guy Johnson, who was endorsed by both the "States-Item" and "Times-Picayune" newspapers. Johnson spent more than $50,000; Shea had to take out a small bank loan. Yet such was Jim Garrison's popularity at the time that Garrison scheduled a victory party for Frank Shea in advance of his victory. Shea won by 523 votes, which became 481 once the voting machines were checked.

Garrison declared that he had struck "another blow to the influence of New Orleans' political organizations." He then rewarded Max Gonzales, who had infiltrated Parish Prison as "Joseph Max Lopez," by making him Shea's Minute Clerk. A few years later, as he was about to fly to Havana to meet with Fidel Castro to discuss the Kennedy assassination on Jim Garrison's behalf, Gonzales, an accomplished pilot, would get into a plane and disappear, never to be seen again.

Almost from the day Frank Shea became a judge he stopped talking to Jim Garrison. Garrison's not going to tell me how to run my courtroom, he told people. Annoyed, Garrison changed the locks on the elevators at Tulane and Broad so that the new judge had to send Max Gonzales down to get a key from Charlie Ward. Shea also became a source for reporter Rosemary James, feeding her what dirt he could find on Jim Garrison.

Shea ran three trials a day and prided himself on moving his docket quickly. You couldn't ask a question as he rushed along. Justice was not served.

Finally, thinking better of waging war with Jim Garrison, Shea sent an emissary to ask Jim what he might do to make amends.

"I'll tell you what to tell him," Garrison said, rankled by Shea's blatant ingratitude. "He can go to the front steps of this building, get a five gallon can of gasoline, pour it over himself and light the match."

In later years, when Jim Garrison was practicing law and having a difficult time, Judge Shea maliciously denied him the privilege of using the judge's private bathroom.

In the presence of Bob Haik, Garrison created another judge. "John, now look…." was all Haik heard Garrison say. He was talking on the telephone to John McKeithen, who had never heard of the man.

"He's named Richard Garvey. A wonderful family," Garrison said. "He supported your election."

"He's got it!" Garrison said triumphantly as he hung up. Garvey would serve on the civil court bench for twenty years. "If I can be of any service to you, please do not hesitate to contact me," Garvey wrote Garrison in his thank-you note.

Garrison got William Hawk Daniells a city judgeship in Baton Rouge. He asked Governor McKeithen to appoint Lawrence Chehardy tax assessor for Jefferson Parish, arguing that Chehardy had been McKeithen's friend. Garrison liked Chehardy for his efforts on behalf of the poor, and for his sympathy for people chafing under unreasonably high property taxes. When Chehardy had to run in his own right, the brother of his predecessor opposed him, arguing that "the Jefferson Parish assessorship…does not belong to Mr. Jim Garrison, district attorney of Orleans Parish." Garrison helped in Chehardy's successful campaign, and Chehardy later remembered, "He fought for me!"

In the summer of 1964, J. Bernard Cocke faced the prospect of running for re-election. Judge Cocke was now sixty-six years old and had presided over Section E since 1944. "For my judicial qualifications," Judge Cocke told voters, "I offer a lifetime devoted to the criminal law."

Two weeks later, Jim Garrison's friend, lawyer Matthew S. Braniff, announced his candidacy. Then he walked into Civil District Court and filed a suit to have Cocke declared ineligible to run on the ground of his age. If Judge Cocke was elected to yet another term, he would have served twenty years or more, and been beyond the retirement age of seventy-five. Judge Cocke could retire now on a pension of $12,000, Braniff pointed out.

Jim Garrison's real candidate was not Braniff, who was serving the old Frank Klein function of stalking horse, but Rudolph Becker, Jr., the father of one of Garrison's assistants. Becker was a figure of no particular distinction who had once served five years as an assistant district attorney.

Furious, Cocke retaliated by attacking the younger Becker, who had been assigned to his court. He was holding court every Friday, "yet only nine of the available Fridays had been used by young Becker," Cocke accused. Becker senior replied: "He should debate me openly and not take the sneak's way out by hitting at me through my son."

Becker's campaign advertisements were authored by Jim Garrison, although they were signed as having been paid for by "Matthew S. Braniff, Attorney-at-Law." One bore the motto: "If this be treason, make the most of it." The funniest of the ads was titled, "The Trouble With Kings (Or: Never on Friday)."

"I never cared much for kings, emperors, Kaisers, sultans or czars," Garrison begins. "That's one of the great things about this country – we don't have too many of these around." Garrison elaborated on his Friday conceit. "The only monarch of any note who worked on Friday," Garrison declares, "was King Farouk – but then he took the rest of the week off!" He also poked fun at Cocke's habit of attacking tardy lawyers and defendants. "I am strongly opposed to jail sentences in the Parish Prison for honest citizens who happened to be a few minutes late."

Another advertisement was designed as a petition: "To Arms, To Arms, Citizens Arise. Defend Your Liberty. We Must Stand Together to Depose the Tyrant J. Bernard 'King' Cocke." Using his facility as a cartoonist, Garrison drew the evil king, adding a list of thirteen tyrants: "Captain Bligh seldom flogged except for sound reasons (i. e. arriving three minutes late on the poop deck)." He also writes: "It was untrue that Cesare Borgia poisoned all his guests at a dinner – only a few were poisoned – the rest were stabbed." These tyrants, Garrison adds, were all "greatly misunderstood."

Garrison also enlisted his literary talent. "It's all very well for a king to have a court," he closes, "but no law court should have a king." In another advertisement, he quoted Cocke's own earlier confession: "I haven't worked on Fridays in 15 years and do not intend to change to please Jim Garrison." A Cocke rejoinder was titled "Firm, You Bet," only for Garrison to get his reply into the paper on the very same day.

Around the margins of Garrison's rebuttal, he pictured: Captain Bligh; the viceroy of Bengal; Caligula; Kubla Khan; Cesare Borgia; and Ivan the Terrible. "All regarded themselves as exceedingly fair men," he wrote, "even though they were firm." Again he utilized the joke about lateness. This time Captain Bligh flogged seamen for "arriving ONE minute late on the poop deck." Kubla Khan, he wrote, spent his Fridays in a "stately pleasure dome." Could there have been another politician in the state of Louisiana – or anywhere else – capable of enlisting the English romantic poet Samuel Taylor Coleridge in a campaign advertisement?

In a statement titled "Why I Am Voting For Rudy Becker," Garrison was serious: "Every time an independent judge is elected our Criminal Court moves forward."

In his reply, Cocke attacked not Becker, but Jim Garrison. The election of Becker, Cocke charged, "will wrap up a neat little package through which the district attorney will be the prosecutor and judge alike." Cocke was no match for Garrison in verbal facility.

"It would be impossible for me to become judge as well as prosecutor," Garrison replied," because, unlike J. Bernard Cocke, I have not acquired the habit of taking long summer vacations." When Cocke accused Garrison of forming his own political machine, Garrison said, "As a product of one of the oldest and most powerful political machines in New Orleans history, Judge Cocke certainly should be an expert on the subject."

The "Times-Picayune" endorsed Judge Cocke, who was also supported by three former district attorneys, Severn T. Darden, Leon D. Hubert and Richard A. Dowling. Other Cocke supporters included Adrian Duplantier; James E. Comiskey; future mayor Moon Landrieu; Edward A. Haggerty, father of the judge; and Clarence O. Dupuy, with whom Jim Garrison warred over Governor McKeithen's supply of patronage. (Dupuy insists that as chair of a five-member group of McKeithen supporters he, and not Garrison, was in charge of McKeithen's patronage.)

Rudy Becker defeated Judge Cocke by ten thousand votes. Afterwards, Garrison admitted: "It took a lot of money to beat Dupuy, all those assessors and the old machine politicians were backing Cocke." In the closing days of the campaign, Becker had to borrow money for television spots from the Bank of Louisiana. Jim Garrison's support, he admitted, had been "the decisive factor in my election." So Jim Garrison had the last word against Judge Cocke. The "right to vote public officials out of office" is not "merely a privilege – it is the life and the very soul of our democracy," Garrison said.

Three years later, Jim Garrison found the opportunity to reward Matthew Braniff. He ran into Braniff at Freddy's, where drinks were ten cents a glass. Now down on his luck. Braniff asked, "Jim, do you have a couple of bucks?"

"If you stop drinking, I'll make you a judge," Jim told Braniff. When Judge Platt retired, Braniff took his place. Every year on the anniversary of that event, Braniff telephoned Jim Garrison to thank him.

Jim Garrison's pleasure in king-making endured for many years. In 1970, he was at Hotel Dieu hospital, recovering from a back operation, when Denis Barry appeared in the hallway in the company of Congressman Hale Boggs. Investigator Steve Bordelon stood in the hallway to ensure that no unwanted visitors gain entry to Garrison's room.

"Does the boss know you're out here?" Bordelon asked Barry. Bordelon put his head in Garrison's door.

"He'll see you," Bordelon said.

Denis Barry went in first. Jim Garrison lay in bed, his hair standing up in tufts around his head, like alfalfa, Barry thought. He was eating green peas with his hand, and appeared to be in excruciating pain.

"Hale Boggs is outside," Barry said.

"What does he want with me?" Garrison said.

"He wants your endorsement."

"Bring him in," Garrison said. The Congressman crept tentatively into Jim Garrison's hospital room.

"Hale! How are you!" Garrison boomed, stretching out his hand. "Congratulations on your re-election!"

Chapter 11:

Pershing Gervais v. Frank Klein

"I regret to say, I trust everyone & am easily fooled."
Jim Garrison

As Jim Garrison lobbied the Louisiana legislature for stronger anti-crime legislation, tension mounted at Tulane and Broad between his chief assistant, Frank Klein, and his chief investigator, Pershing Gervais. Klein had long ago taken note of "the Machiavellian influence which Pershing exercised over Jim Garrison." It was a mistake to say anything critical of Pershing Gervais to Jim Garrison and expect that any correction would be made.

With increasing regularity, Gervais countermanded Klein's orders. When Klein reported this to Garrison, he would be annoyed. Or, Garrison would say, "Gervais should have known better than that." He promised to reprimand Gervais, but he never did. With Jim Garrison now "very seldom" coming out into the field where the workers in his office were, Klein had become "second" to Gervais.

Klein was no match for Gervais. Gervais soon discovered that Klein was living in tight financial circumstances. Gervais advised him to use his job to accumulate money, "like I'm doing." Jim Garrison won't be looking out for me in the future, Gervais predicted. Often Gervais repeated his favorite line: "A man who won't take money can't be trusted."

Many in the office were "frightened of Gervais," Raymond Comstock reports. Once, two investigators asked Pershing for advice in a matter from which Pershing couldn't profit. "Don't bother me," Pershing said. "That's not my problem. That's Klein's problem."

Pershing assessed the troops shrewdly. He had feared Milton Brener, who was not susceptible to his scams. Others, he tested. One day Ross Scaccia remarked about a narcotics arrest, "There's no way we can win that case. I'm going to reject it." When Scaccia wavered, Pershing wanted to be certain.

"I want you to refuse it," Pershing said. Scaccia agreed, then changed his mind and decided to prosecute the case. Pershing hit the ceiling and removed Scaccia as narcotics supervisor. "Pershing, you're dedicated to evil," Scaccia told him one day.

Scaccia learned from his own experience that Jim Garrison was the opposite of Pershing Gervais in his approach to crime. One day Scaccia found a memo from Garrison requesting that he refuse an armed robbery case. Scaccia looked and saw that it was a stone cold armed robbery.

"Jim, I don't think you want to refuse this," he said. "It's one of the worst armed robbery cases I've ever seen. I'm enclosing the file and I want you to read it." Back came a note from Garrison.

"Jesus Christ, Ross," Jim wrote, "You're right. Forget what I said earlier." Scaccia concluded that someone, perhaps a family member, had asked for big-hearted Jim's help in this case, not, of course, bothering to give him all the facts.

Knowing Pershing as "a sneak and a liar," Klein had long been looking into his activities. He knew that Gervais was shaking down those bar operators on Bourbon Street. Pershing authorized some clubs to remain open if they employed only one stripper, but not the Flamingo, which did not pay him off. Sid Davilla's Mardi Gras Lounge and "Papa Joe" Conforto's place allowed B-drinking to thrive, and nothing happened to them. At the Flamingo, Pershing called in the newspapers to take his picture putting a padlock on the door.

When Klein called Superintendent of Police Joe Giarrusso and requested an undercover investigation of the places paying Pershing off, a Gervais spy, Frederick Soulé, immediately told Gervais. Gervais also attempted to maneuver a deal with Carlos Marcello in which Marcello would pay handsomely if the DA's office took only token action against a new type of gambling machine with which he was experimenting. Not wanting to be spotted with Marcello, Pershing sent an intermediary, his old confederate Sal Marchese, now driving a cab. This deal never materialized.

Serving as Pershing's bag man, Marchese collected $1,000 a week for Pershing from the lottery owners. Confronted by one of the policemen attached to Garrison's office, who had spotted them in Pershing's car (he and Marchese met twice a week), Gervais faced him down.

"I didn't know Marchese was collecting that much," Pershing smirked. His scams seem endless to catalogue. They included his taking $100 a week just from the Canal Street Steam Bath, and who knew how many other establishments!

Klein discovered the name of another of Gervais's informants, and that was David Chandler, Jim Garrison's supposed friend. Later Klein would call Chandler "Jim Garrison's enthusiastic biographer," referring sarcastically to that article published under James Phelan's by-line. Klein observed that Chandler seemed to hang out at the Quarter dives patronized by homosexuals.

Gervais retaliated. He kept one of his notorious dossiers on Frank Klein, noting that Klein could have been fired for "major cause on at least eight different occasions." He enlisted Frank Meloche to tabulate all the cases that Klein had "nolle prossed" or simply recommended that sentences be reduced. "I've now got me quite a file on Klein," Gervais told Aaron Kohn.

Bloated with power, Gervais had begun to tell the assistant district attorneys that they did not have to take orders from Klein at all. He told the police officers that if they wanted to get anywhere in the future, they should ally themselves with him, and not with Klein. Then he began to woo the clerical staff. Noticing, Jim Garrison was amused.

Sensing that Frank Klein was on his trail, Pershing began to shadow Jim Garrison, not letting him out of his sight. They went out at night together, but on those nights when Garrison was out of town, Gervais was nowhere to be found. No one knew where he went.

It was 1964, before the arrival of the Warren Commission volumes that would so consume Garrison's attention. Jim told Frank Klein that he wanted to devote his time to his political career. He requested that Klein take the burden of running the office from his shoulders. It was with this authority that Klein made his move against Pershing Gervais.

Jim Garrison was away on National Guard duty at Fort Polk when he received an urgent telephone call from Frank Klein. Klein wanted to fire two stenographers, Laurel Noonan, a sexy redhead who was Frank Shea's mistress, and Carol Boyd. Only a week earlier, Pershing had taken them out to lunch and they returned under the weather. Klein had warned them.

Then, on the Thursday, Klein needed someone to transcribe a statement from an Angola inmate who had cut the tendons on his heel and had been brought to New Orleans. The only stenographer in the office was working on urgent pleadings. The other four were off at La Louisiane, having lunch with Pershing. They all were either mistresses of assistants or police investigators and didn't believe they had to exert themselves overly. When Klein reprimanded Pershing, he denied everything. He had bumped into the women at the restaurant, Pershing claimed.

The next day Judge Bagert reported to Klein that his secretary had heard Laurel Noonan denouncing Klein. If Klein thought he could fire her, Noonan bragged, he was mistaken. She would let him know who was boss. Pershing had told her: "Just tell him to kiss your ass." In this spirit, Laurel had ignored the time clock Jim Garrison had installed, and went about as she pleased.

Out for lunch at the Fontainebleau Motor Hotel on Tulane Avenue and S. Carrollton, Pershing's redoubt, Bagert and D'Alton Williams spotted another office secretary, Lucy Sobecki, in the lounge. In the restaurant proper, Noonan was once more lunching with Pershing. Alerted, Klein had Lucy Sobecki paged and ordered her to return to the office. Back at Tulane and Broad, Klein told Sobecki to type a note to Jim Garrison. Even as Klein was dictating, the telephone rang. It was Pershing.

"Nobody's going to get fired," Pershing said.

Jim Garrison refused to allow Klein to fire the women. Klein, he said, had authority in all things, but not firing. It was during the Cocke-Becker campaign for Criminal Court judge. Garrison told Klein that if one of the stenographers went to Judge Cocke with a lot of stories, they could be used against Becker.

Laurel Noonan would indeed be banished – to a job as the new Judge Becker's secretary. In a deal with Pershing, Sal Marchese would be Becker's Minute Clerk, a position Lou Ivon had hoped for. "If that happens, Pershing would be able to buy anything in Becker's court," Frank Klein predicted, referring to the elevation of Marchese.

When he returned to New Orleans, Jim Garrison found a note. It was a letter of ultimatum. "You've got to make a choice," Frank Klein had written. "It's me or Gervais."

"If you put me in that position, Frank," Garrison said, "it's got to be you."

Everyone in the office thought: if Gervais had demanded that Garrison fire Klein, Gervais would have been gone. Jim Garrison did not take kindly to threats. Pershing, of course, was far too clever to make the mistake of issuing an ultimatum to Jim Garrison.

And so Frank Klein left the office. The story that emerged was that there had been "growing dissension" in the office "over the activities of Pershing O. Gervais," who had undermined Klein's authority, as, indeed, he had.

Klein was hurt. He thought Jim felt "relieved to have me out of there." It took Jim Garrison some time, but finally he realized that firing Klein had been a "bad decision." It had been "stupid" to choose Pershing over Frank Klein. Garrison realized too late that Gervais had been conducting a campaign to get rid of Klein and that Gervais "hated Frank Klein because he could not control him." For a time, Garrison remembered, "Gervais was able to control Lou Ivon, although only temporarily" and because of "rank."

Jim Garrison did not exempt himself from blame. He admitted that Gervais was able to control him, and looked into his own nature and character for the reason. It was, Garrison said, "because, I regret to say, I trust everyone & am easily fooled." Soon enough Garrison understood that he had "dropped [his] best man."

The firing of Frank Klein was a turning point in Garrison's career as district attorney. Four years before his death in 1992, still troubled by the incident, Garrison composed an imaginary dialogue between Klein and Gervais. Klein complains that Pershing "just cannot take off for lunch with one of the secretaries and be gone for two whole hours." An obscene character, Pershing calls one of the stenographers, "Canataloupe Ass." Laurel Noonan appears as "Chastity Reilly."

Gervais tells Klein it is "none of his business."

"Jim's off on Army duty and has left me in command here," Klein tells Gervais.

"Frank, why do you have to be so freaking Germanic, so god-damned structural about everything," Pershing says. When Klein mentions office morale, Pershing says, "Who gives a rat's ass? What really bugs you," Pershing tells Klein, is that "Jim has no objection to members of the office dating each other. But if you were DA, you wouldn't let that happen. You'd be running such a tight ship that everybody'd be walking around like they had a corncob up their ass...."

In matters of sexuality, Jim Garrison's approach was closer to that of Pershing Gervais.

In his story, Garrison also places in Klein's mouth his own reasons for having hired Pershing in the first place. Gervais has made a "substantial contribution to our office," the fictional Klein admits. Then Klein tells Gervais: "you have more street smarts than all the rest of us put together. You know most of the trouble-makers in this town and how to talk to them, how to tell them that we're not kidding about straightening up this city."

In his replacing of Klein, Jim Garrison relied on merit. He chose his assistant with the best record, Charles "Ray" Ward. Pershing got out of the way, flying off to San Francisco for training in "security techniques" (wire taps).

Jim Garrison tried to get Klein a job on one of the state commissions. He called Governor McKeithen's executive assistant, Gus Weill, and so discovered that Clarence O. Dupuy had gotten his brother Milton the powerful position of President of the Orleans Levee Board. "Remember, mother's always watching," Dupuy warned his thirty-five year old brother.

"If Dupuy is honest, then I'm a Japanese admiral," Garrison later said bitterly.

"Henceforth Mr. Garrison will be known as Admiral Garrison of the Japanese navy," Dupuy retorted. So the sands of power shifted. As Clay Shaw remarks in his "diary," referring to New Orleans, "However deep you go there is nothing but mud, built over geologic ages by the Mississippi as it emptied into the Gulf of Mexico."

When in 1965 Clarence Dupuy announced that he was running for the City Council, Garrison flew into action, getting Mayor Schiro to support Dupuy's opponent, Edmond ("Pudgie") Miranne. Dupuy was selling the jobs that came to him from Governor McKeithen, Garrison claimed. Could he prove it?

"This happens in closed rooms," Garrison said, "but it looks like he did." One night at La Louisiane, where both Garrison and Dupuy were regulars, the two engaged in profanities, and Steve Bordelon had to pull Garrison out of the fray.

Garrison supported Miranne, a loyalty Pudgie's friends considered remarkable. Garrison, even as he was facing a tough re-election campaign himself, had no qualms about opposing both the Governor and the Mayor. It was yet another Wilmer. One television advertisement pictured Dupuy as a prize-winning pig with his limbs attached to strings. The puppet master standing above him was John McKeithen. Dupuy was a "pig" because he was hogging patronage.

Clarence Dupuy would serve fourteen years on the City Council. "I didn't give a damn about his power," Dupuy would reflect years later, referring to Jim Garrison, "I had a little of my own."

In 1968, the district attorney's office began an investigation of the levee board. The "Times-Picayune" announced on its front page that hundreds of thousands of dollars of irregularities had been discovered. Milton Dupuy, still President, denied any knowledge or responsibility for the missing funds, and offered to testify before a grand jury. Charlie Ward assigned William Alford to do a two month investigation. Alford was told nothing about the preceding three years of warfare between Jim Garrison and Clarence Dupuy.

Alford had Milton Dupuy indicted on several counts of malfeasance, including overpaying contractors, and payroll extortion – Dupuy had assigned levee board public relations man Alan B. Citron to work on his brother Clarence's 1965 City Council campaign. Clarence Dupuy at once denied the charge.

The case was a plum for twenty-eight year old Alford, who considered the charges against Milton Dupuy air-tight. Better yet, the case had been allotted to Matt Braniff, who, of course, owed his judgeship to Jim Garrison.

Milton Dupuy was represented by Milton Brener, who had at once requested that his client be granted a change of Section since he had been denied a speedy trial. Brener managed to transfer the case into Judge Haggerty's section, only for further delays to bring the case back to Judge Braniff. This did not bode well for Dupuy and Brener.

Brener then filed a motion to quash. This has no basis whatsoever in law, Alford thought. The motion lacked merit entirely. In court, as Alford was arguing the state's position, Judge Braniff suddenly cut him off. Then, to Alford's astonishment, Braniff ruled in favor of Dupuy and quashed the indictments.

Back at the office, Alford sought out Charlie Ward. "I can't believe what just happened," Alford said. "Charlie, we should absolutely appeal. He is flat wrong!"

"I'll let you know," Ward said. He had to talk to Jim Garrison. And then there was silence.

"Aren't we going to appeal?" Alford asked again some time later. Finally Ward told him: "We're not going to appeal." Only still later did Alford discover that Jim Garrison and Clarence Dupuy had resolved their differences, resulting in the case against Milton Dupuy disappearing into the fog of New Orleans politics.

One night, Jim Garrison had walked into Lenfant's restaurant on Canal Street only to find Clarence Dupuy sitting at the bar. There were ten vacant seats to Dupuy's left, but Jim Garrison sat down right next to him.

"Where are you living now?" Garrison inquired. Dupuy was wary. This seemed an odd question from an adversary.

"I'm living in Paris, France," Dupuy said. "I come to work in New Orleans in the morning and return to Paris in the evening."

"Just like you, Dupuy," Garrison said, relishing the verbal challenge. Before the evening was over, the case against Milton Dupuy had evaporated.

Clarence Dupuy was to reappear in Jim Garrison's vista in 1972 when a public service claims department lawyer named Floyd F. Greene, sharing office space with Dupuy, revealed at his alimony hearing that when he was appointed inheritance tax collector by Governor McKeithen, Greene had taken only $700 a month as his salary, kicking back the rest to Dupuy. Over the previous thirteen months, that had amounted to $73,000. Asked why he had given Dupuy all this money, Greene admitted, "because I have an arrangement with him."

At that moment, Jim Garrison was facing charges in federal court that he had bribed pinball gambling owners. Running the day-to-day business of the district attorney's office, John Volz was frustrated at every turn in his efforts to put Clarence Dupuy behind bars.

Being indicted did not phase Dupuy. He was at a convention in Hawaii when he learned of his indictment. Dupuy lit a cigar. Dupuy, who had nerves of steel, turned to his cronies. "Well, boys," he said, "I've just got news I've been indicted. Let's go out and have a good time!"

Greene's lawyer, Lillian Cohen, rejected John Volz's offer of immunity, which would have allowed Greene to testify before a grand jury. The strategy worked. The threat of ten days in jail did not move Greene, who kept his mouth shut. Greene didn't even serve the ten days for contempt. John Volz concluded that the high power defense afforded Greene was to protect Clarence Dupuy.

Governor McKeithen himself made an appearance before the grand jury, arriving in the company of Jim Garrison. He didn't remember Dupuy recommending Greene, McKeithen said. He did not even remember appointing Greene. When Edwin Edwards became governor, and Greene's job went to someone else, Dupuy and Greene pleaded the fifth amendment. Harry Connick in 1974 had no better luck in convicting Clarence Dupuy, who was acquitted of extortion that year.

In December 1964, at La Louisiane, Jim Garrison had spotted at the adjacent table a petite, young blonde woman with strong features and an imperious aspect apparently having lunch with her parents. Having just returned from Greece, where her father worked for the Voice of America, Garrison would soon discover, she had enrolled at the University of New Orleans.

Her name was Phyllis Weinert, and she was well-groomed, well-bred, poised, smart, witty and interesting. She was also Jim Garrison's type. "He liked little bitty women," noted Joyce Wood, still typing out Bills of Information in the office.

"A man will cheat on his wife, but never on his type," Garrison would tell Phyllis. She was nineteen years old, and Jim Garrison was forty-three. She was decidedly his type.

Her nickname was "Candy."

"You're too intelligent to have the name 'Candy,'" Garrison said. He was the only person to call her "Phyllis." A mutual friend intervened and Garrison invited Phyllis to dinner at La Louisiane. She had no idea of his position.

"I have a term paper to type," Phyllis said. She knew better than to seem eager.

"My secretary will do it for you," said the District Attorney of Orleans Parish.

At dinner, he gave her an article about how he had cleaned up Bourbon Street. He did not reveal that he was married and the father of four children. He did ask her to drive him home and drop him off at the corner, so at once she had her suspicions. From then on, they saw each other openly. He invited her to the lunches he held with his inner circle at the Vieux Carre, never referring to the fact that he was married.

When in February 1965 a job opened with United Airlines for a stewardess, Phyllis moved to New York. Jim Garrison attempted to track her down, even enlisting the help of Governor McKeithen when United declined to give him her number. Garrison flew to New York. He asked Phyllis to come back to New Orleans.

She soon discovered, as Pershing had, that when Jim Garrison liked you, you could do no wrong. He was trusting. Once she ordered dinner from a restaurant only for Garrison to compliment her: "What a marvelous cook!" When she confessed that the food had come from Masson's, he replied, "What brilliant choices you made!"

One day, after Phyllis was involved in a minor traffic accident, Jim asked Pershing to drive her home. She offered Pershing a vodka gimlet. Soon he was chasing her around the room, his penis in his hand. She weighed 102 pounds, but physically powerful Pershing, a bruiser, it turned out, was no rapist and she fended him off.

"If you tell Jim," Pershing warned her, "nothing will be gained, except that he'll know you have a big mouth!" Pershing was a wart hog, Phyllis thought. It was only much later that she told Jim Garrison what had happened. "I wish you had told me," he said.

Jim then explained: Pershing's seduction technique was odd. Pershing believed that all he had to do was display his magnificent organ, and at once a woman would succumb.

She discovered his gift for making other people feel intelligent, even as he admired intelligence himself. When he caught her reading "People" magazine, he was indignant. "How can you read that trash!" he said. In the years to come he got her jobs, first as Jimmy Alcock's Minute Clerk, and when Alcock lost his judgeship, she got the same post with Charlie Ward. Phyllis was not intimidated by Jim Garrison and she realized that this made her attractive to him.

He gave her nicknames, just as he did his children. She was "Beagle-Nose," and "Fat Face" and "Monkey." It didn't matter that she was not quite a classic beauty. She was his "type." Soon when friends visited the office, they would ask, "How's Phyllis?" Liz telephoned the office rarely, and when she did, often he wouldn't take her calls.

From the start, Jim Garrison was obsessed by Phyllis Weinert. He was a married man jealous of every man she knew, even as she saw no reason not to see other men – they weren't married, after all. He was fearful that she might prefer someone younger, and waited with his police driver outside the place she lived until a male guest who might be visiting departed. At those times, as his driver circled the block, Garrison was miserable. At one point, he accused her of taking drugs, and demanded that she take a lie detector test. Upset, she agreed, then failed, took it again and passed, although her doctor urged her not to comply.

Everything about her intrigued him, and he regaled his friends with intimate details of how her panties were so good to taste, how "delectable" she was. In later years, when she traveled to Greece, he joked about that: "[You] left in a bikini to raid the beach!" he wrote her.

Sex was fun and playful and humor colored their time together. They played word games like "Facts In Five," a game he had learned that the Kennedys played. She taught him how to do the soft shoe. They played tennis together. Over the many years that she was part of his life, they joked about threesomes, and one day they opened the door and Phyllis spotted a body tucked into the sheets. It turned out to be a life-sized plush rabbit, a Garrison practical joke.

They joked about whippings, and he liked to think of new things that were "kinky." One evening he arrived with a briefcase filled with rope. A quarrel left him stranded, and there was the district attorney in an area of New Orleans where there were no cabs, his briefcase filled with ropes. She never felt they were sneaking around, or hiding. They laughed together and they were friends. Sometimes when they couldn't be together, at campaign functions when only the presence of a wife was acceptable, he sent his secretary Sharon Herkes to keep Phyllis company.

He introduced her to his mother, and Jane plied her with gifts of expensive jewelry. For Mrs. Gardiner, Phyllis was a means of getting rid of her old rival, Liz.

Jim told her he had married Liz only because she was pregnant, and then she said she had a miscarriage. He implied that Liz had lied to him, although he did not say so outright. He wrote her poetry, as in this dedication to a gift of a book of photographs of Greece, its text by author Nikos Kazantzakis:

For Phyllis
Who cares for me
Almost completely –
But not quite,
Who trusts me
Almost completely –
But not quite;
Who is my loveliest love,
My brightest child,
For whom I always shall care,
And who cares for me almost completely –
But not quite...

Love, M.

The "M" stood for "me." Years later, friends like Bob Haik would remember Phyllis as the woman who most intrigued Jim Garrison, the woman he most desired.

On November 16, 1976, they were married at the Unitarian Church in New Orleans. Jane Garrison Gardiner cast a skeptical eye. "That isn't a religion! That's a cult!" she sputtered.

The honeymoon to Puerto Rico was a disaster. He wanted to watch the NFL payoffs and she stormed out, grabbed a taxi and headed for the airport. It was too late, his financial circumstances were more bleak than they had ever been in his life, and the marriage was brief.

Yet he never stopped loving her, and was giving her loans as late as 1986, according to his financial records. Many years after their marriage, at dinner with a blonde companion, he said, suddenly, "Let me tell you about this person I loved," and, overcome by nostalgia, he began to talk about Phyllis.

At the turn of that New Year 1965, Jim Garrison produced a "Report to the People" which ran as a supplement in the January 17th "Times-Picayune." "Progress," it began, "seldom seems to come about automatically and silently." It was a philosophical self-portrait. "To those for whom tranquility and adherence to ancient custom are the supreme values," Garrison wrote, "it must have been a very trying period." Invoking Louisiana populism, he depicted himself as an outsider with higher values. Public servants, he writes, have "not merely the right but the duty to criticize officials who are not doing their best." It was another invocation of Garrison v. Louisiana, of which he remained very proud. He quoted once more from Justice Brennan's opinion for the majority, describing speech concerning public affairs as more than self-expression: "It is the essence of self-government."

"I have no talent for this game," Garrison writes disingenuously, referring to politics. He credits Frank Klein, whom he already missed, noting that in jury trials of twenty-two defendants charged with capital offenses, none had been acquitted. Eleven had received the death penalty, one heading for that facility for mental patients, the East Louisiana State Hospital at Jackson. The remaining ten to went Angola.

As for his office, not a single member of the staff was a political appointee. In December 1964, Governor McKeithen had granted him the power to parole any felon from Orleans Parish committed to Angola, but he had "forbidden my staff to grant paroles in criminal cases." It was, Garrison writes, "the business of the District Attorney to prosecute criminals, not release them from jail." He would not countenance "political favors." Had he not honored this claim, Aaron Kohn would not have granted him so fulsome an endorsement:

> The District Attorney for Orleans Parish is the most powerful, and most important, single official in the City's processes of law enforcement. The vitality with which this authority has been used by the Garrison administration has been an unprecedented deterrent to crime and organized racketeering in New Orleans.

John McKeithen remarked to his assistant Gus Weill that the District Attorney of Orleans Parish was actually the most powerful man in the state of Louisiana. He could accept charges, or refuse them. He could, under the "subpoena deuces tecum," subpoena any records; he could organize twelve people in a room and indict you.

Yet being District Attorney no longer satisfied Jim Garrison. Restless in intellect and spirit, he looked to the political arena. He might run for Mayor, he said. He had been given to know that he would have the financial support of Edgar and Edith Stern. Edith Stern enjoyed the Sears Roebuck-Rosenwald fortune and was a liberal. The Sterns did not hold Jim Garrison's part in the Dombrowski case against him.

At a dinner with Louisiana Supreme Court Justice Walter Hamlin in December 1964, Garrison discussed his future. Hamlin advised him to run for re-election in 1965. Hamlin himself planned to retire in 1968, when he would be seventy. Then Jim Garrison could run for Hamlin's vacant seat on the Supreme Court.

Garrison decided that he preferred to be Governor of Louisiana. He was not shy about this ambition. Referring to one of his many overnight visits with McKeithen, he had remarked, "I got up one morning and walking into the governor's bedroom looked out the window. It was a nice view. You know, I could grow to like it."

Garrison attended Lyndon Johnson's inauguration in January 1965 in the company of Mayor Schiro, Governor McKeithen and his friend oil man, Joseph Rault. Seated in the Louisiana delegation beside Senators Ellender and Long, Garrison was a major figure in Louisiana politics.

By law, John McKeithen could not succeed himself. Early 1965 was not too soon for Jim Garrison to begin his campaign for governor. He wrote a press release announcing his candidacy. Then, on a trip to Shreveport to address a dentists' group, he took with him his favorite of the young assistants, John Volz.

"Hit every radio station and give them this press release," Garrison said.

The plane was crowded and Volz and Garrison could not sit together. As the plane descended, in his booming voice, Garrison called out to Volz: "I think this is the guy's first time flying. He's going in very high, but I guess that's the safest way to do it." Joking, he seemed a man without a care in the world.

They separated. Garrison delivered his speech and Volz distributed the press release announcing that Jim Garrison was casting his hat into the ring for the next gubernatorial race. On their return, Volz was on time, but Garrison had not appeared as the plane was about to take off. Finally, he came running, his raincoat flapping in one hand.

"Look, John!" Garrison said excitedly as soon as he had settled into his seat. In his hand, Garrison held the March 1965 issue of "Esquire" magazine." In it was a story Garrison wanted Volz to read.

"We looked at this in 1963," he said excitedly, referring to an article by Dwight Macdonald on the Warren Report. "There's more to it than meets the eye. That Kennedy thing, one man couldn't have done it!"

When they landed in New Orleans, Jim raced – a pace highly unusual for him – to a newsstand and bought Volz a copy of "Esquire.

"Take this home and read that article!" he ordered. At that moment Jim Garrison began his investigation into the murder of President Kennedy.

John McKeithen needn't have worried about Jim Garrison's ambition to become Governor of Louisiana. But, unaware that the Kennedy assassination had seized his friend's imagination, and with an agenda of his own with respect to the law forbidding him from succeeding himself, McKeithen suggested that Jim Garrison run for Mayor against Victor Schiro. At the end of March, when Garrison accompanied McKeithen on a trip to Chicago, their objective to meet with businessmen in the hope of attracting new industry to Louisiana, Garrison learned that McKeithen planned to run again. McKeithen would maneuver by sending a bill to the legislature to change the law against a governor succeeding himself. It was a ploy even wily old Earl Long never attempted.

Shortly thereafter, Jim Garrison found himself in Washington, D.C. in the company of Congressman Hale Boggs, who had been a member of the Warren Commission, and who further piqued Jim Garrison's curiosity by confiding that Lee Harvey Oswald had been a paid informant of the FBI, while paraffin tests revealed that he had not even fired a rifle on November 22, 1963. "I doubt whether Oswald acted alone," Boggs told Jim Garrison as he nurtured the doubts raised by Macdonald's article.

By April 1965, McKeithen had cobbled out the law that would allow him to run again. Among his opponents would be Garrison's law school classmate John Rarick. "Some folks thought Earl and Huey were crooks and thieves," Rarick wrote his friend Ned Touchstone, "but neither of them had the gall to try and change the constitution to provide for perpetual politics by allowing a governor to succeed himself." In the course of the campaign, Rarick was offered a sizable contribution from Carlos Marcello.

"Big John's already got his," Marcello's emissary confided, referring to McKeithen. Rarick turned him down.

Already immersed in studying the Warren Report, no longer caring who was governor of Louisiana, Jim Garrison endorsed the "proposed Constitutional Amendment No. 1 which would permit a governor of Louisiana to succeed himself." To his endorsement, he added his customary populist spin: "The citizens of this state should be free to choose whomever they want for governor…they should be free to re-elect a governor whom they feel has done a good job."

Garrison continued to help McKeithen. In July 1966, Garrison visited former Congressman Gillis Long, a distant cousin of Earl and Huey, who opposed a second McKeithen term. McKeithen let everyone know that Garrison was to be a guest at the mansion; their mutual friend, Cecil M. Shilstone, defied "any businessman to say that John McKeithen hasn't been good for Louisiana...."

Jim Garrison was immersed in a riddle, one, he said, "that nobody else has been able to solve." In this new chess game, he would bring to "light a truth…." At the beginning, he had no other motive for investigating the Kennedy assassination than that. "This project is so fascinating," he said, "that the idea of any kind of reward for what happens afterwards is so ridiculous that I won't even contemplate it." The truth "was important for its own reasons."

As he studied the twenty-six volumes produced by the Warren Commission, every detail interested him. David Ferrie had not been called as a witness, yet his presence in the crime was apparent. "It was my jurisdiction," Jim Garrison would say when he was asked how he justified investigating a murder that took place in Texas. "It was my duty to locate and prosecute anybody in New Orleans who had something to do with the assassination." He noted that only after the assassination did anyone suggest that an assault on the President be made a federal crime. If some portion of the crime occurred in Louisiana, Garrison thought, it was his responsibility to investigate it.

"Should I," he would ask later when he was in the throes of his investigation, "leave well enough alone and disregard the apparent possibility that the men who planned the terrible murder are among us today? Should I say that the death of John F. Kennedy is not my affair?"

In order to investigate the murder of the President, Jim Garrison had to remain in office. There was no doubt now, in 1965, that Jim Garrison would be running for re-election as District Attorney of Orleans Parish.

Chapter 12:

Is This The End Of Pershing?

"In the weeks to come, you may even be told that I caused the sinking of the 'Titanic'...."

Jim Garrison

"If nominated, I will not run; if elected, I will not serve," Jim Garrison said in 1965 when he was asked if he were running for Mayor. He sat at the head table at a $1,000 a couple dinner at the Roosevelt Hotel to help pay off Lyndon Johnson's losing Louisiana campaign debt.

"I don't think illiterates should be allowed to vote," McKeithen said piously, as he voiced his opposition to Johnson's civil rights bill. McKeithen claimed that this was as true for whites as it was for blacks.

"Vote For Jim Garrison" read a billboard. It did not mention the office for which Garrison was running. So Garrison kept up the charade that he might oppose Victor M. Schiro in the race for Mayor of New Orleans. A wily politician himself, Schiro was notorious for the line, "Don't believe any rumors unless you hear them from me!"

Garrison was now at the height of his power and prestige. It upset him that he did not receive an award in 1965 from the Metropolitan Crime Commission – those prizes went to Joseph Giarrusso and to Juvenile Court Judge James J. Gulotta, Garrison's former law-school classmate, and one of the most humane judges ever to grace the Louisiana bench. Jim sent his friend Willard Robertson to inquire.

Robertson reported Aaron Kohn's answer to Garrison. Garrison had not been selected for an award "because his notorious personal life disqualified him from the requirement that an awardee have a record of integrity in both public and personal life." Garrison had been passed over because of his many love affairs.

"That's my own business," Garrison said.

"You could get one if you straighten out your personal life," Robertson ventured.

"I might refuse it if it's offered to me," Garrison said.

Domestic life remained an uneasy fit. He was a handsome, powerful man who took pleasure in his opportunities in an environment where a Napoleonic double standard prevailed. Phyllis was now an important part of his life. Liz was a "sweet person," he would say. Being home in time for dinner did not appeal to him in any case. When he telephoned and talked to Snapper one day, Liz in the background said, "Ask your Daddy when he's coming home." Snapper did. "I'll talk to you later," his father said then, and the call was over.

Liz telephoned lawyer Lillian Cohen requesting an appointment for her father. It was a matter of real estate, she said. When Mr. Ziegler arrived, however, he wanted to speak about his daughter, Liz. Liz was not happy, he said. They discussed a hypothetical couple and community property law, elliptically talking about "this property he might be selling."

"These people are getting a divorce," Mr. Ziegler said vaguely.

To his close friends, Jim Garrison repeated, "I live a moral life, but I set the rules on what's moral…I'm the best husband and father if you go by my rules." It was never that he was not committed to his family. Liz, for her part, never turned the children against him and in 1973 when he was on trial fighting federal charges, she postponed the divorce, waiting until after he was acquitted. "It might hurt your Dad that we're divorced," she said.

In 1965, as Jim Garrison sought re-election, he could indeed claim that in office he had been honest. He did not accept bribes. No one could buy him, which in the vernacular of New Orleans, meant that he was "undependable." A gambler named Jules Crovetto from Arabi in St. Bernard Parish had been paying off one of Jim Garrison's assistants. This was insurance that none of his four hundred lottery vendors arrested for illegal gambling in Orleans Parish would face trials. Pay-offs were required to ensure that the arresting officer would not appear at the trial.

One of Garrison's assistants was ready to accept considerations for "nolle prosequing" the cases against the vendors. In his heyday, Crovetto had sent five prime Porterhouse steaks to Chep Morrison's house every Friday, accompanied by cash. Was Garrison any different?

Crovetto asked the Chief of Detectives, Ray Scheuering, to introduce him to Jim Garrison. Garrison was, after all, known to believe that gambling was not a crime. He might be bribed.

Crovetto arrived at the Fountain Lounge of the Roosevelt Hotel. It soon became apparent that Jim Garrison was unapproachable, under any conditions. The gamblers found themselves in a situation unique in New Orleans: a public official would not take their money. The assistant district attorney on the take, the one who had blocked prosecutions of the vendors, would not be so fortunate. He was summoned to Jim Garrison's office and summarily fired. If gambling was a victimless crime, and prosecuting the vendors pointless, an assistant district attorney being on the take was criminal.

No matter how careful Jim Garrison was, rumors of corruption seeped from the office. Max Gonzales told an FBI informant that a case could be dropped for $2,000. Another FBI informant, Kay Roberts, a prostitute, reported she heard that for $10,000 prostitutes would not be prosecuted by Jim Garrison's office. The FBI neglected to inform Garrison of any of this, considering that it was more important to protect the informant than to fight crime. "We have a serious security problem in this office," Garrison admitted to Kohn.

One assistant, Alvin Oser, "liked to gamble." Oser was so addicted that he would bet on two roaches running across the floor," John Volz says. In trouble, Oser borrowed $225, interest-free, from Marcello-ally Nick Christiana, the corrupt bail bondsman. Garrison demoted Oser to being a trial assistant, calling Oser "one of my most aggressive, competent men." It was less than a slap on the wrist.

Another assistant, Garrison learned, had solicited a bribe unsuccessfully from Larry Lamarca, the husband of stripper Linda Brigette. Although there were, in fact, three resignations of Garrison assistants from the office, the "States-Item" reported two – with no explanation. It was Charlie Ward who fired Lucy Sobecki, not for her alcoholism, but "because she was a security leak from whom anything about the District Attorney's office could be learned just by buying her a few drinks."

"Our situation is not unlike that of a man who is paddling upstream in a leaking boat," Jim Garrison lamented. "If he stops rowing so as to bail out the water, then he starts slipping downstream. If he stops bailing out the water so as to row, then the boat begins to sink." Then he added, "We shall overcome!" in a defiant invocation of the theme song of the civil rights movement.

Pershing remained entrenched at Tulane and Broad. If a lawyer asked, "what would it cost to make this go away," and balk at the price tag, Pershing would tell him, "Those who have money get a "nolle prosequi," those who want justice get a trial!" Pershing hated lawyers and called them "whores." When he was cornered, his viciousness knew no limits. A few years later, Pershing would summon Lou Trent to his "office" at the Fontainebleau Motor Hotel. The matter at issue was a federal bribery case. Trent's wife, Lillian Cohen, represented the co-defendant.

"You motherfucker!" Pershing threatened Trent. "You're on the verge of going to the bottom of the Mississippi River!"

Garrison continued to attempt to reform his office. He had the locks changed. He no longer permitted police officers to leave reports at the Complaint Desk without securing a receipt. Requests to defer action on police reports had to be done by signature and then be reviewed by another staff member. A "nolle prosequi" salmon-colored card had to include the reasons for the dismissal and the name of the attorney involved. Following every jury trial, the assistant had to make out a red or a green (for victory) card, explaining his strategy and why he believed the case had been won or lost.

Yet another scandal with Pershing at its center erupted in New Orleans. The safe in Clarence's Bar was stolen. By the time it was recovered, the football gambling cards that had been seen in the safe had disappeared. Three men spotted dumping the safe in a canal were arrested. An informant revealed that Clarence Bielosh had paid $600 to a member of Jim Garrison's staff to effect the disappearance of the football cards, which were evidence of illegal gambling practices.

Bielosh confessed: someone in the District Attorney's office had shaken him down for money. He had handed the $600 to one Ronald Gaudin, who was working with police character Charles Quartararo. Gaudin now revealed that Guartararo told him the money was actually going to…Pershing Gervais. On June 11th, the Orleans Parish Grand Jury indicted Clarence Bielosh for perjury.

Joseph Giarrusso inquired whether Pershing would be available for questioning to sort out this mess. On National Guard duty at Fort Chaffe, Arkansas, Garrison was livid. The police had gone "far beyond" their duty to come up with evidence against Gervais, he complained. "Witnesses were cajoled, revisited and cajoled again – and at least one witness had been threatened to come up with evidence that would lead to the DA's investigator."

So once more Garrison affirmed his loyalty to Gervais. "He would never lie to me," Garrison would say two years later. Even when the reputation of the office was at stake, Garrison remained loyal to Gervais. Now he attempted to weather the storm of the Bielosh matter.

Calling the investigation "a Laurel and Hardy comedy," Garrison accused Bielosh of lying when he said he bribed an investigator from the DA's office to overlook the football cards. His re-election at stake, Garrison fought back hard. He prohibited anyone in the office from aiding in the police investigation, calling it "an outlaw, kangaroo, political election-year inquisition."

Behind it all, Garrison charged, was Victor Schiro, a "smirking, smiling, glad-handing ribbon-cutter" who had made "a political weapon of his police department." Garrison was confident that voters would "dump him [Schiro] in the garbage can." Outraged, he charged that "never in memory has another Orleans Parish District Attorney's office been investigated, even when the DA ran a house of prostitution." When Schiro proposed that a "Citizens Committee," including Aaron Kohn, investigate, Garrison declared that he would not permit the mayor to "assume the position of arbiter" even "if he recommended the Queen of England and the President of the United States as members of a committee."

Yet, for all the rhetoric, it seemed as if the law was at last closing in on Pershing Gervais. Pershing had to consent to a polygraph examination. There Pershing denied ever receiving money from Bielosh, Gaudin or Quartararo. Had he ever received money, had he ever asked anyone to destroy football cards held by the police as evidence?

"The answer is no," Pershing said, outsmarting the machine. The Pershing who lied all the time, and admitted it, who once said "It's hard for me to buy a pair of shoes because I give the guy the wrong size," had no trouble defeating a polygraph. Afterwards, he declared it had all been an attempt to "disable" him, a reference to his deaf mute parents. "It will neither kill nor disable me," Pershing declared.

The Bielosh case would not go away. Was this the last of Pershing? Stubbornly persistent in his defense of Gervais, Garrison attacked Mayor Schiro for more illegalities: kickbacks in the purchase of parking meters; funny business in the contract for the Moisant Airport parking lot; irregularities in the development of a land tract. In defense of Pershing, he even took out an advertisement that he titled "The Smear That Failed." Aaron Kohn moved immediately to dissociate himself publicly from Gervais.

When on July 12th, Frank Klein declared himself a candidate for District Attorney, he was at once dismissed from the job Jim Garrison had found for him as attorney for the Louisiana Wild Life and Fisheries Commission. Klein made Gervais a campaign issue. Who better than Klein knew Gervais's dirty dealings, who could document the "reward" Pershing had taken from bail bondsman Chris Baum for the return of the abortionist Frances Welch, and so many other examples?

When Klein accused him of taking $750, Pershing laughed and insisted the figure was $1200, which he had distributed. "I did not get a nickel of that money," Pershing claimed. Pershing referred to his dossier on Klein, and when Klein denied that Pershing had helped him pay off the note on his house, Pershing produced a copy of a canceled check for $130. Yet this "evidence" was peculiar. "Bank of Louisiana" had been written onto Klein's "Bank of New Orleans" check while it was made out, incomprehensibly, to "Central Savings and Loan."

As the election neared, deals were hammered out. It was now that Schiro bounced Pudgie Miranne from his ticket and endorsed Clarence Dupuy. In exchange for Schiro's ending the investigation of Pershing, Garrison pulled the five assistants he had assigned to investigate the Mayor. The perjury charge against Clarence Bielosh disappeared. After meeting with John McKeithen, Frank Klein withdrew from the race, as did mob lawyer G. Wray Gill. Another candidate, Burton Klein, withdrew as soon as he realized that, despite Jim Garrison's opposition to Clarence Dupuy, Garrison still enjoyed McKeithen's support.

Jim Garrison's opponent would be Judge Malcolm O'Hara, the one "sacred cow" he had considered "a friend of the office."

"Doesn't surprise me," Pershing said. "Let's get him!"

Aggressively, O'Hara attacked Jim Garrison for threatening judges "who oppose him with smear and political ruin." He accused Garrison of having been in a courtroom only three times – to be sworn in, to defend himself for defamation, and to prosecute Judge Cocke. But the centerpiece of O'Hara's campaign was Pershing Gervais and the Bielosh case.

Speaking before the Young Men's Business Club, Garrison continued to defend Pershing. He was "an asset to the office," Garrison said. He was "one of the finest men I have ever known." Would he retain Gervais if he were re-elected? "My answer is a resounding yes," Garrison said. But the issue of Gervais would not go away.

On September 9th, 1965, the winds of Hurricane Betsy gusted to over 125 miles an hour over New Orleans. Hundreds of tugs and barges and ships sank. Called to help, Jim Garrison donned his National Guard uniform, cowboy boots and a yellow leather pistol belt with a six-shooter, although he hated guns. As the winds raged, Malcolm O'Hara was in the midst of a tirade against Pershing Gervais. O'Hara called Gervais a "sordid figure" who "casts a shadow on every one of Garrison's strange actions." O'Hara could go no further. The power went out and the room was plunged into darkness.

Pershing Gervais resigned his position as chief investigator for the District Attorney of Orleans Parish on that day, . He called his resignation "ironic to the point of comedy," but there had been no alternative. Jim Garrison would not have been re-elected with the albatross of Gervais in residence at Tulane and Broad. The "Times-Picayune" wrote that Pershing's departure was "long overdue," adding that "Mr. Garrison never should have placed him in a position of trust." The litany of Pershing's escapades and crimes was known to many: those pay-offs Denis Barry had uncovered; the publicity about the Frances Welch pay-off; the Bielosh case; and other incidents where Pershing had approached lawyers with pending court cases "offering his services for cash."

Kohn wondered what to do. Garrison's office was, he believed, certainly an improvement over Richard Dowling's. Malcolm O'Hara's loyalty "to the senior members of the Mills gambling syndicate" and his obstruction of justice regarding graft payments to the New Orleans police by this group when O'Hara served as legal adviser to the grand jury in the Leon Hubert administration, was troubling. Kohn hesitated.

Then, on September 13th, O'Hara launched an attack on Jim Garrison worthy of Hurricane Betsy. He had Jim Garrison's official military records, O'Hara announced, records that revealed that Garrison had been granted a "medical discharge" by the Army. Garrison had suffered from a "neurosis" and an "anxiety reaction" when he rejoined the Army on his way to Korea, O'Hara announced. That Freud viewed all human beings as, to one degree or another, neurotic, was irrelevant, whether or not Freud's work was even known to O'Hara. What counted was what O'Hara could make the voters believe.

There is an "ugly force" in Jim Garrison, O'Hara charged, that "drives him to destroy anyone who fails to bow to his will." Garrison had "a Napoleonic complex," O'Hara insisted, no matter that this particular complex referred to people of less than average height attempting to compensate for their puny size with an aggressive exercise of power. Jim Garrison was six foot six inches tall.

In a campaign debate, Garrison asked O'Hara where he obtained those privileged confidential records. From "a close friend of yours," O'Hara lied. O'Hara claimed that he had been trying to contact this friend for permission to release his name, another obvious lie.

The source of the records was no friend of Jim Garrison's. It was Raymond Huff, United States Collector of Customs in New Orleans and the former commander of the Louisiana National Guard, as well as a close friend of right-wing anti-Communist Guy Banister. It irritated Huff that Jim Garrison had appeared on television during Hurricane Betsy in his National Guard uniform, in violation, Huff thought, of military law. Garrison was using the Guard for his own political ends," Huff complained to Aaron Kohn, and the new National Guard commander, now Adjutant General Erbon W. Wise, could not control him.

"I consider him very dangerous," Huff said darkly. "Something ought to be done about it."

Huff launched a campaign to prevent Jim Garrison's re-election. He visited Governor McKeithen, but got nowhere. He visited arch-segregationist Leander Perez, believing that Perez had become "disenchanted" with Garrison. Huff attempted to fan racist sentiment against Jim Garrison with the assistance of Garrison's own record.

That past spring, Garrison had taken a strong stand against the perpetrators of racist nighttime fire bombings in New Orleans, bombings that followed a CORE protest march in favor of voting legislation and voting rights for African American people. One bomb hit a white church that held interracial meetings. Another bomb found its way to the home of the Reverend Albert D'Orlando of the First Unitarian Church, a civil rights activist. A pipe bomb exploded outside the CORE regional office with organizer Michael Lesser inside.

Against these racist bombings, Jim Garrison had acted swiftly and decisively. "If I was running for office and had to seek the support of the Klan, I would rather not have the office," Garrison said. He planned to charge everyone involved, juveniles and adults alike. There is no place in New Orleans, Garrison said on July 31st, in the midst of his campaign against O'Hara, "for night riders or other hoodlums or groups who think they are above the law and try to take the law into their own hands." He understood the emotions arising from the issue of integration, Garrison added, but "the rule of law must prevail." These words and actions further account for the widespread support the black community offered Jim Garrison.

The case involving the fire bombers was to drag on until May of 1966 as crosses were burned all over New Orleans. That May, the last of four men connected to five of the 1965 fire bombings would be arrested. Ross Scaccia presented the case to the grand jury, exposing that the accused had indeed been members of the Ku Klux Klan.

Jim Garrison would be praised by Dr. Joseph D. Beasley and Virginia Y. Collins of the Citizens Committee on Bombings, as having offered "a significant service to the City of New Orleans." In 1966, Leander Perez, Jr., a lawyer and still a Garrison supporter, acted in concert with the sheriff of St. Bernard Parish to stop a Klan rally. Apparently it was not a question of like-father, like-son. In 1968, three men charged with arson in the fire bombing of D'Orlando's home pleaded guilty.

Huff tried everything he could think of to short-circuit Jim Garrison politically. He lamented that Garrison's earlier prosecution of that reckless driver who killed Leander Jr.'s wife continued to resonate with the Perez family. Huff also feared that Garrison still enjoyed "Times-Picayune" support because as an assistant district attorney he had nolle prosequied the case against the wife of publisher Jack Tims, who killed someone while driving under the influence. Tims "never forgets a favor," Huff thought. Now Tims had "created a monster."

Huff did make some headway with National Guard Brigadier General Leonard E. Pauley, who complained about Garrison's wearing his uniform in political situations, even on a television press conference. Garrison had been habitually late for Guard duty. He had pleaded that he had been delayed by meetings with the Governor, which was no excuse. Or he would leave early, flying off in Governor McKeithen's private plane. Garrison's activities "indicated an indifference and lack of interest." Pauley reported that Garrison's "only interest in the Guard was that it provided him with a title."

Garrison replied that he loved the Guard. It was "more important to him than anything else, including political position and authority." He invoked his defense of a battalion commander on whose watch an accident had occurred. Garrison had wanted to give him another chance. He could not imagine leaving the Guard, Garrison said.

Four years later, Jim Garrison would begin to understand that the enmity of Raymond Huff was political. Huff had worked closely with Guy Banister and the CIA and had been involved in the overthrow of President Arbenz of Guatemala in 1954. He was a CIA asset, and long before Jim Garrison's investigation of the Kennedy assassination became public, Huff was already at work attempting to sabotage Garrison's career.

In the midst of his 1965 re-election campaign, Garrison rocked some of the wrong boats. He brought before the Orleans Parish grand jury Captain William L. Heuer, Jr., who testified that he had paid legislators and state officials in behalf of legislation for the Crescent River Port Pilots Association. Was Garrison attacking the legislature anew? It wasn't, Garrison explained to the public, "an overall investigation of the members of the Legislature…most of the members of the Legislature I know are basically very honest men." It wasn't his fault if the evidence was proving otherwise.

In his attacks on Garrison, O'Hara alternated between the Army psychiatric records and the matter of Gervais. "Possession of another man's army record carries a federal penalty of up to ten years in prison," Garrison said, sardonically, "just about the length of time remaining in O'Hara's judicial term." Moreover, O'Hara was "lying by omission," referring to only part of the record. This, of course, was true.

O'Hara countered that he refused to believe that Pershing had departed from Jim Garrison's sphere. "There are sinister elements who had built a strong wall around Garrison," he said, two weeks after Gervais "resigned." O'Hara then produced more evidence of scandal: Oser's loan from Nick Christiana, whom Garrison had investigated for attempting to bribe members of the state legislature, among other Christiana crimes.

Garrison had charged a Christiana employee, Leo Radalat, delaying the case just as Oser got his loan. John Volz convicted Christiana and Oser had quickly repaid the loan. On the subject of Oser and Christiana, the press was entirely on O'Hara's side. Don't you have any regulations against assistant district attorneys borrowing money from bail bondsmen? Garrison was asked.

"When you go into a hotel," Garrison said, "Do you see a sign saying don't bring snakes into the bathtub?"

O'Hara knew that a dope peddler named Paul Milo Van De Bogart had not been prosecuted, although the FBI had been informed of his operation. In two of the cases raised by O'Hara, involving lawyers Bernie Horton and Monk Zelden, Garrison discovered that the files had disappeared from the office. He hadn't known it about them.

Jim Garrison fought Malcolm O'Hara with his literary skills, his penchant for satire, and his facility with caricature, those talents he had enlisted in his campaign to replace the Criminal Court judges. His theme was the mystery of why a judge would "trade his higher prestige, salary, and security for the job of district attorney." One advertisement, "A Warning About 'Hired Guns,'" pictured a tiny figure in huge glasses and a ten gallon hat, with two pistols in his holsters. "The fastest draw on the bench," is the caption. O'Hara, Garrison implied, was in the pay of his underworld connections, as indeed, O'Hara would later be accused in the Red Strate trial. Then, as always, Jim Garrison attacked organized crime with passion:

> In the Old West when the new town marshal got too rambunctious it was not uncommon for a certain element, which felt it owned the town, to import a professional gun fighter or hired assassin….

O'Hara, Garrison charged, was on the take. "The other way," he wrote, "is to meet the judge in a private room, lock the door, and lay on the table a consideration so large that it will offset his loss in case he is elected D.A. Which method was used to get the Judge to run? One guess." O'Hara was not his own man, Garrison charged, but was on assignment, and that assignment was "to attempt a job of character assassination." As always, hyperbole was Garrison's forte:

> In the weeks to come, you may even be told that I caused the sinking of the Titanic, red ants, the recent hurricane, the loss of the Pelicans, oyster fever and the explosion of the Hindenburg at Lakehurst, New Jersey.

The judicial canon of ethics decreed that O'Hara should first have resigned from the bench if he wanted to run, Garrison said. O'Hara had attempted to solve that problem by taking a leave of absence and enlisting his father, now retired Judge William O'Hara, to take his place.

A memorable O'Hara campaign poster pictured the Jolly Green Giant faced by a "David" armed with rock and sling. The caption reads, "Green, yes…jolly…no." A Garrison-drawn cartoon pictured a judge in robes entering a machine, and emerging as a district attorney in a double-breasted suit.

The most amusing of Jim Garrison's advertisements was a full page that ran in the "Times-Picayune" on October 30th. In bright orange letters against a black background, in a cemetery peopled by ghosts, a banner headline splashes across the page: "Speaking of Halloween."

The tombstones are inscribed: Rackets; Political Favoritism; Lottery Operators; Illegal Bail Bondsmen. The text is pure Garrison:

> "What about O'Hara's ghost stories? Halloween is a time for stories of ghosts and goblins and witches. When has the Halloween season witnessed so many tales of make-believe as Judge O'Hara is spinning for the people of New Orleans? The Judge has revived the lost art of spinning yarns in a way that would make Ananias, Baron Munchausen and the Mayor of Bayou Pom Pom turn vampire green with envy."

Above a sorrowful orange pumpkin, Garrison writes: "Who.oo.o.o is Behind O'Hara?"

When Marshall Brown endorsed O'Hara, Garrison wondered whether Brown had roped in Governor McKeithen as well. McKeithen denied it.

On WDSU television, on November 1st, the campaign drew to its nasty close. Garrison still wondered who was funding O'Hara's "expensive smear campaign." He speculated that O'Hara might even be funded by backers of Lyndon Johnson, with Senator Allen Ellender collecting a favor from Lyndon "to beat me now so I can't run against him for the Senate." O'Hara spent $50,000 to Jim Garrison's $27,000. Marshall Brown later admitted that he had raised $18,000 for O'Hara. Many thought the figure was closer to $25,000.

Having retreated to the Fontainebleau Motor Hotel, where he sat enthroned in a big chair as if he were Louis XIV, and which was to be his headquarters for years to come, Pershing remained close to Garrison. Together they discussed O'Hara's funding. Pershing traced the money back to McKeithen, who, he speculated feared that Jim Garrison's power might endanger the Governor's bid for a second term. McKeithen friends Brown and Dupuy were enthusiastic O'Hara supporters. Jim Garrison had noted too that things were no longer going well between him and the Governor:

> I go to John's office and tell him what is wrong and what I suspect about Brown and Dupuy...he is surprised. He looks me in the eye – sort of like a preacher. He is sincere and he says, "Jim, I wouldn't betray you," and he almost has tears. He shows me his governor's chair and says, if I suspect him to take back the chair and I leave believing him again – all the way back to New Orleans.

Charges and counter-charges were hurled until election day. O'Hara charged that Jim Garrison had forced McKeithen to get Frank Klein out of the race because he knew too much. O'Hara said there had been a lunch at La Louisiane attended by Garrison, McKeithen, Willard Robertson and Marshall Brown. After lunch, at four in the afternoon, the Governor had contacted O'Hara. He owed a debt to Jim Garrison, McKeithen admitted, urging O'Hara to withdraw from the race. The following day, in what was obviously a deal, Governor McKeithen had endorsed Jim Garrison, and Clarence Dupuy for the City Council.

Replying, Garrison acknowledged that the Governor had met with O'Hara, but only to ask him to remain in the race. "No incumbent lucky enough to have O'Hara as his opponent would want him out of the race," he said. He denied that he asked the Governor to persuade O'Hara to drop out.

In one of his efforts, Huff was successful. Tims had seen the error of his ways and the "Times-Picayune" accused Garrison of "selfish political maneuvering" in masterminding the meeting of McKeithen and O'Hara, "to get the judge out of the race." The newspaper expressed no outrage at O'Hara's expropriation and use of Garrison's private medical records.

The "Times-Picayune" decided to endorse neither candidate. On the day before the election, former district attorney Leon Hubert, once Jim Garrison's Tulane law school teacher, and then his boss, and having served as a Warren Commission lawyer, went on the air in support of Malcolm O'Hara.

Jim Garrison defeated Malcolm O'Hara 82,460 to 47,324.

Chapter 13:

The Cupid Doll

"This is very much like the squid which, when attacked, injects black fluid into the eyes of his opponent."
Jim Garrison

New Orleans crime continued to clone itself. The District Attorney continued to blame the police for not supplying evidence and the police blamed the District Attorney for not pressing cases. The sentencing for armed robbery, as Garrison assistant John Dolan remembers, was "as swinging as a rusty gate."

Jim Garrison came out for the death penalty for armed robbery. "Undoubtedly, there will be some hysterical voices complaining that this is a very discourteous way to treat robbers," Garrison said with sardonic humor. "Things are long past the stage where we can solve this problem by inviting these particular criminals to tea for a heart-to-heart talk and a discussion of their frustrations in early childhood." He invited opponents of the death penalty "to examine in the morgue the bodies of [the] victims." He insisted that the crime problem could not be solved by "broadening the poverty program" or with "more stylish uniforms for the prisoners."

He was so vehement that the ACLU accused him of "hysteria." Numa Bertel says that Garrison never intended making armed robbery a capital offense. Rather, he was making a point, and he got what he wanted: a bill with a 99 year sentence for armed robbery where injury resulted. Parole would be possible only after thirty-three years.

Garrison defended the new law. In reply to a WDSU editorial, he said that "an armed robber is a vicious criminal, and the most vicious armed robber is usually the person who has never been convicted. This is the nervous bandit, this is the man that will shoot when his victims resist, this is the man who has made up his mind to kill if he has to. This is the man who, with premeditation to murder, loads his weapon and decides that he will use it if he has to...."

The new 99 year sentence became a useful plea bargaining tool. Bertel prosecuted the first case handled after the new statute was passed. The defendant pled guilty and was sentenced by Judge Bagert to fifty years, an unheard of sentence up to that time.

In the next case Bertel handled, the sentence was a "Phillips 66," a 66 year sentence. In neither case was there even injury to the victim.

While Garrison focused on crime, Pershing focused on one particular scam. From his Fontainebleau "office," he would telephone families that had a child who had violated the law and was facing charges. "I can fix this for you," Pershing said, although he could not. Pershing took their money, usually two or three thousand dollars. If the case went the right way, and the child wasn't charged, Pershing seized the credit, although he had had nothing to do with the decision.

With the fifty percent of cases that went the other way, Pershing had a ready answer.

"The sons of bitches!" Pershing said. "They took the money and didn't do anything for us!"

Pershing telephoned Bertel. "You've got a vice case," Pershing told Bertel. "Do you have a case? Call me when you get the file." It was a variation on the scam.

"Have you spoken to Pershing lately?" Garrison asked Bertel. Then Garrison laughed. "I just got a call from Pershing saying you were on the take and I'd better get rid of you." Pershing had this time underestimated Jim Garrison. "I told him you picked the wrong guy," Garrison said.

One day soon after this conversation, Bertel spotted Pershing standing in front of the Criminal Courts building. "Friend, don't be upset with me," Pershing said in his most disarming way. "I thought if I moved you out I could get someone who would cooperate with me!" Pershing was not quite gone and would not be for some years. In 1969, when Charlie Ward was stepping down as first assistant, and Judge Frank Shea wanted to sponsor John Volz to take Ward's place, Shea used Pershing as his intermediary. Shea knew Pershing still had some control over what happened in the office and liked Volz because Volz wouldn't compete with him for bribes. Volz got the job. When that power structure moves, it really moves, investigator Lynn Loisel remarked then.

Jim Garrison and Pershing were walking up the steps of the Criminal Courts building one morning, Pershing having picked Garrison up. His .45 was prominently in his belt. A reporter came up to them.

"Jim, what should I tell my editor?" the reporter said.

"You tell him, FUCK YOU!" Garrison boomed. Everyone in the neighborhood heard it. Yet it wasn't only Garrison on whom Pershing Gervais exerted his vulgar influence. If Jim had a weakness for Damon Runyon types, so did others, and after Gervais left the office, Jimmy Alcock and Volz, two straight arrows, often went for coffee at the Fontainebleau where they sat with Pershing, being happily entertained.

In the autumn of 1966, as he was studying what happened to President Kennedy, Jim Garrison sponsored a repeal of the double-good-time-law for criminals. In this year of the Miranda v. Arizona decision, he opposed a magistrate taking a prisoner out of police custody when he was arrested without a warrant, arguing that the prisoner would not be available for line-ups. He lost this one. He remained unafraid of the "beneficiaries of the amiable fixes" getting scratched.

Garrison also favored strong federal gun control laws. "Any criminal type, any ex-con, any pill head who wants to get hold of a gun can do it with no trouble whatsoever," he said. So he placed himself at war with the National Rifle Association. His opposition to lax regulations regarding the possession of weapons was prescient. Unless the state and national legislatures provide us "with some means of controlling the proliferation of dangerous weapons," he said, "things are going to be worse than they are now and we better get used to it."

He introduced a bill to make it a crime for finance companies to charge more than sixteen percent simple interest. "The loan sharks gauge people," he said, "they suck the blood out of people and we wanted to try to do something about it." He opposed possession of LSD and the sale of pornography to minors. When a woman became pregnant in prison, he urged that Louisiana create "a modern correctional system," adding his customary literary touch: "There is an old adage that 'love laughs at locksmiths.' This is particularly true in the antiquated, politically-oriented correctional system in the state of Louisiana."

Irony graced his tough stand on crime. He spoke out against a new Code of Criminal Procedure that imposed restrictions on freedom of speech, "not even incorporated in Soviet law." He continued to invoke Garrison v. Louisiana, "one of the fundamental basic principles of democracy – a right to comment on and to criticize government officials." As was his wont, he was available to help the little guy. A man named Gus Blaviano was cheated by the Jacobson Young car dealership: Jim Garrison got him back his $600 within the hour. A Mr. Ellis Irwin wanted to know if he could get the television stolen from his car back from the police. Frank Meloche sent the "Boss" a quick note that it had been done, so swiftly had the matter been handled.

Not that you could walk right in and see Jim Garrison. Reverend D. Norwood complained and received an ironic note: "If you require that the District Attorney be a person who is available to you at your convenience," Garrison wrote, "then I do indeed think it would be a good idea for you to help elect someone who is less involved with his work than I am." A woman whose husband knew Jim Garrison in the National Guard wrote that he and his brother had been cheated out of their deceased father's property. She received an appointment.

Edgar Labat and Clifton Alton Poret had been convicted of "aggravated rape" on March 23, 1953 by an all-white jury. The effort to set them free was spearheaded by Labat's attorney, Bruce Waltzer, one of the Dombrowski defendants. In 1962, Labat had demanded to be released, arguing that nine years in a death cell constituted cruel and unusual punishment, a motion denied by District Judge John R. Rarick. In 1963, Labat argued he had been arraigned without benefit of counsel, while "members of the Negro race had been systematically excluded from the Grand Jury." Both Labat and Poret were African American.

In August 1966, both Labat and Poret, now having sat on death row at Angola for nearly fourteen years, were released by the United States Court of Appeals For The Fifth Circuit. Judge John Minor Wisdom wrote that not only Negroes, but "all daily wage earners" had been excluded from the Orleans Parish grand jury. Garrison assistant Lolis Elie suggests that Garrison could have done more for the rights of African Americans, certainly by integrating the Orleans Parish grand jury. That Elie is correct, and that Garrison might well have agreed, is reflected in the excessive anger with which Garrison greeted Judge

Wisdom's ruling: This ruling, Garrison said, "may have deprived the state of Louisiana of a fair trial...this should be good news to criminals everywhere."

"What are your career plans?" Garrison had asked Elie when he hired him in 1963.

"I want to become a judge," the future civil rights defense lawyer said.

"Maybe in fifty years," Garrison mused. Two years later, Elie was offered a traffic court judgeship. He turned it down.

Garrison assigned Louise Korns to do research on the issue of the racial make-up of the grand jury. Korns found a Louisiana law stating that anyone attacking the composition of a jury must themselves be a member of that race or sex so excluded. She also found that the U.S. Supreme Court had denied certiorari in a case affirming that Negroes were not discriminated against in the selection of juries in Orleans Parish. Korns concluded that the recent Labat decision would not be "binding on the courts in Louisiana."

Only on March 19, 2008, did the United States Dupreme Court rule conclusively on this issue — on a Louisiana murder case. In Snyder v. Louisiana, the Court decided by a 7-2 decision that the death penalty case against Allen Snyder had to be reversed because African Americans had been obviously and deliberately excluded from the jury: "prosecurtor used peremptory strikes to eliminate black prospective jurors who had survived challenges for cause." Justice Samuel Alito delivered the opinion for the court.

Determined to retry Labat and Poret, Garrison now located the victim as well as the two witnesses. All were nervous. The victim did not want her new married name released. In his effort "to indict them again and try them again," Garrison was thwarted, while the ACLU attacked him for prejudicing their right to a fair trial. Labat and Poret pled guilty to the lesser charge of attempted rape and received a sentence of time served. In 1971, Poret, unregenerate, was found guilty in upstate New York of attempting to rape a fifty-two year old woman.

If later, by Charlie Ward and others, Jim Garrison was accused of being a "leftist," it was hardly so. When it came to crime, he was conservative. The ACLU, he charged, has "drifted so far to the left that it is now almost out of sight." The ACLU, Garrison went on, was "the same outfit which attempted to prevent legislation making it unlawful for persons to aid the Viet Cong and making it unlawful for them to interfere with movements of our troops or sending supplies to our troops." If he was, at this very moment, attempting to discover who had killed President Kennedy, it was not because he was predisposed to support the other side in the conflict in Vietnam.

Delivering the commencement speech at Louisiana Tech in Ruston, Louisiana in August 1966, Garrison applauded how America had "steadily defeated Communist aggression" in Greece, Korea and Cuba. He added, "We will end the Communist aggression in Viet Nam." He drew on his own war experiences, arguing that "it is not beyond the realm of possibility that our own children will die in concentration camps somewhere."

This was the note he sounded in the foreword he composed for his former assistant Ralph Slovenko's book, "Crime, Law and Corrections." Garrison titled his essay, "A Heritage Of Stone," the stone standing for the deaths man has visited on man.

Man, Garrison writes, "is one of the most aggressive creatures the world has known," comparable to the piranha. Primitive man, he considers, "felt the need for empathy as much as he would have felt the need for a lawn-mower. His descendants have not done much better." Garrison catalogues the weapons man has constructed in post-modern literary style: "the cross; the bowl of hemlock; the nearly obsolete T.N.T. bomb; the obsolescent atom bomb; and the currently popular hydrogen bomb."

Meanwhile prosecutor Garrison notices, "this marvelous, rational creature murders every hour, commits a rape every twenty-six minutes, a robbery every five minutes, an assault every three minutes...." The epitome of man's degradation, Garrison writes, the fount of evil, were the Nazis: "In the looking-glass world produced by the Nazi culture, truth was an enemy, compassion a stranger, only the innocent were punished, only the guilty were rewarded and the meek inherited the earth."

In this remarkable essay, Garrison envisions a bleak destiny for mankind. Slovenko included in his book one of the photographs Garrison had snapped at Dachau concentration camp, of a victim in his final agony. Garrison closes his brilliant text with someone chancing upon a human skull: "Perhaps he will pick it up, looking through the goggled sockets at the dusty hollow where a handful of grey tissue once took the measure of the universe." At Dachau, Garrison had photographed just such a skull. His literary ambition intact, Garrison submitted the piece to "Commentary" magazine, but they turned it down.

Garrison's office fought insanity defenses hard, aided by Coroner Nicholas Chetta, who served on the "lunacy commission" that was charged with making the determination of whether a defendant was mentally capable of assisting in his own defense. In one notorious case during the autumn of 1966, Frank Charles Williams was indicted for two killings, one involving a rape. Milton Brener argued an insanity defense, although the lunacy commission had ruled that Williams was "sane." Yet Williams had already done two hitches at the East Louisiana State Hospital at Jackson, the mental hospital. Brener bargained, and Williams admitted to the rape, while the charge that he had murdered a nineteen year old girl was dismissed. Williams was sentenced to fifteen years.

Chaim Halpern, who was white, was more fortunate. In November 1961, ensconced in one of the "bust-out booths" at the French Casino bar, he had shot, at point blank range, in the abdomen, a dancer named Doris "Cherrie" Payne. Judge Cocke set no bail, and Jim Garrison requested the death penalty.

"I shot her when a voice in my mind told me to," Halpern insisted. His lawyer called him a "Dr. Jekyll and Mr. Hyde schizophrenic," a result of his having been born in a Russian concentration camp. Halpern was found not guilty by reason of insanity and went off to the East Louisiana State Hospital at Jackson.

After three years, he returned to Parish Prison where he edited "The Pelican," a newspaper. Rehabilitation director Mrs. Ruth Kloepfer declared that she had never been afraid of Halpern and Frank Shea let him go. It was this very Mrs. Kloepfer whom Ruth Paine asked to look out for Marina and Lee Oswald when they moved to New Orleans in April 1963; it was this Mrs. Kloepfer who was in telephonic communication with Jack Ruby, Oswald's assassin, during the summer of 1963.

Garrison had long vowed to start a file on people who hadn't been brought to trial because they were incarcerated in a state institution. "This office does not want to deprive a man of his freedom merely because of a clerical error or an oversight by an assistant district attorney or a secretary," he said. He would open a "can't prosecute now" file on cases that "cannot be tried immediately." One of these cases involved Earl Stautmeyer, who had been held illegally at Jackson since 1933, although the charge against him had been dismissed. Garrison assistant Herman Kohlman wrote to the hospital requesting Stautmeyer's release.

Among the most notorious cases of the day was that of Leonard Caesar. Caesar was a successful boxer, having defeated a former lightweight champion named Joe Brown. By 1956, Caesar had become a serial rapist. He bragged that he knew every alley and dwelling in the Quarter. His tactic was to make his victims submit with a knife. He was, Ralph Slovenko concluded, "among the most dangerous persons imaginable." Richard Dowling had charged Caesar with "aggravated rape" of that airline stewardess Judy Chambers, who would be nicknamed "Scrambled Eggs," and been among Jim Garrison's lovers.

Most of Caesar's victims refused to testify, and the police joked that these women even left their doors open, hoping he would come back. Finally, Caesar was indicted and incarcerated at Parish Prison. A phenomenal athlete, he engineered a daring escape, armed with a gun smuggled in by his wife, Nellie. When the warden lunged at the escaping Caesar, Caesar shot him in the groin. (The warden survived).

Now Caesar was on the move. Like Superman, he leapt from balcony to balcony, jumping over fences, scaling walls, climbing up and down drainpipes, and even squeezing through a small opening in an attic. A police officer climbed up to the attic, and was about to open the trap door, then thought better of it.

In pursuit, the police discovered a shoe with a hole in the toe – part of Caesar's big toe had been amputated. They pressed on. From his attic hide-out, Caesar leapt thirty feet to the ground through a hole he had kicked in the brick chimney. Shot in the arm, and then shot twice more, he dashed to a nine foot wooden fence. In yet another feat of daring, he scaled the fence with ease. Felled at last by pellets, covered with blood and writhing on the ground in agony, Caesar reached for his pistol, only to be shot again.

"Don't shoot, you got me," Caesar whimpered, as he lay on the ground, the cops with their feet planted on his body to hold him down. A cop slammed him in the head with a brick for good measure and a priest administered last rites. Certain that he was dead, the police drove Caesar to the hospital. "Had I known he was alive," the cop who hit Caesar with the brick said later, "I would have shot him!"

Even Dr. Chetta had to agree that Caesar, who heard voices telling him that he was Jesus Christ, was unable to assist in his own defense. Awaiting trial, he had spent his time extinguishing imaginary fires in his cell.

The year was 1956. Leonard Caesar was sent off to the East Louisiana State Hospital at Jackson, known in East Feliciana Parish as "East" and later immortalized because Lee Harvey Oswald applied for a job there during the summer of 1963.

In June 1963, nine years later, the doctors at East wrote to Judge Platt and to Jim Garrison, stating that Leonard Caesar was now same and could assist in his own defense. Neither replied. The thought of Caesar back out on the streets was neither politically desirable nor personally appealing.

Two more years passed. In 1965, more letters came from the hospital, insisiting now that Caesar was an "unconvicted criminal." The guards, feeling sorry for Caesar, began to deliver messages to Judge John R. Rarick, presiding at the august Clinton Courthouse, among the most exquisite buildings in the United States, as well as among the oldest functioning courthouses.

"Help me!" Caesar wrote. "I'm being held illegally at the criminal building." Some of his messages were written on toilet paper.

Judge Rarick spoke to the head psychiatrist at East, and decided that it was an outrage. The criminal colony at East was "worse than being in prison." Leonard Caesar applied for a writ of habeas corpus. When Jim Garrison registered his opposition, Rarick was indignant.

"Mr. Garrison has problems of his own down there, and he doesn't understand our problems up here," he said. The heart of the matter was that Leonard Caesar remained locked up without due process. Rarick's sense of justice was offended and he vowed to see the Leonard Caesar matter through. He was determined not to abandon Caesar.

Rarick notified Jim Garrison's office and demanded that they come and get Leonard Caesar. "Try him and if you convict him, send him to prison in my other Parish, [West Feliciana]," Rarick wrote, "but don't expect me to dodge the bullet for you by hiding him in a ward for the insane." They had been law school classmates, but this was not a matter on which Rarick would compromise.

Jim Garrison replied that they didn't want Caesar back because they would have trouble accumulating evidence at this late date. If they had to take Caesar to trial now, they would lose. Rarick was not sympathetic. An advocate of the rights of mental patients, he was outspoken in his refusal to allow political considerations to interfere with justice. He spoke of "the myth of mental illness" and viewed people like Leonard Caesar as "scapegoats of our society." By now, Rarick had six writs from mental patients at East, and he looked into every one of them.

Ralph Slovenko had to agree, even as he was obliged to inform the psychiatrists at East that the district attorney's office was "not particularly anxious to try this case." He admitted that Caesar was legally sane and that "there was no evidence to convict or hold him."

Judge Rarick kept up his pressure. "The criminal court building wasn't erected to cover up other people's mistakes or as a holding base," he argued. "If I find him sane and ready to go to trial, I expect you to come and get him." At the hearing, Rarick did just that. He found Caesar sane and turned him over to the East Feliciana Parish sheriff. New Orleans had thirty days to transfer him or he would be set free. Rarick did stay the effect of the writ of habeas corpus to permit Orleans Parish to appeal his ruling.

Jim Garrison replied with his customary hyperbole. He accused his classmate of allowing a criminally insane prisoner to return to wreak havoc on New Orleans." Rarick was unmoved. "I don't know what Mr. Garrison is driving at," Rarick replied, "because I've never released any of these people." Then he added, pointedly, "I have a Constitution to follow…nowhere in the Constitution is there authority to place a man in a mental institution without due process of law."

Jim Garrison apologized at once. The dispute was all "based on a misinterpretation on your part…." He blamed "States-Item" beat reporter Jack Dempsey for a misleading article. "As a strong advocate of the rights of individuals," Garrison wrote Rarick, "I am predisposed to be in favor of the availability of writs of habeas corpus at every place where a man might be detained." He closed with an encomium to Rarick: "I might add that I hold you personally in the highest regard and would accept your judgment in any habeas corpus proceeding over which you presided."

In one more miscarriage of justice, the Louisiana State Supreme Court ruled that jurisdiction belonged not to Judge Rarick, but to Judge Platt. A new "lunacy hearing" would be held in New Orleans. John Rarick was indignant. "In the meantime the prisoner or inmate, untried, unconvicted, and unsentenced, sits and rots in filthy prisons. One hour, one day, is too long. Justice delayed is justice denied."

Again Leonard Caesar came before sleepy Judge Platt. Platt loked out at prosecutors John Volz and Ralph Slovenko as if they had descended from Mars. It was Slovenko's first case, and Volz was there as mentor. Calling his first witness, Slovenko addressed the jury.

"This is what we are going to prove with this witness," he began. Volz called him back and whispered, "You are allowed to address the jury only in your opening and closing statements."

At the end, Judge Platt ordered Caesar committed back to Jackson, MISSISSIPPI!

John Rarick considered Leonard Caesar a political prisoner. Later he would wonder, "If I hadn't given Caesar a hearing, would he still be in the insane asylum? If so, by now, he would be nuts!" In support of Judge Rarick, the "Times-Picayune" wrote that Caesar had an "absolute constitutional right" to be released from the hospital once he was declared sane.

Caesar plea bargained. "They couldn't prove their case," Rarick perceived. In January 1966, Caesar pleaded to the lesser charge of simple rape and was sentenced to twenty years at Angola. He served seven additional years.

Released in 1973, Leonard Caesar was hired by the New Orleans city department of streets. He never committed another crime, and was guilty only of a minor parole violation that sent him briefly to Parish Prison that summer. He was forty-six years old.

Jim Garrison's fifth and last child, Eberhard Darrow Garrison, was born on February 6, 1966. His birth was announced by the "States-Item" as "New Garrison Heir, Another Heavyweight." Eberhard Darrow was 20.5 inches long and weighed eight and a half pounds.

Jim Garrison was a permissive father. His den was once the living room, and there the children climbed under the desk or crawled onto his lap as he was working. Eberhard and Elizabeth were fond of scribbling on the upstairs wallpaper.

"They're expressing their artistic talent," Jim explained to Liz, who did not take kindly to the defacement.

He did not believe in spanking his children. Once he did spank Jasper, who had done something dangerous. Jasper cried and his father cried even more than Jasper did. Later Elizabeth would call Jim

Garrison a district attorney who did not believe in punishment. If you did something bad, he made you feel as if you had done a dumb thing, as if you were the most irresponsible person in the world.

"What purpose did that serve?" he might say. "Why did you do it?" You'd walk out of the room feeling terrible because you had let down your Dad, Snapper remembers.

Jim Garrison was not a father who attended school meetings or Little League games. It had never been the Cleavers, as Snapper puts it, but they knew that he loved them. As they grew older, they were awarded new nicknames: Jasper, whose given name was "Jim Robinson," was his favorite because, after falling from his bicycle he was to suffer brain surgeries and serious side effects. The others simply accepted that he would always be fondest of Jasper, who was newly named "Raccoon."

Snapper, who was born with a nickname, became "Brown Eyes" and Elizabeth was "Wizawat," "Wizz" for short, or "Queen of the Bayou." The children enjoyed his sense of humor, and Snapper tells the story of his father liking cigars so that one day Judge Chehardy took the band of a fancy label expensive cigar, slipped it onto a $5 cigar, and gave it to him.

"Here's a great cigar!" Chehardy said.

Jim drew in.

"This is really good," he finally said, "Just like a five dollar cigar!"

The Garrison children did not enjoy visits to their grandmother in Laurel, Mississippi. Jane Gardiner made her grandchildren abide by the standards of her era. She forced them to take naps and would not permit them to come to the table unless their hair was combed. You must not come to breakfast in your pajamas. When you sit down at the table, put your napkin on your lap at once. If you grab a cracker, you better eat it. You had manners. Once she wouldn't take Elizabeth out because she didn't like a haircut that Liz had given her.

Yet their father defended Jane. He told his children that he admired her sacrifices, how she had raised her children alone during the Depression, finding work when many men remained unemployed. Once he was watching an old Hollywood movie of the thirties or forties with Snapper. It had a strong woman at its center, Rosalind Russell or Bette Davis, and he said that she reminded him of his mother.

He was proud when two of his sons became lawyers, but he did not urge them to do so.

"I'm thinking of going to law school," Snapper had announced one day.

"Well, you have to make sure you're interested in the profession for the right reasons," Garrison said. "It's a literary profession." It was not about making money. "You have to do what you want, you have to want to do it," he said.

Once Snapper objected when his father gave a cab driver a twenty dollar tip. "He's working hard, Son," Garrison said. "You worry about money too much." And later, in 1988, when he gave the publishers of his memoir, "On The Trail Of The Assassins," more money than they were owed by contract, and Snapper objected, his father held firm: "Son, these people did me a favor," he said. "They published my work when others wouldn't." They always knew how important his investigation of the Kennedy assassination was to him. "When the bullet went through Kennedy's head, it was not the same country," he told Eb.

After Snapper became a lawyer, Jim Garrison said, "Son, you're a fourth generation attorney," and this mattered to him.

He was not "a crying man," as Elizabeth puts it, but there were at least three occasions the family remembers when he did weep. Once, in his last years, the children brought him a CD of the Big Bands, and as he listened to Glenn Miller, he said, "This is beautiful," and then his eyes filled with tears.

In 1990, Elizabeth was getting married to a man named "Fallen," earning her the new nickname of "Fallen Angel." They were in the limousine on the way to the church when Garrison burst into tears. "It's not too late to change your mind," he told his daughter. "If you're not happy, you don't have to go through with it."

His wife Liz remembers another occasion when he cried. He had finally tracked down his father in Arizona, only to discover that Earling R. Garrison had died. Jim Garrison saw his father's death certificate. Under "Family" was the word "None." Then he broke down into sobs and cried like a baby.

In principle, Jim Garrison continued to be opposed to using the power to intervene in the granting of paroles offered to him by Governor McKeithen. Yet it was his effort to gain a pardon that landed him once more on the front pages. Linda Brigette, the "Cupid Doll," arrested by Robert Buras and Norman Knaps in the Bourbon Street crackdowns, was terrified by the prospect of having to serve her two thirty-day jail sentences. Linda had been arrested twice, on January 11th and November 7th, 1963. At her first trial, the prosecutor was Frank Klein. On the bench sat Frank Shea.

Shea had befriended Linda, and when her son got in trouble had traveled with her to Atlanta to iron out the mess. No matter, Shea sentenced her to thirty days. Garrison was furious and accused Shea of attempting to shake down Frank Caracci and Larry Lamarca.

At her second trial, Linda testified that Jim Garrison himself had watched her perform at the request of her attorney, Bentley G. Byrnes, and Garrison had given her permission to use the red velvet couch in her act. Garrison had found "nothing wrong with it." Asked whether the scream that punctuated her act had "sexual significance," Linda denied it. "It's just a way to end the act," she had testified, demurely.

Nor did she in real life scream during sexual intercourse. Then she had turned to prosecutor Al Oser, and demanded, "Do you?"

Judge Brahney promptly sentenced her to an additional thirty days.

When Byrnes died, Garrison's good friend Louis Trent took over Linda Brigette's representation. Now everyone tried to prevent Linda from going to jail. Trent, his wife Lillian Cohen, and a schoolteacher named Rivette Matthews, signed affidavits stating that they did not believe that Linda's act was "obscene." Linda was to remember Frank Klein with bitterness ("Frank Klein did me bad," she told the author), but Klein recommended clemency for Linda and that she not do time.

Pershing chimed in, urging Garrison to help Linda. Linda had no use for Pershing Gervais, however, and when Frank Caracci saw Jim Garrison was about to introduce her to Pershing one day, Caracci had warned her, "Don't mess with him because he ain't no good." It was advice Linda Brigette took.

On August 31st,1966, Lou Trent appeared before the pardon board on behalf of Linda Brigette. Trent had approached Jim Garrison for help with Brigette's pardon. "Since time is of the essence," Trent wrote Garrison, "will you please use your influence in having the pardon signed or the reprieves [there had been four] continued to another date?" Trent requested that Jim Garrison view Linda's act one more time. Instead, Garrison asked Trent for his opinion. Trent said that the act was not obscene, and that was enough for Jim Garrison.

Soft hearted, as a favor to Lou Trent, his friend, with nothing to be gained for himself, but political grief – as would soon become apparent – Garrison gave orders to Jimmy Alcock. At the pardon board meeting, when Linda Brigette's name came up, Alcock said that the District Attorney's office advocated that Brigette be pardoned. Everyone knew that the office policy was either to oppose pardons or to remain silent. In the room on that occasion, Denis Barry was amazed. He exchanged a knowing smile with Lieutenant Governor "Taddy"Aycock. It must have something to do with Jim Garrison's nighttime Quarter life, Barry concluded. Brigette insisted to the author that there were no "goo goo eyes" between her and Garrison, that he was just one more patron who enjoyed her act. The rumor among the police was otherwise, and they laughed about Garrison "yodeling in the canyon," although that may have reflected more envy than fact.

John McKeithen's general rule was that he would grant clemency only if the vote of the pardon board was unanimous. In the case of Linda Brigette, the two sentencing judges, Shea and Brahney, voted no. On September 24th, at Jim Garrison's suggestion, McKeithen nonetheless sent a pardon down from Baton Rouge by taxi. Linda never thanked Jim Garrison (she told the author that she was too shy) and she never saw him again. "That's Jim Garrison," Trent would say, "the more you talked to him, the better your chances of relief were."

At the turn of the New Year 1966, things had been cordial between Jim Garrison and Aaron Kohn, and Garrison had thanked Kohn for his views on a Department of Corrections for Louisiana. Garrison pronounced himself "happy to take any action which you care to suggest." Then everything changed.

Suddenly a brouhaha erupted as Kohn accused Garrison of involvement with organized crime – based on his assistance in securing Linda Brigette her pardon. Kohn fired off a telegram to Governor McKeithen insisting on "the economic importance of Linda Brigette to organized crime, including the Marcello interests in New Orleans." So Kohn's war with Jim Garrison began. As part of his attack, Kohn also accused Linda's husband, Larry Lamarca, of mob connections, although Lamarca was no more connected to the Mafia than anyone in the Quarter who handed over payoffs. Every club owner did, Larry Lamarca included.

New Orleans was amused. At the annual Gridiron Show of the Press Club on October 21st, Linda Brigette appeared in a shimmering evening gown. On stage, she bumped into the actor playing the role of Governor McKeithen.

"Oh, pardon me!" she exclaims.

"Why, certainly!" the "Governor" replies. McKeithen played along and when some time later he asked Linda where she was from (Winnsboro), McKeithen inquired whether she knew a Dr. Funderburk. She did. "That's my wife's uncle!" the Governor said. "No wonder I gave you a pardon!" It turned out that Dr. Funderburk, an obstetrician, had delivered Linda Brigette.

At the Gridiron event, there was a rendition – with variations - of the song from which "Linda" had taken her name:

> When I go to sleep
> I never count sheep
> I count all the pardons for Linda.
> The DA's her defender,
> The evidence was not enough for him,
> The governor must love Linda.
> Or else he owes a debt to Big Jim...
> But miracles still happen,
> The only time she'll serve her 60 days
> Is when Aaron Kohn's the new DA.

Shortly after the Gridiron evening, Jim Garrison was sitting beside the pool at John Volz's apartment complex. A woman strode up in full indignation.

"Mr. Garrison, I cannot believe that you helped that stripper get a pardon!" she said, outraged.

"Well, Madam, obviously I was paid," said Jim Garrison, never one to suffer fools gladly.

Garrison might joke, but Kohn had launched a venomous attack that would continue for more than a decade. He attacked Garrison for his supposed leniency toward a petty criminal named Mike Roach, and coupled this with the Linda Brigette pardon. Over and over Kohn insisted that Garrison's engineering the pardon for Linda Brigette proved that he was tied in with organized crime.

Kohn knew better. As John Tarver, Governor McKeithen's right-hand man, observed, Carlos Marcello had a strong pipeline to the Governor's mansion, and Marcello would have liked nothing better than to have Jim Garrison voted out of office. For Marcello's purposes, Garrison was undependable and unreliable.

According to John Volz, who monitored organized crime strike forces for the Department of Justice after he left Garrison's office, Kohn's picture of the mob in New Orleans was entirely his own invention. Volz, who as a United States Attorney would send Carlos Marcello to jail, found the Marcellos "the most disorganized organized criminals in the country." There was no comparison between them and the crime families in New York and Chicago.

Garrison responded to Kohn's charges that he was connected to organized crime with bewilderment. He issued a nine-page press release: "Neither the director of the Crime Commission, whose imagination seems to be dominated by the specter of organized crime, nor the reporter who wrote the story, bothered to obtain all the facts." Garrison behaved as if the charge that he was connected to organized crime was subject to reason – or evidence.

He made a joke of Kohn's obsession with Linda Brigette: "It is not made clear whether the Cleveland mob or the Chicago syndicate is engineering this one," Garrison said, "but the inference is that it is a pretty big operation, leaving the public perilously exposed to her dangerous dance." Kohn's campaign, Garrison said, was "the silliest thing to come along since the Flat Earth Society's last press release."

As for Mike Roach, Garrison pointed out that he was the first district attorney to accept charges against Roach, for public bribery and solicitation for prostitution: "Mike Roach was in jail because we put him there." He added: "If I was a friend of the mob, why would I have prosecuted him in the first place?"

On WNOE radio, Garrison called the Metropolitan Crime Commission "an organization of essentially totalitarian nature." Kohn's was a "Big Brother operation right out of George Orwell's 1984...it is a kind of super Soviet-type NKVD." Kohn's behavior, Garrison added, rendered dubious the "continued existence" of the Metropolitan Crime Commission.

Kohn would not relent. On WDSU, he called Linda Brigette "something more than a strip teaser. She is also one of the tools of the underworld." If she was out of jail, it was thanks to Frank Caracci, "who is also a key figure in the organized underworld of the French Quarter." Then Kohn added that there were "two top pin-ball racketeers in this city, against whom Garrison has never acted." So history reveals that it was Aaron Kohn who was the inspiration for the federal prosecution of Jim Garrison in the early 1970s, the charge, Garrison's accepting bribes from pinball gambling interests.

Still unaware of Kohn's hidden agenda, Garrison compared Kohn's attacks to "being attacked by three or four flies." He challenged Kohn to connect Linda Brigette to organized crime: It was "a little hard to see just how organized crime is back of my effort to save an unjustly convicted mother of small children from a jail sentence." He reminded Kohn that his conviction record on illegal pinball operators was ninety-eight percent.

Facts were irrelevant. Kohn ignored even one of his own major informants, press agent Jesse Core, who told him it was silly "to think that a dancer could be important to organized crime." When Core wondered how the United States attorney, Louis Lacour, had been "tricked into backing your [Kohn's] position about organized crime," Kohn just laughed.

Then Kohn retorted: hadn't Garrison at a Press Club dinner bumped Core from his table only to invite Larry Lamarca and Brigette to join him and his wife? Hadn't Jim Garrison's trip to New York to visit the offices of district attorneys been financed with an $800 loan from Larry Lamarca? Hadn't Garrison been a guest of one Carl Goldenberg in Phoenix, and even driven in Goldenberg's Rolls Royce to that event when Lamarca and Birgette had sat at his table? And what about Garrison's new white brick house at 4600 Owens Boulevard, built by Frank Occhipinti? Kohn ignored that Garrison had a fat mortgage on the house, for which he paid $60,000, hardly a cut-rate figure in those days. Garrison would take most of the rest of his life to pay off this mortgage, and he would do so only with the money he earned twenty years later from Oliver Stone's "JFK" film about his Kennedy investigation. By then he had to take out second and third mortgages.

Kohn's facts were wrong, although that never stopped him, as Judge Adrian Duplantier told the author. Kohn charged that Garrison had obtained Linda Brigette's divorce for her, although it was Denis Barry; Garrison hated to appear in civil court. When Kohn accused Garrison of being a lender in a mortgage loan to Mike Roach, which had been notarized by Garrison's then-partner Barry on October 5, 1961,

Barry explained that Roach had signed the papers in Barry's office, and Garrison had merely witnessed the signatures on the mortgage. "Mr. Garrison did not own any part of the funds nor did he derive any benefit from the transaction," Barry tried to explain to Kohn. Barry himself was simply the attorney for a local mortgage company and enlisted Garrison because he required signatures for notarization.

Acerbic when he wanted to be, Barry then laced into Kohn:

> I find it incredible to believe that you would take the above routine transaction and clothe it with a monstrous motive. You should realize that this mortgage occurred seven months before Mr. Garrison became District Attorney....attempting to connect this mortgage with your present personal feud can only be an example of any means justifying the end.

Even Barry, shrewd as he was, could not penetrate Kohn's motive. Governor McKeithen, less courageous, whimpered on WNNR radio that he would have granted Linda Brigette another reprieve rather than a pardon had he known that his action would create this much excitement. He called the pardon a "political error."

Garrison charged Kohn with accusing him of "guilt by association," what Kohn had always done. He repeated his favorite metaphor about the squid blinding its adversary: "This is very much like the squid which, when attacked injects black fluid into the eyes of his opponent." It seemed too absurd. On WDSU, Garrison quoted Mark Twain: You must get the facts first. Then you can go ahead and distort them.

When Louis Lacour stated that the arrest of Carlos Marcello in New York made it "obvious that there is organized crime in this area," Garrison challenged him to appear before the Orleans Parish grand jury. Lacour pleaded executive privilege. Garrison then sent a telegram to the United States Attorney General, Nicholas Katzenbach, demanding that Lacour be allowed to testify. Garrison invited the press to examine his office files. Calling Kohn's statements "the big lie," he insisted that he had fought organized crime: clip joints, narcotics, gambling, bail bonding, loan sharks, and had convicted every abortionist in the city.

Then he subpoenaed Aaron Kohn to the grand jury to produce the evidence he claimed he had in his files of organized crime in Orleans Parish. "We will undoubtedly learn that I have been seen on a street car at the same time as Bugsy Schwartz, the famous burglar," Garrison joked, "Or that I was in New York City at the same time as Machine-Gun Brady."

"Put up or shut up!" Garrison told Kohn.

Kohn arrived at Tulane and Broad with a thirty-pound box of papers and two heavy briefcases. Jim Garrison left him cooling his heels on a bench outside the grand jury room for several hours, later admitting he had done it to "humiliate" Kohn. No information of factual probity about organized crime emerged from Kohn's testimony. He insisted that Linda Brigette was "an asset to the Marcello mob interests in New Orleans," but this was not fact. He offered the innuendo of a relationship between Marcello and Municipal Court judge Andrew Bucaro, who had "attempted to intimidate a police officer." He invoked "illegal courtesy paroles," but these Jim Garrison himself had publicly opposed.

When it was over, Garrison laughed. Kohn had sought the indictment of Bucaro "because he found a seventeen-year-old school girl guilty of violating a municipal ordinance." After Kohn's three hours, Garrison said sardonically, the MCC "should turn its attention to raising camellias," since Kohn's press release was ludicrous. (Kohn wrote that Linda Brigette "is to the strip joint operator what a gun is to an armed robber. Just as you cannot return a gun to a convicted armed robber, you shouldn't return a convicted stripper to the strip joints which profit on her illegal acts").

Charlie Ward accused Kohn of using "charges of organized crime to create scandal," noting that Kohn had "never once produced any evidence before any jury which resulted in any conviction in any court in Louisiana – State or Federal." Katzenbach had never replied to Jim Garrison's request that he give Lacour permission to testify, even as Lacour now admitted that the crimes he had in mind were, in fact, federal crimes, and "to inform a Parish grand jury of these facts could serve no useful purpose, in that they have no authority to act on these matters." Whatever Carlos Marcello did, Lacour admitted, separating himself from Kohn, it was the federal government that had to stop him.

Jim Garrison retorted that "they are going to put away their Ace Investigator Kits and are going to return to their offices and gardens," elaborating on the camellia conceit. Unwilling to let go of the issue, Kohn insisted that "Carlos Marcello is behind Lamarca" and hired a former FBI agent named John Daniel Sullivan to take Jim Garrison up on his 1962 offer and inspect his files. Garrison gave Sullivan access with sarcasm: "We will even have a member of our staff assist him in finding his way back to his hotel at the end of the day." Sullivan in turn complained that he was being "watched" while he worked in the records room. Sullivan's efforts came to an end when he died at home in a shotgun blast that was ruled an accident.

Now Jim Garrison issued a memorandum to "All Members Of The Staff." No certified or registered mail – or mail of any other kind – was to be accepted from the Metropolitan Crime Commission. Should any arrive, it was to be "placed in a brown envelope and sent back to this organization without being opened." No member of the staff was to communicate "with this discredited association." The reason was "the policies of prevarication of the Managing Director."

Aaron Kohn had seized on the Linda Brigette pardon as if Jim Garrison had committed the crime of the century. His over-reaction was so extreme that it should have given anyone pause. What, indeed, could have driven Kohn, who had praised Garrison's work consistently from 1962 to 1965, to such hysteria?

From the hindsight of history, the answer seems apparent. By the autumn of 1966, Aaron Kohn had learned that Jim Garrison was investigating the Kennedy assassination. Kohn had joined a much larger campaign already in place to ensure that Garrison be thwarted in his efforts.

Kohn's source for his information that Garrison was studying the Kennedy case was David Chandler, one of Kohn's "network of informants," as police officer Mike Seghers puts it. Close to Garrison, Chandler had encouraged him in this effort. Garrison had shared his doubts about the Warren Report with Chandler often.

"You're in a unique position to get to the bottom of this," Chandler had told him, "because you can subpoena people. A lot of the principal people involved hung around New Orleans. You can ask questions. You can do something amazing." It had been Chandler who had suggested to Jim Garrison that "Clay Bertrand," who had telephoned Dean Andrews and told him to go to Dallas to represent Lee Harvey Oswald, could only be Clay Shaw, the managing director of the International Trade Mart. During that summer and fall, even Chandler had to admit: "Using Kohn's own definition there isn't organized crime in the political limits of New Orleans. There is in the metropolitan area, which includes Jefferson Parish, the redoubt of the Marcellos."

What Jim Garrison did not notice was that Aaron Kohn had been involved in the cover-up of the Kennedy assassination from the beginning. Only a week after the assassination, the Metropolitan Crime Commission had published a pamphlet filled with facts about Lee Harvey Oswald's background, with a photograph of Oswald on its cover. Oswald had "acted alone," Kohn had written - before the Warren Commission had even convened. Kohn had so much information about Oswald so quickly that years later, working for the House Select Committee On Assassinations in the late 1970s, former New Orleans homicide detective L. J. Delsa paid Kohn a visit.

"Mr. Kohn, let me ask you one question," Delsa began. "Only a week after the assassination, how did you get this picture? How did you get so much information?"

"We got avenues," Kohn said.

"This is evidence," Delsa persisted. "How did you come into possession of this evidence?" Delsa gained neither an answer to that question nor another interview with Kohn.

By 1966, Jim Garrison was so deeply immersed in his investigation into the assassination of President Kennedy and in the Warren Commission volumes that he could talk of nothing else. What Aaron Kohn said or did mattered not at all. You could tell him the house was burning, and they had to get out, Denis Barry's wife Barbara observed, and he would still be talking about the Kennedy case. "Did I tell you…." he would begin, and you knew, only if you were interested in the Kennedy assassination could you gain his attention.

Those closest to him did not encourage Jim Garrison in his single-minded effort to investigate the Kennedy assassination.

Jack Bremermann sent his old friend a postcard: "Is this another Wilmer?" Jim Garrison did not reply.

Liz evinced no interest at all.

"I'm investigating the assassination of President John Fitzgerald Kennedy," Jim told Phyllis. Phyllis looked at him and thought: he's off the wall. He had always trusted the government. What was this? Then she attributed his sudden political reversal to Hale Boggs, who had filled his head with stories of how the Warren Commission had suppressed information, and who had revealed to Garrison how dubious he was about the Commission's "Report."

Ever "playing for results," Pershing Gervais at once distanced himself from Garrison's Kennedy probe. Garrison would not be thanked by the government for these efforts, Pershing perceived at once. The only White House Jim Garrison would be visiting, Pershing said, was "the White House in Jackson." In his nasty way, Pershing was referring to the monumental Greek revival main building at the East Louisiana State Hospital, its pillared façade resembling the Presidential residence in Washington, D.C.

"Garrison is obsessed with the investigation," Pershing reported to FBI Special Agent Regis Kennedy; Aaron Kohn was not the only person for whom Gervais functioned as an informant. Regis Kennedy, Pershing knew, reported not only to the Special Agent in Charge in New Orleans, but also directly to Headquarters.

Pershing wanted "Big Regis," as Dean Andrews dubbed the tall, red-haired agent, to know that he had urged Garrison "to forget the matter." Pershing assured the FBI that he "would not assist Garrison in his investigation." Nothing he said could change Garrison's mind, Pershing added.

The only contact he himself had with the investigation had been a call he received from David Ferrie, Pershing claimed. This was another of Pershing's lies. By the time he contacted Big Regis, Pershing had made an appearance at Tulane and Broad where he had interviewed Jack Martin. Self-preservation governed Pershing's actions, always. He continued to tell Jim Garrison that in searching for President Kennedy's assassins, he was running around in circles and getting nowhere.

It wasn't that Garrison's friends opposed the investigation out of respect for national authority. Few in Louisiana trusted the federal government, with many experiencing a dizzying, visceral revulsion for what they called "the Fed." This feeling, an expression of the culture of states' rights, is reflected in the story, famously, of Governor Earl Long's reply to Leander Perez, who was infuriated by a challenge to the oil depletion allowance.

"The Feds have the atom bomb," Uncle Earl warned his friend. "What are you going to do now, Leander?"

"I wouldn't piss on Washington D.C. if the place was on fire," Pershing said. "But I'm not going to sign up in a suicidal crusade of telling the whole world that the government's been lying."

Pershing, whose name would appear on a secret CIA list of its plants in Jim Garrison's office, was not shy about admitting to his fear of repercussions. I've "acquired this habit of breathing," Pershing said. There would be no "kamikaze missions" for him, his definition of what Jim Garrison had embarked upon.

For Pershing, there had always to be "a plus," as his friend Mike Seghers says. Investigating the Kennedy assassination offered none. Later, when people complained to Pershing about Jim Garrison's probe, he had a ready answer: "Go tell the FBI!"

Jim Garrison, no Pershing Gervais, would go on to compare the indifference of people to the assassination of President Kennedy, their unquestioning acceptance of the flawed Warren Report, to the willful ignorance of residents of Dachau who walked by the concentration camp and pretended that "they didn't know what that smoke was that was pouring out of the crematorium."

"Nothing else matters," Jim Garrison was to declare on Dutch television refering to his investigation. As his personal sacrifices mounted, he remained, for the rest of his life, dedicated to his search for the truth about what had happened to President Kennedy.

APPENDIX:

WHO WAS JACK MARTIN?

The level of Jack Martin's connections would give anyone pause. Inexplicably, Jack enjoyed access to highly placed sources, rendering it at once a mistake to conclude that Jack Martin was not taken seriously in New Orleans and elsewhere, as reporter and future assistant district attorney Herman Kohlman knew from his days working on the "Times-Picayune," and as Jim Garrison also came to know.

Among others in New Orleans, "States-Item" reporter and CIA asset himself, Hoke May, appreciated Jack Martin as, always, a credible source. Jack Martin knew a great deal about Dr. Mary Sherman, the orthopedic surgeon who was murdered under extraordinary circumstances. He knew about her connections with Dr. Alton Ochsner. Hoke May confirmed that Dr. Sherman knew Jim Garrison's chief suspect, David Ferrie, even as Dr. Sherman's cancer researches took her to the U.S. Public Health Hospital where Lee Harvey Oswald alighted briefly during his time in New Orleans.

Jack Martin also knew the precise moment when federal agents would kidnap Carlos Marcello and deport him to Guatemala; and, some years later, Jack knew in advance that Jim Garrison would be taken to the Wildlife and Fisheries building for booking when he was arrested on those bogus charges that he had accepted bribes from illegal pinball gambling interests. When Garrison was driven up, Jack Martin stood in the crowd that had gathered to wait for him.

What Garrison would never discover for certain, not through all the years that he investigated the assassination of President Kennedy, was that Jack Martin worked for government intelligence. Thomas Edward Beckham knew it because Jack Martin was his handler. But by the time Beckham was to come forward with this information, he had lived a lifetime as a con man, even for a time becoming a Rabbi, to the ultimate disillusionment of several of his Parishioners who had been seduced by his charm, energy and spiritual certitude and formidable knowledge of the Torah. For historians lacking an appropriate skepticism, Beckham had long been the quintessential impeachable source.

Jack Martin admitted that he was "probably responsible for Thomas Beckham first becoming a priest." For years, Beckham feared Jack and would only talk to this author once he was certain that Jack Martin was dead.

The one thing about Beckham that surprised people, not least those who consider themselves his victims, was, finally, that he seemed never to face any consequences. His activities themselves rendered Beckham thoroughly impeachable and allowed him to continue unimpeded. They also guaranteed his survival.

After Jim Garrison became involved with Jack Martin as a source, after Garrison began his pursuit of Beckham, the CIA quickly issued a document stating that Jack of New Orleans, also known as John J. Martin of Louisville, was not their acknowledged former employee, Joseph J. Martin. They were responding to a report from "the Most Reverend Christopher Maria Stanley" of Louisville, himself a dubious character, wrapped in the cloak of a marginal religious sect. Stanley had reported to the FBI that "John J. Martin" had been associated with David Ferrie, and that Martin claimed "not only to have been in the Air Force during World War II, but also to have worked for CIA."

In the course of their denial that Joseph and Jack were one and the same, CIA quickly stopped investigating the identity of the New Orleans Jack Martin. "OS (Office of Security) does NOT believe identical nor do I," writes CIA's Scott Miler, following up on a request from one J. L., of Counter Intelligence (CI/R&A), the research and analysis group, whose name is redacted from the 1998 document release. "Have agreed with OS no further action and think this proper." CIA then issued a document exposing that Joseph J. Martin, who ostensibly retired from the Agency in June 1958 when he was an "Intelligence Assistant," was as erratic a personality as the Jack Martin of New Orleans.

Joseph, like Jack, engaged in "rambling talk," habitually making unwelcome telephone calls to the CIA Watch Office, and once to the Director of Central Intelligence himself. As in New Orleans, Jack was known to be of "unsound mind," so the CIA described Joseph. The FBI added that Joseph James Martin was a "nut." Joseph was also employed by several airlines, even as "Jack Martin" of New Orleans enjoyed that intimate relationship with Richard Robey of the Federal Aviation Agency.

Joseph was alcoholic; Jack was alcoholic. Joseph, a Roman Catholic, sneered, belligerently, that he "wouldn't vote for Kennedy." Jack associated with several of those involved in the plot to kill President Kennedy, among them the patsy Lee Harvey Oswald and David Ferrie, his sometime handler, not to mention Guy Banister, at whose offices Oswald and Jack both perched. Joseph and Jack even looked alike, sharing a small mustache and a puny physique. Was this all a coincidence?

In 1998, the CIA released a document admitting that among those they utilized in their operations were several people grouped under the name "Jack Martin." One of the names, CIA acknowledges, "(Jack Martin)" was "generic." There were three 201 files on different people whose names were variations on "Jack Martin" and none of whom was the admitted, if obstreperous, CIA employee "Joseph James Martin."

These three Jack Martins, all bearing different middle initials, were listed on another CIA document, along with their "AINS" numbers or internal CIA File Subject Identification Numbers. AINS were "Agency Identification Numbers," as CIA explains, "not necessarily suggesting an "employee relationship." In contrast, was the "EIN," which was an "Employee Identification Number." On the list of those with AINS in the CIA security files were: Jack Martin; Jack M. Martin; Jack S. Martin; and a Lawrence J. Martin.

"Not necessarily" employees, they may indeed have been employees, or, if not employees, then assets. Among those listed on the same document with AINS numbers were such known CIA assets as Richard Case Nagell, Frank Fiorini (Frank Sturges), Cesar Diosdado and George de Mohrenschildt. One might ask why, if Joseph James Martin were the only CIA Martin, would the Agency admit to using the name "Jack Martin" "generically"? (Another of those to use the "Martin" surname as an alias was one of the Watergate burglars, CIA operative Virgilio R. Gonzalez).

What CIA had accomplished, as New Orleans former homicide detective L. J. Delsa suggested to the author, is "plausible deniability" in the very name "Jack Martin." CIA need not fear that its relationship with the New Orleans Jack would emerge because you would never be able to figure out if the man in question was the right "Jack Martin."

As on behalf of the House Select Committee On Assassinations, Delsa interviewed the "Jack Martin" who was part of Jim Garrison's investigation into the Kennedy assassination, he concluded that Jack Martin was "hard core" CIA. That he was an intelligence agent was at once obvious to seasoned investigator Delsa.

It was, of course, "Jack S. Martin" (aka Edward Stewart Suggs) who telephoned the New Orleans field office of the FBI to report that Jim Garrison was conducting an investigation "concerning the Lee Harvey Oswald case." It was this Jack who also confided to the FBI that Thomas Edward Beckham "was associated with Oswald and assisted Oswald in passing out leaflets", which Beckham denies. On another occasion, Martin called the head of the CIA field office in New Orleans, claiming that Jim Garrison's chief investigator, Louis Ivon, had enlisted him to request that the head of the local CIA office, Lloyd Ray, call Ivon "at his unlisted number."

Jack S. Martin's file included a Dallas Police Department report of his having been arrested on a murder charge in 1952 only for him to be released on bond and the murder case dismissed three months later. No explanation was provided. It is apparent that Martin's stay in the psychiatric ward at Charity Hospital in New Orleans later in the decade was following a script common to many involved in the Kennedy assassination, either as witnesses or participants.

Martin, who committed himself, just as he would later advise an innocent young Beckham to commit himself to a mental hospital in Mandeville, was rendering himself impeachable. It worked: A report issued by Charity Hospital in January 1957 diagnosed Martin with "sociopathic personality disturbance, antisocial type."

Jack spelled out the problem in the disjoined 1968 affidavit he authored for Jim Garrison with Banister runner, David Lewis: "No one could possibly afford for the 'cat to get out of the bag,' as it were," Martin writes with respect to who was involved in the plot to murder President Kennedy. "So it was," he adds, "that either certain people must not be (1) available, or (2) creditable…They must not be able to tell, or they must not be believed. In short, all became 'dead,' either figuratively, or literally, so to speak."

As author Penn Jones and others were to report, many Kennedy assassination witnesses did meet untimely ends, becoming "unavailable." Among the New Orleans witnesses who died inopportunely was a Clinton resident named Andrew Dunn being held in the Clinton jail on a charge of public intoxication; Dunn was found hanged in his cell – while lying flat in his bunk.

Another premature death was that of nineteen-year-old Gloria Wilson, who had been spotted in East Feliciana Parish in the company of Lee Harvey Oswald during the summer of 1963; the source for this information was Gloria's lover in Eunice, Louisiana, Norman (Sam) Dunnehoe, who swore Garrison investigator Anne Dischler to secrecy, imploring her never to utter his name during his lifetime. The doctor who did the autopsy on Gloria, Dr. Richard Munson, said, "That woman was murdered." The cause of death, he determined, was a septic infection, the result of a botched abortion with a blunt instrument. Oswald, a friend of Dr. Munson's named Hadley Hudnall says, stayed sometimes with Gloria on St. Helena Street, three blocks east of the Clinton Courthouse.

Other Garrison witnesses who suffered violence before they could testify at the trial of Clay Shaw included the Reverend Clyde Johnson, who was beaten up badly the day before he was scheduled to testify, then shot to death a few months later. And, of course, Jack Martin's cohort, David Ferrie, died the week before Jim Garrison could charge him.

Jack Martin and Thomas Edward Beckham lived to tell what they knew – but as impeachable witnesses who would not be believed no matter what they said. They joined others, like Marina Oswald, who changed her story so many times that no one could believe anything she said.

In the preceding narrative, the reader first makes the acquaintance of ubiquitous Jack as he just happens to be passing the time of day outside the office of bail bondsman Hardy Davis – just as Davis is about to be offered a bribe from Richard Dowling, running for re-election as District Attorney of Orleans Parish. Dowling's opponent, of course, was Jim Garrison.

Jack Martin was later to inform Jim Garrison that the CIA contributed to his campaign against Dowling. The CIA backed "several opposing political candidates" in the campaign to ensure that Dowling would be defeated, Martin confided. He called it an "ironic joke" in the light of Garrison's later suggestion that Lee Harvey Oswald was a CIA asset. In 1968, Martin reminded Garrison that he and his partner, Joe Newbrough, had been present when the contribution came in to

Garrison's law office. "Yes," Martin wrote in that fifty-five page "Affidavit," "you took the seat vacated by Dowling, partially with C.I.A. funds!"

The identification of the Jack Martin in the Garrison story awaits further confirmation, and is the subject of a pending FOIA suit, as of October 2007 on Administrative Appeal. It is useful to note, however, that the very intrusion of "Jack Martin" into Jim Garrison's life suggests what Garrison was up against, both as he attempted to navigate the shoals of New Orleans politics, and, shortly, what he would face as he pursued his investigation into the murder of President Kennedy.

When Garrison took up his pen to write the story of his investigation, the book that would become "On The Trail Of The Assassins," published in 1988, by Sheridan Square Press, his plan was in the very first scene to dramatize Jack Martin sitting across from him and being interrogated. The title of the chapter would be "Man Under The Oak Tree," an image Garrison borrowed from William March, a novelist he admired. The metaphoric "man under the oak tree" represents those who, simply by propinquity, become witnesses to a crime. Martin would be "acting nervous," Garrison writes. Martin would admit "he knew Ferrie and Banister that summer, but won't say what they were up to. You decide not to push him at this point."

During these years in New Orleans, Jack Martin sat under more than one oak tree.

Notes

Foreword

Information in the foreword derives from interviews with Donald Deneselya, December 8, 2007, December 11, 2007 and subsequent occasions, with Louis Ivon and with John R. Rarick. For the HSCA document referenced in connection with Mr. Deneselya's testimony: HSCA, 180-101110-10145. Record Series: SECURITY CLASSIFIED FILES. Agency file Number: JFK-171. Date: 09/26/78. 4 pages. NARA. See also: Transcript of FRONTLINE program #1205 broadcast November 13, 1993, available at http://www.pbs.org. Files of the false defector Robert Webster are available at NARA.

Chapter 1

Page

1— "It's just Mr. Jimmy": Interview with Peggie Baker, May 26, 1998.

1— "keeping blacks from walking": Interview with Jim Garrison, July 29-August 9, 1977 for HSCA. Present are Jonathan Blackmer, L. J. Delsa, Gaeton Fonzi and Clifford Fenton. NARA.

2— "rather eccentric in his views": Carl D. Lynch to Mrs. Alfred Garrison, October 25, 1964. Appendix to "A Short History of the Garrison Family of North Carolina and Their Descendants." Courtesy of Lyon Garrison.

2— Patrick Henry County, 1764: Carl D. Lynch to Mrs. Alfred Garrison, October 25, 1964.

2— For the portrait of T. J. Garrison, see "History of Crawford County, Iowa." (Published by the S. J. Clarke Publishing Co., 1911), p. 67.

2— T. J. is relieved to see Clarence Darrow depart: Jim Garrison, "On The Trail of the Assassins: My Investigation and Prosecution of the Murder of President Kennedy" (Sheridan Square Press: New York, 1988), p. 8.

2— the Garrison House...Silk Stocking Row: "Garrison's Roots Found in

Denison," by Richard Osterhohn. Omaha "World Herald." April 1, 1967.

2— "why didn't we keep cash": Jane Garrison Gardiner: "To Whom It May Concern," November 7, 1971. Courtesy of Lyon Garrison.

2— Lillian Garrison listens to the new records: Mrs. Ray H. Thompson to Jim Garrison, April 3, 1967. Courtesy of Lyon Garrison.

3— the circus came to Des Moines: Fragment of a History of the Robinson family, pp. 32-33. Begins with William McFarren Robinson. The Garrison Family Papers. NARA.

3— Portrait of William Oliver Robinson: "On The Trail of the Assassins," p. 9.

4— Jim Garrison registers at hotels as W. O. Robinson: "Ibid., p. 220n.

4— Jim Garrison gets out of the tub, puts on his mother's hat: Pearl Rank Heiden to Mrs. Ethel Thompson, March 8, 1967. This letter is also the source of the story of Jim Garrison hiding in the oven. Courtesy of Lyon Garrison.

4— "to sit with Carothers and Judy": "Garrison's Roots Found In Denison."

4— at four he could read: Interview with Mrs. Liz Garrison, January 11, 1998.

5— Earling Carothers changes his name to "Jimmy": Interview with Elizabeth Garrison, January 11, 1998.

5— Jimmy shaves off his eyebrows: Interview with Phyllis Kritikos, May 29, 1998.

6— "Daddy in drag": Conversation with Virginia Garrison, May 28, 1998.

6— the troubles of Earling R. Garrison: See "Garrison's Roots Found In Dennison"; "Earling Garrison Lodged In Jail Here On Sunday," "Denison Review," April 23, 1930; "Judge Peter J. Klinker Holds Court Here Sat.," "The Denison Bulletin," April 30, 1930.

6— Jane Garrison describes Evansville: Jane Gardiner to "Simpson": January 16, 1970. Courtesy of Lyon Garrison.

6— "We were stuck up in Evansville": Notes of Interview with Jim Garrison. Courtesy of Zachary Sklar.

6— Jim Garrison was to remember having to place cardboard in his shoes: Interview with Phyllis Kritikos, May 29, 1998.

7— running away from something: Interview with William Alford, May 28, 1998.

7— Condolences from the members of the Mississippi Society, DAR: Undated. Mrs. James S. Lawson, Chaplain, Mississippi Society to Miss Garrison. Courtesy of Lyon Garrison.

7— Mike Tyson wouldn't last a round: Notes of Interviews with Jim Garrison. Courtesy of Zachary Sklar.

7— he drew his strength from her: Interview with Mrs. Liz Garrison, January 11, 1998.

7— Jimmy didn't have a bicycle: Interview with Dr. Bernard Jacobs, April 14, 2000.

7— Jimmy sets off a firecracker and is expelled from the Boy Scouts: Interview with Mrs. Liz Garrison, January 11, 1998.

7— Jimmy sits drawing pictures and shrugs when his neighbor comments: Interview with the late Walter Gemeinhardt, May 31, 2000.

8— for descriptions of Fanny Campbell's boarding house: Interview with Loraine Chadwick, June 15, 2000; Martha Ann Samuel, June 10, 2000; C. Jackson Grayson, Jr., January 6, 2000; Marcie Ann Little, June 19, 2000; Mickey Parlour Bremermann, July 30, 31, 1999.

8— you had to be in the social register: To Dick. From: Marge. March 20, 1967. Papers of Richard N. Billings, Assassination Archives and Research Center, Washington, D. C. (AARC).

9— Ruth Bayer Francis takes care of Jimmy and Judy: Interview with Miss Francis's niece, Mrs. Lenore Ward, August 7, 2000.

9— very tall gangling fellow: Conversation with Richard Gaille, April 22, 2000.

9— for a portrait of Jim Garrison's high school years, see Alvin Gottschall, "Growing Up In New Orleans" (Vantage Press: New York, 1997). Gottschall includes the story of being accused of parking violations by the new District Attorney of Orleans Parish.

9— nose was clogged up: Interview with Alvin Gottschall.

10— "didn't want to go to school." Letter to Joan Mellen from Michael H. Bagot, August 14, 2000.

10— Michael Bagot visits Garrison: Interview with Michael Bagot, October 8, 2000.

10— "lost in space": Conversation with Judge Charles Schwartz, July 24, 2000.

10— he ate his lunch all by himself: Interview with John Clemmer, June 1, 2000.

10— "Do you have a pencil?" Conversation with Edwin H. Gebhardt, April 17, 2000.

10— "How do you like this?" Conversation with Herbert Barton, June 2, 2000.

10— "those stupid fools": Alvin G. Gottschall, "Growing Up In New Orleans," p. 40.

11— he spoke of his father with disdain: Interview with Wilma Baker, May 26, 1998.

11— the Baker girls gave parties on Saturday nights: Interviews with Alvin Gottschall; Peggie Baker; Wilma Baker; Pat Gore; Fred Gore.

11— so they could have the boys to themselves: Gottschall, p. 47.

11— "Swing music, which so many people still love": Jim Garrison to The Willard Alexander Agency, June 23, 1982. Courtesy of Lyon Garrison.

12— Mrs. Garrison hires a private investigator to bring Judith back: Interview with Mrs. Liz Garrison, May 28, 1998.

12— he used big words: Interview with Pat Gore, July 18, 2000.

13— "why don't you come to the Jackson Barracks?" Ibid. Jim Garrison had to lie about his age to enlist.

13— he led a movement for students to stop shaving: Conversation with Allen B. Koltun, June 2, 2000.

13— Jane Garrison followed: Interview with Mrs. Liz Garrison, May 28, 1998.

Chapter 2

15— "New Orleans coffee": Powell A. Casey, "Try Us: The Story of the Washington Artillery in World War II" (Claitor's Publishing Division: Claitor's Books: Baton Rouge, 1971), p. 6.

15— the cot was far too short: Interview with Elizabeth Garrison, May 28, 1998.

15— "That's the dummies' kid": Rosemary James, "Pershing Gervais – Man or Myth?" "New Orleans" magazine (July 1970), p. 62.

15— carrying concealed weapons: "Sheriff of West Feliciana First Tyson Case Witness," "Times-Picayune," April 2, 1953, p. 21.

15— blackjack and brass knuckles: Gene Bourg,"The Long Checkered Career of One Pershing Gervais": City Hall Report. "New Orleans States-Item."

16— a controlling influence: Jim Garrison to Zachary Sklar, June 1, 1988. AARC. "He was able to control me because, I regret to say, I trust everyone and am easily fooled."
16— a man who cared for him: Interview with Phyllis Kritikos, February 6, 2002. Kritikos would become Jim Garrison's second wife.

16— "wild cat and were-wolf": Jim Garrison, "Coup D'Etat" (Unpublished). p. 18 of 12. D. C. AARC.

16— for a description of Camp Shelby, see "Try Us: The Story of the Washington Artillery in World War II."

16— "erotic attachment": Interview with Robert Haik, January 9, 2000.

16— "love the army": James, p. 58.

17— "tent pegs in a honeymoon bed": Jim Garrison to Pershing Gervais, September 6, 1942. Courtesy of Darrow Gervais.

17— he teaches "illiterates, mental neurotics, and physically disabled": Jim Garrison to Pershing Gervais, November 1, 1942.

17— "the Black Hole of Calcutta": Jim Garrison to Pershing Gervais, May 15, 1943.

18— Jim Garrison describes his wartime experiences flying a Grasshopper in "A Piper Cub Over Germany," included in "New Orleans Goes To War, 1941-1945," an oral history of New Orleanians during World War II, compiled by Brian Altobello. 1990. pp. 134-136. Courtesy of The Williams Research Center, 410 Chartres Street, New Orleans, Louisiana 70130.

20— "pick up the bodies": Memorandum. January 16, 1984. To: Stadiem. From: Garrison. Re: Characteristics Of The Grasshopper. Courtesy of Lyon Garrison.

20— brand new Grasshopper: Ibid.

20— Jimmy Gulotta would scoff at the Air Medal: Interview with Judge James J. Gulotta, January 9, 1998.

20- "What I saw there has haunted me ever since": Jim Garrison, interview, Playboy magazine.Vol.14, No 10 (October 1967), p. 178.

20— "machine-gunned to death": Jim Garrison, "Foreword – A Heritage of Stone," "Crime, Law and Corrections, ed. Ralph Slovenko. (Charles C. Thomas; Springfield, Illinois, 1966), p. xx.

21— lawyers…judges: Ibid., p. xxi.

21— Jane Garrison moves to Laurel: See Gardiner v. Gardiner, No. 40433. Supreme Court of Mississippi, March 25, 1957, Decided.

21— "on the basis that his efficiency index was below 3.5": Federal Bureau of Investigation Report: 2/1/51. File No. 67-35908. February 20, 1951. Courtesy of the US Department of Justice.

21— Jim catches amoebic dysentery in Mexico: Interview with Joseph E. Allain, January 24, 2001.

21— Jane paid far too much attention to Jim: Interview with Brucie Rafferty, August 10, 2000.

21— For Mrs. Gardiner's stay at Fanny's, see also: Interview with Loraine Chadwick, June 15, 2000.

22— Brooks Brothers suits: Interview with Robert Haik, January 9, 2000.

22— glum: Interview with Loraine Chadwick.

22— never pushed himself on other people: Interview with Marcie Ann Little, June 19, 2000.

22— ever having been a teenager: Interview with Mickey Parlour Bremermann, July 31, 1999.

22— he was afraid of people: Interview with Judge James J. Gulotta, January 9, 1998.

22— "that's kind of silly": Interview with C. Jackson Grayson, Jr., January 6, 2000.

22— "it was my great happiness to see you all enjoying yourselves": Interview with Loraine Chadwick.

22— he was never cruel: Interview with C. Jackson Grayson, Jr.

23— a United States Senator: Interview with Alvin Gottschall, March 6, 1998.

23— "with the minimum of effort": Interview with Judge Thomas Wicker, June 5, 2000.

24— best student he ever had: Interview with C. J. Morrow as recounted by Wilmer Thomas, July 24, 2000.

24— then he was consumed: Interview with Judge James J. Gulotta, January 9, 1998.

24— moot court team: "Winners Listed in Moot Cases," New Orleans "Times-Picayune," April 3, 1947, p. 14.

24— a cartoonist: Interview with Vance Gilmer, January 4, 2001.

24— "did you mention that outline?" Interview with Warren Garfunkel, June 2, 2000.

24-25— Jim and John R. Rarick at a demonstration: Interview with John R. Rarick, July 28, 2000.

25— he never mentioned that he had been to Dachau: Interview with Rene Lehmann, June 16, 2000; Interview with Warren Garfunkel, June 14, 2000.

25— a hypochondriac: Interview with H. John Bremermann, July 30, 1999.

25— he is allergic to lint: Military Records of James C. Garrison, 1951 Report. AARC.

25— "if you feel someone is guilty": Interview with Peggie Baker, May 26, 1998.

26— "once you know love": Interview with Wilma Baker, July 22, 2000.

26-Delta airline scene with Mindy: Interview with Peggie Baker.

27— "the word is pronounced 'indefaTIgable'": Interview with Martha Ann Samuel, June 10, 2000.

27— the nurse has an identical twin: Interview with Joe Allain, January 24, 2001.

27— Jane Pitcher: Interviews with Mickey Parlour Bremermann and Vance Gilmer.

27— the model in the fluffy jacket: Interview with Vance Gilmer.

27— Rosemary Pillow couldn't get a job: Interview with Rosemary Pillow, April 24, 2000.

27— decided he would become a Professor of Law: Interview with Denis A. Barry, May 20, 1998.

28— "I'll bet you can't": Interview with H. John Bremermann.

28— "I'm going to do it": Interview with C. Jackson Grayson, Jr.

28— Jim and Wilmer Thomas share a love of mischief: Interview with Judge Marcel Livaudais, June 9, 2000.

28— grab your rear end: Interview with Vance Gilmer.

28— Wilmer creates his own library: Interview with Jack Benjamin, May 31, 2000.

29— why not make a mockery of it?: Interview with Wilmer Thomas, July 24, 2000.

29— brought up on banking fraud charges: Interview with Robert Haik, May 30, 2000.

29— Wilmer would run on the "Nazi ticket": Interview with Wilmer Thomas, March 7, 2001.

29— "Hotsy, totsy, I'm a Nazi": Interview with Rosemary Pillow, April 23, 2000.

29— passionate desire to help the underdog: Interview with Judge James J. Gulotta, January 9, 1998.

30— he considered working for an oil company: Interview with Vance Gilmer, January 4, 2001.

30— he would give up the law: Interview with Jay Teasdel, January 16, 2000.

30-Garrison and the FBI: Interview with H. John Bremermann.

30-Nigel Rafferty's wedding: Interview with H. Jackson Grayson.

31-Jim Garrison's short stories are available in the Garrison papers at the National Archives.

Chapter 3

33— "Politics is something anyone can succeed at": Interview with C. Jackson Grayson, Jr.

33— you practically had to be a member of the Boston Club: Interview with Lillian Cohen, August 8, 2000. Miss Cohen was a prominent New Orleans attorney herself.

34— "an immense favor if you didn't mention Judy": Interview with Wilma Baker, July 22, 2000.

34— For Jim Garrison's application to the FBI, medical records and the FBI's own reports, see FBI file, Part I, available from the Federal Bureau of Investigation.

34— he saw Dr. Matthews at LSU: Military Records: Garrison, James C. Captain – 11165863. AARC.

34— "one of the most promising young lawyers": "NO #67-4715. Reference: Bulet to New Orleans, dated 1-5-51. Details: All of applicant's references...FBI. Report made at New Orleans, Louisiana. 1-13-51. Bureau Applicant -- Special Agent. NARA.

35— Captain of the Artillery: The document begins, "The President of the United States of America..." The date is January 17, 1951. Courtesy of Lyon Garrison.

35— "a pleasant, friendly personality, etc.": See FBI file.

35— "rather distracted and absent–minded": The easiest way to obtain this document is: "Life" magazine Office Memorandum. To: Billings, Haskell, The Garrison Watchers. From: Angeloff. Papers of Richard N. Billings. Georgetown University. Special Collections. Box 2, folder 14.

35— "Greek Drama has always bored me.": Questionnaire filled out by Jim Garrison, February 19, 1984. NARA.

35— the choice of remaining with the Bureau: Interview with H. John Bremermann.

35— "if I can ever... be of any service to the FBI": James C. Garrison to J. Edgar Hoover, June 29, 1951. FBI file.

35— "just couldn't make it": Medical report by Marshall L. Fowler. 1st Lt. MC. Garrison, James C. Captain, 0-1165863. (1951). AARC.

35— on Garrison's combat fatigue: Interview with Bill Preston, July 30, 2000. Preston had discussed their mutual experiences in World War II with Jim Garrison.

36— flying toward the enemy: Memo to: Stadiem. From: Garrison, January 16, 1984.

36— "I find myself accomplishing little of value": James C. Garrison to J. Edgar Hoover, August 17, 1951. FBI file.

36— "an honorable discharge or release": J. Edgar Hoover to Captain James C. Garrison, August 30, 1951. FBI file.

36— "I know this sounds crazy": Medical report by Marshall L. Fowler.

37— "either a neurasthenia, or a hypochondriasis": Douglas J. Page, Colonel. ARTY-RA President. Appended to FBI document 89-69-3250, Agency file: 124-10251-10247.

37— "over-solicitous mother": Military Report (1951) on Garrison, James C. Captain. 0-1165863 by Marshall L. Fowler.

37— he had grown to resent her: Interview with Phyllis Kritikos, May 29, 1998.

37— did not reply to her letters: Jane Gardiner to Robert Haik. Undated. Courtesy of Lyon Garrison.

37— "the word 'lease' in Louisiana": Jim Garrison's master's thesis is available in the Garrison Family Papers collection at NARA.

37— Jim decides to give up the law: Interview with Jay Teasdel, January 16, 2000. Jim Garrison's ambivalence about the law was a persistent theme of their conversations. Garrison told Teasdel he hoped that he would never have to practice law.

38— "decidedly promising": A. L. Fierst to Jim Garrison. July 23, 1952. The Garrison Family Papers.

38— dinner at Antoine's: Interview with H. Jackson Grayson, Jr.

39— "just do it": Interview with Jasper Garrison, January 11, 1998.

39— Garrison's "salty" vocabulary: Interview with Dr. Robert Heath, May 25, 1999.

39— Garrison cherished his set of Dickens: Interview with Elizabeth Garrison, January 11, 1998.

40— "Be anything but a lawyer": Interview with Jasper Garrison, January 11, 1998.

40— for Chep Morrison's use of the press and a public relations firm, see Edward F. Haas, "DeLesseps S. Morrison and the Image of Reform: New Orleans Politics, 1946-1961" (Louisiana State University Press: Baton Rouge, 1974), pp. 36-37, 41.

40— bored with the law, he tried politics: Interview with Jay Teasdel.

40- 200,000 unpaid traffic tickets: "Traffic Tickets Jam Is Placed At 200,000 by Schiro," "Times-Picayune," April 7, 1951, p. 1.

40— Jim Garrison is appointed Deputy Safety Commissioner: "Garrison Named Aid of M'Closkey," "Times-Picayune," May 13, 1952, p. 33.

40— McCloskey says he's backing Ike: "Times-Picayune," September 24, 1952, p. 6.

40— "We USED to like Ike": "Times-Picayune," November 3, 1952, p. 24.

40— traffic prosecutor: "Special Traffic Prosecutor Due," "Times-Picayune," January 14, 1954, p. 8.

41— "an arm of the law": Ibid.

41— "a flagrantly contemptuous action": "Traffic Ticket Crackdown Set," "Times-Picayune," February 17, 1954, p. 1. See also: "Traffic Court's Penalty Scored," "Times-Picayune," March 12, 1954, p. 44.

41— "I'll get her to the head of the line": Interview with Mickey Parlour Bremermann.

42— special envelope: "Proposed Parking Violation Ticket Has Envelope In Which To Put Fine," "Times-Picayune," March 16, 1954.

42— "inertia on the part of the Judge: "Inertia in Traffic Court Blamed For Ticket

Chaos" by Walter Goodstein. "Times-Picayune," April 11, 1954, p. 1.

42— Judge Sperling insists the court clerk processed traffic tickets: "Sperling Denies 'Inertia' Charge," "Times-Picayune," April 13, 1954, p. 1.

43— "It is somewhat analogous to the defensive reaction": "Garrison Issues Statement In Reply To Traffic Judge," "Times-Picayune," April 14, 1954, p. 5. See also,
"Sperling Calls For Clerk 'With Good Business,'" "Times-Picayune," February 19, 1954, p. 9.

43— "Saturday Is A Holiday": "M'Closkey Will Ask New Court," "Times-Picayune," April 15, 1954, p. 1.

43— he was less interested in notoriety: Interview with G. Harrison Scott, June 9, 2000.

43— "an excellent job": "Safety Council Backs Garrison," "Times-Picayune," April 14, 1954, p. 5.

43— "Judge Sperling Will Be Able To Get Tough:" "Bill Seeks New Judicial Power." "Times-Picayune," May 12, 1954, p. 24.

43— he praised the "untiring effort": "Cops Are Lauded In Traffic Case," "Times-Picayune," May 15, 1954.

43— "Human nature being what it is": "Traffic Ticket 'Fix' Ban Is Urged," "Times-Picayune," May 20, 1954, p. 28.

44— Chep Morrison went before a City Council committee: "Council Okays Traffic Court," "Times-Picayune," June 22, 1954, p. 22.

44— "I don't want to be a traffic court judge": Interview with Numa Bertel, October 9, 2000.

44— Garrison's appointment to Darden's office: "Two Appointed Assistant DA's," "Times-Picayune," January 5, 1954, p. 7.

44— "parley," the deal that made Garrison an assistant district attorney: Interview with Judge Adrian Duplantier, February 6, 2001.

44— not a tough opponent: Interview with Milton Brener, May 27, 1998.

44— "he was devastating": Interview with Donald V. Organ, January 10, 2000.

45— moved slowly: Interview with Milton Brener.

45— he didn't care whether the sun came up: Interview with G. Harrison Scott.

45— easy on plea bargains: Interview with Phillip Foto, January 7, 2000.

45— "close the door when you're finished": Interview with Herman Kohlman, May 19, 1998.

45— he prosecuted lottery operators: "Alleged Gaming Chiefs Accused; Pair Held As Operators of Lottery Firms," "Times-Picayune," October 4, 1956, p. 26.

45— the doctor used blue ink: "La. High Court Annuls Decree: Doctor Found Not Guilty Of Using Wrong Ink," "Times-Picayune," March 27, 1956, p. 39.

45-"the cops own this town": A. J. Liebling, "The Earl Of Louisiana" (Louisiana State University Press: Baton Rouge and London), p. 168.

45— In a 1967 BBC interview, Pershing Gervais refers to himself as a "door crasher." NARA.

46— "what did I do, officer?" Interview with William Alford, May 28, 1998.

46— seizing narcotics from addicts and pushers: The source is Patrick J. Horrigan, a former New Orleans police officer. Investigative Report. July 31, 1967. Reported by Aaron Kohn. Papers of the Metropolitan Crime Commission (MCC). NARA.

46— "a lousy $21 a week": Rosemary James, "Pershing Gervais – Man or Myth?" p. 55.

46— he loads up his car with groceries: Interview with John Volz, May 21, 1998.

46— "We ARE the cops!" Interview with Ross Scaccia, January 6, 2000.

47— Pershing uses Sal Marchese as an intermediary with Carlos Marcello: Raymond Comstock interview with Aaron M. Kohn. MCC.

47— Grosch collected $150,000 in bribes: Haas, p. 185.

47— one of the best safe crackers in the city: Interview with Denis A. Barry, May 17, 1998.

47— Grosch's informant was Gervais himself: Interview with Raymond Comstock, April 30, 2001.

47— I told you I was lying: Interview with G. Harrison Scott. A variation was Pershing's "Didn't I tell you I was lying to you?"

47-"carry the safe out": Interview with Herman Kohlman. May 17, 2001.

47— Pershing sells his favors at Norma Wallace's: Christine Wiltz, "The Last Madam: A Life In The New Orleans Underworld" (Faber and Faber: New York, 2000), p. 128.

47— Pershing kept dossiers on everyone he knew: Interview with Frank Meloche, June 11, 2000.

47— "did you ever give money?": "Bray Describes Graft Methods," "Times-Picayune," June 20, 1957, p. 34.

48— "That was crime that was organized": Pershing Gervais would always claim that it was police graft that represented in New Orleans crime "that was organized": James, "Pershing Gervais – Man or Myth?" p. 55.

48— Norma Wallace on organized crime in New Orleans: Wiltz, p. 84.

48— Aaron Kohn's history as an FBI agent can be reviewed from his FBI file, available from the Department of Justice.

48— Hoover refused to promote him: "I do not believe this should be done. Select someone else outside the division": Memorandum For the Director. April 20, 1932. U.S. Department of Justice, Bureau of Investigation letter signed by Clyde A. Tolson.

48— "superior": Memorandum for the Director from H. H. Clegg. February 16, 1937, Kohn FBI file.

48— "know-it-all": W. R. Glavin. May 29, 1937. Report on Aaron M. Kohn. Special Agent, Detroit Division. May 1, 1937. FBI file.

48— "cocksure": Report of Inspector Foxworth. Inspection. Philadelphia Office. November 16-24, 1937. FBI file.

49— "eastern area": Memorandum for the Director by H. H. Clegg. January 4, 1937. FBI file: 62-022-65. Aaron Kohn FBI file.

49— an FBI man had been found in the whorehouse: W. V. McLaughlin, Special Agent in Charge, to John Edgar Hoover. Personal and Confidential. December 16, 1938. Kohn FBI file. Aaron Kohn FBI file.

49— the Chicago police retaliated: U.S. Government Memorandum. To: Mr. A. H. Belmont. From Mr. F. J. Baumgardner. Subject: Chicago, Illinois, Police Department Cooperation, Bureau file. 67-14051. June 17, 1952. FBI file.

49— Kohn had offered bribes: Office memorandum. United States Government. To: Director, FBI. From: SAC, New Orleans (33-165-A). Subject: Aaron M. Kohn. GIIF. January 2, 1953. FBI file.

49— investigating "political murders": SAC New Orleans to Director, FBI. January 14, 1953. Subject: Aaron M. Kohn. General Investigative Intelligence File. FBI file.

49— Kohn arrives in New Orleans: "Ex-G Man Kohn Arrives in N.O., Starts Police Dept. Probe," "New Orleans Item," June 10, 1953, p. 7.

49— it was most unusual for Hoover to clear the record: Interview with H. John Bremermann, December 28, 2000.

49— "of their own city government": Chianelli Is Reindicted In Finance Safe Theft," "Times-Picayune," September 5, 1953, p. 1.

49— "inexcusable carelessness": E. P. Coffey, "Memorandum For File." September 12, 1934. FBI file.

50— "a policeman has been prevented": "Police Probers Ask Public's Aid," "Times-Picayune," August 12, 1954.

50— "I always thought he was for sale": Interview with Vance Gilmer, January 4, 2001.

50— a register of ex-convicts: Aaron M. Kohn to Mr. Hepburn Many, U. S. Attorney. September 20, 1957. FBI file. See also Aaron M. Kohn to Councilman Glenn P. Clasen, September 16, 1957.

50— whether bingo was legal: "Report on Bingo Probe Prepared," "Times-Picayune," March 22, 1956, p. 12.

50— "be most circumspect in any dealings with Kohn": Mr. Tolson. R. T. Harbo. Special Citizens Investigating Committee of the New Orleans Commission Council. November 4, 1953.

50— Hoover reminded his over-zealous former employee: J. Edgar Hoover to Aaron M. Kohn, July 2, 1959. FBI file.

50— Banister is appointed by Chep Morrison to investigate subversives: "Probe

Ordered on Subversives," "Times-Picayune," March 21, 1956, p. 1. See also, "Banister Named First Red Prober," "Times-Picayune," March 22, 1956, p. 27.

50— "in a log cabin": From: Banister, Guy. Title: Biographical Sketch. 180-10096-1011. 007272 [5 of 6]. Originator: New Orleans District Attorney. NARA.

50-51— Banister supervises raids on the Puerto Rican Nationalist Party: Memorandum for File. From: Guy Banister. Re: Nationalist Party of Puerto Rico. November 28, 1962. The memo is to Banister's own files.

51— Banister resembles Charles Bickford: Mary H. Brengel to Daly, Martin. HSCA. 180-10077-10263. 007546. NARA.

51— "Mr. Spic and Span": Jim Garrison to Zachary Sklar, August 29, 1988. AARC.

51— Morrison demanded that Banister stop meeting with Kohn: Haas, p. 211.

51— "police character": "Appeals Heard In Police Cases," "Times-Picayune," July 9, 1953, p. 26.

51 — Pershing was given a sixty-day suspension for "conduct unbecoming an officer" while Marchese was fired: "Chief Fires Marchese, Is Suspending Gervais," "Times-Picayune," March 30, 1953, p. 1.

51— a woman "separates you from your money": Interview with Mike Seghers, June 6, 2000.

52— The Bucket of Blood: See "Trial Arranged In Saloon Case," "Times-Picayune," February 11, 1955, p. 6; "Melito, Gervais Ruling Delayed," "Times-Picayune," March 4, 1955, p. 33; "Gervais Freed On Bar Charge," "Times-Picayune," May 20, 1955.

52— "outrageous accusation": "Gervais Assails 'Informer' Label," "Times-Picayune," December 23, 1953, p. 32.

52— Gervais's reports were sprinkled with names ending in a vowel: Interview with Numa Bertel, February 6, 2001.

52— "frequented a whorehouse": Interview with Judge Adrian Duplantier, February 6, 2001.

52— "Get out!" Ibid.

52— "individuals not consistent with law enforcement": "Kohn told To Produce

More Scheuering Data," "Times-Picayune," January 20, 1955, p. 4.

52— "A most effective job": Ibid.

53— One of three "bagmen": "Paternostro's Appeal Heard," "Times-Picayune," September 11, 1959, p. 23.

53— Guy Banister's concurrence: "Pasternostro's Ouster Upheld," "Times-Picayune," January 29, 1960, Section 2, p. 6.

53— Kohn buttonholes Garrison: Investigative Report. February 29, 1956. Date of investigation: February 20, 1956. Reported by: CI #1. MCC.

53— "as of oil and water": Interview with H. John Bremermann, December 28, 2000.

53-54— Jim Garrison at the "Practicing Law Institute": Jot pad for notes and questions. Notes re: Jury Trials. The Garrison Family Papers. NARA.

Chapter 4

55— "How do you know if you're in love?" Interview with Peggie Baker, June 6, 2000.

55— The Peter Murtes case: "Trial Continued in Murtes Case," "Times-Picayune," November 30, 1956, p. 18; "Jury's Verdict Clears Murtes," "Times-Picayune," December 20, 1956, p. 1.

55— Seven black teenagers: "Teen-Age Negro Beating Denied," "Times-Picayune," February 21, 1957, p. 3.

55— Narcotics convictions: "7 1-2 years Given On Dope Counts," "Times-Picayune," March 7, 1957, p. 23; "Dope Possessor Gets Eight Years," "Times-Picayune," March 13, 1957, p. 32; "Dope Roundup Results Listed," "Times-Picayune," May 3, 1957, p. 11.

55— refused charges: "Cop Is Cleared In Slaying Case," "Times-Picayune," June 7, 1957, p. 3.

56— "malfeasance, misfeasance…": "Grand Jury Planning Inquiry on Dayries," "Times-Picayune," July 16, 1957, p. 1.

56— "tactics 'underhanded'": "Supt. Dayries Accuses Kohn: Effort to Confuse Public Charged by Police Head," "Times-Picayune," March 24, 1956, p. 40.

56— "to improve law enforcement in this city": "12 Witnesses Called For Hubert Hearing," "Times-Picayune," July 18, 1957, p. 11.

56— Garrison assigned to assist the Metropolitan Crime Commission: "MCC Loaned Garrison," "Times-Picayune," July 18, 1957, p. 11.

57— "hooked": "Police Firing Laid To Mayor," "Times-Picayune," August 17, 1957, p. 16.

57— Marc Antony a Kohn informant: Investigative Report – Confidential. October 14, 1957. MCC.

57— "about face": Investigative Report – Confidential. October 14, 1957. MCC.

57— A "public hearing" on the alleged communication: "Hearing Asked On Morrison," "Times-Picayune," September 12, 1957, p. 4.

57— to get hold of Mr. Antony: "Met Jury Head, Mayor Admits," "Times-Picayune," August 30, 1957, p. 1.

58— "there's nothing at all sinister": "Hearing Asked On Morrison," "Times-Picayune," September 12, 1957, p. 4.

58— Aaron Kohn's version of these events: Garrison had telephoned him: Interview with Aaron Kohn, "Life" magazine memorandum from David Chandler to Rowan, Orshefsky, Billings, et. al. March 6, 1967. Papers of Richard N. Billings, Georgetown University.

58— "playing the game": Investigative Report. Confidential. October 31, 1957 Report of a September 17, 1957 lunch between Kohn and Marc Antony. MCC.

58— "indictments had been typed": Interview with Joyce Wood, June 10, 2000. The information about Marc Antony's arrest in New York comes from Wood. Wood typed indictments for several district attorneys, including Darden, Hubert, Dowling and Garrison.

58— Garrison argued that he couldn't change the minds of the grand jurors overnight: Investigative Report, March 10, 1958. Received from CI #1. MCC.

58— convicting of negligent homicide: "Driver Guilty In Auto Death," "Times-Picayune," September 20, 1957, p. 6.

59— Morrison had few friends: Milton Brener, "The Garrison Case: A Study In The Abuse Of Power" (Clarkson N. Potter: New York, 1969), p. 3.

59— "complete impartiality and fairness": "Garrison Seeks Assessor Post," "Times-Picayune," December 7, 1957, p. 32.

59— "I post additional signs": Brener, p. 3.

59— "scarcely a glowing triumph": James H. Gillis, "Notes From City Hall: Defeat Is Worst Since 1904!" "Times-Picayune," February 9, 1958, Section 2, p. 14.

60— "impossible...all over": Brener, pp. 3-4.

60— "play his cards right": Investigative Report. Received From CI #1. March 10, 1958. Reported by Aaron M. Kohn. MCC.

61— Jim Garrison investigates voting irregularities in the District Attorney Race: "Voting May Be Probed By Jury," "Times-Picayune," March 13, 1958, p. 10.

61— he appoints Fontenot: "Dowling Granted Suspensive Appeal From Rainold Ruling," "Times-Picayune," March 15, 1958, p. 1; "Voting May Be Probed By Jury," "Times-Picayune," March 13, 1958, p. 10.

61— "the start Mr. Garrison has made": "Vote Probe Start," "Times-Picayune," March 15, 1958, p. 10.

61— Richard Dowling is declared the winner: "Supreme Court Decides Dowling Is DA Nominee," "Times-Picayune," March 21, 1958, p. 1.

61— Jim distinguished himself: "2 Million Bonds Theft Is Charged," "Times-Picayune," April 2, 1958, p. 1.

61— Hubert assigns him to investigate the Pinner issue: "D.A.'s Asst. Pinner Resigns Abruptly," "Times-Picayune," March 28, 1958, p. 1.

61— sounding board of public opinion: "Police Advisor Unit Is Formed," "Times-Picayune," June 15, 1958, p. 6.

62— "wild drinking parties": Investigative Report From CI #180. March 29, 1967. MCC.

62— you should be married: Interview with Jay Teasdel.

62— they went for a coke: Interview with Liz Garrison, January 11, 1998.

62— "I dare you": Interview with Lenore Ward, August 7, 2000.

62— Mississippi Magnolia: Interview with John Volz, June 13, 2000.

62— she never wanted to go home: Interview with Numa Bertel, February 6, 2001.

62— little pixie: Interview with Lenore Ward, August 8, 2000.

62— little doll: Interview with Lillian Cohen, October 8, 2000.

62— praising her legs: Interview with Jay Teasdel.

62— he consulted his friends on how to get her into bed: Interview with C. Jackson Grayson, Jr.

63— father figure: Interview with Numa Bertel, February 6, 2001.

63— a bad reputation: Interview with Iris Kelso, May 19, 1998.

63— lost opportunity: Interview with Phyllis Kritikos.

63— Evelyn Jahncke: Interview with Phyllis Kritikos, June 16, 2000.

63— Uptown debutante world: Garrison had an aversion to the Uptown debutante world. Interview with Jay Teasdel, January 19, 2001.

63— Jim must marry better: Interview with Vance Gilmer, January 4, 2001.

63— his mother ruined him: Interview with Bob Haik, January 9, 2000.

63— different man: The consensus among his friends was that he would never be a family man. Interview with Judge James J. Gulotta, January 8, 1998.

63— "nothing to do with morality": Interview with John Volz, July 31, 2001.

63— Jim told both Denis Barry and Bob Haik that he had to marry Liz because she was pregnant: Interviews with Barry and Haik.

64— "why don't you two guys get together?" Interview with Denis Barry, May 20, 1998.

64— "How do you build a practice?" Interview with Robert Haik, May 30, 2000.

64— Barry complained about it to Jordan Brown: Interview with Jordan Brown, June 3, 2000.

64— borrowed from a finance company: Interview with Warren Garfunkel, June 2, 2000.

65— both sides of the fence: Interview with Christine Wiltz, September 25, 1998.

65— excellent as a trial lawyer: Interview with Denis Barry.

65— "good religion is the only thing": "Good Religion 'Saved Me,' Asserts Driver of Truck" by Fritz Harsdorff, "Times-Picayune," January 28, 1960, Section 1, p. 1.

66— the "Claribel": See Nos. 4274, 4277: Civ. A. No. 10795, Division D. United States District Court For The Eastern District of Louisiana, New Orleans Division. 222 F Supp. 521; 1963. Dist. Lexis 7893. Jim Garrison's Memorandum for State of Louisiana versus Drexel Brister and John Carver. Twenty-Second Judicial District Court, Parish of St. Tammany. Memorandum in behalf of defendants, May 31, 1960. Harry Connick files of Jim Garrison's papers. NARA.

66— three black youths: "Three Acquitted In Slaying Case," "Times-Picayune," December 13, 1958, p. 28.

66— robbing and beating: "Five Acquitted of $10 Robbery," "Times-Picayune," May 15, 1959, Section 2, p. 2.

66— sailors whistled: Interview with Steve Jennings, May 26, 1998.

66— obscenity and weapons charges: "Stripper Fined $500 By Judge," "Times-Picayune," January 14, 1960, Section 2, p. 2.

66— a sixteen year old boy named Lester Lee Hall: "French Quarter Resident Slain," "Times-Picayune," June 30, 1960, Section 1, p. 8; "50 Questioned in Slaying Case," "Times-Picayune," July 1, 1960, Section 1, p. 11; "Juveniles Blame Each Other In Hold-Up Death, say Police," "Times-Picayune," July 8, 1960, p. 1; "Boy, 16, Admits Fatal Gunshot," "Times-Picayune," July 9, 1960, Section 1, p. 5; "Teen-Agers Face Murder Charge," "Times-Picayune," July 13, 1960, Section 1, p. 23; "2 Boys Indicted In Murder Case," "Times-Picayune," July 28, 1960, Section 1, p. 6; "Murder Trial Takes Recess," "Times-Picayune," March 28, 1961, Section 1, p. 6; "Youth Is Guilty In Murder Case," "Times-Picayune," March 29, 1961, Section 1, p. 1. See also Interview with Denis Barry.

66— The Fernando Rios Case: All from the "Times-Picayune": "Three Students Testify...." January 23, 1959, p. 1; "Guide Death Up To Grand Jury," October 1, 1958, p. 1; "Probe Involves Guide's Wallet," October 1, 1958, p. 14; "Charge Filed In Guide Death," October 3, 1958, p. 19; "New Evidence In Guide Death,"

October 9, 1958, p. 2; "Grand Jury To Hear Case Against Tulane Students," October 14, 1958, p. 40; "Students to Face Trial In Slaying," October 15, 1958, p. 1; "Students Face Trial On November 17," October 21, 1958, p. 9; "Fight Is Made On Indictments," October 31, 1958, p. 12; "Trial of Tulane Trio Continued," November 13, 1958, p. 34; "Rios' Articles Are Requested," November 18, 1958, p. 32; "22 Are Called For Riots Case," December 4, 1958, p. 12; "Murder Trial Slated Today," January 20, 1959, p. 2; "Jury Completed For Trial of Three in Guide Slaying," January 21, 1959, p. 1; "Boast in Fatal Beating Is Told," January 22, 1958, p. 1; "Jury Acquits 3 Students Tried in Slaying of Guide," January 24, 1959, p. 1; "Trio May Face Robbery Trial," January 27, 1959, p.7; "New Indictment of Trio Flayed, Challenges Sounded by Attorneys of Students," January 28, 1959, p. 16; "Acquitted Trio Indicted Anew," January 28, 1959, p. 1; "Ruling Delayed In Case of 3 Tulane Students," June 16, 1959, Section 1, p. 15; "Rehearing Aim In Youths Case," November 3, 1959, Section 1, p. 8; "Students Held Liable to Trial," June 1, 1960, Section 2, p. 2; "Drop Charge Studied," October 7, 1959, Section 2, p. 2; "Bond-Set Time Extended by DA," February 14, 1959, p. 12; "D.A. Seeking Trial of Three," February 6, 1959, p. 12; "Platt Receives Students' Case," January 29, 1959, p. 26; "Theft Sentence Suspended Here," October 28, 1964, p. 14.

67— For disposition of the Fernando Rios case: Civ. No. 862. United States District Court for the Eastern District of North Carolina, Wilmington Division. 209F. Supp. 927; 1962. U.S. Dist. LEXIS 3572. October 18, 1962.

67— "closely associated with Communists": "Federationist Head Accused," "Times-Picayune," December 18, 1959, Section 3, p. 17.

67— he never accepted bribes: Interview with Walter Hammer, March 4, 2001.

67— lunch companion was Milton Brener: Interview with Milton Brener, May 27, 1998.

67— Jim carried a little black book: Interview with Barbara Barry Ward: July 11, 2001.

67— Tuesday afternoons: Interview with Denis Barry.

67— trouble meeting his share of the expenses: Investigative Report. May 31, 1962. MCC.

68— could be found at the racetrack: Interview with G. Harrison Scott. When the first race started: Interview with Warren Garfunkel, June 2, 2000.

68— "senile": Interview with Denis Barry, May 20, 1998.

68— it would be easy: Interview with Judge Louis P. Trent, December 10, 2000.

68— the CCDA endorses challengers: "CCDA Endorses Candidate List," "Times-Picayune," June 10, 1960, Section 1, p. 1.

68— defying tradition: "Disunity Seen As Cause Of CCDA's Poor Showing," Notes From City Hall by James H. Gillis, "Times-Picayune," July 31, 1960, Section 2, p. 5.

68— you never run against a sitting judge: Interview with Denis Barry.

68— "you do not have a full-time judge": "13th Ward CCDA Backing Ticket," "Times-Picayune," June 14, 1960, Section 3, p. 2.

68— "dangerous and most undemocratic": "Candidate Hits Monopoly Idea," "Times-Picayune," June 7, 1960, Section 2, p. 2.

68— "there is a constant cold war": "Litigation Cost Is Pledged," "Times-Picayune," July 8, 1960, Section 2, p. 6.

69— "reclining judge": "Support Asked by Fitzmorris; Proposed to Operate Office From City Hall," "Times-Picayune," July 9, 1960, Section 3, p. 4.

69— "cases dismissed, charges reduced": "Garrison Sees Facts Omission," "Times-Picayune," July 14, 1960, Section 2, p. 6.

69— Garfunkel learned: Interview with Warren Garfunkel, June 14, 2000.

69— "I run on my record": Interview with Warren Garfunkel, June 2, 2000.

69— "deserted as the North Pole": "Platt Record Is Challenged," "Times-Picayune," July 17, 1960, Section 1, p. 20.

69— "young attorney": "Times-Picayune" endorsement: "Judicial Contests," July 14, 1960, Section 1, p. 18.

69— "interested enough to make their voices: "J. C. Garrison Thanks Voters," "Times-Picayune," July 29, 1960, Section 3, p. 21.

69— "I keep late hours": Consider, however, the source. Hugh Aynesworth went to New Orleans apparently for the purpose of discrediting Jim Garrison, as his reports to the FBI and his correspondence with Richard Billings make abundantly clear: "To: Nation, Sanders, Iselin, From: Carter and Aynesworth in New Orleans. Re: Garrison Backgrounder. February 24, 1967. "Newsweek" telex. AARC. Quoted by David Chandler in "The Devil's DA," "New Orleans" Magazine. November 1966.

70— civil rights demonstrators disturb the peace: "Picketers Arrested in N. O," "Times-Picayune," August 29, 1961, Section 1, p. 12; "Bucaro Defers Trial of Three," "Times-Picayune," August 30, 1961, Section 1, p. 8; "Picketing Case Suspect Freed," "Times-Picayune," September 1, 1961, Section 3, p. 8; "Two Get 90-Day Jail Sentences," "Times-Picayune," September 9, 1961, Section 1, p. 7.

Chapter 5

71— "ass closed": Interview with Walter Hammer.

71— "sold cases like crazy": Interview with Joyce Wood.

71— "you could buy your way": Interview with John Volz, January 15, 2000.

71— Louis LaCour is bribed: Conversation between Jack Martin and Louis Ivon. November 22, 1967. Transcript. NODA. NARA.

72— he had made a lot of money during the Depression: Joseph Newbrough interviewed by William Davy, April 3, 1995. Courtesy of Mr. Davy.

72— Jack Martin: Description provided by Jim Garrison's secretary, Sharon Herkes, by Thomas Edward Beckham, March 30, 2002, and interview with L. J. Delsa, December 7, 2005.

73— Jim Garrison declares his candidacy: "Ex-DA Chief Aid In Race For Job," "Times-Picayune," October 13, 1961, Section 1, p. 1.

73— "the last guy in the world": Interview with Dr. Frank Minyard, January 8, 1998.

73— "furious about how Dowling": To: Nation, Sanders, Iselin. From: Carter and Aynesworth, New Orleans. Re: Garrison Backgrounder. "Newsweek" Inter-office Memo. February 24, 1967. NARA.

74— "unbelievable": "Candidates Rap Record of D.A.," "Times-Picayune," October 24, 1961, Section 1, p. 4.

74— rain water dripping from his lapels: William R. Klein to Jim Garrison, May 4, 1967. NARA.

74— Jim Garrison asks Bob Haik to approach Schiro: Aaron M. Kohn interview with Bob Haik. Investigative Report. May 31, 1962. MCC.

74— "Are you still in the race?": Brener, "The Garrison Case," p. 5.

74 — "more oysters": "Verbal Blasts Mark D.A. Race," "Times-Picayune," December 28, 1961, Section 1, p. 5.

75— "strip-clip joints": "D.A. Criticized On Club Gifts," "Times-Picayune," October 24, 1961, Section 1, p. 4.

75— "habits of mis-information": "Dowling Ready To List Donors," "Times-Picayune," November 9, 1961, p. 6.

75— "Jefferson Parish, maybe": "Panel Discussion Is Held On Orleans Area Crime," "Times-Picayune," October 13, 1961, Section 2, p. 5.

75— Jim resigned: "Garrison Quits Position In City," "Times-Picayune," January 16, 1962, Section 1, p. 6.

75— "Times-Picayune" sided with Kohn: Editorial. November 10, 1961, Section 1, p. 12.

75— Kohn's questionnaire is available in the papers of the MCC.

75— the candidates for district attorney debate: "DA Candidates Discuss Issues," "Times-Picayune," January 15, 1962, Section 2, p. 4.

75— he sounded and looked like a district attorney: Brener, pp. 5-6.

76— Projecting sincerity: David Chandler to Richard N. Billings, March 23, 1967. Papers of Richard N. Billings. Georgetown University.

76— they knew it was all over: Interview with Judge Adrian Duplantier.

76— Burton Klein, looking for scandal, writes to the FBI: Burton G. Klein to Director, Federal Bureau of Investigation. In Re: James C. Garrison. New Orleans, Louisiana. January 22, 1962. Subject: JAMES CAROTHERS GARRISON. See also: To: SAC, New Orleans. From: Director, January 26, 1962 and To: Director, FBI. From: SAC, New Orleans. Re: James C. Garrison, Former Special Agent. January 29, 1962. Garrison FBI file.

77— "if you raise one hundred dollars": Internal Memo, "Newsweek" magazine, February 24, 1967.

77— "Everybody else was home watching Garrison....": James Phelan, "The Vice Man Cometh," "Saturday Evening Post," June 8, 1963, p. 69. This article was in fact written by David Chandler.

77— the type of needle used to inject horses: Interview with Judge Thomas

Wicker, June 5, 2000.

77— Jim got the names of the dealers from narcotics police: Interview with Denis A. Barry, May 20, 1998.

77— a female impersonator: "Acquittal Ends Narcotics Case," "Times-Picayune," June 23, 1960, Section 1, p. 5.

77— "I busted that nigger wench" was how Comstock described his arrest of Welch: Raymond Comstock interview with Aaron Kohn. Investigative Report. June 18, 1968. Date of investigation: September 19, 1964. MCC; Interview with Raymond Comstock.

78— "to oppose organized crime": "Will Stop Dope Sale—Garrison," "Times-Picayune," January 27, 1962, Section 2, p. 7; "Garrison Vows Anti-Dope Fight," "Times-Picayune," January 26, 1962, Section 1, p. 17.

78— "they want a new district attorney": "Returns Bring Runoff for DA," "Times-Picayune," January 28, 1962, Section 1, p. 1.

78— "You can type, right?" Interview with Carol Boyd, July 22, 2002.

78— "free and independent of politics": "Garrison Stays Independent," "Times-Picayune," February 1, 1962, Section 2, p. 6.

78— "I'm a Unitarian": See letter by Mary Helen Brengel. May 14, 1967. House Select Committee On Assassinations. 007546. Mary H. Brengel to Martin Daly, May 14, 1967. NARA.

79— Doane attempts to shake down Hardy Davis: Hardy Davis, "Aiming For The Jugular In New Orleans" (Ashley Books: Port Washington, New York, 1976), pp. 13-14.

79— Jack Martin's bad check: "Bad Check Laid To Henry Hautot," "Times-Picayune," March 13, 1958, p. 74; "Hautot Check Charge Voided," "Times-Picayune," March 14, 1958, p. 5.

79— See Appendix. Martin's information was always worth checking out: Interview with Herman Kohlman, December 1, 2000.

80— Perez would be excommunicated: "Segregation Figures Are Excommunicated," "Times-Picayune," April 17, 1962, Section 1, p. 1.

80— sixteen pinball operators: Investigative Report. March 28, 1962. Reported by Carol Goodrich. MCC.

80— the issue bogus: Interview with Donald V. Organ, January 5, 2001.

81— "wet mop": Brener, p. 6.

81— Dowling utilizes the Marc Antony matter: "Dowling Blasts 'False Issues,'" "Times-Picayune," January 27, 1962, Section 2, p. 7.

81— a "hack": "Dowling Slaps At His Critics," "Times-Picayune," February 24, 1962, Section 3, p. 21.

81— Myth versus Facts": "Times-Picayune," March 2, 1962, Section 1, p. 22; "Garrison Sues DA For $75,000," "Times-Picayune," March 3, 1962, Section 3, p. 2.

81— thanking a strip-joint operator: "Dowling Knew Of Aid, Charge," "Times-Picayune," March 3, 1962, Section 3, p. 23.

82— John F. Kennedy has sexual relations with Angie Dickinson on the day of his inauguration: Richard Reeves, "President Kennedy" (Simon & Schuster: New York, 1993), p. 35.

83— "I belong there": Interview with Robert Haik.

83— "get out of my way": Interviews with Barbara Barry Ward and Robert Haik.

83— "she was a dragon": Interview with Iris Kelso, May 19, 1998.

83— John Leavines does not get a job with the new district attorney: Investigative Report. May 10, 1962. MCC.

83— Jim Garrison and Denis Barry visit Washington: Interview with Denis A. Barry; "Bob Kennedy, Jim Garrison Talk," "Times-Picayune," March 13, 1962, Section 1, p. 17; "Garrison Will Appoint Boesch," "Times-Picayune," March 14, 1962, Section 3, p. 4.

84— Chep Morrison suggested that Jim Garrison be an alternate choice for United States Attorney: Haas, p. 286.

85— Jim Garrison visits New York: "Garrison To Crack Down On Bail Bonding Credit," "Times-Picayune," March 22, 1962, Section 1, p. 1.

85— "any DA's office which would consider the Crime Commission as an opponent": Investigative Report. August 27, 1973. Date of activity: April 26, 1962. Reported by Carol Goodrich. MCC.

85— "perpetual attack on the Southern way of life": "Schiro Defends Stand On Talks," "Times-Picayune," March 24, 1962, Section 3, p. 3.

85— Clay Shaw invited: Clay Shaw to Hon. Hale Boggs, April 18, 1962; Hale Boggs to Clay Shaw, April 30, 1962. Papers of Clay Shaw. NARA.

85— "strength of diversity": The text of President Kennedy's speech in New Orleans was printed in the "Times-Picayune," May 5, 1962, Section 2, p. 2.

86— "wears the badge of no local political party": "Garrison and Others Sworn," "Times-Picayune," May 8, 1962, Section 1, p. 4.

Chapter 6

87— "banana republic": Interview with Gordon Novel, January 16, 2000.

87— "like a smog": Interview with Jim Garrison by Richard N. Billings. Undated. 94 pages. Papers of Richard N. Billings.

87— the judge opened his palm: Interview with Ralph Slovenko, January 25, 2001.

87— "a good lawyer doesn't need law books": Interview with Louis Ivon, January 8, 1998.

88— Items on Jim Garrison's desk. See: "Is Garrison Faking? The DA, The CIA and the Assassination" by Fred Powledge. "The New Republic," June 17, 1967.

88— Barry would be Special Assistant: "Garrison Picks Barry for Post," "Times-Picayune," March 8, 1962, Section 1, p. 20; "Brener To Head Anti-Dope Unit," "Times-Picayune," April 14, 1962, Section 2, p. 2.

88— they considered hiring Harry Connick: Interview with Denis A. Barry.

88— nobody was above the law: Interview with John Volz, March 13, 2001.

88— "delegated the details": Jim Garrison, "Coup d'Etat" (unpublished). p. 10 of 3. AARC.

88— "tempering justice with mercy was not an everyday occurrence": Interview with William Porteous, July 5, 2000.

89— "Frank, do you think it was one of your relatives?" Interview with Numa Bertel, October 9, 2000.

89— "heart of gold": Interview with William Alford.

89— John Volz is sent to argue against capital punishment, in which he believes: Interview with John Volz, March 12, 2001.

89— no jail time: Interview with Judge Louis P. Trent, October 8, 2000.

89— Jim McPherson came in to argue: Interview with Jim McPherson, January 9, 2000.

89— Ray McGuire pleads for the driver: Interview with Ray McGuire, March 2, 2001.

90— Garrison co-signs a note for Earl Landry: Jim Garrison to Henry Sibley. August 21, 1967. New Orleans Public Library Garrison Collection.

90— Michael Karmazin: "Karmazin To Be DA's Assistant," "Times-Picayune," April 1, 1962. Section 1, p. 12.

90— Ralph Whalen was astonished: Interview with Ralph Whalen, January 8, 2000.

90— the first woman assistant: Interview with Louise Korns, July 13, 2001.

91— "I like the way you won the election": Interview with Ross Scaccia, January 6, 2000.

92— testified voluntarily in federal court: Jim Garrison interviewed by Richard N. Billings.

92— Damon Runyonesque: Interview with William Alford, May 28, 1998.

92— needed a break: Interview with John Dolan, May 16, 2000.

92— Raymond Comstock would have made a better chief investigator: Interview with Robert Buras, June 3, 2002.

92— Pershing was feared: Interview with Frank Meloche. Denis Barry suggested to the author that Garrison thought he could keep an eye on Pershing.

92— if he had to fire anyone, he would get them a better job: Interview with William Alford, May 29, 1998.

92— Pershing controlled the vice squad: Interview with Frank Meloche, November 27, 2000.

93— "a distorted view of Jim": William R. Alford, Jr. to Joan Mellen, March 5, 1998.

93— "efficient law enforcement": "Gervais To Be Prober For DA," "Times-Picayune," May 10, 1962, Section 1, p. 5.

93— "Devil Incarnate." Interview with John Volz, January 15, 2000. Rosemary James termed him "the Devil's Own": "Perching Gervais: Man Or Myth?" p. 39.

93— "naïve about people": Investigative Report. July 21, 1966. Date information received, June 10, 1966. Conversation between Aaron M. Kohn and D'Alton Williams. MCC.

93— "the good guys and the bad guys": "The Star-Spangled Contract" (McGraw-Hill Book Company: New York, 1976), p. 293.

93— he continued to work as an informant: Interview with Louis Ivon, October 9, 2000.

93— "Jim is a little naïve": Investigative Report, August 29, 1973. Date of activity March 28, 1962. Reported by Carol Goodrich. MCC.

94— "lie like a rug": Interview with Raymond Comstock, May 29, 1998.

94— "Pershing won't let you in": Interview with Edward Sapir, June 8, 2000.

94— electric chair skull cap: Internal "Newsweek" memo: Garrison Backgrounder. February 24, 1967.

95-Mr. Bird: Interview with Joyce Wood.

95— "filthy mess": Memorandum for File. May 11, 1962. MCC.

95— "a Chinese whorehouse in a hurricane": Jim Garrison, "Coup D'Etat," p. 3 of 1.

95— one hundred files missing: "Case Records Vanish From Office of DA," "States-Item," October 19, 1962.

95— an abortionist, a thief, a heroin dealer: "Dane Accused of $14,000," "Times-Picayune," May 20, 1962, Section 1, p. 1; "Man Arrested in 1960 Hold-Up," "Times-Picayune," May 22, 1962, Section 1, p. 2; "Narcotics Sale Charge Accepted," "Times-Picayune," May 23, 1962, Section 1, p. 9.

96— Garrison charged Christiana: Jim Garrison interview with Richard N.

Billings.

96— reduce the time in which bonding companies: "DA Seeks To Alter Bonds Law," "States-Item," June 1, 1962.

96— "we don't need more money in the budget": "Garrison Tells Plans to Legion," "Times-Picayune," April 27, 1962, Section 1, p. 16.

96— "an African bazaar": "Office Honesty New DA Pledge," "Times-Picayune," May 10, 1962, Section 1, p. 27.

96— "Charge them anyway": Interview with Philip Foto, January 7, 2000.

96— the doctor and the cop on Lake Pontchartrain: Interview with Ralph Slovenko, April 5, 2001.

97— "a hurricane, a cyclone, or an earthquake": Interview with Numa Bertel, June 5, 2000.

97— "I don't want them charged": Interview with John Volz, June 13, 2000.

97— Jim Garrison and the Catholic Church: Interview with William Alford, March 19, 2001.

97— blacks have Garrison's picture in their homes: Interview with Dr. Frank Minyard.

97— "unconstitutional": "Garrison Gives Views In Talks," "Times-Picayune," May 17, 1962, Section 1, p. 26.

98— "involved in political campaigns": "Crime Control Shy – Garrison," "Times-Picayune," May 31, 1962, Section 4, p. 7.

98— Garrison addresses graduates at the New Orleans Police Academy: "Police Cadets Finish Course," "Times-Picayune," June 17, 1962, Section 1, p. 20.

98— "prosecute two": "Prosecute Two, Garrison Asked," "Times-Picayune," May 11, 1962, Section 2, p. 2. See also: "Garrison Says Probe Ordered," "Times-Picayune," May 9, 1962, Section 2, p. 2.

99— Kohn now began to demand more files: Interview with Denis Barry.

99— sent Barry a long memo: Aaron Kohn to Denis A. Barry, II: May 15, 1962. MCC.

99— "divided loyalties": Investigative Report. May 21, 1962. MCC.

99— refused to prosecute: Interview with William Alford.

99— "forfeiture at once": Memorandum on File: May 11, 1962, from Aaron M. Kohn. MCC.

99— Judge Wimberly on the Medina case: "Woman Charged in Morals Case," "Times-Picayune," May 19, 1962, Section 2, p. 2; "Bond Reduced In Morals Case," May 30, 1962, Section 1, p. 10.

100— "all of this builds up": Investigative Report, June 8, 1962. MCC.

100— at the suggestion of Pershing Gervais, Jim Garrison agrees to prosecute Kleinfeldt and Dowling: Interview with Numa Bertel, February 6, 2001.

100— "poking motion": "Kleinfeldt's Case Quashed," "Times-Picayune," July 27, 1962, Section 2, p. 5.

100— secrecy of grand jury proceedings: "DA Staff Broke Law Is Charge," "Times-Picayune," September 25, 1962.

100— "indiscreetly malicious": "Action Illegal, Says Dowling," "Times-Picayune," August 18, 1962, Section 2, p. 4.

100— only in 1971: "Malfeasance Charge Ends," "Times-Picayune," April 20, 1971, Section 1, p. 20.

101— "Just another day at Tulane and Broad": Interview with Louis Ivon, January 8, 1998.

101— "the office that plays together": Interview with Joyce Wood.

102— uncashed checks in his desk: Interviews with Frank Minyard, Numa Bertel.

102— the incursions of his mother: Interview with Sharon Herkes.

Chapter 7

105— upstart DA: Jim Garrison interviewed by Richard N. Billings for "Life" magazine article on organized crime in New Orleans. AARC.

105— "I never think of consequences": Jim Garrison interviewed by the BBC, 1967. AARC.

105: "Didn't I tell you I was lying to you?" Interview with G. Harrison Scott.

106— "incredible": Jim Garrison interviewed by Billings.

106— "down the rabbit hole": "The Vice Man Cometh" by James Phelan, p. 67.

106— "no obligations": Jim Garrison interviewed by Billings.

106— his long belly hanging over tight pants: this description of Pershing Gervais is courtesy of Raymond Comstock, May 29, 1998.

106-111— William Livesay's story: Interviews with Livesay, December 20, 31, 2000 and January 14, 15, 16, 2001.

107— Andrews used profanity: Interview with Ralph Slovenko, January 25, 2001.

107— "You're the judge": Interview with Ralph Slovenko, April 14, 1998.

107— Hardy Davis did Livesay a favor: Livesay interviews and Hardy Davis, "Aiming For the Jugular in New Orleans." Livesay's and Davis's accounts of the incident are virtually identical.

108— "I'll beat the shit out of you": "Aiming For The Jugular in New Orleans," p. 26.

108— "possibly frequent the Gaslight Bar": Warren Commission Exhibit 3104. Vol. 26. pp. 732-733.

108— "homosexual clique": "Aiming For The Jugular in New Orleans," p. 25.

109— "a Gervais operation": Interview with Louis Ivon, May 28, 2002. Police officer Lester Otillio concurs. Interview with Lester Otillio.

109— a "professional homosexual": Investigative Report, March 20, 1963. Date information received March 20, 1963. MCC.

109— "committing an indecent act": "Bail Bondsmen Get Subpoenas," "Times-Picayune," June 16, 1962, Section 3, p. 5.

111— "because he gave information to this office": "Garrison Hits Jail Term Cut," "Times-Picayune," November 21, 1963, Section 1, p. 29.

111— "they had clearly violated the defendant's constitutional rights": Campaign advertisement: "What About O'Hara's Ghost Stories?" "Times-Picayune,"

October 30, 1965, Section 1, p. 20.

111— William Livesay was pardoned by Governor John J. McKeithen on May 25, 1971, having served six years. He went on to become Executive Vice-President of the Louisiana Jaycees, and later a successful realtor in another state.

111— "clutch of professional politicians": "Garrison Hits At Politicians," "Times-Picayune," August 23, 1963.

111-112— "if you want to get a mule's attention": James Phelan, "The Vice Man Cometh," p. 70.

112— B-drinking: I am indebted to Barbara Bennett, Robert Buras, Linda Brigette, Gordon Novel, and William Livesay for their descriptions of B-drinking and of the 1960s French Quarter in general.

112— "cool the beef": Interview with William Livesay, March 24, 2001.

112— glove: "B-Drink Fees Paid—Stripper," "Times-Picayune," December 10, 1962, Section 2, p. 8.

113— kiss her breasts: Interview with Barbara Bennett.

114— "Hot Water Sue": Jack Dempsey interviewed by Jim DiEugenio, Peter Vea and William Davy, September 2, 1994. Courtesy of Mr. Davy.

114— Jim Garrison goes off to War College: Aaron Kohn finds an opportunity to get his name into the newspapers: "Garrison going to War College," "Times-Picayune," July 7, 1962, Section 1, p. 4.

115— Texas Lounge: "Women Booked in A B-Drink Case," "Times-Picayune," June 23, 1962, Section 2, p. 2.

115— undercover agents: "Woman Posed as Waitress," "Times-Picayune," June 27, 1963, Section 1, p. 9.

115— Aubrey Young, a bartender: Interview with John Tarver, February 1, 2001.

115— Lucy Sobecki poses as a Madam: Interview with Andy Partee, June 28, 2000.

116— Barry spent nine straight days in court: Interview with Denis A. Barry.

116— "there was no hanky panky": Interview with Joseph Oster, June 30, 2000.

116— Pershing exempted those who were paying him off: Interview with John Volz, July 17, 2001.

116— never exempted those with connections to organized crime: Interview with William Alford, May 28, 1998.

116— Sinopoli had borrowed money from Peter Marcello: "Peter Marcello Loan Told," "Times-Picayune," January 9, 1963, Section 2, p. 6.

116— "making General Grant explain": Jim Garrison interview with Richard Billings.

116— Pershing collects from card games: Notes of Jack N. Rogers on Pershing Gervais. June 14, 1963. Papers of Jack N. Rogers. Courtesy of Anne Rogers Gentry.

117— much of value vanishing: Interviews with Barbara Bennett, February 6, 2001. Interview with John and Dotty Clemmer, June 1, 2000.

117— Rickey Planche knew Shaw as "Clay Bertrand": Interview with Rickey Planche, May 21, 2005.

117— "interpretive dancing...drag queens": Interview with Suzanne Robbins, November 29, 1999.

118— Caracci was always fair to Linda: Interview with Linda Brigette, July 28, 2001.

118— two left feet: Interview with Joan Bovan, January 10, 2000.

118— when she went to the toilet: Interview with Lillian Cohen, December 10, 2000.

119— the Spinato brothers were nailed: Interview with Robert Buras, January 17, 2002.

120— "is to kill me": "The Vice Man Cometh."

120— "like a pit bull": Interview with Carol Boyd, July 22, 2002.

120— an army that had a mission: Press statement by Jim Garrison. March 7, 1963. Papers of the New Orleans District Attorney's Office (NODA). NARA.

120— "why capture the hill and end all the fun": "The Vice Man Cometh," p. 70.

120— "state of emergency": So Jim Garrison declared his war on vice: See "Quarter Vice Drive Opening," "Times-Picayune," August 7, 1962, Section 1, p. 1; "Six Arrested As Klein Leads Raids on Bourbon Clubs," "Times-Picayune," August 10, 1962, Section 1, p. 1; "10-Point Action Urged by MCC," "Times-Picayune," August 10, 1962, Section 1, p. 16; "Bars May Lose Liquor License," "Times-Picayune," August 10, 1962, Section 1, p. 30; "Many Clubs In Quarter Still Dimly Lit As Ever," "Times-Picayune," August 11, 1962, Section 1, p. 1; "Quarter Raids Net 12 Persons," "Times-Picayune," August 12, 1962, Section 1, p. 1.

120— six clubs: Investigative Report, November 2, 1962. Date information received, September 5th and 6th, 1962. MCC.

120-121— maroon Oldsmobile…fender benders: Interview with Louis Ivon and Dr. Frank Minyard, January 8, 1998.

121— "colored" guests: "Quarter Business Loss Laid To Anti-Mix Laws," "States Item," September 7, 1962.

121— "the economics of Bourbon Street": "Strip Circuit Reform," "Times-Picayune," September 21, 1962, Section 1, p. 16.

121-122— "The Vice Man Cometh" was not written by James Phelan but by David Chandler: "Life" magazine internal memo, March 5, 1967. Lang for Rowan For Newsfronts, Billings, Copy TXT, Miami Bureau. The following note is appended by David Chandler: "I did a manuscript, 'Garrison: Demagogue Or Crusader?' in 1963 which was subsequently used by 'Saturday Evening Post' under title 'Vice Man Cometh' by James Phelan. Since the 'Post' only changed about 500 words of the manuscript, I suppose we are free to quote it. I can send the original manuscript if you prefer…." See the papers of Richard N. Billings.

122— "Only the individual can do anything": Interview with Denis A. Barry.

122— "funny and friendly": Interview with Patricia Chandler, May 22, 1998.

122— Jimmy Moran never sent a bill: Interview with Walter Hammer.

122— assignation": "Padlock Order For Night Club," "Times-Picayune," December 15, 1962, Section 1, p. 1.

123— "What can I do for you today, Charlie?" Interview with Joyce Wood.

123— It was nobody's business: Investigative Report, January 14, 1963. Information received: January 9, 1963. MCC.

— "refreshing and reassuring": Aaron Kohn praises Jim Garrison: "Garrison Given Praise By Kohn," "Times-Picayune," August 25, 1962, Section 3, p. 23. See also Aaron Kohn to Jim Garrison, August 23, 1963. MCC.

— "considerable progress": Aaron M. Kohn to Jim Garrison, August 23, 1962. "I hope that this office": Jim Garrison to Aaron Kohn, September 6, 1962. MCC.

— "a period of unprecedented use of the DA's powers": Investigative Report. December 21, 1962. Date of Activity: December 19 and 20, 1962. MCC.

Chapter 8

126— redecorating the office: See "City Hall Report: Critics Gloat Over DA's Furnishings" by Iris Kelso. "States-Item," August 25, 1962, p. 13.

126— Denis A. Barry is the source regarding Jim Garrison's lack of ability as an administrator. Investigative Report. December 3, 1962. Date information received November 30, 1962. MCC.

126— Cocke ran the Dowling office: Interview with Numa Bertel, February 6, 2001.

127— "Go get your degenerate boss": Interview with Frank Meloche, November 27, 2000.

127— "he slipped that man into Parish Prison": "States Item," August 31, 1962, p. 1.

127— palming the balls: Interview with William Alford.

128— "the white man should have known better": Interviews with Louis P. Trent and Walter Hammer.

128— "there is a conspiracy among the judges": Brener, "The Garrison Case," p. 16.

128— "sacred cows of India": "Prison Crowding Laid To Judges," "States-Item," October 31, 1962, p. 1.

128— Garrison is persona non grata: "City Hall Report; Jurist, DA Feud 'Like Old Times,'" by Iris Kelso. "States-Item," August 18, 1962.

128— the first time the judges ever worked: "Judges To Meet On DA Charges," "States-Item," November 1, 1962, p. 1.

129— peace conference: "Garrison, 6 Judges Hold Private 'Peace Meeting,'" "States-Item," November 7, 1962, p. 1.

129— "racketeer influences": "Garrison, 6 Judges Hold Private 'Peace Meeting.'"

129— the only judges on whom Kohn had nothing: Investigative Report, January 2, 1963. Date information received: January 9, 1963. MCC.

130— "that's ridiculous": "Garrison Top Aid Dismisses Charge," "Times-Picayune," November 9, 1962, Section 1, p. 11. See also, "DA's Office Hit For Dismissing Judges' Charge," November 10, 1962, Section 1, p. 1.

130— "the case is unsubstantiated": "Efforts to Charge Garrison Blocked," "States-Item," November 8, 1962, p. 1.

130— ten point "crash" program: "DA Offers 10-Point Plan For Parish Jail," "Times-Picayune," November 11, 1962, Section 1, p. 1. Editorial, "Criminal Trials Speed-Up," November 12, 1962, Section 1, p. 14.

130— "Gold Medal": Letter to the Editor, "States-Item," November 12, 1962.

130— the judges meet with Jack P. F. Gremillion: "Judges Will Discuss DA With Gremillion," "States-Item," November 10, 1962, p. 1.

130— "just put it in a law book": Interview with John Tarver, January 14, 2000.

130— JPFG: See, for example, Jack P. F. Gremillion to Brother Beckham (Thomas Edward Beckham). August 14, 1962. Courtesy of Thomas Edward Beckham.

130— "apologize for what?" "On the Police Beat," "States-Item," November 17,1962.

131— "if this were Hungary": "Garrison Tells Of Grievances," "Times-Picayune," November 15, 1962.

131— "loud, boisterous and rough with women": "Padlock Club, Judge Orders," "Times-Picayune," January 10, 1963, Section 1, p. 1.

132— Garrison dropped the charge: "DA Drops Charge Against Woman," "Times-Picayune," February 26, 1963, Section 1, p. 3.

132— the object of the operation: Memo to his Assistants: "Morals Cases Are Dismissed," "Times-Picayune," March 9, 1963, Section 2, p. 8.

132— "your office is too busy blaming the vacation-minded judges": "Judge Frees Suspect Here, Blasts DA Aide," "States-Item," November 28, 1962; "Garrison Hits Judge's Blast Against Aide," "States-Item," November 29, 1962.

132— flip his goatee: Jack Dempsey interview with Jim DiEugenio, taped September 2, 1994.

132— "simple kidnapping": "Kidnap Count Is Reduced," "Times-Picayune," January 8, 1963, Section 1, p. 2.

132— "inasmuch as this is the same J. Bernard Cocke": "DA Replies to Judge Cocke," "Times-Picayune," January 9, 1963, Section 1, p. 5.

133— he agreed to represent Jim: The discussion of Garrison v. Louisiana from Don Organ's point of view: Interview with Donald V. Organ, January 10, 2000, and subsequent conversations in New Orleans and Maine.

133— "King James The First": Papers of Jim Garrison from the Harry Connick files. NARA.

136— "I'm no ruffian": Interview with Donald V. Organ.

136— the instructions a judge might have given to the jury: Interview with Donald V. Organ, February 5, 2001.

137— "Washington Post" series: "Battle Over New Orleans Vice Arrays Stubborn DA Against Stubborn Judge," "Washington Post," February 9, 1963.

137— "valiant fight to rid the city of crime": "Times-Picayune," March 1, 1963.

137— "throw anybody in jail": Investigative Report. March 7, 1963. Date Information received: March 6, 1963. MCC.

137— "for some time my attorneys have been working: "LA High Court Upholds Conviction of Garrison," "States Item," June 4, 1963. "Court Upholds DA Conviction," "Times-Picayune," June 5, 1963.

138— Jim Garrison could not refuse: Interview with Numa Bertel.

138— Deutsch as an ambulance chaser: Interview with Wilmer Thomas, July 6, 2000.

138— scenes in Washington during the arguing of Garrison v. Louisiana: Interview with Robert Haik.

140— "The Lawyer and The Bill of Rights," "The American Criminal Law Quarterly," Volume 3, Spring 1965. Number 3, pp. 146-155.

141— "there is no element of this controversy": "DA Has No Jurisdiction, View," "Times-Picayune," November 6, 1962 and "DA Report Distorted, says Stevens," November 6, 1962.

141— Doubleday as a gay hang-out: See "Madame John Dodt's Legacy #19" by Jon Newlin. "Ambush" magazine 2000. Volume 15, Issue 26.

141— Frederick A. Soulé: "Obscene Book Sold, Is Charge": "Times-Picayune," June 18, 1963, Section 2, p. 4.

141— "the most filthy and pornographic book": "Times-Picayune," June 21, 1963, Section 1, p. 7.

141— "cheap political expedient": "Offer In Novel's Case Pondered," "Times-Picayune," June 24, 1963, Section 1, p. 3.

141— the bookstore would not reorder: "Truce In Smut Case Possible," "Times-Picayune," June 27, 1963, Section 3, p. 9.

141— for the history of James Baldwin's book being seized by the New Orleans police: See also: "Book Charges Refused by DA," "Times-Picayune," June 19, 1963; "Offer In Novel's Case Pondered," "Times-Picayune," June 26, 1963; "Citizens Group Raps Garrison," "Times-Picayune," June 20, 1963, Section 1, p. 30; "Case Dismissed Involving Book," "Times-Picayune," September 11, 1964, Section 1, p. 4.

142— Garrison speaks before the United Press International Newspaper Association: "Criminal Libel 'Obsolete'—DA," "Times-Picayune," October 18, 1964, Section 1, p. 15.

142— "I am always interested in any complaints": Jim Garrison to Honorable Bernard J. Bagert, August 26, 1966. New Orleans Public Library. See also: Bernard J. Bagert to Jim Garrison, August 26, 1966.

142— "have been issuing orders": Joseph I. Giarrusso To All Branches Of This Department. New Orleans Public Library.

142— "You're not going to see my files anymore, Judge": Interview with William Alford.

Chapter 9

145— "the integrity of the judiciary may be involved": "Indicted Judge Defends Stand," "Times-Picayune," February 14, 1963, Section 1, p. 1. See also in the matter of the charges against Judge J. Bernard Cocke: "Wimberly Not To Hear Motion," "Times-Picayune," January 12, 1963, Section 2, p. 2; "Action in Cocke Trial Is Sought," "Times-Picayune," February 2, 1963, Section 1, p. 15; "Battle Over New Orleans Vice Arrays Stubborn DA Against Stubborn Judge" by James E. Clayton, "The Washington Post," February 9, 1963; "Contempt Case Judge Is Named," "Times-Picayune," February 12, 1963, Section 1, p. 1; "Judge Indicted by Grand Jury," "Times-Picayune," February 13, 1963, Section 1, p. 1; WWL-TV editorial, February 13, 1963; "Enter Cocke Case, DA Asks Gremillion, "States-Item," February 14, 1963; "Cocke Trial Set Feb. 20; Bagert Recuses Himself," "Times-Picayune," February 15, 1963, Section 3, p. 3; "Garrison Staff Will Prosecute," "Times-Picayune," February 16, 1963, Section 3, p. 22; "Cocke Decision Soon –Gardiner," "Times-Picayune," February 19, 1963, Section 1, p. 1; WWL-TV Editorial, February 19, 1963; "Cocke Control of DA's Claimed," "Times-Picayune," February 19, 1963, Section 1, p. 3; "Cocke Is Ruled Innocent In Contempt Case," "Times-Picayune," February 21, 1963, Section 1, p. 1; "Cocke Ruled Innocent Again," "Times-Picayune," February 22, 1963, Section 1, p. 5; "4 Garrison Cases Refused By Cocke," "States-Item," March 22, 1963.

146— "need not fear being charged by me with defamation": "Judge Accuses D.A. Of 'Fakery'," "Times-Picayune," March 14, 1963, Section 1, p. 25.

146— a plump $60,000: Investigative Report. March 7, 1963. Date information received: March 6, 1963. MCC.

146— Pershing spies on Denis Barry: Investigative Report, January 14, 1963. Date information received: January 9, 1963. MCC.

146— Denis Barry catches Pershing: Interview with Denis A. Barry. In return for a secret share: Investigative Report. February 12, 1963. Subject (1) Orleans Parish District Attorney: Jim Garrison. (2) Attorneys: Denis Barry II. Date information received: February 8, 1963. MCC.

147— "If you just stick to doing your duty": Interview with William Porteous, July 5, 2000.

148— not making use of the evidence: "Giarrusso Asks Padlock Action," "Times-Picayune," March 7, 1963, Section 1, p. 1.

148— "padlocking a bird cage...drunk leans upon a lamppost": "'Status Quo' Attitude Rapped," "Times-Picayune," March 8, 1963, Section 1, p. 8.

148— "an army which has an enemy hill surrounded": Press Statement by Jim Garrison. March 7, 1963. Available in papers of the MCC.

148— "an old New Orleans custom": "Times-Picayune," May 16, 1963, Section 1, p. 1.

148— "doctored" and "fully of orchestrated": "9 Policemen Charged By DA," "Times-Picayune," May 17, 1963, Section 1, p. 10.

148-149— Mayor's Special Committee: Memorandum. March 20, 1963. MCC. See also: Memorandum To: Fellow Members of the Mayor's Special Committee to Negotiate District Attorney Garrison – Police Superintendent Giarrusso Conflict. From: Aaron M. Kohn. Subject: Recommendations for Committee Consideration. MCC

149— "only an underling": Memorandum. March 14, 1963. Subject: (1) Mayor Victor N. Schiro (2) Orleans Parish District Attorney Jim Garrison (3) NOPD Supt. Joseph Giarrusso (4) MCC Project: NOPD. MCC.

149— Rock of Gibraltar: "Top Police Officials Major Vice Probe Foes, says DA," "States-Item," March 20, 1963.

149— "preserving the status quo of the rackets": "Giarrusso Hits Back At Critic," "Times-Picayune," May 28, 1963, Section 1, p. 16.

149— "somebody from the United Nations": "Garrison Raps Mayor, Police," "Times-Picayune," May 25, 1963, Section 1, p. 1.

149-- "nothing but words": "No Cooperation Pledged by Schiro, says Garrison," "States-Item," August 29, 1962, p. 1.

149— "if Mr. Garrison has any knowledge": "Challenge Issued by Giarrusso," "States-Item," August 30, 1962, p. 1.

149— "at the very top of the police force": "Garrison Blames Policymakers For Vice Drive Apathy," "States-Item," August 31, 1962, p. 1.

149— "monumental disinterest": "DA Blasts Police Drive Apathy," "States-Item," August 27, 1962, p. 1. See also: "Mayor Orders Cops Help DA In Clean-Up," States-Item," August 28, 1962.

150— Garrison and Giarrusso come to an understanding: "DA, Giarrusso Hold Meeting," "Times-Picayune," June 2, 1963, Section 1, p. 1.

150— "the whole upper structure of the police": Interview with Numa Bertel,

February 6, 2001.

150— "cooperate with those bums": Investigative Report: May 30, 1963. Date information received: May 29, 1963. MCC.

150— "pseudo-detective": Aaron Kohn to Jim Garrison, June 10, 1963. MCC.

150— "lunatic-fringe": Aaron Kohn to Jim Garrison, November 7, 1963. MCC.

151— Jack Martin files a suit against Jim Garrison and Pershing Gervais: Civil District Court For the Parish of Orleans. No. 412-747. Filed: June 11, 1963. Jack S. Martin, ex rel State of Louisiana vs. Jim Garrison, District Attorney, Parish of Orleans, et. Pershing Gervais, et John Doe, et Joan Doe, et al. to the Honorable, the Civil District Court for the Parish of Orleans. NARA. The dismissal is "Order" No. 412-747, 14th of June, 1963.

150— Frank Klein was exasperated: Investigative Report. June 20, 1963. Date information received: June 16, 1963. MCC.

150— Giarrusso leads raids: "5 Bourbon Street Strip Clubs Raided," "Times-Picayune," May 3, 1963, Section 1, p. 1.

151— Kohn informs to the FBI: See Kohn's Memo to Frank J. Klein, April 15, 1963. Re: Old Southport Club (Riverside Inn). In his own hand, Kohn writes: "4/19/63. Gave copy of above to FBI agt. Regis Kennedy."

151— "a grown man has been tugging": Investigative Report. April 4, 1963. Date information received: March 20, 1963. MCC.

151— "Truth is stranger than fiction": Message slip to Aaron Kohn from Jim Garrison. July 18, 1963. MCC.

152— "the old shell game": Jim Garrison to Aaron Kohn, April 5, 1963. MCC.

152— "I am applying for the job": "DA Enters Race For State Post," "Times-Picayune," June 3, 1963, Section 1, p. 12.

152— "He might win": Interview with Adrian Duplantier, February 6, 2001.

152— the newspapers would not support: Investigative Report. May 30, 1963. Date information received: May 29, 1963. MCC.

153— as an independent: "DA May Ask Job As Independent," "Times-Picayune," June 6, 1963, Section 1, p. 30.

153— "anything else to do but shoot him": Obituary for Jack P. F. Gremillion, "Times-Picayune," March 3, 2001.

153— "I do not consider the incumbent competent": "Garrison drops Out of LA Race," "Times-Picayune," August 21, 1963.

153— rigid-looking: Interview with Gus Weill, January 14, 2000.

153— "won't you h'ep me": Interview with Numa Bertel.

153-154— he and Marshall Brown agreed: Interview with Mrs. Ellen Brown, April 17, 2001.

154— "throw off the yolk": "M'Keithen Hits Federal Moves," "Times-Picayune," June 30, 1963, Section 1, p. 22.

154— McKeithen denounces Morrison: Interview with John Tarver, February 23, 2001.

154— According to Numa Bertel, Garrison liked Chep Morrison: Interview with Numa Bertel.

154— Morrison cocktail party: "Morrison Host At Party Here," "Times-Picayune," November 26, 1962, Section 1, p. 22.

154—Garrison was McKeithen's most prominent supporter: "Notes From City Hall: CRD Organization Now Divided Into Four Parts" by James H. Gillis. "Times-Picayune," October 10, 1963.

154— "Come to Antoine's": Interview with Robert Haik.

155— he would have gone after Jim Garrison with an ax: Interview with Gus Weill.

155— his coat-tails were weak: Interview with John Tarver.

155— "That's the first ultimatum": Memorandum. June 27, 1963 by Aaron M. Kohn. MCC.

156— "I wouldn't imagine even Carlos...." Investigative Report, June 18, 1968. Date of investigation: September 19, 1964. Interview with Raymond Comstock. MCC.

156— According to Raymond Comstock, Garrison isolated himself from the investigators: Interview with Raymond Comstock, May 29, 1998.

156— you could buy an allotment to Section B: Memorandum to Mr. George Denegre. From: Ben L. Upton. Re: Metropolitan Crime Commission (District Attorney's Advisory Committee). May 15, 1963. MCC.

156— that Baum had paid off Gervais emerged only in Garrison's 1965 campaign for re-election: "Baum Paid DA's Aide $750 –Klein," "Times-Picayune," July 13, 1965, Section 1, p. 1.

157— "we put every one of the abortionists in the penitentiary": Garrison interview with Richard N. Billings.

157-158— the abortion cases: For the Pailet case, see: all from the "Times-Picayune": "Abortion Charge Made In Arrest," October 6, 1962, Section 1, p. 16; "Police Lawyer Is Suspended," October 9, 1962, Section 1, p. 26; "Four Abortion Counts Accepted," October 12, 1962, Section 1, p. 6; "PBI Attorney Accused, Quits," October 27, 1962, Section 1, p. 17; "Lanne Cleared, Is Reinstated," November 7, 1962, Section 1, p. 20; "Garrison takes Step Against Judge," September 20, 1963, Section 1, p. 6; "Lanne Enters Innocent Plea," September 20, 1963, Section 1, p. 12; "State Insists Woman Be Tried," September 24, 1963, Section 1, p. 9; "Judge Alters Pailet Ruling," September 25, 1963, Section 3, p. 2; "Ex-PBI Prober Asks Damages," September 25, 1963, Section 3, p. 2; "Judge Is Asked to Recuse Self," September 26, 1963, Section 1, p. 3; "Review Denied in Pailet Case," September 27, 1963, Section 1, p. 5; "Three Testify in Pailet Trial," September 28, 1963, Section 1, p. 8; "Lanne Names 21 in Damage Suit," October 9,1963, Section 1, p. 15; "Midwife Given 7-Year Term," October 15, 1963, Section 1, p. 8; "One Held In Theft From Mrs. Pailet," October 18, 1963, Section 1, p. 1; "Probe 90-Day Reprieve of Mrs. Pailet, DA Urges," October 19, 1963, Section 1, p. 1; "Pitcher Won't Probe Reprieve," October 22, 1963, Section 1, p. 1; "Hegeman File Innocent Plea," November 6, 1963, Section 1, p. 1; "Abortion Case Figure In Prison," January 17, 1964, Section 3, p. 5; "Bond Forfeited In Theft Case," January 18, 1964, Section 1, p. 13; "Abortion Case Term Is Upheld," June 9, 1964, Section 2. p. 2; "Convicted Abortionist's Clemency Appeal Dropped," August 13, 1964, Section 1, p. 19; "Full Pardon For Woman, Plea," January 12, 1967, Section 1, p. 12; "Pardons Board Hears Appeal," November 17, 1964, Section 1, p. 9.

157— "she had not gone into total retirement": Jim Garrison to Aaron Kohn, June 3, 1965. MCC.

157— "dealing in misery": "Conviction Ends Abortion Trial," "Times-Picayune," October 1, 1963, Section 1, p. 16.

157— Lanne and Banister visit the FBI: FBI Airtel: To: Director, FBI. From: SAC, New Orleans. March 8, 1967. 89-69-1637. NARA.

158— "we had them on the run": Raymond Comstock interviewed by Aaron Kohn.

158— "I understand that you're leaving": Interview with Raymond Comstock.

158— raising the salaries of the judges: "Garrison Attacks Report By N.O. Bar Committee," "Times-Picayune," November 15, 1963, Section 1, p. 1.

159— "have difficulty recognizing progress": "Garrison Plans Talk In Florida," "Times-Picayune," October 9, 1964, Section 3, p. 19.

Chapter 10

161— Louisiana's struggle against integration: See the two pamphlets published by the Joint Legislative Committee on Un-American Activities published by the State of Louisiana: "Activities of the Southern Conference Educational Fund, Inc. In Louisiana," Part I, November 19, 1963. Report No. 4, and Part 2, April 13, 1964. Report No. 5.

161— "The Negro race is not capable": "Pfister Notes La. Subversion, Private Investigators' Applications Heard," "Times-Picayune," September 22, 1960, Section 1, p. 28.

162— "Communist-financed": Testimony of Robert Morris before the Louisiana Legislature. Joint Committee on Un-American Activities. Communist Propaganda Infiltration in Louisiana. Baton Rouge: The Committee, 1962, pp. 46-47.

162— Asked whether he was a member of the Communist Party, Hunter Pitts O'Dell invoked his fifth amendment privilege both in April of 1956 before Senator James Eastland's Senate Subcommittee on Internal Security, and again in 1958 before the House Un-American Activities Committee.

162— "They're Communists": David J. Garrow, "The FBI and Martin Luther King, Jr.: From 'Solo' to Memphis (W. W. Norton and Company: New York, 1981), p. 61.

162-163— John F. Kennedy orders Dr. Martin Luther King, Jr. to get rid of Levison and O'Dell: See: Taylor Branch, "Parting The Waters: America In The King Years, 1954-63 (Simon and Schuster: New York, 1988), p. 838.

163— "Marx coming to the White House": Branch, p. 809.

163— CORE efforts in the State of Louisiana: Demonstrations were held in Plaquemine and in Clinton: "Police Employ Tear Gas, Make Plaquemine Arrest,"

"Times-Picayune," August 20, 1963, Section 1, p. 4; "March In Plaquemine Fails," "Times-Picayune," August 21, 1963, Section 1, p. 6; "Negroes Demonstrate Despite Order of Judge," "Times-Picayune," August 22, 1963, Section 1, p. 30; "Civil Rights Demonstration Is Stalled in Plaquemine," "Times-Picayune," Section 1, p. 4; "Will Not Be Intimidated, Say Plaquemine Leaders," "Times-Picayune," Section 1, p. 25.

163— Dombrowski is arrested at gun-point: "Frank T. Adams, "James A. Dombrowski: An American Heretic, 1897-1983" (University of Tennessee Press: Knoxville, 1992), p. 263.

164— not on the list of Communist front organizations: "Raids On SCEF Rapped By King," "Times-Picayune," October 7, 1963, p. 22.

164— "Call me an integrationist": "Times-Picayune," October 6, 1963, Section 1, p. 7.

165— "no confidence whatsoever" in Robert F. Kennedy: "FBI Not Tabbed On Raid–Rogers," "Times-Picayune," October 6, 1963, Section 1, p. 1.

165— this was "correct": CONVERSATION CARTE BLANCHE, WDSU radio, New Orleans. Transcript of a news documentary, aired October 31, 1963.

165— "the last living genuine liberal": Jim Garrison at New Orleans Conference, September 21-23, 1968. Transcript available from AARC, Washington, D. C.

166— Milton Brener and William A. Porteous III concur: Interview with Milton Brener, May 27, 1998; Interview with William Porteous, July 5, 2000.

166— "on advisement": See "Data Studied in SCEF Raids," "Times-Picayune," October 15, 1963, Section 1, p. 13.

167— "all Gremillion's show": Interview with Bruce Waltzer, September 20, 2000.

168— "can we deny the state the basic right?": James A. Dombrowski et. al. v. James H. Pfister, Individually, etc. et. al. Civ.A. No. 14019. United States District Court for the Eastern District of Louisiana. New Orleans Division. 227 f. Supp. 556; 1964. U. S. Dist. Lexis 8828. February 20, 1964.

167— on linking integration with Communism: "Two Attorneys Blast Charges," "Times-Picayune," June 31, 1964, Section 1, p. 7.

167— seized material now inadmissible: "Court Rejects SCEF Evidence," "Times-Picayune," June 17, 1964, Section 2, p. 2.

167— failed to prove that Dombrowski: "Court Rejects SCEF Evidence," "Times-Picayune," June 17, 1964, Section 2, p. 2.

168— Korns authors a brief "pro se": Supreme Court of the United States. October term, 1964. No. 52. Brief on Behalf of Jim Garrison, Appellee, on appeal from the United States District Court for the Eastern District of Louisiana, New Orleans Division. Jim Garrison, District Attorney For The Parish of Orleans; Charles R. Ward, First Executive Assistant District Attorney for the Parish of Orleans; Louise Korns, Assistant District Attorney For the Parish of Orleans; John Volz, Assistant District Attorney For The Parish of Orleans.

168— "how many Communists would you have to find:" "Subversive Activities Law Argued Before Tribunal," "Times-Picayune," January 26, 1965, Section 1, p. 5.

168— "bad faith": United States Supreme Court. Dombrowski v. Pfister, 380 U.S. 479 (1965). Dombrowski Et. Al. v. Pfister, Chairman, Joint Legislative Committee On Un-American Activities of the Louisiana Legislature, Et Al. Appeal From The United States District Court For The Eastern District of Louisiana. No. 52. Argued January 25, 1965. Decided April 26, 1965.

169— Louisiana Senate votes to retain the Joint Committee: "Un-American Activities Unit Retained By Senate, Bill Gains Approval by 37 to 2 Vote," "Times-Picayune," June 30, 1964, Section 1, p. 4.

169— "they have nothing on these people": For a copy of Senator Eastland's letter, turn to the website of John Salter, a field secretary for SCEF: www.hunterbear.org/creative.htm. In May, 1969, nine of the members of the Louisiana Un-American Activities Committee, faced with a damage suit, retracted the charge that Dombrowski, Smith and Waltzer were "subversives": "We find that there exists no basis for the charges that any of these parties have taken any steps that threaten the safety and well-being of the state or the nation, or that they are guilty of any un-American activities." At this, Dombrowski, Smith and Waltzer dropped their suit. See "Group's Charge Retracted," "Times-Picayune," May 3, 1969, Section 4, p. 22.

169— Jim Garrison's duty under the law: Interview with William Porteous, March 8, 2001.

169— could have done much less: Interview with the late Arthur Kinoy, March 6, 2001. In his memoir, "Rights On Trial: The Odyssey Of A People's Lawyer (Harvard University Press: Cambridge, 1983), Kinoy does not mention either Jim Garrison or the role of the Orleans Parish district attorney's office in the Dombrowski case.

170— For the quickie parole story, see: "Undercover Man Beaten But Aids Dope Round-Up," "Times-Picayune," April 30, 1963, Section 1, p. 1; "Task-Force Raid on Bourbon Street," "Times-Picayune," May 4, 1963, Section 1, p. 12; "Paroles Mistake, LA Office Admits," "Times-Picayune," February 21, 1964, Section 1, p. 1; "Two Bought Their Freedom – Convict," "Times-Picayune," April 3, 1964, Section 1, p. 1; "Halt Open Quiz On Two Special Paroles Is Bid," "Times-Picayune," April 7, 1964, Section 1, p. 1; "Testimony Halted by Wrist Slashing," "Times-Picayune," April 9, 1964, Section 1, p. 1; "Shift In Parole Inquiry," "Times-Picayune," April 10, 1964, Section 1, p. 13; "Board Charges Rights Denied," "Times-Picayune," April 11, 1964, Section 1, p. 1; "DA Will Not Go To Meeting," "Times-Picayune," May 1, 1964, Section 1, p. 11; "Inmates Deride Quickie Paroles," "Times-Picayune," May 2, 1964, Section 3, p. 28; "Parole Board Chief Target," "Times-Picayune," May 5, 1964, Section 1, p. 1; "Stand Pat On Parole," editorial, "Times-Picayune, "May 5, 1964, Section 1, p. 8; "DA To Study Move For Pardon Inquiry," "Times-Picayune," June 3, 1964, Section 1, p. 1: "DA To Seek Open Probe of Pardons," "Times-Picayune," June 4, 1964; "Bar Group Deplores DA Blasts At Pardon Board," "Times-Picayune," Section 2, p. 4; "DA Hits Back At Bar Group," "Times-Picayune," Section 1, p. 7; "Pardon and Parole Reform Urgent," "Times-Picayune" editorial, June 10, 1964, Section 1, p. 10; "Bar Unit Raps Garrison Anew," "Times-Picayune," June 12, 1964, Section 2, p. 2; "Bribery behind Bill," "Times-Picayune," July 7, 1964, Section 1, p. 1; "FOP Speakers Hit Bondsmen," "Times-Picayune," July 10, 1964, Section 1 , p. 5; "Politics-Free Board Is Goal," "Times-Picayune," August 11, 1964, Section 1, p. 1; "Judges Oppose Clemency In All Cases, Board Told," "Times-Picayune," November 13, 1964, Section 1, p. 6; "Crime To Grow, Garrison says," "Times-Picayune," November 22, 1964, Section 1, p. 1; "Virtual Parole Veto Power Given To New Orleans DA," "Times-Picayune," December 12, 1964.

170— "people worry about the crime 'syndicate'": "The Vice Man Cometh," p. 71.

170— blood and guts school of politics: Interview with John Tarver, January 31, 2001.

171— "conspiracy to commit such offenses": "Views Of Open Hearing Given," "Times-Picayune," February 29, 1964, Section 1, p. 18.

171— "if you will excuse the expression": Jim Garrison to Aaron Kohn, February 28, 1964. MCC.

171— "democracies in general prefer": "States-Item," April 8, 1964.

171— Haggerty agreed: "Judge Grants Open Probe of Paroles," "Times-Picayune," March 10, 1964, Section 1, p. 1.

172— bad check laws: Chamber of Commerce News Bulletin, April 17, 1964.

173— "focused the public's and the legislature's attention": "Parole Reform Climate Ideal," by Iris Kelso, "States-Item," March 27, 1965. See also: "Convicts' Parole Cases Complex" by Iris Kelso and Rosemary Powell, "States-Item," March 4, 1965.

173— "an exceptionally promising career": "Long-Range Look At Mayor's Race" by Hermann Deutsch, "States-Item," May 19, 1965.

173— McKeithen offers Jim Garrison a bank charter: Interview with Numa Bertel; Interview with Phyllis Kritikos.

173— "Obtaining A Charter For A State Bank," Memo by Louise Korns, August 16, 1965. Courtesy of Lyon Garrison.

174— "How'd you like to represent a new business?": "Not A Dollar's Worth of Interest in L L & T – Garrison," "Times-Picayune," October 10, 1968, Section 1, p. 3. See also:"Gremillion Is Indicted By Federal Grand Jury" by Gordon Gsell, "Times-Picayune," February 15, 1969, Section 1, p. 1.

175—Garrison was not exaggerating in his disdain for the Louisiana legislature. John Tarver summed agrees that it was a "corrupt outfit": Interview with John Tarver, Governor McKeithen's, Administrative Assistant, calls the Louisiana legislature of that day a "corrupt outfit." January 31, 2001.

175— Christiana a long-time Marcello associate: Investigative Report. June 18, 1968. Date of investigation, September 19, 1964. Reported by Aaron M. Kohn. MCC.

175— "muckraking of the parole board": Aaron Kohn to Jim Garrison, July 31, 1964. MCC.

175— "structure changes": Jim Garrison to John McKeithen. May 27, 1964. New Orleans Public Library.

176— "who do you want?" Interview with Sharon Herkes, June 10, 2000.

176— "You're not going to be happy married to a Jew": Interview with Louis P. Trent, December 10, 2000.

177— scheduled a victory party: Brener, "The Garrison Case," p. 24.

177— "another blow to the influence of New Orleans' political organizations": "Notes From City Hall: Effect of Runoff Vote Told: Influence of Political Units

Hurt" by James H. Gillis, "Times-Picayune," September 8, 1963, Section 2, p. 2.

177— Frank Shea becomes a source for Rosemary James: David Chandler, Memo. Papers of Richard N. Billings. Chandler writes: "P.S.: Pershing has been important source for R as, to lesser degree, Judge Frank Shea."

177— "light the match": Interview with John Volz, March 12, 2001.

177— private bathroom: Interview with Phyllis Kritikos, June 16, 2000.

177— "John, now look": Interview with Robert Haik.

178— William Hawk Daniells: Jim Garrison to Honorable John J. McKeithen, October 6, 1966. New Orleans Public Library.

178— Jim Garrison makes Lawrence Chehardy tax assessor: Interview with the late Lawrence Chehardy, January 9, 1998.

178— "I offer a lifetime devoted": "Cocke To Seek Return To Post," "Times-Picayune," May 26, 1964, Section 1, p. 12.

178-180— the Becker-Cocke campaign: "Braniff Enters Race For Judge," "Times-Picayune," June 14, 1964, Section 1, p. 22; and "Change Needed, Says Candidate," June 24, 1964, Section 3, p. 3; "Becker Assails Cocke Remark," July 15, 1964, Section 3, p. 19.

179— "The Trouble With Kings": "Times-Picayune," July 24, 1964, Section 1, p. 15.

179— "To arms, To arms": "Times-Picayune," August 24, 1964, Section 1, p. 12.

179— "Thirteen Infamous Tyrants & Their Facts" by Jim Garrison. Papers of Jim Garrison. Garrison Family Papers. NARA.

180— "Why I Am Voting For Rudy Becker," "Times-Picayune," July 24, 1964, Section 1, p. 17.

180— "independent judge": "We Need…A New Kind of Judge," "Times-Picayune," August 31, 1964, Section 1, p. 12.

180— Braniff, not surprisingly, threw his support to Becker: "Elect Becker, Braniff Urges," "Times-Picayune," July 29, 1964, Section 3, p. 7.

180— "long summer vacations": "Cocke Claim Is Incorrect – DA," "Times-

Picayune," August 13, 1964. Section 1, p. 4.

180— the "Times-Picayune" endorses Cocke: "Judge Cocke Seems Best Qualified," July 15, 1964, Section 1, p. 12.

180— Dupuy and Garrison warred over patronage: Interview with Clarence O. Dupuy, June 20, 2002.

180— "the old machine politicians who were backing Cocke": Investigative Report. September 3, 1964. Reported by Aaron M. Kohn. MCC.

180— "very soul of our democracy": "Oath of Office Taken By Judge," "Times-Picayune," January 5, 1965, Section 1, p. 8.

180-181— Braniff replaces Judge Platt: "Criminal Court Position Filled," "Times-Picayune," March 30, 1967, Section 1, p. 7. "Judge Braniff Assumes Bench," April 1, 1967, Section 1, p. 7.

180-181— Braniff telephones Jim Garrison every year: Interview with Lyon Garrison; Interview with Judge Thomas A. Early, January 10, 1998.

181— "Hale Boggs is outside": Interview with Denis A. Barry.

Chapter Eleven

183— "I trust everyone": Jim Garrison to Zachary Sklar, June 1, 1988. AARC.

183— "Machiavellian influence which Pershing exercised": Interview with Frank Klein by Aaron Kohn. August 18 and 19, 1964. Investigative Report: September 22, 1964. MCC.

183— Frank was "second": Aaron Kohn interview with Raymond Comstock. Investigative Report, June 18, 1968. MCC.

184— "There's no way we can win that case": Interview with Ross Scaccia, January 6, 2000.

185— "I didn't know Marchese was collecting that much": Investigative report. October 5, 1964. Date information received: October 2, 1964. The source is Denis Barry. MCC.

185— the Canal Street Steam Bath: Lynn Loisel is the source, testifying in open court: "DA Fired Gervais For 'Shakedowns,'" "Times-Picayune," September 13, 1973.

185— "I've now got me quite a file on Klein": Pershing Gervais to Aaron Kohn, October 6, 1964. MCC.

185-186— Frank Klein wanted to fire two stenographers: Investigative Report: September 22, 1964. MCC.

186— mistresses of assistants: Interview with Sharon Herkes and Joyce Wood, June 10, 2000.

186— the time clock: "Time Clock Put In Office Of DA," "Times-Picayune," August 9, 1963, Section 1, p. 8. The time clock was eventually removed.

186— Pershing would be able to buy anything": Investigative Report, September 8, 1964. MCC.

187— "You've got to make a choice": Jim Garrison to Zachary Sklar, May 22, 1988. AARC.

187— if Gervais had demanded: Interview with John Volz, March 12, 2001.

187— "growing dissension": "States-Item," August 18th, 1964. Red Comet edition. TOP GARRISON AIDE KLEIN QUITS, DISPUTE REPORTED." The headline was in bold face. See also: all from "Times-Picayune," "Ward Acting DA in Coming Week," August 16, 1964, Section 1, p. 26; "Klein Quits DA Post; Dissension Blamed," August 19, 1964, Section 1, p. 1; "Shea Assails Press Report," August 20, 1964, Section 1, p. 19; "Klein to Leave DA's Payroll," September 29, 1964, Section 1, p. 19.

187— "relieved to have me out of there": Investigative Report, September 8, 1964. MCC.

187— "bad decision...stupid": Jim Garrison to Zachary Sklar, June 2, 1988. AARC.

187— "dropped my best man": Jim Garrison to Zachary Sklar, May 31, 1988. AARC.

187— an imaginary dialogue between Klein and Gervais: "Second Scene between Klein & Gervais," July 14, 1989. Courtesy of Lyon Garrison.

188— "mother's always watching": "M. E. Dupuy Elected Head of Orleans Levee Board," "Times-Picayune," June 23, 1964, Section 1, p. 1.

188— "I'm a Japanese admiral": Internal memo "Newsweek". To: Nation, Sanders, Iselin. From: Carter and Aynesworth. February 24, 1967. NARA.

188— "there is nothing but mud": The Diary of Clay Shaw is available in the papers of Clay Shaw. NARA.

188— "this happens in closed rooms": Transcript of broadcast, WWL-TV. November 1, 1965. Memorandum. January 5, 1966. Reported by Aaron M. Kohn. MCC.

189— hundreds of thousands of dollars of irregularities: "Jury to Probe Levee Board," "Times-Picayune," April 26, 1968, Section 1, p. 1.

189— Alford had Milton Dupuy indicted: All from "Times-Picayune": "Jury to Probe Levee Board; Subpoenas are Issued For Two Members," April 26, 1968, Section 1, p. 1; "Dupuy Offers To Be Witness; Volunteers to Testify in Grand Jury Probe," April 27, 1968, Section 1, p. 1; "Dupuy Faces Indictment, action taken By Orleans Parish Grand Jury," July 12, 1968, Section 1, p. 1; "Dupuy Asking Speedy Trial; Transfer of Court is Attorney's Request," August 6, 1968, Section 3, p. 2; "Trial of Dupuy Slated Aug. 21, Set For Orleans Levee Board President," August 7, 1968, Section 1, p. 17; "Trial of Dupuy Case Delayed, September Date Appears Earliest Possible," August 8, 1968, Section 1, p. 19; "Court Quashes Dupuy Charges, Judge Rules On All Counts," November 9, 1968, Section 1, p. 1; "DA Won't Fight Braniff Ruling, Won't Appeal Quashing of Dupuy Indictments," November 23, 1968, Section 1, p. 14.

189— Clarence Dupuy denied the charge: "Dupuy Faces Indictment," "Times-Picayune," July 12, 1968, Section 1, p. 1.

190— "we should absolutely appeal": William Alford attempts to convict Milton Dupuy: Interview with William Alford, March 19, 2001.

190— "I've living in Paris, France": Interview with Clarence O. Dupuy, June 20, 2002.

190— Greene had taken only $700 a month: "Greene Is Paid $700 Per Month," "Times-Picayune," February 3, 1972, Section 1, p. 1.

190— "let's go out and have a good time": Interview with Louis P. Trent, June 21, 2002.

191 — kept his mouth shut: "DA Office Probes Charge Dupuy Given 'Kickbacks,'" "Times-Picayune," January 28, 1972, Section 1, p. 7.

191---Governor McKeithen makes an appearance in the company of Jim Garrison: "More Are Due To Testify; Greene Held In Contempt," "Times-Picayune," February 11, 1972, Section 1, p. 1.

191— well-bred, poised, smart: Interview with Sharon Herkes, March 13, 2000. These were the terms in which Jim Garrison talked about Phyllis with Herkes.

191— "little bitty women": Interview with Joyce Wood, June 10, 2000.

191— "a man will cheat on his wife": Interview with Phyllis Kritikos, May 29, 1998. The story of her meeting with Jim Garrison and their relationship is from this and interviews on January 11, 2000; June 16, 2000; October 9, 2000; February 5, 2002.

195— none had been acquitted: In May of 1965, a defendant charged with rape was in fact acquitted. Ernest Jones, Jr. was acquitted of manslaughter after fatally shooting a man in an argument "with a Negro woman" in September of 1963. This was not quite an exception. See "Slaying Figure Wins Acquittal": "Times-Picayune," September 11, 1963, Section 2, p. 12.

195— the most powerful man in the state of Louisiana: Interview with Gus Weill, January 14, 2000.

195— the support of Edgar and Edith Stern: HSCA interviews of Jim Garrison with Jonathan Blackmer and L. J. Delsa. July-August 1977. NARA. On audio cassette. 002220.

195— He could have had all the money he needed: Jim Garrison interviewed by Richard N. Billings. 1967. Papers of Richard N. Billings, Georgetown.

195— Garrison's dinner with Walter Hamlin: Investigative Report, December 14, 1964. Reported by Aaron M. Kohn. MCC.

196— "grow to like it": quoted in David Chandler, "The Devil's DA," "New Orleans" magazine. November 1966, p. 32.

196— "Hit every radio station": Interviews with John Volz, May 21, 1999; May 12, 2000.

196— "Look, John!" Interview with John Volz, May 21, 1999.

197— Garrison accompanies Governor McKeithen to Chicago: "Garrison Is With McKeithen On Industry-Seeking Chicago Trip," "Times-Picayune," March 30, 1965, Section 1, p. 11.

197— "I doubt whether Oswald acted alone": To Billings and Haskell. "Life" magazine internal memo from Holland McCombs – Dallas. May 18, 1967. Interview with Henry Wade. AARC.

197— Hale Boggs nurtured Garrison's doubts: Interview with Phyllis Kritikos. January 11, 2000.

197— McKeithen decides to run again by changing the law: Charles A. Ferguson, "Louisiana Politics," "States-Item," April 24, 1965.

197— Earl and Huey were crooks: John R. Rarick to Ned Touchstone, April 28, 1965. Papers of Ned Touchstone. Louisiana State University at Shreveport. Interview with John R. Rarick, July 9, 2000.

—

197-"Big John's already got his": Interview with John R. Rarick, February 3, 2001.

197-198— "free to choose whomever they want": "Garrison Backs Amendment No. 1," "Times-Picayune," November 7, 1966, Section 2, p. 12.

198— Jim Garrison visits Gillis Long: "Gillis Long, DA Talk 'Politics,'" "Times-Picayune," July 15, 1966, Section 1, p. 7.

198— "hasn't been good for Louisiana": "Defense Given by Shilstone," "Times-Picayune," October 5, 1966, Section 1, p. 22.

198— "nobody else has been able to solve": Jim Garrison interviewed by Richard N. Billings.

198— "It was my jurisdiction": Jim Garrison in "Beyond JFK." Documentary film by Danny Schecter and Barbara Kopple.

198— "should I say that the death of John Kennedy is not my affair?" From: "Insert A of a draft of a letter regarding charges made by James Phelan. Undated. Garrison family papers. NARA.

Chapter Twelve

199— "if nominated, I will not run": "Urged to Enter Race – Garrison," "Times-Picayune," May 28, 1965, Section 1, p. 2.

199— "don't believe any rumors": Interview with Judge Louis P. Trent, August 3, 2001.

199— his notorious personal life: Memorandum. April 30, 1965. Date information received: April 23, 1965. From: Aaron M. Kohn. MCC.

200: "I'll talk to you later": Interview with Lyon Garrison

200— he was undependable: Interview with John Volz, June 11, 2002.

200— Jules Crovetto tries to bribe Jim Garrison: Interview with Louis Crovetto. February 6, 2002.

201— the FBI did not inform Jim Garrison of Kay Roberts' allegations: FBI. Memorandum to Director, FBI. From: SAC, New Orleans. Subject: Dissemination of critical information to other agencies. New Orleans Division AR. Criminal Influence In Local Agencies. September 22, 1965. 66-6353-2874. 4 pages ("This information was not disseminated to James Garrison").

201— solicited a bribe unsuccessfully: E. C. Upton, Jr. to Jim Garrison, December 19, 1966. MCC.

202— "paddling upstream in a leaking boat": Jim Garrison to Aaron Kohn. Personal and Confidential. May 18, 1965. MCC.

201— the "States-Item" reports two resignations: "2 Assistant DA's Quit In Shakeup," May 19, 1965.

201— "a few drinks": Investigative Report. March 11, 1965. Date information received: March 10, 1965. Reported by Aaron M. Kohn. MCC.

202— "those who have money get a "nolle prosequi": Interview with Burton Klein, April 5, 2001.

202— Pershing calls lawyers "whores": Interview with Mike Seghers, January 13, 2000.

202— "the bottom of the Mississippi River": Interview with Judge Louis P. Trent, October 8, 2000.

203— Bielosh is indicted for perjury: "Perjury Indictment Names Owner of Bar," "Times-Picayune," June 11, 1965, Section 1, p. 1. It was the lead story that day. See also: "Giarrusso OK's PBI Pair Probe," "Times-Picayune," June 12, 1965, Section 1, p. 1.

203— "he would never lie to me": Jim Garrison interviewed by Richard N. Billings.

203— "a Laurel and Hardy comedy": "DA Will Probe Investigation," "Times-Picayune," June 13, 1965, Section 1, p. 24.

203— "an outlaw, kangaroo, political, election-year": "Garrison Bars Staff On Probe," "Times-Picayune," June 16, 1965, Section 3, p. 2.

203— "a house of prostitution": "DA Will Make Record Public," "Times-Picayune," June 21, 1965, Section 2, p. 4.

203— the Queen of England and the President: "Will Ask Citizens' Probe of Bielosh Case –Schiro," "Times-Picayune," June 22, 1965, Section 2, p. 4.

203— Pershing is questioned: "Motives For Inquiry Hidden, Gervais Says," "Times-Picayune," June 24, 1965, Section 1, p. 1.

204— Garrison demanded an investigation of Mayor Schiro: "Garrison asks Schiro Quiz," "Times-Picayune," June 25, 1965, Section 1, p. 1, and "If Illegalities Act, Schiro's Reply to DA," June 26, 1965, Section 1, p. 1.

204— "the smear that failed": "Times-Picayune," June 28, 1965, Section 2, p. 4.

204— Pershing's reward from Chris Baum": "Baum Paid DA's Aide $750 – Klein," "Times-Picayune," July 13, 1965, Section 1, p. 1.

204— Pershing produces a copy of a check: "Gervais Offers Check As Proof," "Times-Picayune," July 14, 1965, Section 1, p. 2.

204— the perjury charge against Clarence Bielosh: Brener, "The Garrison Case," p. 38.

204— Gill withdrew: "Gill Quits DA Post Race," "Times-Picayune," September 2, 1965, Section 1, p. 9.

204— "let's get him": quoted in David Chandler, "The Devil's DA," "New Orleans" magazine, November 1966, p. 90.

205— Pershing resigned: "Gervais Quits; 'Trick' – O'Hara," "Times-Picayune," September 10, 1965, Section 1, p. 11. See also Editorial, "The DA's Chief Investigator," September 10, 1965.

205— Garrison didn't like guns: see William W. Turner, "Rearview Mirror: Looking Back At The FBI, the CIA and Other Tails" (Penmarin Books: Granite Bay, California, 2001), p. 139.

205— "sordid figure": "Lust For Power Charged To DA," "Times-Picayune," September 10, 1965, Section 1, p. 11.

205— the information about Pershing's shaking down lawyers comes from the testimony of Lynn Loisel during Jim Garrison's trial in federal court in 1973: "DA Fired Gervais For 'Shakedowns'" by Lanny Thomas and Allan Katz, "Times-

Picayune," September 13, 1973, Section A, p. 2.

205— "to the senior members of the Mills gambling syndicate: Investigative Report. September 28, 1965. Dates information received: September 22, 27 and 28, 1965. Reported by Aaron M. Kohn. MCC.

206— an "ugly force": "O'Hara Charges DA Has Anxiety," "Times-Picayune," September 13, 1965, Section 1, p. 18.

206— "I consider him very dangerous": Investigative Report, July 3, 1965. Date information received: July 1, 1965. Reported by Aaron M. Kohn. See also for Garrison's relationship with the National Guard: "Resume of Conversation – General Pauley and Colonel Garrison – September 18, 1965. Courtesy of General Erbon W. Wise.

207— "and had to seek the support of the Klan": "DA Disowns Possibility Of His Running For Mayor," "Times-Picayune," April 6, 1965, Section 1, p. 1.

207— "night riders or other hoodlums": "Warning Given On Bombings," "Times-Picayune," July 31, 1965, Section 1, p. 7.

207— "a significant service": "Fire Bombings Arrests Hailed," "Times-Picayune," June 4, 1966, Section 1, p. 6.

207— Leander, Jr. stops a Klan rally: "Officials Halt Klan Meeting," "Times-Picayune," July 10, 1966, Section 1, p. 1.

208— Captain William L. Heuer, Jr.: "Heuer To Face Quiz Thursday," "Times-Picayune," October 16, 1965, Section 1, p. 16.

209— "sinister elements": "Crusade Urged By O'Hara," "Times-Picayune," September 25, 1965, Section 2, p. 2.

209— Most agree that it was a "vicious campaign": Interview with Judge Louis P. Trent, April 23, 2001.

209— Kohn noticed Christiana's relationship to Carlos Marcello: Aaron Kohn to Jim Garrison, October 2, 1965. MCC.

209— "a sign saying don't bring snakes": Interview with John Volz, June 11, 2002.

209— the files had disappeared from the office: Jim Garrison to Aaron Kohn, June 4, 1965. MCC.

209— the FBI had been informed: "O'Hara Blasts DA Handling of Dope Case," "States-Item," October 12, 1965. See also "Garrison Target of O'Hara Speech," "Times-Picayune," October 15, 1965, Section 1, p. 14.

209— on Garrison's campaign posters: See To: Billings. From: Haskell. 3/23/67. Garrison bio. AARC.

211— "smear": "Threats Made, O'Hara Charges," "Times-Picayune," September 8, 1965, Section 3, p. 8.

211— Marshall Brown admitted to raising $18,000 for O'Hara: Investigative Report. November 28, 1966. Date information received: November 25, 1966. Reported by Aaron M. Kohn. MCC.

211— "all the way back to New Orleans": quoted in Chandler, "The Devil's DA," p. 90.

211---See also: "Would Relate Details – O'Hara," "Times-Picayune," October 26, 1965, Section 1, p. 5.

211— "no incumbent lucky enough": "McKeithen Confirms He had Meeting With O'Hara," "Times-Picayune," October 28, 1965, Section 1, p. 23.

212— "to get the judge out of the race": "District Attorney Debate," Editorial. "Times-Picayune," November 1, 1965, Section 1, p. 12.

Chapter 13

213— "as swinging as a rusty gate": Interview with John Dolan, April 10, 2001.

213— "a heart to heart talk": "Death Penalty Is Sought," "Times-Picayune," November 23, 1966, Section 1, p. 1.

213— "hysteria": For the ACLU response, see "Times-Picayune," November 25, 1966, Section 2, p. 3.

213— he never intended making armed robbery a capital offense: Interview with Numa Bertel, April 10, 2001.

213— "an armed robber is a vicious criminal": "Answer to Editorial Criticizing Proposed Legislation re: Armed Robberies." Garrison Collection. New Orleans Public Library.

214— "Have you spoken to Pershing lately?" Interview with Numa Bertel, October 9, 2000.

214— "I thought if I moved you out": Interview with John Volz, June 11, 2002.

215— "amiable fixes": Jim Garrison, Letter to the Editor of the "States-Item," March 17, 1965.

215-any criminal type": "Changes Urged To Bar Murder," "Times-Picayune," September 3, 1966, Section 1, p. 15.

215— unless the state and national legislatures: "Changes Urged To Bar Murder."

215— "loan sharks gauge people": "Convict Good-Time Repeal Goal Of DA," by Patsy Sims. "States-Item," April 18, 1966. See also: "Garrison Asks For Two Laws," "Times-Picayune," June 2, 1966, Section 1, p. 12.

215— "modern correctional system": "Better Prison Policies Urged," "Times-Picayune," June 4, 1966, Section 1, p. 6.

216— "not even incorporated in Soviet Law": "D.A. Compares Criminal Code To Soviet Law," "States-Item," June 8, 1966. See also: "Garrison Hails LA. Senate Unit," "Times-Picayune," June 23, 1966, Section 2, p. 8.

216— within the hour: Gus Glaviano to Mr. James Garrison, September 16, 1966. New Orleans Public Library. Frank Meloche to "Boss": October 2, 1966. New Orleans Public Library. See also: Ellis C. Irwin to Mr. Jim Garrison, October 6, 1966. Irwin thanks both Garrison and Meloche.

216— "available to you at your convenience": Jim Garrison to Reverend D. Norwood, September 15, 1966. New Orleans Public Library.

216— a woman writes to Jim Garrison about her husband: Mrs. Ruel Rossi to Jim Garrison, September 2, 1966. New Orleans Public Library.

217— "deprived the state of Louisiana": "Rapists May Get Freedom Soon," "Times-Picayune," August 18, 1966, Section 2, p. 2.

217— "good news to criminals everywhere": "DA Hits Ruling On Release Of Death Row Pair," "Times-Picayune," August 17, 1966, Section 2, p. 7. See also: "DA Statements Harmful – ACLU," August 27, 1966, Section 2, p. 77, and "Garrison Locates Victim of Labat and Poret Rape," August 19, 1966, Section 1, p. 1; "Pair Won't Be Released Without Fight – Gremillion," August 30, 1966, Section 1, p. 6.

217— Louise Korns to the research: See Memorandum, October 25, 1966. To: All Assistant District Attorneys. From: Louise Korns. Re: Jury Selection As Affected

By Race, Sex, etc, and Memorandum. November 21, 1966, To: All Assistant District Attorneys. From: Louise Korns. Re: Selection of Juries in Orleans Parish. NARA.

217— Poret is found guilty in 1971: "Poret Again In Rape Case," "Times-Picayune," April 2, 1971, Section 1, p. 11.

217— "I want to become a judge": Interview with Lolis Eli, June 3, 2000.

218— "steadily defeated Communist aggression": "Fight To Retain Freedom, Garrison Tells Graduates," "States-Item," August 5, 1966. NARA.

218— "A Heritage of Stone," in "Crime, Law and Corrections," ed. Ralph Slovenko (Charles C. Thomas: Springfield, Illinois, 1966), pp. xvii-xxv.

219— Garrison submits the article to "Commentary": Warner J. Dannhauser to Jim Garrison, October 25, 1966 and James H. Brown, Jr. to Jim Garrison, October 2, 1966. New Orleans Public Library collection.

219— Chetta is skilled at wiping away an insanity defense: Interview with Ralph Slovenko, April 5, 2001 and Interview with Ross Scaccia, April 5, 2001.

219— Frank Williams is judged sane: "Killer Suspected Adjudged Sane," "Times-Picayune," October 22, 1966, Section 1, p. 1.

219— "this office does not want to deprive a man of his freedom": "DA Will Start New Case File," "Times-Picayune," October 30, 1962, Section 1, p. 7.

220— "dangerous persons imaginable": Ralph Slovenko to Joan Mellen, March 6, 2001.

220— For an account of the capture of Leonard Caesar, see, "Caesar Still Alive, Condition Critical," "Times-Picayune," May 1, 1956, p. 1. Interview with Robert Buras, September 21, 2007.

221— Judge Rarick receives messages from Leonard Caesar: Interview with John R. Rarick, April 5, 2001.

221— Rarick was indignant. John Rarick tells this story in "The Leonard Caesar Case," "Notes For A Biography," Unpublished. Courtesy of John R. Rarick.

222— Six writs from mental patients: John R. Rarick to Ned Touchstone, April 5, 1964. Ned Touchstone papers. LSU-Shreveport.

222— "no evidence to convict or hold him": See "Caesar Release Stayed" and

"Report Denied in Caesar Case," "Times-Picayune," February 24, 1965, Section 2, p. 12. Slovenko argues that he was misquoted. Dr. Butler said, obscurely, that Slovenko "never gave me any indication that the district attorney's office was trying to railroad Leonard Caesar." Slovenko points out in his book, "Psychiatry In Law/Law In Psychiatry," that it wasn't until 1972 with Jackson v. Indiana that the United States Supreme Court set a time limit on confinement for pretrial commitment for incompetency to stand trial. During Leonard Caesar's time, commitment for incompetency was tantamount to confinement for life.

222— Rarick did stay the effect of his writ: "Caesar Release Stayed 20 Days," "Times-Picayune" February 23, 1965, Section 2, p. 12.

222— "I hold you personally in the highest regard": Jim Garrison to John R. Rarick, February 22, 1965. Courtesy of John R. Rarick.

222— Louisiana State Supreme Court ruled: 247 La. 1108. State ex rel. Leonard Caesar v. Lionel Gremillion, acting superintendent of East Louisiana State Hospital. No. 47665. Supreme Court of Louisiana, June 7, 1965. Rehearing denied July 2, 1965. 176 "Southern Reporter," 2nd Series.

223— Volz was there as mentor: Interview with John Volz, April 18, 2001.

223— "If I hadn't given Caesar a hearing": Interview with John R. Rarick, September 7, 2000.

223— "absolute constitutional right": "Another Problem at Jackson Hospital," "Times-Picayune," February 23, 1965, Section 1, p. 8.

223— "they couldn't prove their case": Interview with John R. Rarick, April 10, 2001.

223— Caesar released: "Convicted Escape Artist, Rapist Ends Prison Term," "Times-Picayune," May 18, 1973, Section 1, p. 4.

223— he was forty-six years old: "Parole Break Said of Ceaser [sic]," "Times-Picayune," August 31, 1973, Section 3, p. 2.

223-224: Garrison as father: Interviews with Lyon Garrison, Elizabeth Garrison, and Eberhard Garrison and Liz Garrison.

226— "Frank Klein did me bad": Interview with Linda Brigette, July 28, 2001.

226— "since time is of the essence": Judge Louis P. Trent to Jim Garrison, September 8, 1966. NARA.

227— "goo goo eyes": Interview with Linda Brigette.

227— "the economic importance of Linda Brigette": MCC telegram, September 27, 1966.

227— "happy to take any action": Jim Garrison to Aaron M. Kohn, January 25, 1966. MCC.

228— "obviously I was paid": Interview with John Volz, April 18, 2001.

228— Kohn's attempt to create publicity for himself over the Linda Brigette pardon was not unconnected to his sense that his welcome in New Orleans may have run its course. Only a year earlier, he had gone to Alabama preaching that Mobile had serious organized crime problems, his way of applying for a new job in Alabama. Then he had written to J. Edgar Hoover, complaining that "at least one FBI agent in the Mobile office" had opposed citizen efforts against organized crime. Hoover saw through Kohn, and perceived, shrewdly, that Kohn's crime investigations were losing ground in New Orleans "and that he was looking for another job." If Kohn could get the people of Mobile in the right frame of mind, Hoover thought, Kohn might be able to obtain a similar job in the Mobile area: See Aaron M. Kohn to J. Edgar Hoover August 2, 1965; FBI report; August 6, 1965, To: SAC, New Orleans. From: Director, FBI. SA Mobile Division. Personnel Matter. "Personal Attention." See also: Mr. Callahan, August 31, 1965. Special Agent. Mobile Division.

229— the Marcellos want Jim Garrison out of office: Interview with John Tarver, January 31, 2001.

229— "Neither the Director of the Crime Commission": Press release. New Orleans District Attorney's Office. September 21, 1966. MCC.

230— "three or four flies": WDSU Close-Up.

230— "dancer could be important": Investigative Report. October 10, 1966. Date information received: October 7, 1966. Reported by Aaron M. Kohn. MCC.

230— a guest: Investigative Report, November 28, 1966. Date information received: November 25, 1966. Reported by Aaron M. Kohn. MCC.

231— "I find it incredible": Denis Barry answers Kohn. Denis A. Barry II to Aaron Kohn, September 26, 1966 and Aaron M. Kohn to Denis A. Barry II, September 29, 1966. MCC.

231— "political error": June Allen Reports. WNNR radio. October 7, 1966.

231— "obvious that there is organized crime in this area": US Grand Jury Probe 'Rock Country' View," "Times-Picayune, " September 30, 1966, Section 1, p. 1.

231— he had fought organized crime: "Garrison Raps News Media On Stripper Story," "States-Item," October 13, 1966, p. 26 and "MCC to Be Exposed – DA," "Times-Picayune," October 13, 1966, Section 1, p. 21.

231— on a street car at the same time as Bugsy Schwartz": "Jury Calls MCC Chiefs, Evidence on Organized Crime Is N.O. Aim," "Times-Picayune," September 27, 1966, Section 1, p. 1.

232— For Aaron Kohn's appearance before the Orleans Parish grand jury, see videotaped Kohn statement for WDSU-TV, September 24, 1966 and press release of the same date. MCC.

232— "Put up or shut up!": "Put Up Or Shut Up, DA's Word To Kohn," "Times-Picayune," September 25, 1966, Section 1, p. 1.

232— "humiliate Kohn": To: Billings. From Haskell. March 23, 1967. Jim Garrison bio.

232— "raising camellias": "Jury Fails To Indict; 'Raise Camellias,' DA Tells MCC," "Times-Picayune," September 30, 1966, Section 1, p. 1.

232— "Ace Investigator Kits": "MCC Presented No Evidence – DA," "Times-Picayune," October 18, 1966, Section 3, p. 2.

232— Carlos Marcello is behind Lamarca: Memorandum. September 29, 1966. MCC.

232-233— John Daniel Sullivan inspects the files of the District Attorney: Investigative Report. October 21, 1966. Date information received: October 19, 1966. Reported by John D. Sullivan. MCC.

233- "Finding his way back to his hotel": Press Release. Office of the District Attorney, October 19, 1966. See also: "Gun Blast Kills Prober For MCC," "States-Item," October 24, 1966, p. 11; "DA Office Held Target Of Plot," "Times-Picayune," October 27, 1966, Section 3, p. 2; "DA Resources Not Used—Kohn," "Times-Picayune," November 10, 1966, Section 1, p. 22.

233— no certified or registered mail: Memorandum. December 27, 1966. To: All Members of the Staff. From: Jim Garrison, District Attorney. Re: Mail from M.C.C. New Orleans Public Library Collection.

233— "network of informants": Interview with Mike Seghers, January 6, 2000.

233— Chandler is a Kohn informant: Aaron M. Kohn to David Chandler, November 18, 1966. MCC. As late as November 3, 1967 Jim Garrison, unaware Chandler was betraying him, spoke of being "personally fond" of David Chandler. See Jim Garrison to Melvin Belli, November 3, 1967. NARA. See also: Chandler's essay, "The Devil's DA" in the November 1966 issue of "New Orleans" magazine.

234— "We got avenues": Interview with L. J. Delsa, January 12, 2000.

234— another Wilmer?: Interview with H. John Bremermann.

234— Liz evinced no interest: Interview with Mark Lane, February 6, 1998.

234— Phyllis thought: he's off the wall: Interviews with Phyllis Kritikos.

235— "the White House in Jackson": Interview with Herman Kohlman, March 21, 1998.

235— Pershing informs to Regis Kennedy: Interview with Raymond Comstock.

235— "I wouldn't piss on Washington, D.C.": "Second Scene Between Klein & Gervais" by Jim Garrison. July 14, 1989.

236— "there had always to be a plus": Interview with Mike Seghers, January 13, 2001.

236— "what that smoke was": Jim Garrison interviewed by the BBC.
1967. NARA.

APPENDIX

237--Herman Kohlman, op. cit. p. 79. Interview with Herman Kohlman, December 1, 2000. Hoke May finds Jack Martin a credible source: Hoke May in conversation with New Orleans journalist and University of New Orleans professor, Don Lee Keith. The Don Lee Keith papers. Courtesy of the late Don Lee Keith.

238----On how Thomas Edward Beckham became a priest: Investigation Interview Schedule 005213. Name: Jack S. Martin. 12/6/77. Robert Buras and Lawrence Delsa. 2-6-78. NARA

238----On Beckham's knowledge of the Torah: Conversation with Tammy Beckham, March 20, 2008.

238--For the document regarding Joseph James Martin: Agency: CIA. 104-

10300-10323. Record Series: JFK 80T01357A. From: Stevens, M.D. To: D/Chief, Security Research Staff. Title: Memo Re Joseph James Martin. Date: 04/06/67. 5 pages. Subjects: Martin, J. J. NARA.

238--For the memo from Scott Miler: Assassinations Records Review Board. Agency: CIA. 104-10170-10134. JFK. 80T01357A. September 1998. CIA. Title: Routing Record Sheet Re Jack J. Martin. 05/01/67. One page. Subjects: Martin, Jack J. JFK 64-25:F4 1998.02.21.12:01:39:216108. See also: CIA 104-10170-10134. From: Withheld. To: Mr. Scott Miler. Title: Speed Letter The Attached FBI Report DBB 73951. Contains A Reference To A John J. Martin. 03/20/67. JFK 64-25:F4.1998.02.21.11:59:53:280108.

239--For the CIA's reference to a "generic" Jack Martin: CIA. 104-10331-10189. JFK. Agency File Number: PROJFILES-CORRESPONDENCE. From: Wickham. C/IMS.EXT Supp Group. To: C/JFK Declass Project/HRP/OIM/DA. Title: Memo: DO Response to Quest For Files On Selected Names From HSCA Investigation. Date: 08/24/1998. Pages: 2. ARRB Request. NARA.

239--For the list of people with AINS numbers: CIA Special Collections. New Memo/Standard. 11 August 1998. Memorandum For: J. Barry Harrelson, Gary Breneman. From: Frieda P. Omasta. Office: ADA/IRO. Subject: Re: PRIORITY - Name Traces For JFK/ARRB - Andrew (Andy) Anderson. Reference: CIA IR-19/DA/IRO 32b. NARA.

239--Remarks of L. J. Delsa on Jack Martin, Interview of Delsa with the author, New Orleans, December 7, 2005.

240--Jack Martin informs to the FBI: FBI 124-10040-10174. Agency file number: 62-109060-4407. From: SAC, NO. To: Director, FBI. 01/17/67. NARA.

240--On Martin's call to the CIA asking that they telephone Louis Ivon: Director, Domestic Contact Service. From: Chief, New Orleans Office, Lloyd A. Ray. 3 March 1967. Re: Musulin/Ray telecom 3 Mar 67. NARA.

240--On Jack Martin's connection with a Dallas murder: D.K. Rogers, Detective, Criminal Intelligence Section to Captain W.F. Dyson, July 6, 1967. Subject: Criminal Intelligence (1) Jack Martin aka Jack S. Martin, True name of Edward Stewart Suggs, W M 47 DS 41771.

240--On Charity Hospital and Jack Martin: Hospital Record dated January 28, 1957. From: U.S. Department of Justice, Federal Bureau of Investigation, 6/21/68. State Police, Baton Rouge, Louisiana. Attention: General Thomas D. Burbank. Re: Edward Steward [sic] Suggs.

241--On the death of Gloria Wilson: Conversation with Hadley Hudnall,

December 9, 2005. Clinton Courthouse, Clinton, Louisiana. Conversations with Anne Dischler.

241-242--Jack Martin's "Affidavit" (with David Lewis) is available at NARA.

242--Jim Garrison on Jack Martin: Notes For A Book. 3. "Man Under The Oak Tree." NARA.

INDEX

Printed in the United States
115403LV00003B/502-522/P

9 780977 465729